Romanian Gr

Mika Sarlin

Romanian
Grammar

2nd ed.

2014

©Mika Sarlin 2014

Manufactured by Books on Demand GmbH, Norderstedt, Germany.
Published by Books on Demand GmbH, Helsinki, Finland.

ISBN: 978-952-286-898-5

Contents

Preface

This book intends to be a comprehensive grammar of modern Romanian for foreign students. It is based on the Finnish version originally published in 2009. However, many changes and enlargements have been made in order to make this book more suitable for English speaking readers.

In this grammar, special attention has been given to the rich morphology of Romanian, including the many irregularities and sound changes. The book includes e.g. very detailed lists of Romanian verbs with all their sound changes. Since this is an advanced grammar, basic knowledge of traditional grammatical terms is assumed. However, the grammatical explications have been kept as short and simple as possible, and more space is given to examples, declension and conjugation tables, word lists, etc. Most of the example sentences are taken from modern sources, mainly from different online newspapers.

This grammar follows the latest norms published by the *Academia Română: Gramatica limbii române* (2008), *Gramatica de bază a limbii române* (2010), *Dicționar ortografic, ortoepic și morfologic al limbii române DOOM* (2007), *Dicționarul explicativ al limbii române DEX* (2009), *Enciclopedia limbii române* (2006).

In this second editions many small corrections and some additions have been made.

September 28th 2014

The author

PHONETIC SYMBOLS

Vowels

i	close unrounded front vowel
e	mid unrounded front vowel
ɨ	close unrounded central vowel
ə	mid unrounded central vowel
a	open unrounded central vowel
u	close rounded back vowel
o	mid rounded back vowel
ø	mid rounded front vowel
y	close rounded front vowel
ⁱ	voiceless, asyllabic

Semivowels and semiconsonants

w, u̯	semiconsonantic and semivocalic u
j, i̯	semiconsonantic and semivocalic i
e̯	semivocalic e
o̯	semivocalic o

Consonants

p	voiceless bilabial stop
b	voiced bilabial stop
t	voiceless denti-alveolar stop
d	voiced denti-alveolar stop
k	voiceless velar stop
g	voiced velar stop
kʲ	voiceless palatalised velar stop
gʲ	voiced palatalised velar stop
s	voiceless alveolar fricative
z	voiced alveolar fricative
ts	voiceless denti-alveolar affricate
ʃ	voiceless postalveolar fricative
ʒ	voiced postalveolar fricative
tʃʲ	voiceless palatalised postalveolar affricate
dʒʲ	voiced palatalised postalveolar affricate
f	voiceless labiodental fricative
v	voiced labiodental fricative
h	voiceless glottal fricative
x	voiceless velar fricative
ç	voiceless palatal fricative
l	voiced alveolar lateral
r	voiced alveolar trill
m	voiced bilabial nasal
ɱ	voiced labiodental nasal
n	voiced alveolar nasal
ŋ	voiced velar nasal
ŋʲ	voiced palatalised velar nasal

About the Romanian language

Romanian is spoken by ca. 24 million people. It is the official language of Romania (ca. 19.4 million) and Moldova (ca. 2.8 million), where it is often been known as the Moldovan language[1]. It also has an official status in the autonomous province of Vojvodina in Serbia (ca. 35 000). Romanian is also one of the official languages of the European Union.

Apart from Romania, Moldova and Vojvodina, some Romanians also live in Ukraine (ca. 410 000), Russia (ca. 180 000), other parts of Serbia (ca. 40 000) and Hungary (ca. 15 000). In Israel, about 218 000 people are of Romanian origin. In Ukraine, Romanian has been declared a regional language in the villages of Bila Tserkva (Rom. Biserica Albă) and Tarasivtsi (Rom. Tărăsăuți)[2].

After 1989, many Romanians have moved to Western Europe. In 2010 there were ca. 800 000 Romanians in Spain and over 1 million in Italy.

The name 'Romanian language' usually refers to the main dialect, *Dacoromanian*. The other Romanian dialects are less widely spoken. These dialects are: *Aromanian* (or *Macedo-Romanian*), which is spoken by some 200 000 people in Albania, Bulgaria, Greece and Macedonia[3]; *Megleno-Romanian* (spoken by ca. 5 000 people in Moglena, Greece and in Macedonia[4]); and *Istro-Romanian* (spoken by only ca. 500-1500 people in Istria, Croatia[5]). The Dacoromanian dialect is further divided into subdialects (*grai*), but the dialectal differences are quite small. Southern dialects are spoken in Oltenia, Muntenia and Dobrogea, while northern dialects are spoken in Transylvania and Moldova.

Romanian is a Romance language, which means it has developed from Latin just like Spanish, Portuguese, French and Italian. The Roman emperor Trajan conquered Dacia in 101-106, but the Roman rule lasted only for a short time, and in 271 emperor Aurelian pulled the Roman army and administration out of Dacia. However, this short period was enough to latinize the area.

---

[1] The name Moldovan was used in the Soviet Union. In the declaration of independence of Moldova (27/8/1991) the language was called Romanian, but in the constitution (29/7/1994) it was again called Moldovan. On December 5th 2013 the Constitutional Court of Moldova ruled that the official language is Romanian.

[2] http://www.kyivpost.com/content/ukraine/romanian-becomes-regional-language-in-bila-tserkva-in-zakarpattia-region-313373.html.

[3] http://www.ethnologue.com/14/show_language.asp?code=RUP. Aromanian is one of the official languages in the town of Kruševo (Macedonia).

[4] http://www.ethnologue.org/show_language.asp?code=ruq

[5] http://www.ethnologue.org/show_language.asp?code=ruo

During the Migration Period, Proto-Romanian was separated from the other Romance areas and at the same time it was split into the above mentioned dialects. Because of its isolation, Romanian has evolved quite differently from the other Romance languages. Sound changes typical to Romanian include e.g. *qu* → *p, gu* → *b, ct* → *pt, l* → *r*.

Latin	Romanian	Spanish	Italian	French
aqua *water*	apă	agua	acqua	eau
quattuor *four*	patru	cuatro	quattro	quatre
lingua *language*	limbă	lengua	lingua	langue
octo *eight*	opt	ocho	otto	huit
lac(tem) *milk*	lapte	leche	latte	lait
sol(em) *sun*	soare	sol	sole	soleil
caelum *sky*	cer	cielo	cielo	ciel

Romanian has also maintained some Latin sounds that have changed into other sounds in the other Romance languages, e.g. the diphthong *au*.

Latin	Romanian	Spanish	Italian	French
aurum *gold*	aur	oro	oro	aur [or]
audire *to hear*	auzi	oír	udire	ouïr

Perhaps the most noticeable feature of Romanian is the declension of nouns and adjectives. Like Latin, Romanian has three genders: masculine, feminine and neuter. Romanian has also retained some of the Latin cases. The declension is further complicated by the fact that the definite article is a suffix in Romanian (Sp. *el estudiante*, It. *lo studente*, Fr. *l'étudiant*, Rom. *studentul*).

The Romanian conjugation of verbs differs somewhat from the other Romance languages as well. For example, the future is formed in Romania with the Latin verb *velle* (*volo cantare* → Rom. *voi cânta*), whereas in the other Romance languages a suffix formed from the Latin verb *habere* is used (*cantare habeo* → Sp. *cantaré*, It. *canterò*, Fr. *chanterai*).

During the Middle Ages, Church Slavonic became the language of civilization in Romania and the written use of Latin was forgotten. A huge number of loanwords entered Romanian, especially from Slavic languages, but also from Greek, Turkish and Hungarian. These loanwords give an exotic flavour to Romanian compared to the other Romance languages.

The oldest remaining Romanian text is the letter of *Neacșu* from 1521. It is written using the Cyrillic alphabet, which was in use until 1862. Because of Soviet influence, the Cyrillic alphabet was used in Moldova until 1989, but the Moldovan alphabet differed somewhat from the one used in Romania[6]. Some people still use the Cyrillic alphabet, especially in Transnistria[7].

Apart from changing the alphabet, the language was also otherwise strongly re-latinised during the 19th century. The vocabulary experienced great changes and new words were borrowed, especially from French. It has been estimated that as much as 40% of the modern Romanian vocabulary has been borrowed from French. About 80% of the Romanian vocabulary is of Latin origin, coming either directly from Latin or as loan words from other Romance languages. Nowadays new words are borrowed mainly from English.

---

[6] For more information see e.g. http://ro.wikipedia.org/wiki/Alfabetul_chirilic_român and http://ro.wikipedia.org/wiki/Alfabetul_chirilic_moldovenesc.
[7] The T. G. Ševčenko University in Tiraspol has a department of the Moldovan language (Катедра де филоложие молдовеняскэ). This is the only university in the world that still teaches "Moldovan" in Cyrillic script.

Sounds of Romanian and their spelling

Consonant sounds

The Romanian language has the following consonant phonemes:

	Bilabial	Labiodental	Alveolar	Postalveolar	Velar	Glottal
Stops	p b		t d		k g	
Fricatives		f v	s z	ʃ ʒ		h
Affricates			ts	ʧ ʤ		
Nasals	m		n			
Laterals			l			
Trills			r			

In Romanian, the voiceless stops are unaspirated, just as in French, Italian and Spanish.

As in the other Romance languages, the consonants /t, d, ts/ are laminal denti-alveolars: they are pronounced with the blade of the tongue against the alveolar ridge, leaving the tip of the tongue against the teeth (and therefore traditionally called *dentals*[8]), unlike English /t/ and /d/, which are apical (pronounced with the tip of the tongue against the alveolar ridge). Also /s/ and /z/ are laminal (like in English, Italian, etc., but not like in North Iberian Spanish) and pronounced with the blade of the tongue, not with the tip of it.

In Romanian, the lateral /l/ is always clear (like the first *l* in English *little*), and never dark (as the second *l* in *little*). The Romanian /r/ is a trill, like in Italian.

The sounds /ʃ, ʒ, ʧ, ʤ/ are not so clearly rounded as in English, and in the standard Romanian /ʧ/ and /ʤ/ are always slightly palatalised[9].

The other consonants are pronounced as in English.

---

[8] According to Academia (DEX, ELR) also /l, n, r/ are dentals. *Limba română comtemporană* (1985, p. 72) calls all the consonants /t, d, s, z, ts, l, r/ 'dental (alveolar)'. Canepari (2007: 350) classifies /t, d, s, z, ts/ as dentals and /l, n, r/ as alveolars.

[9] They are pronounced hard in Maramureș ([ʧ, ʤ]) and as fricatives in Moldova ([ʃ, ʒ]).

Double consonants occur only in some compound words formed usually with a prefix:

înnoda	[inno'da]	to tie
transsiberian	[transsiberi'an]	Siberian train

Some of the most important allophones of the Romanian consonants include:

/k/	[kʲ][10]	voiceless palatalised (prevelar) stop, used before [e, i, j, ⁱ]
/g/	[gʲ]	voiced palatalised (prevelar) stop, used before [e, i, j, ⁱ]
/h/	[x]	voiceless velar fricative, used at the end of a word, before another consonant and after a consonant (except before [i, j, ⁱ]).
	[ç]	voiceless palatalised (prevelar) fricative, used before [i, j, ⁱ]
/n/	[ŋ]	voiced velar nasal, used before [k, g, x].
	[ŋʲ]	voiced palatalised (prevelar) nasal, used before [kʲ, gʲ, ç].
	[m]	voiced bilabial nasal, used before [p, b, m].
/n, m/	[ɱ]	voiced labiodental nasal, used before [f] and [v].

The other consonants are also slightly palatalised before [e, i, j, ⁱ], but this palatalisation is not as noticeable as with the velar consonants /k, g, h/.

The voiced consonants [b, d, g, v, z, ʒ, ʤʲ] can loose their voice in front of the unvoiced consonants [p, t, k, f, s, ʃ, ʧ, ʦ], and vice versa:

absolut	[abso'lut, apso'lut]	absolute
fotbal	['fotbal, 'fodbal]	football

Some authors recommend pronouncing according to the spelling, while others prefer the voice assimilation, especially the devoicing[11].

Vowel sounds

Romanian has seven vowel phonemes and one asyllabic vowel:

close vowels:	/i/	/ɨ/	/u/
mid vowels:	/e/	/ə/	/o/
open vowel:	/a/		

asyllabic vowel: /ⁱ/

Only the vowels *o* and *u* are rounded; all the other vowels are unrounded. The Romanian vowels /i, e, a, o, u/ are very similar to equivalent vowels in languages such as Spanish, Modern Greek or Croatian (i.e. languages with three degrees of openness).

---

[10] Although Academia considers [kʲ] and [gʲ] to be phonemes (*ochi* /o-kʲ/, not /o-k-ⁱ/), in this grammar [kʲ] and [gʲ] are counted as allophones of /k/ and /g/. This question has been the subject of heated discussion since the 1960s. For discussion, see Turculeț (2010).

[11] Tătaru (1999) gives [abso'lut] and ['fotbal], Calotă & Vlădulescu [apso'lut] and ['fotbal/fodbal].

The vowel /i/ is a close front unrounded vowel, like the English /iː/ (as in *eat*). It is much closer than the English /ɪ/ (as in *it*).

The vowel /e/ is a mid front unrounded vowel like the English /e/ (as in *get*).

The vowel /a/ is an open central unrounded vowel. It is not pronounced as far back in the mouth as the English vowel /ɑː/ (as in *father*) and it is more open than the English /ʌ/ (as in *son*).

The vowel /o/ is a mid back rounded vowel. It is slightly more open than the British English /ɔː/ (as in *law*) as clearly closer than the British English /ɒ/ (as in *hot*).

The vowel /u/ is a close back rounded vowel. The Romanian /u/ is pronounced further back in the mouth than the English /uː/ (as in *do*) and it is closer than the English /ʊ/ (as in *put*).

The vowel /ə/ is a mid central unrounded vowel. It is pronounced slightly further back and is more open than the English /ɜː/ (as in *learn*). The Romanian /ə/ can occur both in stressed and unstressed syllables.

The vowel /ɨ/ is a closed central unrounded vowel. It has no equivalent in English. It is somewhat similar to the Russian ы.

In some foreign words (French or German) the vowels [ø] and [y] are used: *bleu* [blø] 'light blue', *ecru* [eˈkry] 'ecru (colour)'.

Comparison of Romanian and British English (received pronunciation) vowels[12]:

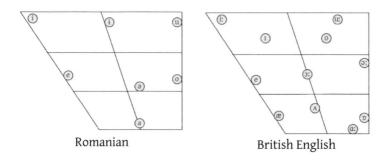

Romanian   British English

---

[12] Based on Canepari (2007) and Roach (2004).

Asyllabic *i*

One of the special features of Romanian phonetics is the short, weak, voiceless [ⁱ], known as *i şoptit*, the whispered *i*[13]. It occurs only at the end of a word, where it palatalises the final consonant[14]. This sound differs from the other vowels in that it does not form a syllable[15]. However, it is spelled with the letter *i* (see p. 28).

The sound [ⁱ] must not be confused with the sound [i], which also occurs at the end of a word:

pom	[pom]	(one syllable)	tree
pomi	[pomⁱ]	(one syllable)	trees
pomii	[pomi]	(two syllables)	the trees

This sound also occurs in compound words formed with *câteşi-, fieşi-, oareşi-* and *ori-*:

câteşitrei	[kiteʃⁱ'trei̯]	all the three
oricare	[orⁱ'kare]	anyone

The asyllabic *i* can occur after the consonants /p, b, k, g, ts, z, ʃ, ʒ, f, v, h, m, n, l, r/.[16] After [tʃ, dʒⁱ] the asyllabic -*i* is not audible, since these consonants are always palatalised in Romanian:

faci	[fatʃ]	you do
mergi	[merdʒⁱ]	you go

Because of the regular sound changes [t → tsⁱ, d → zⁱ, s → ʃ] (see p. 35), the asyllabic *i* does not usually occur after the consonants [t, d, s]. Exceptions are the consonant groups [ʃtⁱ] and [ʒdⁱ][17]:

creşti	[kreʃtⁱ]	you grow
nădejdi	[nə'deʒdⁱ]	hopes (pl.)

The sounds [sⁱ] occurs in *mătăsi* [mə'təsⁱ], which is the genitive and dative form of *mătase* 'silk', and in the names of the Thrakian tribes *bessi* [besⁱ] 'Bessi' and *moesi* [moesⁱ] 'Moesi'. The sounds [tⁱ] occur in *starosti*, the plural form of the word *staroste* 'starosta, the elder of a guild'.

---

[13] Technically, this sound could be called a voiceless palatal approximant. It is much weaker than the German voiceless palatal fricative in *ich*.

[14] In other interpretations, the final consonant is palatalised and the [ⁱ] itself is not pronounced at all.

[15] For this reason in *Limba română contemporană* (1985: 64) [ⁱ] is classified as a allophone of the semivowel [j]. In some studies both [ⁱ] and [j] are classified as allophones of [i]. Because of the opposition [pomi – pomⁱ] and because semivowels occur only in diphtongs, in this grammar [ⁱ] is counted as a seperate phoneme.

[16] However, the difference between [ʃ, ʒ] and [ʃⁱ, ʒⁱ] is not clearly audible even for native Romanian speakers (Spinu 2007: 303), although the difference is made in articulation.

[17] [ʒdⁱ] occurs only in the plural forms of *nădejde* 'hope' and *deznădejde* 'despair'.

Diphthongs and hiatus

When two vowels occur in the same syllable, they form a diphthong. The rising diphthongs start with a semiconsonant [j] or [w] or a semivowel [e̯] or [o̯] and end with a more prominent full vowel.

The rising diphthongs of Romanian are:

starting with [j]:	[ja, je, jo, ju]
starting with [w]:	[wa, wə, wɨ]
starting with [e̯]:	[e̯a, e̯o][18]
starting with [o̯]:	[o̯a]

E.g.:

		but			
iar	[jar]	but	*ziua*	['zi.wa]	the day
miere	['mje.re]	honey	*două*	['do.wə]	two
iod	[jod]	iodine	*plouând*[19]	[plo'wɨnd]	raining
iubi	[ju'bi]	to love			
mea	[me̯a]	my			
vreo	[vre̯o]	any			
foarte	['fo̯ar.te]	very			

There is also the diphthong [we] that occurs only in some loanwords like *western* ['westərn] 'Western (film genre)'. In verb forms like *înșeuez* 'I saddle' it is usually replaced by [wə]: [ɨnʃe'wəz][20].

Romanian also has falling diphthongs that start with the prominent full vowel and end with a weaker semivowel [i̯] or [u̯]. These semivowels are pronounced with less friction (or no friction at all) than the semiconsonants [j, w] occurring in rising diphthongs.

The falling diphthongs of Romanian are:

ending in [u̯]:	[au̯, eu̯, iu̯, ou̯, əu̯, ɨu̯][21]
ending in [i̯]:	[ai̯, ei̯, ii̯, oi̯, ui̯, əi̯, ɨi̯]

---

[18] In the diphthong [e̯o] the semivowel [e̯] is usually pronounced as rounded, so a more detailed transcription would be [ø̯o].

[19] The diphthong [wɨ] is very rare and only occurs in the gerund form of *ploua* and *oua*.

[20] Calotă & Vlădulescu, 2003: 97, Buia 2006:148-149. Calotă & Vlădulescu even suggest the spelling *(eu) înșeuăz, (tu) înșeuăzi, să înșeuăze*.

[21] According to the latest norm, there is no diphthong [uu̯]: *ambiguu* [am.bi.gu.u].

E.g.:

au	[au̯]	they have	*ai*	[ai̯]	you have
leu	[leu̯]	lion	*trei*	[trei̯]	three
fiu	[fiu̯]	son	*mii*	[mii̯]	thousands
nou	[nou̯]	new	*noi*	[noi̯]	new (pl.)
rău	[rəu̯]	bad	*uita*	[ui̯'ta]	to forget
râu	[riu̯]	river	*răi*	[rəi̯]	bad (pl.)
			câine	['kii̯.ne]	dog

Notice that the letters *iu* are used both for the diphthongs [iu̯] and [ju].

Colloquially, some speakers use a semiconsonant or a semivowel also in words starting with a vowel ([ʲ] before [e, i], [ᵊ] before [a, ə, i] and [ʷ] before [o, u])[22]. This is done especially with older Romanian words:

om	[om ~ ʷom]	human
in	[in ~ ʲin]	flax, linseed
acest	[a'ʧest ~ ᵊa'ʧest]	this

In such cases the vowel is also pronounced more closed than usually. Some people might also pronounce newer loanwords like this. However, according to the normative pronunciation rules, the semiconsonant is added only with some pronouns and forms of the verb *fi* (see p. 27).

Two vowels following each other do not necessarily form diphthongs, since the vowels can belong to different syllables. Compare:

seară	['se̯a.rə]	evening	*licean*	[li.ʧe.'an]	pupil
leu	[leu̯]	lion	*leucit*	['le.u.'ʧit]	leucite
au	[au̯]	they have	*saună*	['sa.u.nə]	sauna

Usually older words have diphthongs while in newer words the vowels belong to different syllables. However, there are no strict rules about this, and a good dictionary should be consulted to determine the accurate pronunciation.

In older Romanian words and grammatical suffixes the hiatus is usually avoided by adding a more or less weak semiconsonant [j] or [w] (transcribed in this grammar as [ʲ, ʷ]) between the two vowels:

familie	[fa'miliʲe]	family	*aur*	['aʷur]	gold
fiii	['fiʲi]	the sons	*râul*	['riʷul]	the river
cailor	['kaʲilor]	to the horses	*lua*	[lu'ʷa]	to take
puilor	['puʲilor]	to the chickens	*știut*	[ʃti'ʷut]	known
oilor	['oʲilor]	to the sheep			
apropia	[apropi'ʲa]	to come closer			

This kind of pronunciation should be avoided with neologisms.

---

[22] Vasiliu 1965: 95-96.

Thus in Romanian, two vowel letters like *ai* can mean either a diphthong ([ai̯]), hiatus ([a.i]) or even a sequence of a vowel, semiconsonant and a vowel ([aʲi]).

When two of the same vowels follow each other, they always belong to different syllables:

liceele	[li.'t͡ʃe.e.le]	the secondary schools
alcool	[al.ko.'ol]	alcohol
copiilor	[ko.'piʲi.lor]	to the children
fiind	[fi.ʲind]	being

An exception is -*ii* at the end of a word, which can mean a diphthong [ii̯], two syllables [i.ʲi] or even just one vowel [i] (see p. 28).

Triphthongs

Triphthongs are formed with two semivowels/semiconsonants and one ordinary full vowel. The Romanian triphthongs are [jau̯, jeu̯, jou̯, jai̯, jei̯, joi̯, wai̯, wau̯, ea̯u̯, ea̯i̯, oa̯i̯, eo̯a, jo̯a], e.g.:

iau	[jau̯]	I take
eu	[jeu̯]	I
maiou	[ma.'jou̯]	undershirt
tăiai	[tə.'jai̯]	you were cutting
iei	[jei̯]	you take
i-oi da	[joi̯ da]	I will give him/her
înșeuai	[ɨn.ʃe.'wai̯]	you saddled
înșeuau	[ɨn.ʃe.'wau̯]	they saddled
rouăi	['ro.wəi̯]	of the dew (genitive)
beau	[be̯au̯]	I drink
beai	[be̯ai̯]	you were drinking
rusoaică	[ru.'so̯ai̯.kə]	Russian woman
pleoape	['ple̯oa.pe]	eyelids
creioane	[kre.'jo̯a.ne]	pencils

The apparent triphthong *uea* in verbal forms like *înșeuează* 'he saddles' is usually pronounced as [wa]: [ɨnʃe'wazə][23].

Just as with diphthongs, three vowels following each other do not necessarily form a diphthong, since they can belong to different syllables.

---

[23] Calotă & Vlădulescu, 2003: 97, Buia 2006:148-149. Calotă & Vlădulescu even suggest the spelling *înșeuază*.

Stress

In Romanian the word stress can change the meaning of the word. The stress is usually on the last or second to last syllable of the word stem.

E.g. the placement of the stress in the word *copii* changes the meaning:

copii	children (from *copil* 'child')
copii	copies (from *copie* 'copy')

In the declension of the substantive and adjectives the stress stays on the same syllable:

stea, niște stele, stelele	star, stars, the stars
timp, timpuri, timpurile	time, times, the times

The only exceptions are: *noră: nurori* 'daughter in law', *soră: surori* 'sister, nurse' and a few nouns ending in -o like: *radio: radioul, radiouri* 'radio', *trio: trioul, triouri* 'trio', *zero: zeroul, zerouri* 'zero'.

In the conjugation of verbs, some endings are unstressed while some are stressed:

cântă	he/she sings (present)
cântă	he/she has sung (simple perfect)

The placement of stress in verb conjugation is explained in more detail in the chapter on verb morphology.

Intonation

Declarative sentences have a falling intonation:

Mama vine.	Mother is coming.
['mama ↘'vine]	

In a yes/no-question the intonation rises on the last stressed syllable and falls after it. The most stressed element is at the beginning of the sentence.

Vine mama?	Is mother coming (or not)?
['vine ↗'ma↘ma]	
Mama vine?	Is mother coming (or father)?
['mama ↗'vi↘ne]	

If the stressed element is at the end of the yes/no-question, the intonation rises on the last syllable:

> Mama **vine**?   Is mother coming (or going)?
> ['mama 'vi ↗ne]

If the question includes a choice, the intonation first rises and then it descends after the conjunction *sau* 'or':

> Vine mama sau tata?   Is it mother or father who is
> ['vine ↗'mama sau̯ ↘'tata]   coming?

In questions containing an interrogative pronoun or an adverb the intonation falls:

> Când vine mama?   When is mother coming?
> [↘kɨnd 'vine 'mama]

Alphabet

The letters of the Romanian and their names are:

A a	[a]	Î î	[ɨ (din i)]	Ș ș[25]	[ʃe, ʃɨ]
Ă ă	[ə]	J j	[ʒe, ʒɨ]	T t	[te, ti]
Â â	[ɨ (din a)]	K k	[ka, kapa]	Ț ț	[tse, tsi]
B b	[be, bɨ]	L l	[le, el, lɨ]	U u	[u]
C c	[tʃe, kɨ]	M n	[me, em, mɨ]	V v	[ve, vɨ]
D d	[de, dɨ]	N n	[ne, en, nɨ]	W w	[dublu ve,
E e	[e]	O o	[o]		dublu vɨ][26]
F f	[fe, ef, fɨ]	P p	[pe, pɨ]	X x	[iks]
G g	[dʒʲe, gʲe, gi]	Q q	[ky][24]	Y y	[igrek][27]
H h	[haʃ, hɨ]	R r	[re, er, rɨ]	Z z	[ze, zet, zɨ]
I i	[i]	S s	[se, es, sɨ]		

Capital letters are used as in English:

- At the beginning of a sentence.
- With personal and place names: *Ion, Bucharest, România*.
- With historical events: *Renaștere* 'Renaissance', *Primul Război Mondial* 'First World War'.
- With historical time periods: *Evul Mediul* 'Middle Ages', *Antichitatea* 'Antiquity'.

---

[24] The earlier name [kiṷ] is no longer recommended.
[25] The letters *ș* and *ț* have a comma, not a cedilla. However, because the correct letters are not included in all fonts, the cedilla is often used. The Turkish letter *ş* is often used in print instead of the Romanian *ș*.
[26] Double *v*, not double *u* as in English.
[27] *I grec* 'Greek i'.

- With celebrations: *Crăciun* 'Christmas', *Anul Nou* 'New Year', *Ramadan* 'Ramadan'.
- With organizations and companies (*Organizaţia Naţiunilor Unite* 'United Nations', *Biblioteca Naţională a României* 'National Library of Romania').

Only the first word is capitalised in titles and headlines (*Evenimentul zilei* (a journal), *O scrisoare pierdută* (a play)) and with names of departments of organizations and companies (*Compartimentul de limbi romanice* 'Department of Romance Languages').

Notice that capital letters are not used in Romanian for points of the compass (*nord* 'North'), nationalities (*român* 'Romanian'), languages (*engleză* 'English'), days of the week (*luni* 'Monday') nor months of the year (*ianuarie* 'January').

The Romanian orthography is quite phonological and most sounds are written with one letter. The sounds /a, o, u, e, p, b, t, d, v, f, m, n, h, l, r, z/ are spelled with the same letter while /ʒ/ is spelled with *j*, /ə/ with *ă*, /ts/ with *ţ* and /ʃ/ with *ş*. However, the orthography of the following sounds varies:

- /i/ is spelled usually with *i*, but an unstressed /i/ at the end of a word is usually spelled with *ii*.
- /ɨ/ is spelled with *î* at the beginning and at the end of a word. Otherwise it is spelled with *â*.
- /k/ is spelled with *c*, except before *e* and *i*, when it is spelled with *ch*.
- /g/ is spelled with *g*, except before *e* and *i*, when it is spelled with *gh*.
- /tʃ/ is spelled *c* before *e* and *i* and otherwise with *ci* or *ce*.
- /dʒ/ is spelled *g* before *e* and *i* and otherwise with *gi* or *ge*.
- The semiconsonants and semivowels [i̯/j, u̯/w, e̯, o̯] are spelled with *i, u, e, o*.
- The asyllabic *i* is spelled with *i*.

The letters *k, q, w* and *y* occur only in foreign words, where they are pronounced as closely as possible to the language of origin:

K k	*afrikaans* [afriˈkans], *kilo* [ˈkʲilo], *ketchup* [ˈkʲetʃap]
Q q	*quasar* [kwaˈsar], *quechua* [ˈkʲetʃua], *quaestor* [ˈkvestor]
W w	*watt* [vat], *western* [ˈwestərn], *weekend* [ˈui̯kend][28]
Y y	*yoga* [ˈjoga], *lady* [ˈledi], *byte* [bai̯t]

Pronunciation of vowel letters

a   is pronounced as [a]:

an	[an]		year
masă	[ˈmasə]		table
lucra	[luˈkra]		to work

---

[28] According to most sources, Romanian does not have the diphthong [wi]. However, Buia (2006: 96) gives the pronunciation [ˈwikend].

â, î Both *â* and *î* represent the sound [ɨ]. The letter *â* is used inside a word:

cuvânt	[ku'vɨnt]	word
când	[kɨnd]	when
râu	[riu̯]	river

At the beginning and at the end of a word the letter *î* is used:

începe	[in'ʧepe]	to begin
coborî	[kobo'rɨ]	to take down

The word-initial letter *î* is kept in compound words and after prefixes:

bineînțeles [bineɨntse'les]		of course
reîncepe [reɨn'ʧepe]		to begin again

In conjugation of verbs, the letter *î* changes into an *â* inside a word:

coborând [kobo'rɨnd]   taking down

The letter *î* is also used in some family names:

Pîrvulescu ~ Pârvulescu
Frîncu ~ Frâncu

Before 1993, [ɨ] was always spelled with *î* (*cuvînt, cînd, coborînd*), except in the word *România* and its derivations (*român, românește* etc.). Some publishers still use the old orthography. In Moldova the new orthography became official in 2010-2011.

These rules should also be respected while transcribing Cyrillic names. However, in practice the usage varies greatly:

Vâborg (~ *Vîborg*)	Vyborg
Kârgâzstan (DEX 2009)	Kyrgyzstan
~ *Kîrgîzstan* (DEX 1998)	

The vowel [ɨ] is usually not pronounced in fast speech when preceded by another vowel:

casa întreagă ['kasa(ɨ)n'tre̯agə]	the whole house
bineînțeles [bine(ɨ)ntse'les]	of course

After an *i* the letter *î* is pronounced as [i] (the sound [ɨ] does not occur after the sounds [i, j, ʲ]):

nemaiîntâlnit [nemajintɨl'nit]   unencountered

ă is pronounced as [ə]:

casă	['kasə]	house
văd	[vəd]	I see

After an *i* the letter *ă* is pronounced as [e] (the sound [ə] does not occur after [i, j, ͥ]):

ochii ăia	['okʲi'eja]	those eyes

The vowel [ə] usually disappears in fast speech when it is followed by [a]:

o casă albă	[o'kas(ə)'albə]	a white house

e   is usually pronounced as [e]:

ecou	[e'kou̯]	echo
expert	[eks'pert]	expert

However, in the following words *e* is pronounced as [je]:

personal pronouns: *eu* [jeu̯], *el* [jel], *ei* [jei̯], *ele* ['jele]
polite pronoun: *dumneaei* [dumnʲea'jei̯]
all the verb forms of *fi* starting with *e*:
    present: *eşti* [jeʃtʲ], *este* ['jeste], *e* [je]
    imperf.: *eram* [je'ram], *erai* [je'rai̯], *era* [je'ra],
           eram [je'ram], *eraţi* [je'ratsʲ], *erau* [je'rau̯]

E is pronounced as [je] also when it is used to transcribe the Cyrillic *е*:

Elţin	['jeltsin][29]	Yeltsin

In diphthongs and triphthongs, *e* is pronounced as a semivowel [e̯]:

neagră	['ne̯agrə]	black
beau	[be̯au̯]	I drink

However, in the following pronouns *ea* is pronounced as [ja]:

ea	[ja]	she
ceea	['t͡ʃeja]	that (thing)
aceea	[a't͡ʃeja]	that
aceeaşi	[a't͡ʃejaʃʲ]	the same

After another vowel the pronunciation [e̯a] is recommended in loanwords:

coreean	[kore'e̯an (kore'jan)]	Korean

After the consonants /k, g/ the diphthongs starting with [e̯] are merged with the consonant (see the consonants *ch* and *gh*).

The letter *e* is also used for the writing of the consonants [t͡ʃ, d͡ʒʲ] (see the consonants *c* and *g*).

---

[29] Pronounced in Russian as ['jeltsin] and therefore sometimes transcribed as *Elţîn*.

i   is pronounced as [i] at the beginning of a word and inside it:

imita	[imi'ta]	to imitate
copil	[ko'pil]	child
ființă	[fi'ʲintsə]	being

In diphthongs and triphthongs, *i* is pronounced as a semiconsonant [j] before another vowel and a semivowel [i̯] after:

iar	[jar]	but
cai	[kai̯]	horses

The diphthong [ii̯] occurs at the end of a word only when the first *i* is part of the word stem and the second one is part of a suffix:

copii	[ko'pii̯]	children
* știi*	[ʃtii̯]	you know

After the consonants /k, g/ the diphthongs starting with [j] are merged with the consonant (see the consonants *ch* and *gh*).

At the end of a word, after a consonant, an unstressed *i* is pronounced as [ⁱ]:

pomi	[pomⁱ]	trees
ești	['jeʃtⁱ]	you are

However, in the sound group cons. + *l/r* + *i*, the final *i* is pronounced as [i]:

metri	['metri]	metres
urli	['urli]	you scream

Exception:
azvârli	[az'vɨrlⁱ]	you throw

Even in some foreign words and proper names the unstressed final *-i* is pronounced as [i]:

swahili	[swa'çili]	Swahili
Coresi	[ko'resi]	Coresi (a name)

At the end of a word, a stressed *-i* is pronounced always as [i]:

auzi	[au'zi]	to hear
construi	[konstru'ʲi]	to build
pustii	[pusti'ʲi]	to ravage, to devastate

The suffix *–ii*, which occurs e.g. in the definite masculine nominative and accusative plural and in the definite feminine genitive and dative singular, is pronounced as [i]:

pomii	['pomi]	the threes
metrii	['metri]	the metres
caii	['kaʲi]	the horses
limbii	['limbi]	of the language

At the end of a word, *-iii* is pronounced as two syllables according to the morphological structure of the word:

copiii	[ko'piʲi]	the children
fiii	['fiʲi]	the sons
pustiii	[pus.ti.ʲiị]	I have devastated

The letter *i* is also used for the writing of the consonants [tʃ, dʒʲ] (see the consonants *c* and *g*).

o   is usually pronounced as [o]:

pom	[pom]	tree
frumos	[fru'mos]	beautiful
omorî	[omo'rɨ]	to kill

In diphthongs and triphthongs, *o* is pronounced as a semivowel [o̯]:

foarte	['fo̯arte]	very
creioane	[krejo̯ane]	pencils

At the beginning of a syllable, *oa* is pronounced as [wa]:

oameni	['wamenʲ]	men
găoace	[gə'watʃe]	shell

u   is usually pronounced as [u]:

un	[un]	one
lung	[luŋg]	long

In diphthongs and triphthongs, *u* is pronounced as a semiconsonant [w] before another vowel and a semivowel [u̯] after:

ziua	['ziwa]	the day
citeau	[tʃi'te̯au̯]	they were reading

Pronunciation of consonant letters

b   is pronounced as [b]:

braț	[brats]	arm
bob	[bob]	bean, grain

c   is pronounced before *e* and *i* as [ʧ]:

face	['faʧe]	to do
cer	[ʧer]	sky
cine	['ʧine]	who
scenă	['stʧenə]	stage
accent	[ak'ʧent]	accent

In colloquial speech, [stʧ] is pronounced often as [ʃʧ]: ['ʃʧenə]. This pronunciation is not recommended.

Before another vowel, *ci* or *ce* are pronounced as [ʧ] (i.e. there is no [j] or [e̦] after a palatalised consonant):

ciot	[ʧot]	tree stump
ceas	[ʧas]	clock
serviciu	[ser'viʧu]	work

However, if the following vowel belongs to a different syllable, both vowels are pronounced:

licean	[liʧe'an]	pupil (at the secondary school)

Also a stressed *i* is pronounced before another vowel:

sălciu	[səl'ʧiu̦]	tasteless

At the end of a word an unstressed *ci* is pronounced as [ʧ]:

faci	[faʧ]	you do
nici	[niʧ]	not even

In some nouns (mostly compound words) the sound [ʧ] occurs before another consonant. In this case too it is spelled with *ci*:

nicicum	[niʧ'kum]	no way
cincisprezece	[ʧin(ʧ)spre'zeʧe]	fifteen
Pecica	['peʧka]	Pecica (a city)

In all other cases (i.e. before the other vowels, before a consonant and at the end of the word) *c* is pronounced as [k]:

casă	['kasə]	house
crede	['krede]	believe
fac	[fak]	I do

ch   Before *e* and *i* the sound /k/ is spelled *ch*. It is pronounced as a palatalised [kʲ] and the letter *h* is not pronounced at all:

chelner	['kʲelner]	waiter
chimie	[kʲi'miʲe]	chemistry
chiasmă	[kʲi'asmə]	chiasm

The sounds [j, ę, ⁱ] merge with the preceding palatalised consonant:

chiar	[kʲar]	just
cheamă	['kʲamə]	he/she calls
ochi	[okʲ]	eye

d is pronounced as [d]:

deget	['dedʒʲet]	finger
nud	[nud]	naked

f is pronounced as [f]:

frate	['frate]	brother
pantof	[pan'tof]	shoe

g is pronounced before *e* and *i* as [dʒʲ]:

ger	[dʒʲer]	frost
girafă	[dʒʲi'rafə]	giraffe

Before another vowel, *gi* or *ge* are pronounced as [dʒʲ] (i.e. there is no [j] or [ę] after a palatalised consonant):

giulgiu	['dʒʲuldʒʲu]	shroud
georgian	[dʒʲor'dʒʲan]	Georgian
geam	[dʒʲam]	window, glass

However, if the following vowel belongs to a different syllable, both vowels are pronounced:

geografie	[dʒʲeogra'fʲe]	geography

Also a stressed *i* is pronounced before another vowel:

hangiu	[han'dʒʲiu̯]	innkeeper

At the end of a word an unstressed *gi* is pronounced as [dʒʲ]:

dragi	[dradʒʲ]	dear (pl.)
fugi	[fudʒʲ]	you run

In all other cases (i.e. before the other vowels, before a consonant and at the end of the word) *g* is pronounced as [g]:

gând	[gɨnd]	thought
gumă	['gumə]	rubber
greu	[greu̯]	heavy ; difficult
drag	[drag]	dear

Notice that there is no digraph *ng* in Romanian and both letters have their own phonetic value ([ŋg] or [ndʒʲ]):

englez	[eŋ'glez]	English
miting	['mitiŋg]	meeting
sânge	['sɨndʒʲe]	blood

gh   Before *e* and *i* the sound /g/ is spelled *gh*. It is pronounced as a palatalised [gʲ] and the letter *h* is not pronounced at all:

ghețar	[gʲe'tsar]	iceberg
ghindă	['gʲində]	acorn
unghie	['uŋʲgʲiʲe]	nail

The sounds [j, e̦, ⁱ] merge with the preceding palatalised consonant:

Gheorghe	['gʲorgʲe]	George
gheață	['gʲatsə]	ice
unghi	[uŋʲgʲ]	corner

h   is usually pronounced as [h]:

hartă	['hartə]	map
zahăr	['zahər]	sugar

Before the letter *i* it is pronounced as a palatalised [ç]:

arhitect	[arçi'tekt]	architect
monahi	[mo'naçⁱ]	monks

At the end of a word, before a consonant and after a consonant (but not before *i*), it is pronounced [x]:

monah	[mo'nax]	monk
hrană	['xranə]	food, nourishment
arheolog	[arxeo'log]	archaeologist

The letter *h* is not pronounced in the groups *chi, che, ghi, ghe* (see above). The letter *h* is also silent in some foreign words like *charismă, Thailanda, Afghanistan ~ Afganistan*.

j   is pronounced as [ʒ]:

juca	[ʒu'ka]	to play
joi	[ʒoi̯]	Thursday

l   is pronounced as [l]:

ladă	['ladə]	box
cal	[kal]	horse

m is usually pronounced as [m]:

mamă	['mamə]	mother
pom	[pom]	(fruit) tree

Before the consonants *f* and *v* it is pronounced as a labiodental [ɱ]:

amfiteatru	[aɱfite'atru]	amphitheatre
tramvai	[traɱ'vai̯]	tram

n is usually pronounced as [n]:

noi	[noi̯]	we
an	[an]	year

Before sounds [k, g, x] it is pronounced as a velar [ŋ]:

încă	['iŋkə]	still
englez	[eŋ'glez]	English
înhuma	[iŋxu'ma]	bury

Before sounds [kʲ, gʲ, ç] it is pronounced as a palatalisezed verlar [ŋʲ]:

unchi	[uŋʲkʲ]	uncle
unghi	[uŋʲgʲ]	corner
branhie	['braŋʲçʲe]	gill

Before the consonants *p, b* and *m* it is pronounced as [m]:

input	['imput]	input
înmiit	[immi'ʲit]	thousandfold

Before consonants *f* and *v* it is pronounced as a labiodental [ɱ]:

inferior	[iɱferi'or]	inferior
învăța	[iɱvə'tsa]	to teach

p is pronounced as [p]:

papă	['papə]	pope
dulap	[du'lap]	cupboard

r is pronounced as [r]:

rar	[rar]	rare
rege	['redʒʲe]	king

Notice that the word *roma* 'Romani' can also be spelled as *rroma*.

s is pronounced as [s]:

sus	[sus]	above
casă	['kasə]	house

ş   is pronounced as [ʃ]:

şi	[ʃi]	and
aşa	[a'ʃa]	so

t   is pronounced as [t]:

tată	['tatə]	father
trezi	[tre'zi]	to wake up

ţ   is pronounced as [ts]:

ţară	['tsarə]	country
îţi	[itsⁱ]	to you

v   is pronounced as [v]:

vară	['varə]	summer
bolnav	[bol'nav]	ill

x   is usually pronounced as [ks]:

pix	[piks]	pen
xilitol	[ksili'tol]	xylitol

Between two vowels, *x* is pronounced either as [ks] or [gz]. The correct pronunciation must be learnt individually with every word:

taxi	[tak'si]	taxi
exemplu	[eg'zemplu]	example

z   is pronounced as [z]:

zi	[zi]	day
zăpadă	[zə'padə]	snow

Syllabification

The syllabification is done according to the following rules:

- Diphthongs and triphthong are not divided (*pia-tră, pleoa-pă*).
- Vowels in hiatus belong to different syllables (*sa-u-nă, e-po-pe-e*).
- A single consonant or a semiconsonant between vowels is grouped with the following syllable (*ca-sa, soa-re, no-uă*). *Ch* and *gh* are treated as single consonants (*u-re-che*), *x* is a single consonant in writing but two in pronunciation (*ta-xi* [tak.'si]).
- Two consonants between vowels belong to different syllables (*car-te, aş-tep-ta*).
- However, combination *p, b, t, d, c, g, f, v, h + r/l* is inseparable (*tea-tru, cu-pru, ti-tlu, a-tlet*).
- When there are three or more consonants between vowels, only the first consonant belongs to the preceding syllable (*as-tru, lin-gvist*).

- Exceptions: *lp-t, mp-t, mp-ț, nc-ș, nc-t, nc-ț, nd-v, rc-t, rt-f, st-m* (*sculp-ta, punc-tu-a-ți-e, ast-mul*).
- Combined words and derivations can also be divided according to their structure (*i-ne-gal ~ in-e-gal, de-ze-chi-li-bru ~ dez-e-chi-li-bru*).

Sound changes

One of the characteristics of Romanian is the very frequent sound changes that occur in the declension of nouns and adjectives and in the conjugation of verbs. Although many sound changes are regular, the rules have many exceptions. The consonant changes are more regular and predictable than the vowel changes.

Consonant changes

The regular consonant change occur when the endings *-i* or *-e* (or endings starting with these vowels) are added to the stem of a noun, adjective or verb. The following consonants and consonant groups are affected:

[k, g] + *e/i* → [tʃ, dʒʲ]	*mic* 'small' → pl. *mici*
	ac 'needle' → pl. *ace*
	drag 'dear' → pl. *dragi*
	catalog 'catalogue' → pl. *cataloage*
s + *i* → *și*	*frumos* 'beautiful' → pl. *frumoși*
	lăsa 'to leave' → *lași* 'you leave'
st + *i* → *ști*	*specialist* 'specialist' → pl. *specialiști*
	asista 'to assist' → *asiști* 'you assist'
str + *i* → *ștri*	*albastru* 'blue' → pl. *albaștri*
	mustra 'to blame' → *muștri* 'you blame'
sc/șc + *e/i* → *ște/ști*	*muscă* 'fly' → pl. *muște*
	mișca 'to move' → *miști* 'you move'
t + *i* → *ți*	*student* 'student' → pl. *studenți*
	arăta 'to show' → *arăți* 'you show'
d + *i* → *zi*	*verde* 'green' → pl. *verzi*
	vedea 'to see' → *vezi* 'you see'

In the verbs belonging to the third and fourth conjugations, these sound changes occur in "reversed order", e.g.:

[dʒʲ] → *g*	*merge* 'to go' → *merg* 'I go'
zi → *d*	*auzi* 'to hear' → *aud* 'I hear'

The exceptions to these rules are extremely rare.

On the other hand, the following types of consonant change are rarer and must be learnt individually with every word:

l/n + *i* → *i* [i̯]	*cal* 'horse' → pl. *cai*
	vin 'I come' → *vii* 'you come'
z → *j*	*obraz* 'cheek' → pl. *obraji*

Vowel changes

The vowel changes are more irregular and must be learnt individually with every word. The vowel changes occur more often in older vocabulary, whereas newer words are often unaffected.

The most frequent vowel change is the diphthongisation of the vowels *o* and *e* in stressed syllables:

- The vowel *o* changes to *oa* when the following syllable has the vowel *ă* or *e*:

pot	→ *poate*	I can → he/she can
	→ *poată*	→ he/she can (conj.)
frumos	→ *frumoasă*	beautiful (m. sg. → f. sg.)
	→ *frumoase*	→ (f. pl.)
oi	→ *oaie*	sheep (pl. → sg.)
moi	→ *moale*	soft (pl. → sg.)

- The vowel *e* changes when the following syllable has the vowel *ă*:

negru	→ *neagră*	black (m. sg. → f. sg.)
seri	→ *seară*	evening (pl. → sg.)

- The diphthong *ie* changes to *ia* in the same environment (*ie* → *iea* → *ia*):

iese	→ *iasă*	he/she goes out (ind. → conj.)
pietre	→ *piatră*	stone (pl. → sg.)
iepe	→ *iapă*	mare (pl. → sg.)

- After the consonant *ş* the change *e* → *ea* occurs as *a* → *e* (only in stems):

aşeze	→ *aşază*	he/she sits (conj. → ind.)

Other vowel changes include e.g.:

- The change *a* → *ă* occurs in verb conjugation when the stress shifts from the stem to the ending:

las	→ *lăsa*	I leave → to leave

- The change $a \rightarrow ă$ ($ia \rightarrow ie$) occurs in nouns before the ending -*i*:

ladă	$\rightarrow$ *lăzi*	box (sg. $\rightarrow$ pl.)
băiat	$\rightarrow$ *băieți*	boy (sg. $\rightarrow$ pl.)

- The changes $ă \leftrightarrow e$ (before *e* and *i*) $\leftrightarrow a$ (before *ă*) occur after labial consonants (*p, b, f, v, m*):

văd	$\rightarrow$ *vezi*	$\rightarrow$ *vadă*	I see, you see, he/she sees (conj.)
măr	$\rightarrow$ *meri*		apple tree (sg. $\rightarrow$ pl.)
păr	$\rightarrow$ *peri*		pear tree (sg. $\rightarrow$ pl.)
	pere	$\rightarrow$ *pară*	pear (pl. $\rightarrow$ sg.)
	fete	$\rightarrow$ *fată*	girl (pl. $\rightarrow$ sg.)

- A few words have the rarer vowel change $â \rightarrow i$, e.g.:

cuvânt	$\rightarrow$ *cuvinte*	word (sg. $\rightarrow$ pl.)
vând	$\rightarrow$ *vinde*	I sell $\rightarrow$ to sell

The sound changes are explained in more detail in the chapters concerning the declension of nouns and adjectives and the conjugation of verbs.

Nouns and articles

Romanian nouns have three different genders (masculine, feminine and neuter), two numbers (singular and plural), and five cases (nominative, accusative, genitive, dative and vocative).

There are two degrees of definiteness (indefinite and definite), which are expressed with the indefinite and definite articles. Apart from these, traditional grammar includes a further two articles: the genitive and the demonstrative article.

Gender

As a general principle, most Romanian nouns can be classified into different genders according to their form, as follows:

Masc.	Neuter	Fem.
Nouns ending in a consonant Nouns ending in -*u* Nouns ending in -*i*		
		Nouns ending in -*ă* Nouns ending in -*a*
Nouns ending in -*e*		

Since masculine and neuter nouns have the same form, the gender of these nouns must be learnt individually with every noun. In contrast, feminine nouns are usually easy to recognise. Nouns ending in -*e* can be of any gender.

Masculine

Masculine nouns end in a consonant or in the vowels -*u* or -*e*, rarely in -*i*.

Exceptions:

- Some nouns ending in -*ă* referring to human males are masculine: e.g. *papă* 'pope', *popă* 'priest', *tată* 'father', *vodă* 'voivode, prince'.
- Some new loanwords end in -*a* or -*o*: e.g. *koala, boa, euro, dingo*.

The following nouns are usually masculine:

- nouns referring to human males (*Ion, Mircea, bărbat* 'man', *frate* 'brother').
- names of mountains (*Carpați* 'Carpathians', *Anzi* 'Andes').

- months (*ianuarie* 'January', *mai* 'May').
- trees (*arbore* 'tree', *pom* '(fruit) tree', *păr* 'pear tree', *prun* 'plum tree').
- numbers (*un trei* 'a three').
- letters and sounds[30] (*un A, un B, un alfa, un beta*).
- musical notes (*do, re, mi*).

Feminine

All the feminine nouns end in a vowel, usually in -*ă* or -*e*, more rarely in -*a*.

Exceptions:

- There are a few feminine nouns that end in -*i*. These include: *zi* 'day', some days of the week (*luni* 'Monday', *marţi* 'Tuesday', *miercuri* 'Wednesday', *joi* 'Thursday', *vineri* 'Friday'), *tanti* 'aunt (fam.)' and a few foreign words such as *kiwi* ['kivi], *lady* ['ledi].
- Feminines ending in -*o* are extremely rare, the most common being *cacao*. Also e.g. *imago* 'imago (biol.)'.
- Some words for languages end in -*u*: *zulu, urdu, bantu*.
- Some foreign words end in a consonant: *babysitter, miss, cover-girl*.

Long infinitives (-*are, -ere* etc.), nouns ending in -*ie* (except the names of months) and nouns formed with the suffixes -*tate* or -*iune* are feminine (e.g. *lucrare* 'work', *familie* 'family', *compatibilitate* 'compatibility', *naţiune* 'nation').

The following nouns are usually feminine:

- nouns referring to human females (*Maria, Ioana, femeie* 'woman', *fată* 'girl').
- names of countries and islands (*Finlanda* 'Finland', *România* 'Romania', *Sardinia, Corsica*).
- continents (*Africa, America, Antarctida, Asia, Australia, Europa*).
- fruits and flowers (*pară* 'pear', *prună* 'plum', *garoafă* 'carnation').
- days of the week (*luni* 'Monday', *marţi* 'Tuesday').
- seasons (*iarnă* 'winter', *primăvară* 'spring', *vară* 'summer', *toamnă* 'autumn').
- languages (*engleză* 'English').

Many nouns referring to human beings or animals have special forms for male and female:

- Sometimes a different word is used:

bărbat	femeie	man	woman
tată	mamă	father	mother
frate	soră	brother	sister
fiu	fiică	son	daughter

---

[30] The Latin letters can also be neuter: *un A, niște A-uri*. The names of sounds are always masculine: *un A, niște A*.

băiat	fată	boy	girl
ginere	noră	son-in-law	daughter-in-law
cal	iapă	horse	mare
cocoş	găină	rooster	chicken
bou, taur	vacă	ox, bull	cow
berbec	oaie	ram	ewe
motan, cotoi	pisică	tomcat	cat
câine	căţea	dog	bitch

- The feminine form is often formed with different suffixes such as *-ă, -toare, -că, -oaică, -iţă, -esă, -ină*:

student	studentă	student
profesor	profesoară	teacher
cumnat	cumnată	brother-in-law, sister-in-law
socru	soacră	father-in-law, mother-in-law
bunic	bunică	grandfather, grandmother
scriitor	scriitoare	writer
traducător	traducătoare	translator
conducător	conducătoare	leader
român	româncă	Romanian man, woman
ţăran	ţărancă	peasant
turc	turcoaică	Turk, Turkish man, woman
lup	lupoaică	wolf, she-wolf
actor	actriţă	actor, actress
doctor	doctoriţă	doctor
pictor	pictoriţă	painter, artist
duce	ducesă	duke, duchess
principe	principesă	prince, princess
erou	eroină	hero, heroine
rege	regină	king, queen

- Rarely, the masculine form is formed from the feminine form:

gâscă f.	gâscan m.	goose, gander
mierlă f.	mierloi m.	blackbird
vulpe f.	vulpoi m.	vixen, fox

The masculine plural form of nouns referring to humans is also used when talking about both males and females:

actori	actors
bunici	grandparents
fraţi	siblings
socri	parents-in-law

Some nouns have a third form for referring to both male and female:

copil, copii m.	child
om, oameni m.	human, people
părinte, părinți m.	parent

With animals, in some cases the masculine form is used for referring to the whole species, while in others the feminine is used:

cal m.	horse
lup m.	wolf
câine m.	dog
găină f.	chicken
oaie f.	sheep
vacă f.	cow
vulpe f.	fox
pisică f.	cat

However, most animals have only one grammatical gender.

Neuter

The neuter nouns refer usually to inanimate things. Just like masculine nouns, neuter nouns end usually in a consonant or in the vowels -u, -e, -i. Most of the nouns ending in -ou are neuter[31].

Exceptions:

- Some foreign words end in -o: *radio, trio, kilo.*
- Neuters ending in -a are extremely rare: *cinema, lila* 'lilac (colour)'.

Words formed with the suffixes -ment, -mânt, -ism are neuter, just like the nouns made from the verbal supine forms (e.g. *argument* 'argument', *mormânt* 'grave', *comunism* 'communism', *ras* 'shave').

Neuter nouns include:

- colours (*negru* 'black colour', *albastru* 'blue colour', *verde* 'green colour', *lila* 'lilac colour').
- senses (*auz* 'hearing', *miros* 'smell', *gust* 'taste').

In the singular, Romanian neuter nouns act like masculine nouns, but in the plural they act as feminine nouns.

---

[31] There are only three masculine nouns ending in -ou: *bou* 'ox', *erou* 'hero', *bardou* 'hinny'.

Exceptions to the gender rules

Exceptions to the gender rules mentioned above are quite frequent. For example, many nouns referring to humans or animals have only one grammatical gender:

- always masculine:

rector	head teacher, school principal
decan	dean
struț	ostrich
hipopotam	hippopotamus
elefant	elephant

- always feminine:

persoană	person
rudă	relative
victimă	victim
vedetă	star
balenă	whale
furnică	ant
muscă	fly

- always neuter:

star	star
model	model
animal	animal
macrou	mackerel

All these nouns can naturally refer to both males and females. When talking about animals, the natural gender can be distinguished using the words *mascul* 'male' and *femelă* 'female': *un cangur-mascul, un cangur-femelă* 'male/female kangaroo', *o girafă-mascul, o girafă-femelă* 'male/female giraffe'. Notice that the grammatical gender does not change.

Many nouns referring to (traditionally male) professions have only a masculine form, which can be used also for women:

amiral	admiral
soldat	soldier
istoric	historian
ministru	minister
politician	politician
președinte	president
medic	medic
președintele finlandez Tarja Halonen	the President of Finland Tarja Halonen

ministrul turismului Elena Udrea		Tourism Minister Elena Udrea
Doamna președinte!		Mrs. President!

Some (traditionally female) professions only have a feminine form:

moașă	midwife
bonă	nanny

If needed, compound words like o *femeie-soldat* 'a female soldier' and *un bărbat-moașă* 'a male midwife' can be used.

The other gender rules have some exceptions as well. For example, the flowers *trandafir* 'rose' and *toporaș* 'viola' are masculine, while the fruit *măr* 'apple' is neuter.

In some words, a change in gender also changes the meaning (and the plural form). Nouns like these include:

un cap, capi	m.	chief, leader
un cap, capuri	n.	cape, headland
un cap, capete	n.	head
un cot, coți	m.	cubit
un cot, coate	n.	elbow
un cot, coturi	n.	bend, curve
un ghid, ghizi	m.	guide (person)
o ghidă, ghide	f.	guide (person) (rarely used)
un ghid, ghiduri	n.	guidebook
un ochi, ochi	m.	egg
un ochi, ochiuri	n.	fried egg
un kiwi, kiwi	n.	kiwifruit
o kiwi, kiwi	f.	kiwi (bird)
un măr, meri	m.	apple tree
un măr, mere	n.	apple (fruit)
un pas, pași	m.	step
un pas, pasuri	n.	mountain pass
un râs, râși	m.	lynx
un râs, râsuri	n.	laughter
un timp, timpi	m.	tempo (music)
un timp, timpuri	n.	time ; tense
un umăr, umeri	m.	shoulder
un umăr, umere	n.	coat hanger
un zmeu, zmei	m.	dragon
un zmeu, zmeie	n.	kite

Number

In the different genders the regular plural endings are as follows:

Masc.	Fem.	Neuter
-i	-e, -i, -le, (-uri)	-e, -uri, (-i)

Since the choice of the plural ending is not always predictable, the correct plural form must usually be learnt individually with every noun. The different sound changes in the stem of the nouns complicate the matter further.

With some new loanwords the same form is used both for singular and plural.

Plural of masculine nouns

The plural ending for masculine nouns is -i. There are also some invariable masculine loanwords.

Masculine nouns ending in a consonant

After a consonant the plural ending -i is pronounced as [-ⁱ]:

an, ani	year
lup, lupi	wolf
cerb, cerbi	moose
pantof, pantofi	shoe
elev, elevi	pupil
ucigaş, ucigaşi	murderer
profesor, profesori	teacher

The ending -i causes regular consonant changes (see p. 35) and several unpredictable vowel changes. The consonant changes occur in all nouns ending in the following consonants:

$t \rightarrow t$:
student, studenţi	student
bărbat, bărbaţi	man

$d \rightarrow z$:
doctorand, doctoranzi	graduate student
ghepard, gheparzi	cheetah

$s \rightarrow ş$ ($x \rightarrow cş$):
pas, paşi	step
urs, urşi	bear

index, indecşi	index finger
sfinx, sfincşi	sphinx

st → şt

artist, artişti	artist
gimnast, gimnaşti	gymnast

sc → şt (rare)

mosc, moşti	musk deer
vasilisc, vasilişti	basilisk

[k] → [t͡ʃ]

porc, porci	pig
nuc, nuci	walnut tree

[g] → [d͡ʒ]

fag, fagi	beech
meteorolog, meteorologi	meteorologist

Regular consonant changes also occur in foreign words not yet adapted to the Romanian orthography:

boss, boşi	boss
watt [vat], waţi	watt
byte [baįt], byţi	byte
yard [įard], yarzi	yard

The sound change *sc → şt* does not occur with a few nouns referring to nationalities (*basc, monegasc, etrusc, morisc, osc, volsc*). These nouns have the sound change [sk] → [st͡ʃ] instead (see the conjugation of adjectives, p. 108).

The following consonant changes are irregular and occur in only a few words:

z → j:

obraz, obraji	cheek
praz, praji	leek
boz, boji	danewort, dwarf elder (plant)
mânz, mânji	foal

l → -:

copil, copii [-į]	child
cal, cai [-į]	horse
miel, miei [-į]	lamb
colonel, colonei [-į]	colonel

The diminutive suffix *-el* behaves the same way:

tinerel, tinerei	youngster

Most of the masculine nouns ending in *-z* or *-l* are regular:

englez, englezi	Englishman
amiral, amirali	admiral

The vowel changes must usually be learnt individually for every word. The most frequent vowel change types are *ea* → *e* and *ia* → *ie*:

european, europeni	European man
coreean, coreeni	Korean man
licean, liceeni	pupil
băiat, băieți	boy
belgian, belgieni	Belgian

The vowel change *ă* → *e* is rarer and it occurs only after a labial sound (*m, b, p, v, f*):

păr, peri	hair ; pear tree
măr, meri	apple tree
făt, feți	foetus
văr, veri	cousin

In a few words the vowel change *ă* → *e* occurs in an unstressed syllable:

umăr, umeri	shoulder
ienupăr, ienuperi	juniper
seamăn, semeni	fellow man
geamăn, gemeni	twin
mesteacăn, mesteceni	birch

The following two words have the vowel change *â* → *i*:

tânăr, tineri	young man
sfânt, sfinți	saint

Totally irregular masculine nouns are:

om, oameni	man, people
leah, leși (old-fashioned)	Pole

Some words ending in *man* have an English type plural *-meni*:

businessman ['biznismen], businessmeni	businessman
gentleman [-men], gentlemeni	gentleman
yesman [iesmen], yesmeni	yes man

Exceptions:

barman [-man], barmani	barman
cameraman [-man], cameramani	cameraman

Notice also the following nouns having *-men* in the singular:

tenismen, tenismeni	tennis player
congresmen, congresmeni	congressman

Masculine nouns ending in a vowel

If a masculine noun ends in one of the vowels *-e, -u*[32] or *-ă*, this vowel is removed before the plural ending. After cons. + *l/r* the plural ending is pronounced as [i] and after a vowel it is pronounced as [i̯] (see the pronunciation of *i*, p. 28):

câine, câini [-ʲ]	dog
peşte, peşti [-ʲ]	fish
rege, regi [-ʲ]	king
litru, litri [-i]	litre
metru, metri [-i]	metre
leu, lei [-i̯]	lion
fiu, fii [-i̯]	son
bou, boi [-i̯]	ox
popă, popi [-ʲ]	priest
papă, papi [-ʲ]	pope

The regular consonant changes occurring with these nouns are *t → ţ, d → z, str → ştr*:

t → ţ:

dinte, dinţi	tooth
frate, fraţi	brother
tată, taţi	father

d → z:

erede, erezi	heir
custode, custozi	custodian
gâde, gâzi	executioner (colloq.)

str → ştr:

astru, aştri [-i]	celestial object
ministru, miniştri [-i]	minister

The sound change *st → şt* does not occur in the word *staroste, starosti* (old-fashioned) 'starosta, the elder of a guild'.

Vowel changes are rarer:

soare, sori	sun
şarpe, şerpi	snake
cumătru, cumetri [-i]	god father

---

[32] Nouns ending in a cons. + *l/r* + *u* or a diphthongs ending in *-u*.

Masculine nouns ending in -*i* have the same form for both singular and plural:

ochi, ochi	eye
unchi, unchi	uncle
pui, pui	chicken
maori [-i], maori [-i]	Maori
colibri, colibri	hummingbird

Invariable masculine nouns

The names of letters[33], musical notes and numbers are invariable (the plural is identical to the singular form):

A, A	A (sound, letter)
beta, beta	beta (Greek letter)
do, do	do (musical note)
zece, zece	ten (number, school grade)

Colloquial nouns formed by the suffix -*ilă* are also invariable:

sărăcilă, sărăcilă	pauper (colloq.)
orbilă, orbilă	blind (a person who does not notice what is going on)

Masculine nouns ending in -*a*, -*o* or in a stressed vowel are new loanwords. The plural form of these nouns is identical to the singular:

koala, koala	koala bear
judoka, judoka	judoka
anşoa, anşoa	anchovy (fish)
boa, boa	boa snake
euro, euro	euro
dingo, dingo	dingo (dog)
avocado, avocado	avocado tree
mango, mango	mango tree
acaju, acaju	mahogany
gnu, gnu	wildebeest

However, the following three nous have a plural ending in -*i*:

picolo, picoli	piccolo
flamingo, flamingi	flamingo
paparazzo [-tso], paparazzi [-tsi]	paparazzi

Other invariable loanwords include (mostly nouns ending in a cons. + *u*[34]):

guru, guru	guru
nandu / nandu, nandu / nandu	nandu, Darwin's Rhea (a bird)

---

[33] The Latin letters can also be neuter: *A, A-uri.*
[34] Other than nouns ending in a cons. + *l/r* + *u.*

emu, emu	emu (a bird)
kamikaze, kamikaze	kamikaze

Some foreign words are only used in the singular:

bebe [be'be or 'bebe]	baby
papa	papa, father
vodă	voivode, prince

Plural forms of masculine nouns

Noun type	Plural	
cons.		*lup, lupi*
-e		*câine, câini*
cons. + *l/r + u*	-i	*litru, litri*
vowel + *u*		*leu, lei*
-ă		*popă, popi*
-i		*ochi, ochi*
-o, -a, -u	-	*dingo; koala; guru*
Irreg.	*om, oameni; flamingo, flamingi, leah, leşi...*	

Plural of feminine nouns

The plural ending for feminine nouns is *-e, -i, -le* or (rarely) *-uri*. The general rule is that *-e* is used with nouns ending in *-ă, -i* with nouns ending both in *-ă* or *-e*, and *-le* with nouns ending in a stressed *-a*.

Feminine nouns ending in -ă

The plural ending for feminine nouns ending in *-ă* can be either *-e* or *-i* [ʲ], and therefore the ending must be learnt individually with every word.

Plural ending in -e:

casă, case	house
profesoară, profesoare	teacher
prună, prune	prune

Plural ending in -i:

limbă, limbi	language
maşină, maşini	car
inimă, inimi	heart

Some words can have different plural endings in different meanings:

vară, vere	cousin
vară, veri	summer

The regular consonant changes (see p. 35) are *d* → *z*, *t* → *ț* before *i* and *sc/șc* → *șt*, [k] → [tʃ], [g] → [dʒʲ] before *i* or *e*:

d → *z:*

coadă, cozi	tail
oglindă, oglinzi	mirror

t → *ț:*

poartă, porți	port
hartă, hărți	map

sc, șc → *șt:*

muscă, muște	fly
broască, broaște	frog
pușcă, puști	gun, rifle

[k] → [tʃ]

marcă, mărci	mark
pisică, pisici	cat

[g] → [dʒʲ]

pungă, pungi	bag
creangă, crengi	bough

The sound change *sc* → *șt* does not occur in a few nouns referring to nationalities (*bască*[35], *monegască, etruscă, moriscă, oscă, volscă*). These nouns have the sound change [sk] → [stʃ] instead (see the conjugation of adjectives, p. 108). Also some other words behave the same way:

frescă, fresce	fresco
ască, asce	ascus
odaliscă, odalisce	odalisque

As can be seen from the examples above, nouns ending in *-că* or *-gă* (except those ending in *-scă*) usually form their plural with the ending *-i*. Exceptions (plural with *-e*) include the nouns formed by the suffixes *-ancă, -oaică, -logă* and a few others:

ucraineancă, ucrainence	Ukrainian woman
norvegiancă, norvegience	Norwegian woman
leoaică, leoaice	lioness
biologă, biologe[36]	biologist
colegă, colege	colleague
algă, alge	alga, algae

---

[35] The regular sound change occurs in the meaning 'baret (hat)': *bască, băști.* 'Baret' can also be a neuter: *basc, bascuri.*

[36] Usually the masculine form *biolog, biologi* is used even when talking about female biologists. Similarly e.g. *astrolog(ă)* 'astrologist', *filolog(ă)* 'philologist' etc.

The most frequent vowel change types are *ea → e, ia → ie, oa → o*:

fereastră, ferestre	window
seară, seri	evening
piață, piețe	city square
viață, vieți	life
școală, școli	school
boală, boli	disease

The vowel change *a → ă* is quite common with the plural ending *-i*:

barbă, bărbi	beard
ladă, lăzi	box
stradă, străzi	street
țară, țări	country

The vowel change *a → e* occurs only after a labial sound:

fată, fete	girl
masă, mese	table
pană, pene	feather
vară, veri	summer
zăpadă, zăpezi	snow

Some feminine nouns have the sound change *ă → e* in an unstressed syllable:

lepădă, lepede	swan
tabără, tabere	camp
sâmbătă, sâmbete	Saturday
geamănă, gemene	twin girl

The following sound changes are rarer:

â → i:

vână, vine	vein
sfântă, sfinte	saint
sămânță, semințe	seed
tânără, tinere	young woman

ă → e:

cumătră, cumetre	godmother

Irregular feminine nouns are:

soră, surori	sister ; nurse
noră, nurori	daughter-in-law
mână, mâini	hand
piuă, pive	mortar

Feminine nouns formed by the diminutive suffix -*ică* form their plural with the suffix -*ea* (pl. -*ele*):

iubițică, iubițele	love (fam.)
minciunică, minciunele	little lie
păsărică, păsărele (păsărici)	small bird

Exception:

mămică, mămici	mummy

Feminine nouns ending in -e

Feminine nouns ending in -*e* usually form their plural with the ending -*i*, which is pronounced as [ⁱ] after a consonant and [i̯] after a vowel:

pâine, pâini [-ⁱ]	bread
lege, legi	law
ordine, ordini	order
vulpe, vulpi	fox
idee, idei [-i̯]	idea
epopee, epopei	epic
diaree, diarei	diarrhoea
moschee, moschei	mosque

The regular consonant changes occurring with these nouns are *t* → *ț*, *d* → *z*, *st* → *șt*:

carte, cărți	book
parte, părți	part
lespede, lespezi	flagstone
poveste, povești	tale, story

The consonant change *d* → *z* does not occur with the nouns *nădejde, nădejdi* 'hope' and *deznădejde, deznădejdi* 'despair'.

The only possible vowel changes are *a* → *ă*, *oa* → *o*:

floare, flori	flower
lucrare, lucrări	work

The consonant *l* disappears in three words:

cale, căi [-i̯]	way, path, road
piele, piei [-i̯]	skin ; leather
vale, văi [-i̯]	valley

Feminine nouns formed with the ending -*toare* denoting people have a plural that is identical to the singular:

dansatoare, dansatoare	dancer
muncitoare, muncitoare	worker

| scriitoare, scriitoare | writer |
| trecătoare, trecătoare | walker |

Other nouns ending in *-oare* have the regular plural ending *-ori*:

| scrisoare, scrisori | letter |
| trecătoare, trecători | mountain pass |

Also some other feminines ending in *-e* have a plural identical to the singular form:

canoe, canoe	canoe
dragoste, dragoste	love
matrice, matrice	matrix
aloe, aloe	aloe
vetrice, vetrice	tansy
leghe, leghe	league (about 3 miles)

Scientific names ending in *-ee* behave the same way:

cefalee, cefalee	headache
orhidee, orhidee	orchid
rozacee, rozacee	Rosaceae, the rose family
onomatopee, onomatopee	onomatopoeic word

Some nouns have alternative plural forms:

| cicatrice, cicatrice / cicatrici | scar |

Feminine nouns ending in *-ie*

The plural ending of these nouns is *-ii* [iị] after a consonant, and *-i* [ị] after a vowel:

lecție [-iʲe], lecții [-iị]	lesson
hârtie, hârtii	paper
familie, familii	family

femeie [-je], femei [-ị]	woman
cheie, chei	key
lămâie, lămâi	lemon

The sound changes are quite rare:

a → ă:
baie, băi	bath
odaie, odăi	room
vrabie, vrăbii	sparrow

oa → o:
oaie, oi	sheep
ploaie, ploi	rain
zoaie, zoi	dish water

A few nouns ending in *-ie* have the same form in the plural, e.g.:

căsoaie, căsoaie	big house
gruie, gruie	crane
strigoaie, strigoaie	ghost

Feminine nouns ending in -a

Feminine nouns ending in stressed *-a̠*, *-e̠a̠*, or *-i̠a̠* form their plural with the ending *-le (-ea → -ele, -a → -ale, -ia → -iele / -iale)*:

cafe̠a, cafe̠le	coffee
ste̠a, ste̠le	star
măse̠a, măse̠le	molar tooth
lale̠a, lale̠le	tulip
pijam̠a, pijam̠ale	pyjama
sof̠a, sof̠ale	sofa, couch
z̠a, z̠ale	link (in a chain)
boia, boiele	ground pepper
nisfia, nisfiele	old Turkish coin
raia, raiale	raya (administrative unit of the Ottoman Empire)
But:	
şa, şei	saddle

In contrast, feminine nouns ending in an unstressed *-a* behave in various ways. These are new loanwords and the norm has varied with many nouns[37]. Some nouns have the same form in the plural:

papaia, papaia	papaya
tuia, tuia	thuja (plant)
cola, cola[38]	cola (drink)
mantra, mantra	mantra

Some nouns do not have a plural at all:

yoga	yoga
yucca	yucca (plant)
paranoia	paranoia

Scientific names have a plural (*-a → -e, -ia → ii*):

drosera, drosere	sundew (plant)
cineraria, cinerarii	cineraria (plant)
tibia, tibii	tibia, shinbone

---

[37] In the dictionary DOOM[2] many nouns ending in *-a* and *-ia* have been changed to regular nouns ending in *-ă* or *-ie* (e.g. *sauna → saună*). Many plural forms have also been given to previously invariable nouns.

[38] According to DOOM[2] the plural of *coca-cola*® is *coca-cola*, but that of *pepsi-cola*® is *pepsi-cole*!

Some other words have a plural as well:

salsa, salse	salsa
ikebana, ikebane	ikebana

Some words have two alternative forms in the singular:

leva / levă, leve	leva (Bulgarian currency)
pizza / pizză, pizze [-ts-]	pizza
puma / pumă, pume	puma, cougar

Feminine nouns ending in -i

The plural of feminine nouns ending in *-i* is identical to the singular form:

luni, luni	Monday
marți, marți	Tuesday
miercuri, miercuri	Wednesday
joi, joi	Thursday
vineri, vineri	Friday
kiwi, kiwi ['kivi]	kiwi (bird)
okapi, okapi [o'kapi]	okapi (animal)
lady, lady [ledi]	lady

An important exception is:

zi, zile	day

Other feminine nouns

Feminine nouns ending in *-o-*, *-u* or a consonant are foreign words. Usually these words do not have a plural at all, and if the plural exists, it has the same form as the singular:

cacao	cacao
urdu	Urdu (language)
bantu, bantu	a Bantu language, Bantu languages
Afklärung	Enlightenment
cover-girl, cover-girl	cover-girl
miss, miss	beauty queen

But:

babysitter [bebi'sitər], babysittere[39]	babysitter

Feminine plural ending with -uri

A few feminine noun form their plural with the ending *-uri* [ur[i]]. Many of these are mass nouns that in the plural have the meaning 'different types of':

alamă, alămuri	brass, brass utensils
aramă, arămuri	copper, copper utensils

---

[39] However, the masculine form *babysitter, babysitteri* is more frequent.

blană, blănuri	fur coat
but: blăni / blănuri	fur
carne, cărnuri	meat
ceartă, certuri	quarrel
ceață, cețuri	fog
cerneală, cerneluri	ink
dulceață, dulcețuri	sweets, jam
but: dulceți	pleasant things
favoare, favoruri	favour
făină, făinuri	flour
gheață, ghețuri	ice, drifts of ice
greață, grețuri	nausea
iarbă, ierburi	grass, herbs
lână, lânuri	wool
but: lâni	wool of one sheep
leafă, lefuri	salary
lipsă, lipsuri	absence, lack, need
marfă, mărfuri	merchandise
mătase, mătăsuri	silk
mâncare, mâncăruri	food, dish
but: mâncări	eating (inf. pl.)
otravă, otrăvuri	poison
sare, săruri	salt
treabă, treburi	work
verdeață, verdețuri	green, green groceries
vreme, vremuri / vremi	time
zeamă, zemuri	juice, sauce

The word *brânză* behaves similarly:

brânză, GD brânze	cheese
brânzeturi	types of cheese

Plural forms of feminine nouns

Noun type	Plural	
-ă	-e	*casă, case*
	-i	*limbă, limbi*
	-uri (rare)	*marfă, mărfuri*
-e	-i	*carte, cărți*
	-e	*scriitoare, scriitoare*
	-uri (rare)	*mătase, mătăsuri*
cons. + ie	-ii	*familie, familii*
vowel + ie	-i	*cheie, chei*

Noun type	Plural	
-e<u>a</u>	-ele	*stea, stele*
-<u>a</u>	-ale	*pijama, pijamale*
-a	-a	*tuia, tuia*
	-e	*puma, pume*
-i	-i	*marți, marți*
Irreg.	*mână, mâine; soră, surori; noră, nurori; șa, șei; zi, zile...*	

Plural of neuter nouns

The plural ending for neuter nouns is usually *-e* or *-uri* [ur^i], more rarely *-i.*
Some neuter nouns have a plural that is identical to the singular.

Neuter nouns ending in a consonant

Since both the endings *-e* and *-uri* occur in nouns ending in a consonant, the
plural form must usually be learnt individually for every noun.

Plural ending in -e:
grad, grade	degree
punct, puncte	point
sat, sate	village

Plural ending in -uri:
loc, locuri	place
timp, timpuri	time
tren, trenuri	train

Neuter nouns formed with the suffixes *-ment, -ent, -aj, -ism, -tor, -sor* have a
plural ending in *-e:*

accent, accente	accent
instrument, instrumente	instrument
sondaj, sondaje	opinion poll
latinism, latinisme	Latinism
motor, motoare	motor
ascensor, ascensoare	lift

Nouns made from supine forms (see p. 264) have a plural ending in *-uri:*

cules, culesuri	harvest
ras, rasuri	shave

With some words both endings are accepted:

tunel, tunele / tuneluri	tunnel
nivel, nivele / niveluri	level

Neuter nouns have fewer sound changes than nouns of other genders. Sound changes occur only when the plural ending is -*e*. The most frequent change is the vowel change *o* → *oa*:

os, oase	bone
avion, avioane	airplane
creion, creioane	pencil

The vowel changes *ea* → *e*, *ia* → *ie* are very rare:

briceag, bricege	pocket knife
lighean, lighene	wash basin
toiag, toiege	staff, wand

The vowel change *ă* → *e* occurs in stressed syllables only after a labial consonant:

măr, mere	apple
ovăz, oveze	oat, oat field
băţ, beţe	stick

Some words have the change *ă* → *e* in an unstressed syllable, e.g.:

numắr, numere	number
umắr, umere	coat hunger
geamắt, gemete	moan
greabắn, grebene	withers

The change *â* → *i* occurs in the word *cuvânt* and in the suffix -*mânt*:

cuvânt, cuvinte	word
mormânt, morminte	grave
jurământ, jurăminte	oath

The only regular consonant change is [k] → [tʃ] and [g] → [dʒʲ] before -*e*:

ac, ace	needle
catalog, cataloage	catalogue

Neuter nouns ending in -u

The unstressed -*u* disappears before the ending (*u → e, u → uri*). Nouns ending in a consonant + *r* + *u* or in -*plu* usually have the plural ending -*e*, while those ending in a consonant + *l* + *u* use the ending -*uri*:

Plural in -e:

teatru, teatre	theatre
centru, centre	centre
templu, temple	temple
exemplu, exemple	example

Plural -uri:

cablu, cabluri	cable
titlu, titluri	title
ciclu, cicluri	cycle
trianglu, triangluri	triangle

Exceptions:

lucru, lucruri	thing
cifru, cifruri	code

The only word with a sound change is *căpăstru, căpestre* 'bridle'.

The stressed -*u* is kept. The plural ending is -*uri*:

igl̲u̲, igluuri [i.'glu.ʷurⁱ]	igloo
tab̲u̲, tabuuri	taboo

Neuter nouns ending in -*ou* always have a plural ending in -*uri*:

cadou [-o̲u̲], cadouri [-o.ʷurⁱ]	gift
ecou, ecouri	echo
stilou, stilouri	fountain pen

With nouns ending in -*eu* both endings occur:

muzeu [-e̲u̲], muzee [-e.e]	museum
liceu, licee	secondary school

careu [-e̲u̲], careuri [-e.ʷurⁱ]	square
eseu, eseuri	essay

Neuter nouns ending in -*iu* usually form their plural with the ending -*i*:

deceniu [-ju], decenii [-i̲i̲]	decade
exercițiu, exerciții	exercise
participiu, participii	participle
teritoriu, teritorii	territory

Exceptions are nouns ending in a stressed -*i̯u,* which form their plural either with -*e* or -*uri*:

sicriu [-iy̯], sicrie [-iʲe]	coffin
bisturiu, bisturie	scalpel
burghiu, burghie	drill
meniu [-iy̯], meniuri [-i.ʷurʲ]	menu
interviu, interviuri	interview
pariu, pariuri	betting
pliu, pliuri	pleat, fold
chipiu, chipie/chipiuri	peak cap

Other exceptions are very rare:

doliu [-ju], doliuri [-jurʲ]	mourning
luciu, luciuri	lustre, brilliancy
giulgiu, giulgiuri	shroud

Neuter nouns ending in -e

Neuter nouns ending in an unstressed -*e* usually have the same form in the plural:

nume, nume	name
pronume, pronume	pronoun
spate, spate	back
apendice, apendice	appendix
laringe, laringe	larynx

Exceptions:

dulce, dulciuri	dessert, sweets
lapte, lăpturi (rare)	milk, different kinds of milk, milk products
(sânge), sângiuri (old-fashioned)	murder

Nouns ending in a stressed -*e* have plurals ending with -*uri*:

piure, piureuri	puré
file, fileuri	filet
pate, pateuri	pâté

Neuter nouns ending in -i

With nouns ending in a diphthong both plural endings (-*e,* -*uri*) occur:

Plural in -e:

tramvai, tramvaie	tram
gunoi, gunoaie	garbage
război, războaie	war

Plural in -uri:

grai, graiuri	voice, speech
nai, naiuri	Pan's pipe
stei, steiuri	cliff

Some compound nouns have the same form both in the singular and the plural:

portchei, portchei	key-ring
parascântei, parascântei	spark arrestor

Neuter nouns ending in *-ci* have the plural forms *-ce* or *-ciuri*:

bici [bitʃ], bice [bitʃe]	whip
brici, brice	razor
meci [metʃ], meciuri [metʃuri]	match
puci, puciuri	putsch

Nouns ending in *-chi, -ghi* take the plural ending *-uri*:

trunchi, trunchiuri	tree trunk
unghi, unghiuri	angle

Nouns ending in a stressed *-i̯* have a plural ending *-uri* as well:

taxi̯, taxi̯uri [-i.ʷurⁱ]	taxi
schi̯, schi̯uri	ski

However, those ending in an unstressed *-i* [i] are invariable:

ki̯wi [-i], ki̯wi [-i]	kiwifruit
tsunami, tsunami	tsunami

Neuter nouns ending in -o and -a

Nouns ending in *-o* are loanwords with plurals ending in *-uri*:

motto [-o], mottouri [-o.ʷurⁱ]	motto
duo, duouri	duo
tempo, tempouri	tempo
studi̯o, studi̯ouri	studio

In a few words the stress shifts in the plural form:

radio, radioouri	radio
trio, triouri	trio
zero, zerouri	zero

However, some neuter nouns ending in *-o* have the same form in the singular and plural:

kilo, kilo	kilogram
mango, mango	mango (fruit)

avocado, avocado	avocado (fruit)
sombrero, sombrero	sombrero

Neuter nouns ending in *-a* are loanwords as well. They have the plural ending *-uri*:

cinema, cinemauri	cinema (colloq.)
anșoa, anșoauri	anchovy paste

Some Latin words are neuter plurals (*acta, addenda, corrigenda, miscellanea, varia*).

Irregular neuter nouns

Totally irregular neuter nouns include:

cap, capete	head
caro, carale / carouri	diamonds (in a card game)
atu, atale / atuuri	trump
rău, rele	harm, mischief

The word *ou* has an irregular plural ending *-ă*:

ou, ouă	egg

Some nouns ending in *-u* have a plural ending in *-ie*, e.g.:

curcubeu, curcubeie	rainbow
frâu, frâie	rein
grâu, grâie / grâne	wheat (fields)
pârâu, pâraie	brook
zmeu, zmeie	kite

The plurals of letters of the alphabet are formed with *-uri*[40]:

B, B-uri ['beʷurⁱ, 'biʷurⁱ]
M, M-uri ['meʷurⁱ, 'emurⁱ, 'miʷurⁱ]
W, W-uri [dublu'veʷurⁱ, dublu'viʷurⁱ]
Y, Y-uri ['igrekurⁱ]

Sometimes a word may have different plurals in different meanings:

brâu, brâie	belt, waist
brâu, brâuri	a certain folk dance
mijloc, mijlocuri	middle, waist
mijloc, mijloace	means
raport, raporturi	relation, connection
raport, rapoarte	report, statement
timbru, timbre	stamp
timbru, timbruri	tone

---

[40] The Latin letters can also be invariable masculine nouns: *un B, niște B.*

Plural forms of neuter nouns

Noun type	Plural	
cons.	-e	*grad, grade*
	-uri	*loc, locuri*
-u	-e	*teatru, teatre; muzeu, muzee*
	-uri	*lucru, lucruri; eseu, eseuri*
-iu	-ii	*exercițiu, exerciții*
-e	-e	*nume, nume*
-i	-ie	*tramvai, tramvaie*
	-iuri	*taxi, taxiuri*
-u̱, -e̱, -o, -a	-uri	*iglu, igluuri; file, fileuri; studio, studiouri; anșoa, anșoauri*
Irreg.	*cap, capete; ou, ouă; rău, rele; mango, mango; curcubeu, curcubeie...*	

Singular nouns

Many abstract Romanian nouns occur only in the singular form:

curaj	courage
fizică	physics
frică	fear
importanță	importance
sete	thirst
socialism	socialism
biologie	biology

Likewise, many mass words occur only in the singular:

miere	honey
aur	gold
oxigen	oxygen

Some other words are also used only in the singular:

vodă	voivode
bade	uncle (= an older man)
nene, (colloq.) neică	uncle (= an older man)
taică	dad (colloq.)

Plural nouns

Romanian has some nouns that only occur in the plural forms. These include:

anale f.	annals
angli m.	Angles (Germanic people)
aplauze n.	applause
blugi m.	jeans
lenjuri n.	underwear
ochelari m.	glasses
șale f.	small of the back
viscere n.	viscera
zori m./f.	dawn

Cases

Romanian nouns have five cases (nominative, accusative, genitive, dative and vocative). For the usage of cases see p. 278.

However, the declension of nouns is quite simple, since the accusative always has the same form as the nominative, and the dative always has the same form as the genitive. Thus the nouns have only three different forms: nominative-accusative, genitive-dative and vocative.

Nominative-accusative case

The nominative and accusative form of the noun is the base form given in dictionaries.

Formation of the genitive-dative

Many Romanian nouns do not have a specific ending for the genitive and dative case. In fact, the case can usually be deduced from the form of the article, not from the noun itself.

Masculine and neuter nouns

All the masculine and neuter nouns have in the genitive-dative the same form as in the nominative-accusative (both in singular and plural).

E.g. *un student* 'a student':

		Article	Noun
Singular	NA	un	student
	GD	unui	
Plural	NA	nişte	studenţi
	GD	unor	

Other examples:

un câine → unui câine		a dog
nişte câini → unor câini		
un euro → unui euro		a euro
nişte euro → unor euro		
un tren → unui tren		a train
nişte trenuri → unor trenuri		
un sat → unui sat		a village
nişte sate → unor sate		

Feminine nouns

With feminine nouns the genitive-dative singular usually has the same form as the nominative plural (and thus ends in *-e, -i* or *-le*). The genitive-dative plural always has the same form as the nominative-accusative plural (ending in *-e, -i, -le* or *-uri*). E.g. *o studentă* 'a student':

		Article	Noun
Singular	NA	o	studentă
	GD	unei	
Plural	NA	nişte	studente
	GD	unor	

Other examples:

casă, case	→ unei case, unor case	house
carte, cărţi	→ unei cărţi, unor cărţi	book
stea, stele	→ unei stele, unor stele	star
zi, zile	→ unei zile, unor zile	day
şa, şei	→ unei şei, unor şei	saddle
dragoste, dragoste	→ unei dragoste, unor dragoste	love, affection
drosera, drosere	→ unei drosere, unor drosere	sundew (plant)

Exceptions are:

- Feminine nouns that do not have a plural form. The genitive-dative singular form is formed based on the same principles used to form the plural, i.e. with the endings -i, -e:

  ➢ Nouns ending in -ă have a genitive-dative in -e or -i:

suficiență, suficiențe	sufficiency
frică, frici	fright
aritmetică, aritmetici	arithmetic

  Some nouns, such as *rouă* 'dew', *cocă* 'dough', *frișcă* 'whipped cream', *vlagă* 'energy', *joacă* 'play', *iască* 'polypore', *pască*[41] 'Easter bread', *vogă* 'vogue' do not have a indefinite genitive form at all[42].

  ➢ Nouns ending in -e have a genitive-dative in -i:

creativitate, creativități	creativity
miere, mieri	honey
rușine, rușini	shame
liniște, liniști	peacefulness

  Exceptions:

cinste, cinste	honour	linte, linte	lentil
foame, foame	hunger	sete, sete	thirst
justețe, justețe	justice	tuse, tuse	cough
lene, lene	laziness	urbe, urbe (old-fash.)	city

- Feminine nouns that have a plural form ending in -uri (see p. 55). These nouns also have a genitive-dative singular form ending in -e or -i:

  Genitive and *dative singular ending in -e:*

alamă, alame	ceartă, certe	lipsă, lipse
aramă, arame	greață, grețe	

  Genitive and dative singular ending in -i:

blană, blăni	favoare, favori	leafă, lefi	sare, sări
carne, cărni	făină, făini	marfă, mărfi	treabă, trebi
ceață, ceți	gheață, gheți	mătase, mătăsi[43]	verdeață, verdeți
cerneală, cerneli	iarbă, ierbi	mâncare, mâncări	vreme, vremi
dulceață, dulceți	lână, lâni	otravă, otrăvi	zeamă, zemi

  The genitive-dative plural form of these nouns has the same form as the nominative (*unor alămuri*, etc.).

---

[41] DOOM[2]. DEX98 gave *păști* for the nominative plural and for the genitive-dative.
[42] Forms such as *unei rouă* etc. are extremely rare. However, some of these nouns have the definite genitive-dative.
[43] No sound change *s* → *ș*!

- The following two words have different genitive-dative singular forms in different meanings:

o soră, unei surori nişte surori, unor surori	sister
o soră, unei sore nişte surori, unor surori	nurse
o piele, unei piei nişte piei, unor piei	leather
o piele, unei pieli nişte piei, unor piei	skin

- Feminine nouns ending in an unstressed -a and having a plural in -a (or not having a plural at all), also use the nominative form in the genitive-dative:[44]

papaia, unei papaia	papaya
mantra, unei mantra	mantra
paranoia, unei paranoia	paranoia
yucca, unei yucca	yucca

- Also the nouns ending in a consonant or in -o do not have a special genitive-dative form and the nominative is used instead:

cacao, unei cacao	cacao
miss, unei miss	beauty queen
cover-girl, unei cover-girl	cover-girl

- The word *nea* 'snow' (non-standard, colloq.)' does not have a genitive-dative form at all.

Declension of feminine nouns

Singular		Plural		
NA	GD	NA	GD	
-ă	-e			*casă, case, case, case*
	-i			*limbă, limbi , limbi, limbi*
	-e	-uri		*lipsă, lipse, lipsuri, lipsuri*
	-i	-uri		*marfă, mărfi, mărfuri, mărfuri*
-e	-i			*carte, cărți, cărți, cărți*
	-e			*scriitoare, scriitoare, scriitoare, scriitoare*
	-i	-uri		*carne, cărni, cărnuri, cărnuri*
cons. + ie	-ii			*familie, familii, familii, familii*

---

[44] Nouns ending in cons. + a (except in -ca, -ga) can sometimes be seen with a genitive and dative ending in -e (*unei mantre, unei nirvane*). Since the norm for the plural form is -a, but for the definite genitive is -ei, the norm for the indefinite genitive is not clearly expressed in DOOM[2].

Singular		Plural		
NA	GD	NA	GD	
vowel + *ie*	-i			*cheie, chei, chei, chei*
-e<u>a</u>	-ele			*stea, stele, stele, stele*
-<u>a</u>	-ale			*pijama, pijamale, pijamale, pijamale*

Formation of the vocative

There are no strict rules for the formation of the vocative case, and the usage varies greatly. Many nouns do not have a separate vocative form at all, and the nominative form is used instead. The use of the vocative is becoming less frequent in the standard language and it is being replaced by the nominative. The vocative forms are used in spoken language, especially in Muntenia.

Masculine and neuter singular

The vocative ending for masculine and neuter singular is either -*e* or -*ule*. Both of these endings occur with nouns ending in consonants, and with some nouns -*e* is preferred while others use -*ule*. In modern language -*ule* is more productive.

doctor: doctore!	doctor!
bărbat: bărbate!	man!
prieten: prietene!	friend!
domn: domnule!	sir!
om: omule!	human!
bunic: bunicule!	grandfather!
animal: animalule!	you beast!
idiot: idiotule!	idiot!
scriitor: scriitorule!	writer!

The ending -*e* can cause several sound changes, e.g.:

Domn: Doamne!	God!
cetățean: cetățene!	citizen!
văr: vere!	cousin!
tânăr: tinere!	young man!
luceafăr : lucefere!	morning star!
amic: amice	friend!

With many masculine nouns both endings are possible:

profesor: profesore!, profesorule!	teacher!
băiat: băiete!, băiatule!	boy!

copil: copile!, copilule!	child!
poet: poete!, poetule!	poet!

The form ending in -*e* is more neutral, while the one ending in -*ule* often has an endearing, ironic or even derogatory or demeaning tone.

Nouns ending in -*e* or -*ă* have a vocative form identical to the nominative:

frate: frate!	brother!
rege: rege!	king!
tată: tată!	father!
popă: popă!	priest!

Nouns ending in a diphthong or in -*i* [ⁱ] use the ending -*ule*:

fiu: fiule!	son!
erou: eroule!	hero!
pui: puiule!	my son!
unchi: unchiule!	uncle!

Nouns ending in a consonant + *l/r* + *u* have the vocative ending -*e*:

maestru: maestre!	master!

The proper nouns ending in a consonant or in a consonant + *l/r* + *u* usually have the vocative ending -*e*. The other proper nouns ending in -*u* have -*ule*:

Ion: Ioane!	Ion!
Tudor: Tudore!	Tudor!
Alexandru: Alexandre!	Alexandru!
Barbu: Barbule!	Barbu!
Nicu: Nicule!	Nicu!
Popescu: Popescule!	Popescu!

Other proper nouns have a vocative identical to the nominative:

Vasile!	Vasile!
Gheorghe!	Gheorghe!
Andrei!	Andrei!
Mihai!	Mihai!

Colloquially, the proper names ending in -*a* and the common nouns ending in -*ă* and -*e* that are declined like feminine nouns (see p. 76) also have the vocative ending -*o*:

Toma: Toma!, Tomo! (colloq.)	Toma!
Mircea: Mircea!, Mirceo (colloq.)	Mircea!
popă: popă!, popo! (colloq.)	priest!
bade: bade!, badeo! (colloq.)	uncle (= an older man)

Exception:

tată, taică (colloq.)	father!

Feminine singular

The feminine singular vocative ending is *-o (-ă → -o, -ie → io, -e → eo)*, but this can only be used in the standard language with a handful of feminine nouns and with proper nouns:

bunică: bunico!	grandmother!
soră: soro![45]	sister!
fetiță: fetițo!	girl!
copilă: copilo!	child!
Ana: Ano!	Ana!
Ioana: Ioano!	Ioana!
Maria: Mario!	Maria!

The vocative ending in *-o* is more frequent in colloquial style. Some colloquial vocative forms may also have a pejorative meaning:

fată: fato!	girl! (peor.)
vacă: vaco!	you cow!
vulpe: vulpeo!	you vixen!
oaie: oaio!	you stupid women (lit. sheep)

Because of this colloquial tone, the standard language tends to prefer the nominative form (*bunică!, Ana!, Maria!*).

Apart from these forms, especially in Transylvania, Maramureş and Moldova, proper nouns without the definite article (ending in *-ă, -ie*) are also used as vocative forms (*Ană!, Ioană!, Marie!*).

Most feminine nouns have a vocative identical to the nominative:

mamă!	mother!
doamnă!	madam!

Plural

The vocative plural ending is *-lor*, which is added to the plural form of the noun. Thus the plural vocative is identical to the definite plural dative:

doamnelor şi domnilor!	ladies and gentlemen!
fraţilor!	brothers!
surorilor!	sisters!
fetelor!	girls!
oamenilor!	people!

---

[45] But *soră!* 'nurse'.

However, with most nouns the vocative form is identical to the nominative:

soldaţi!	soldiers!
băieţi!	boys!

Sometimes both forms can be used:

studenţilor!, studenţi!	students!

See also the vocative of adjectives, p. 115.

Indefinite article

Forms of the indefinite article

The article must have the same gender, case and number as the noun it modifies. The indefinite article is declined as follows:

		Masc.	Neuter	Fem.
Sg.	NA	un		o
	GD	unui		unei
Pl.	NA	nişte		
	GD	unor		

The indefinite article does not have the vocative case. The article has the same form in the masculine and neuter.

Thus the indefinite declension of the nouns *bărbat* 'man', *femeie* 'woman' and *animal* 'animal' is as follows:

	Masc.		Fem.	
	Sg.	Pl.	Sg.	Pl.
NA	un bărbat	nişte bărbaţi	o femeie	nişte femei
GD	unui bărbat	unor bărbaţi	unei femei	unor femei

	Neuter	
	Sg.	Pl.
NA	un animal	nişte animale
GD	unui animal	unor animale

Use of the indefinite article

Countable nouns

As in English, the indefinite article is used for indefinite, countable nouns:

Am citit o carte.	I read a book.
Am o maşină.	I have a car.
Este un miracol!	It is a miracle!

In the genitive and dative cases the indefinite article is always used:

cartea unui student	the book of a student
cărţile unor studenţi	the books of some students

When an indefinite noun is used as the subject or direct object, the indefinite article is often omitted in the plural, especially if the noun is placed after the verb or if the noun has some other modifier (e.g. an adjective):

Am citit (nişte) cărţi.	I have read books.
Nu sunt supravieţuitori. (*Adevărul*)	There are no survivors.
Nori negri se adună.	Dark clouds are gathering.

If the noun has no modifiers, the plural indefinite article must be used after a preposition:

pentru nişte prieteni	for (some) friends

Pentru prieteni would have the definite meaning 'for the friends'. For the omission of the definite article, see p. 196. If the noun has a modifier, the difference is clear even without an indefinite article (*pentru zile reci* 'for cold days', *pentru zilele reci* 'for the cold days').

The indefinite article is also omitted when a noun is used as an attributive apposition (see also p. 278):

Ion, *prieten bun,* este român.	Ion, a good friend, is Romanian.

The indefinite article is not compulsory when the noun is preceded by an adverbial adjective (*aşa* 'such', *asemenea* 'similar', *astfel de* 'like this', *altfel de* 'different'):

NA: (o) asemenea situaţie	a similar situation
GD: unei asemenea situaţii =	
a/la asemenea situaţie	

Countable nouns with generic meaning

With countable nouns the indefinite article may also have a generic meaning (the noun is seen as an example of the group):

O maşină este o invenţie utilă.	A car (= any car) is a useful invention.

Here, *o maşina* does not refer to any specific car, but to cars in general. In this case the definite article could also be used (*Maşina este o invenţie utilă.*).

After *ca* 'in the role of' the article is not used:

Ion lucrează ca profesor.	Ion works as a teacher.
Ţelina este cultivată ca plantă culinară.	Celery is cultivated as a culinary plant.

However, after a comparative *ca* 'as' the article is required:

înalt ca un munte	high as a mountain

The indefinite article is also omitted when a noun is used as a predicative to describe (and not to identify) the subject. Nouns used like this express to which group the subject belongs (profession, nationality, sex, etc.):

Sunt profesor de matematică.	I am a maths teacher.
Este fată.	She is a girl.
Este medic.	He/she is a doctor.
L-au ales preşedinte.	They selected him president.
Este iarnă.	It is winter.

Compare with:

Este un profesor foarte bun.	He is a very good teacher.
Este un medic care ştie tot!	He is a doctor who knows everything!

Similarly, when a noun with a descriptive meaning is used as a direct object, the indefinite article is not used:

Căutăm secretară.	We are looking for a secretary.

Căutăm o secretară would mean that we are searching for a certain secretary that has gone missing.

The same is true when a noun with a descriptive meaning is used as the subject of a passive sentence with *se*:

Se caută secretară.	Hiring a secretary (lit. a secretary is looked for)

When a noun expressing a classification is used as a predicative, the article is optional:

Delfinul este (un) mamifer.	The dolphin is a mammal.
„Câine" este (un) substantiv.	"Dog" is a noun.

Uncountable nouns

The indefinite article is not used with uncountable nouns:

Beau cafea.	I am drinking coffee.
Cade zăpadă.	It is snowing.
Mi-e sete / foame / somn / frig.	I am thirsty / hungry / tired / cold.

If the indefinite article is used before an uncountable noun, the meaning changes to something countable:

Vreau o cafea.	I want a (cup of) coffee.

This can also happen, when an uncountable noun has a restrictive modifier:

Mi-e o foame de lup.	I am hungry like a wolf. (as opposed to any other kind of hunger).
Secrete pentru un somn bun.	Secrets for a good night's sleep.

Before uncountable nouns the word *niște* (see p. 192) can be used with a partitive meaning:

Cumpăr (niște) pește.	I am buying (some) fish.
Compare with:	
Cumpăr un pește.	I am buying a fish.
Cumpăr (niște) pești.	I am buying several fish.

Other indefinite determiners

The indefinite article is not used, if the noun is preceded by another indefinite determiners. These include:

- Cardinal and ordinal numerals: *două zile* 'two days', *a doua zi* 'second day'. (The equivalent definite forms are *cele două zile, cel de-a doua zi.*)
- Indefinite pronominal adjectives: *fiecare zi* 'every day', *nicio zi* 'no day', etc.
- Interrogative and relative pronominal adjectives: *care zi* 'which day', *ce zi* 'what day'.

Exceptions:

- The indefinite pronominal adjectives *anumit/anume* 'certain' and *oarecare* 'some' are used with the indefinite article.

- The indefinite pronominal adjective *alt* 'other' can be used both as an indefinite determiner (*altă zi* 'other day') or as a modifier after the indefinite article (*o altă zi* 'another day').
- The indefinite pronominal adjective *tot* requires the definite form: *toate zilele* 'all the days'.

Definite article

Unlike in other Romance languages, the Romanian definite article is a suffix. The different endings are:

		Masc.	Neuter	Fem.
Sg.	NA	*-ul, -le*		*-a, -ua*
	GD	*-ului, -lui*		*-i*
Pl.	NA	*-i*	*-le*	
	GD	*-lor*		

Some nouns referring to persons form their genitive and dative with the article *lui*, which comes before the noun. The same happens with years, months and names of the letters, musical notes etc.

In the vocative the suffix *-ule* occurs, but it has no definite meaning compared with the vocative ending *-e* (see p. 68).

Definite forms of masculine nouns

Singular

In the nominative and accusative case the masculine article usually has the form *-ul*, which is often colloquially pronounced as [-u]:

un student	→ studentul	the student
un om	→ omul	the human
un ochi [-kʲ]	→ ochiul [-kʲul]	the eye
un colibri [-i]	→ colibriul [-i.ʷul]	the hummingbird
un flamingo	→ flamingoul [-o.ʷul]	the flamingo

An unstressed *-u* [u/u̯] disappears before the article:

un metru	→ metrul	the metre
un guru	→ gurul	the guru
un leu [leu̯]	→ leul ['le.ʷul]	the lion ; the leu (currency)
un erou [e.'rou̯]	→ eroul [e'.ro.ʷul]	the hero

A stressed -*u* is kept:

un gnu	→ gnuul ['gnu.ʷul]	the wildebeest
un nand<u>u</u>	→ nand<u>uu</u>l[46]	the nandu

Masculine nouns that end with an unstressed -*e* take the definite article -*le*:

un frate	→ fratele	the brother
un munte	→ muntele	the mountain
un perete	→ peretele	the wall
un rege	→ regele	the king
un ginere	→ ginerele	the son-in-law

The words ending in a stressed -*e* have the article -*ul*:

un E	→ E-ul	the letter E
un M	→ M-ul ['me.ʷul, 'emul]	the letter M

The genitive and dative definite forms can be formed from the nominative: -*ul* → -*ului*, -*le* → -*lui*.

studentul	→ studentului	student
metrul	→ metrului	metre
fratele	→ fratelui	brother
muntele	→ muntelui	mountain

Exceptions

- The definite form of masculine nouns ending in -*ă* is formed with feminine endings: nominative and accusative with -*a*, and genitive and dative with -*ei* [eị] or -*ii* [i]:

NA: un papă	→ papa	pope
GD: unui papă	→ papei	
NA: un popă	→ popa	priest
GD: unui popă	→ popii	

Nouns declined like *papă* include *pașă* 'pasha, a rank in the Ottoman Empire' and *bulibașă* 'Romani leader'. E.g. *naiba: naibii* 'devil' (only used in the definite form) is declined like *popă*.

The definite genitive and dative of masculine nouns ending in -*că* and -*gă* are usually formed with the ending -*ăi*:

agă: aga, agăi	Turkish soldier (hist.)
rigă: riga, rigăi	king (arch.)

---

[46] Or *n<u>a</u>ndu* → *n<u>a</u>ndul*.

Some nouns have various forms for the genitive and dative (*-ăi, -(h)ii, lui*):

> ginerică: ginerica, ginericăi / lui ginerică son-in-law (colloq.)
> taică: taica, taichii / lui taica dad (colloq.)
> neică: neica, neichii / lui neica uncle (colloq.)
> vlădică: vlădica, vlădicăi/vlădicii/vlădichii bishop (hist.)

- The word *tată* 'father' has two sets of definite forms:

> NA: un tată → tata, tatăl father
> GD: unui tată → tatei / lui tata, tatălui

The forms *tatăl, tatălui* are used in the meaning 'God' and when the noun has a modifier (*Tatăl* 'Father', *tatăl lui Ion* 'Ion's father', *tatăl meu* 'my father'). The forms *tata, tatei / lui tata* are used colloquially with the meaning 'my father, your father, etc'.

- A few masculine nouns ending in *-e* also use the feminine definite article:

> bade: badea, badei / lui badea uncle (= older man)
> nene: nenea, lui nenea uncle (= older man)
> hoge: hegea, hogii Muslim priest
> gâde: gâdea / gâdele, gâdei / gâdelui executioner (non-standard)

- Years, letters and words used metalinguistically form their definite genitive and dative with the article *lui*:

> primăvara lui 1995 (= anului 1995) the spring of 1995
> scrierea lui A (= literei A) the writing of the letter A
> scrierea lui 2 (= numărului 2) the writing of the number 2
> scrierea lui și (= cuvântului și) the writing of the word și

- Some masculine nouns do not have definite forms. These include:

  ➢ Names of the months:

> Ianuarie este „luna Verdi" la January is "Verdi month" at the
> Opera Națională (*evz.ro*) National Opera
>
> în ianuarie următor next January

However, the definite genitive and dative are formed with the article *lui*:

> ianuarie, lui ianuarie January
> mai, lui mai May
> august, lui august August

The word *luna* 'month' is often used to avoid declension of the name of the month:

> horoscopul lunii ianuarie the horoscope for January

> Masculine nouns ending in *-a* (e.g. *koala, judoca*) and some of the nouns ending in *-o* (e.g. *dingo, euro, alto, sambo*):

Koala și dingo sunt mamifere.	The koala and the dingo are mammals.
Euro scade, dolarul crește. (*EVZ*)	The euro is falling, the dollar rising.

> Colloquial words formed with the suffix *-ilă*:

năsăilă	big nosed person
sărăcilă	pauper

> A few other nouns like *bebe* 'baby', *vodă* 'voivode'.

The genitive and dative of invariable nouns referring to humans are formed with the article *lui*:

lui dalai-lama	dalai-lama
lui vodă	voivode, prince (hist.)
lui sărăcilă	pauper

Otherwise the invariable form is used also in the genitive and dative:

România refuză să grăbească adoptarea *euro*. (*Adevărul*)	Romania refuses to hurry the adoption of the euro.

The genitive and dative forms are often avoided by using structures like:

ursul koala, GD ursului koala	koala bear

Plural

In the nominative and accusative plural, the masculine article is *-i*, which is added to the plural form of the noun. Since the plural form of masculine nouns is formed with *-i* [^{i}, i̯, i], the definite forms end with *-ii*, which is pronounced as [i]:

un student, niște studenți [-^{i}]	→ studenții [-i]	the students
un frate, niște frați [-^{i}]	→ frații [-i]	the brothers
un om, niște oameni [-^{i}]	→ oamenii [-i]	the humans
un tată, niște tați [-^{i}]	→ tații [-i]	the fathers
un pui, niște pui [pu̯i]	→ puii ['pu.ʲi]	the chicken
un copil, niște copii [-i̯]	→ copiii [-i.ʲi]	the children
un metru, niște metri [-i]	→ metrii [-i]	the metres

The genitive-dative plural article is *-lor*, which is added to the plural noun in the same way. Thus the ending is *-ilor* [-ilor]:

un student, niște studenți [-^{i}]	→ studenților [-ilor]
un frate, niște frați [-^{i}]	→ fraților [-ilor]
un om, niște oameni [-^{i}]	→ oamenilor [-ilor]

un pui, niște pui [pui̯] → puilor [pu.ʲi.lor]
un copil, niște copii [-ii̯] → copiilor [-i.ʲi.lor]

Those masculine nouns that do not have a plural ending in *-i* (e.g. *euro, koala, gnu*) do not have a definite form. If needed, expressions like *monedele euro* 'the euro coins' and *urșii koala* 'the koala bears' can be used.

Thus most of the masculine nouns ending in *-o* have the definite form only in the singular (*mango: mangoul,* pl. *mango* 'mango tree', likewise e.g. *avocado, peso*), whereas some of them are completely invariable (e.g. *euro, dingo*). Only three words are fully declined (*flamingo: flamingoul,* pl. *flamingi, flamingii,* likewise: *picolo, paparazzo*).

Definite forms of masculine nouns

Singular			
cons.	-ul	-ului	*lup: lupul, lupului*
-u	-ul	-ului	*leu: leul, leului*
-u̯	-uul	-uului	*gnu: gnuul, gnuului*
-i	-iul	-iului	*ochi: ochiul, ochiului*
-e	-ele	-elui	*frate: fratele, fratelui*
-ă	-a	-ei	*papă: papa, papei*
		-ii	*popă: popa, popii*

Plural			
-i	-ii	-ilor	*lupi: lupii, lupilor*

Definite forms of feminine nouns

Singular

Nominative-accusative

The feminine nominative and accusative definite article is usually *-a*. If the noun ends with *-ă,* that vowel disappears before the article. Nouns that end with an unstressed *-a* do not change:

o studentă → studenta the student
o casă → casa the house
o carte → cartea [-ea̯] the book
o idee → ideea [-ja] the idea

o papaia	→ papaia	the papaya
o mantra	→ mantra	the mantra

Feminine nouns that end with -*ie*, have a definite form ending in -*ia* (< *ie* + *a*):

o familie [-iʲe]	→ familia [-iʲa]	the family
o cheie [-je]	→ cheia [-ja]	the key

Feminine nouns ending in a stressed -*a* or a stressed diphthong ending in -*a* have the definite article -*ua* [wa]:

o ste<u>a</u>	→ steaua	the star
o lale<u>a</u>	→ laleaua	the tulip
o pijam<u>a</u>	→ pijamaua	the pyjama
o ș<u>a</u>	→ șaua	the saddle
o boi<u>a</u>	→ boiaua	the paprika

The following two nouns have an irregular definite form:

o zi	→ ziua	the day
o cacao	→ cacaua	the cacao

The names of the weekdays that end with a consonant + *i* have a definite form ending in -*ea* [e̯a]:

o luni	→ lunea	the Monday
o miercuri	→ miercurea	the Wednesday

But after a vowel:

o joi	→ joia	the Thursday

Other feminine nouns ending in -*i*, -*o* (e.g. *kiwi* 'kiwi (bird)', *imago* 'imago') do not have definite forms.

Feminine nouns ending in -*u* (e.g. *zulu* 'Zulu language'), a stressed -*e* (*koiné*) or in a consonant (*miss* 'beauty queen') do not have a separate definite form either. If needed, expressions like *păsarea kiwi* 'the kiwi bird', *limba zulu* 'the Zulu language' can be used.

Genitive-dative

The genitive-dative article -*i* is added to the genitive-dative form of the noun. Thus the ending for the definite genitive-dative can be -*ei* [ei̯], -*ii* [i] or -*lei* [lei̯]:

o casă, unei case	→ casei [-ei̯]	to the house
o fată, unei fete	→ fetei	to the girl
o orhidee, unei orhidee	→ orhideei	to the orchid
o carte, unei cărți [-ⁱ]	→ cărții [-i]	to the book
o vreme, unei vremi	→ vremii	to the time
o cheie, unei chei [-ei̯]	→ cheii [-eʲi]	to the key

o idee, unei idei	→ ideii	to the idea
o şa, unei şei	→ şeii	to the saddle
o stea, unei stele	→ stelei [-leị]	to the star
o pijama, unei pijamale	→ pijamalei	to the pyjama
o zile, unei zile	→ zilei	to the day

Exceptions:

- If the noun has a genitive-dative form ending in *-ii*, the definite form is *-iei* [-i.ʲeị] (and not *-iii*):

o familie, unei familii	→ familiei	to the family
o staţie, unei staţii	→ staţiei	to the station

  The sound change *a* → *ă* is cancelled:

o vrabie, unei vrăbii	→ vrabiei	to the sparrow

- The genitive and dative forms of weekdays are not usually used. Expressions like *ziua de luni* 'Monday' are used instead:

programul zilei de miercuri	Wednesday's programme

- For a few feminine nouns ending in *-ă* (some nouns ending in *-că*, *-gă* and the noun *rouă*) the definite genitive-dative ending is *-ăi*:

rouă, GD rouăi	dew
cocă, GD cocăi	dough
pască, GD pascăi	Easter bread
frişcă, GD frişcăi[47]	whipped cream
gigă, GD gigăi	jig

  However, some words do not have a definite dative or genitive form at all. These include *vlagă* 'energy', *joacă* 'play', *iască* 'polypore', *vogă* 'vogue'.

  Some colloquial words may have various different genitive and dative forms:

mămică, GD mămicăi, mămicii, mămichii	mom (diminut.)

- Feminine nouns ending in an unstressed *-a* usually form their definite genitive and dative form with the ending *-ei*:

o cola, unei cola	→ colei	cola drink
o papaia, unei papaia	→ papaiei	papaya

  Some words ending in an unstressed *-a* (mostly loanwords ending in *-ca-*, *-ga*) are invariable, and the nominative form is used also in the genitive and dative. These include *moca* 'caffè mocha', *saga*, *yucca* and *yoga*[48]:

practicarea yoga	the practice of yoga

  However, the word *perestroika* has two alternative definite GD forms: *perestroikăi/perestroicii*.

---

[47] Vintilă-Rădulescu (2009) also gives the form *frişţii*.
[48] The reasons for this are probably phonetic: thus a sound change is avoided in a loanword. Forms like *yogăi* are not accepted in the standard language.

- Also the word *cacao* does not have a definite genitive or dative form[49].

- Some loanwords ending in a consonant and referring to persons form their definite genitive and dative with the article *lui* (as do proper nouns ending in a consonant, see p. 98):

(see p. 98)

miss, lui miss	beauty queen
Also:	
lady, lui lady	lady

Plural

The feminine nominative-accusative plural article *-le* is added to the plural ending of the noun. If the plural ending is *-i*, it is pronounced before the article as a full vowel [i]. The possible endings for the definite feminine plural are thus *-ele, -ile* [-ile], *-lele* and *-urile* [-urile]:

o studentă, niște studente	→ studentele	the students
o carte, niște cărți [-i]	→ cărțile [-ile]	the books
o idee, niște idei [-ei]	→ ideile [-eʲile]	the ideas
o familie, niște familii [-ii]	→ familiile [-iʲile]	the families
o stea, niște stele	→ stelele	the stars
o lalea, niște lalele	→ lalelele	the tulips
o pijama, niște pijamale	→ pijamalele	the pyjamas
o vreme, niște vremuri	→ vremurile	the times

The genitive-dative plural article is *-lor*, which is added to the plural noun in the same way:

studentele	→ studentelor	stelele	→ stelelor
cărțile	→ cărților	lalelele	→ lalelelor
ideile	→ ideilor	pijamalele	→ pijamalelor
familiile	→ familiilor	vremurile	→ vremurilor

Feminine nouns that do not have a plural ending (e.g. *cola, papaia, cover-girl*), do not have a different definite form either[50]. If needed, expressions like *băuturile cola* 'the cola drinks' can be used.

---

[49] The form *cacauei* is not accepted in the standard language.
[50] Forms like *papaiele, coca-colele* are not accepted in the standard language.

Definite forms of feminine nouns

Singular			
-ă	-a	-ei	*casă: casa, casei*
		-ii	*limbă: limba, limbii*
-e	-ea	-ei	*scriitoare: scriitoarea, scriitoarei*
		-ii	*carte: cartea, cărții*
cons. + *ie*	-ia	-iei	*familie: familia, familiei*
vowel + *ie*	-ia	-ii	*cheie: cheia, cheii*
-e<u>a</u>	-eaua	-elei	*stea: steaua, stelei*
-<u>a</u>	-aua	-alei	*pijama: pijamaua, pijamalei*
Irreg.			*zi: ziua, zilei; cacao: cacaua; marți: marțea, (marții)...*

Plural			
-e	-ele	-elor	*case: casele, caselor*
-i	-ile	-ilor	*limbi: limbile, limbilor*
-uri	-urile	-urilor	*lipsuri: lipsurile, lipsurilor*

Definite forms of neuter nouns

Singular

The neuter nominative-accusative definite article is usually *-ul*:

un scaun	→ scaunul	the chair
un timp	→ timpul	the time
un tramvai	→ tramvaiul	the tram
un taxi [-i]	→ taxiul [-i.ᵂul]	the taxi

This article is also used in loanwords ending in *-o* or *-a*:

un motto	→ mottoul [-o.ᵂul]	the motto
un avocado	→ avocadoul	the avocado (fruit)
un studi<u>o</u>	→ studi<u>o</u>ul	the studio
un lila	→ lilaul [-a.ᵂul]	the lilac (colour)

A few nouns ending in -*o* have their word stress changed in the definite form:

un r<u>a</u>dio	→ radi<u>o</u>ul [-o.ʷul]	the radio
un tr<u>i</u>o	→ tri<u>o</u>ul [-o.ʷul]	the trio
un z<u>e</u>ro	→ zer<u>o</u>ul [-o.ʷul]	the zero

If the noun ends in an unstressed vowel -*u* [u/u̯], it disappears before the article:

un teritoriu [-ju]	→ teritoriul [-jul]	the territory
un ou [ou̯]	→ oul [o.ʷul]	the egg
un eseu [-eu̯]	→ eseul [-e.ʷul]	the essay

However, the stressed -*u* is kept:

un iglu	→ igluul [-u.ʷul]	the igloo
un tabu	→ tabuul	the taboo

Neuter nouns ending in an unstressed -*e* use the article -*le*:

un nume	→ numele	the name
un spate	→ spatele	the back

Nouns ending in a stressed -*e* have the regular article -*ul*:

un piur<u>e</u>	→ piur<u>e</u>ul	the purée
un fil<u>e</u>	→ fil<u>e</u>ul	the filet
un pat<u>e</u>	→ pat<u>e</u>ul	the pâté

The definite genitive-dative form can be formed from the definite nominative form: -*ul* → -*ului,* -*le* → -*lui*:

scaunul	→ scaunului	numele	→ numelui
tramvaiul	→ tramvaiului	spatele	→ spatelui
oul	→ oului		

Plural

The neuter nominative-accusative plural article -*le* is added to the plural ending of the noun. If the plural ending is -*i*, it is pronounced before the article as a full vowel [i]. The possible endings for the definite neuter plural are thus -*ele,* -*ile* [-ile] and -*urile* [-urile]:

un scaun, niște scaune	→ scaunele	the chairs
un nume, niște nume	→ numele	the names
un teritoriu, niște teritorii	→ teritoriile [-riʲi.le]	the territories
un timp, niște timpuri	→ timpurile	the times
un taxi, niște taxiuri	→ taxiurile	the taxis

The word *ou* forms its definite form with the ending -*le* as well:

un ou, niște ouă	→ ouăle	the eggs

Neuter nouns that do not have a plural ending (e.g. *kiwi* 'kiwifruit', *kilo*, *mango* 'mango (fruit)', *corrigenda*), do not have a definite form either. If needed, expressions like *fructele kiwi* 'the kiwifruits' can be used.

The genitive-dative plural article is *-lor*, which is added to the plural noun in the same way:

scaunele	→ scaunelor	timpurile	→ timpurilor
numele	→ numelor	taxiurile	→ taxiurilor
teritoriile	→ teritoriilor	ouăle	→ ouălor

Definite forms of neuter nouns

Singular			
cons.	-ul	-ului	*scaun: scaunul, scaunului*
-u	-ul	-ului	*teatru: teatrul, teatrului*
-e	-ele	-elui	*nume: numele, numelui*
-i, -o, -a, -e̲, -u̲	-ul	-ului	*tramvai: tramvaiul, tramvaiului; radio: radioul, radioului; iglu: igluul, igluului*

Plural			
-e	-ele	-elor	*scaune: scaunele, scaunelor*
-uri	-urile	-urilor	*locuri: locurile, locurilor*
-i	-ile	-ilor	*exerciții: exercițiile, exercițiilor*
-ă	-ăle	-ălor	*ouă: ouăle, ouălor*

Use of the definite article

As in English, the definite article is used for specific reference:

Am citit *cartea.*	I read the book.
Am citit *cărțile.*	I read the books.

Unlike in English, in Romanian the definite article is also generally used with names of languages, academic subjects, meals, illnesses and sports:

Engleza este o limbă anglo-friziană. (*Wikipedia*)	English is an Anglo-Frisian language.
Biologia este o știință naturală.	Biology is a natural science.
Am mâncat *cina.*	I had supper.

Diabetul este o boală metabolică.	Diabetes is a metabolic disease.
But: Am diabet.	I have diabetes.
Fotbalul este un sport de echipă.	Football (soccer) is a team sport.
But: Joacă fotbal.	He/she plays football.

As a predicative, the definite article has an identifying meaning:

Sunt profesorul.	I am the teacher.
Compare with:	
Sunt profesor.	I am a teacher.

Unlike in English, the nominal premodifiers (titles) of names are in the definite form in Romanian:

domnul Popescu	Mr. Popescu
Regele Mihai I	King Michael I
Muntele Everest	Mount Everest

The definite article is used when the noun is modified by the adjectival pronoun *tot* 'whole, all', *amândoi* 'both', a collective numerals *toți trei / câteșitrei*, etc., or by the emphatic pronominal adjective *însuși* 'himself, itself':

toate pisicile	all the cats
amândouă pisicile	both cats
toate trei / câteșitrei pisicile	all 3 cats
însuși popa	the pope himself

A special feature of Romanian is that after a preposition requiring the accusative case, the definite article is usually not used (for more examples, see p. 196):

după *dulap*	behind the cupboard
Vorbește în *engleză*.	He/she is speaking in English.

With some nouns referring to body parts and relatives, the definite article can be used instead of a possessive pronoun (see p. 155):

tata	my father

In Romanian, the definite form is also used with geographical names (see p. 100) and with some feminine personal names (see p. 98):

Bucureștiul	Bucharest
România	Romania
Maria	Maria

Before a cardinal or ordinal numeral or an independently used adjective the demonstrative article (see p. 95) is used instead of the definite article:

cei doi prieteni	the two friends
cel al doilea	the second one
cei puțini	the few

Notice also that the definite article is (etymologically) included in some pronouns like *altul, unul,* etc.

Generic meaning

As in English, the definite article can also have a generic meaning (the noun denotes the whole group):

Enotul este un animal nou în fauna României. (*Wikipedia*)	The raccoon dog is a new animal in the fauna of Romania.

Here, *enotul* does not refer to any specific raccoon, but to the whole species.

In Romanian, the definite article is also used with mass nouns with a generic meaning:

Banii nu pot cumpăra *fericirea.*	Money cannot buy happiness.
alb ca *zăpada*	white as snow
Mierea este un produs apicol. (*Wikipedia*)	Honey is a bee product.

Notice also:

Costă 10 lei *kilogramul/litrul.*	It costs 10 lei a kilo/litre.

Other definite determiners

The definite article is not used if an other definite determiner (demonstrative pronoun, a demonstrative article, or a possessive pronoun) precedes the noun:

această mașină	this car
cea mai mare mașină din lume	the biggest car in the world
a mea mașină (rare, poetic)	the car of mine

However, if a demonstrative pronoun, a demonstrative article or a possessive pronoun comes after the noun it modifies, the article must be used:

mașina aceasta	this car
mașina cea roșie	the red car
mașina mea	my car

An exception is the possessive structure type *frate-meu* 'my brother', see p. 155.

Declination models

Masculine nouns

- cons.

		Indefinite	Definite
Sg.	NA	un bărbat	bărbatul
	GD	unui bărbat	bărbatului
Pl.	NA	nişte bărbaţi	bărbaţii
	GD	unor bărbaţi	bărbaţilor

-*u*

		Indefinite	Definite
Sg.	NA	un fiu	fiul
	GD	unui fiu	fiului
Pl.	NA	nişte fii	fiii
	GD	unor fii	fiilor

-*i*

		Indefinite	Definite
Sg.	NA	un ochi	ochiul
	GD	unui ochi	ochiului
Pl.	NA	nişte ochi	ochii
	GD	unor ochi	ochilor

-*e*

		Indefinite	Definite
Sg.	NA	un frate	fratele
	GD	unui frate	fratelui
Pl.	NA	nişte fraţi	fraţii
	GD	unor fraţi	fraţilor

-*ă*, definite GD -*ei*

		Indefinite	Definite
Sg.	NA	un papă	papa
	GD	unui papă	papei
Pl.	NA	nişte papi	papii
	GD	unor papi	papilor

-*ă*, definite GD -*ii*

		Indefinite	Definite
Sg.	NA	un popă	popa
	GD	unui popă	popii
Pl.	NA	nişte popi	popii
	GD	unor popi	popilor

Feminine nouns

-*ă*, GD and plural -*e*

		Indefinite	Definite
Sg.	NA	o studentă	studenta
	GD	unei studente	studentei
Pl.	NA	nişte studente	studentele
	GD	unor studente	studentelor

-*ă*, GD and plural -*i*

		Indefinite	Definite
Sg.	NA	o limbă	limba
	GD	unei limbi	limbii
Pl.	NA	nişte limbi	limbile
	GD	unor limbi	limbilor

-ă, GD *-e*, plural *-uri*

		Indefinite	Definite
Sg.	NA	o alamă	alama
	GD	unei alame	alamei
Pl.	NA	niște alămuri	alămurile
	GD	unor alămuri	alămurilor

-ă, GD *-i*, plural *-uri*

		Indefinite	Definite
Sg.	NA	o marfă	marfa
	GD	unei mărfi	mărfii
Pl.	NA	niște mărfuri	mărfurile
	GD	unor mărfuri	mărfurilor

-e, GD and plural *-i*

		Indefinite	Definite
Sg.	NA	o pâine	pâinea
	GD	unei pâini	pâinii
Pl.	NA	niște pâini	pâinile
	GD	unor pâini	pâinilor

-e, GD and plural *-e*

		Indefinite	Definite
Sg.	NA	o scriitoare	scriitoarea
	GD	unei scriitoare	scriitoarei
Pl.	NA	niște scriitoare	scriitoarele
	GD	unor scriitoare	scriitoarelor

- cons. + *ie*

		Indefinite	Definite
Sg.	NA	o familie	familia
	GD	unei familii	familiei
Pl.	NA	niște familii	familiile
	GD	unor familii	familiilor

- vowel + *ie*

		Indefinite	Definite
Sg.	NA	o cheie	cheia
	GD	unei chei	cheii
Pl.	NA	niște chei	cheile
	GD	unor chei	cheilor

-e, GD *-i*, plural *-uri*

		Indefinite	Definite
Sg.	NA	o vreme	vremea
	GD	unei vremi	vremii
Pl.	NA	niște vremuri	vremurile
	GD	unor vremuri	vremurilor

-ea

		Indefinite	Definite
Sg.	NA	o stea	steaua
	GD	unei stele	stelei
Pl.	NA	niște stele	stelele
	GD	unor stele	stelelor

-a

		Indefinite	Definite
Sg.	NA	o pijama	pijamaua
	GD	unei pijamale	pijamalei
Pl.	NA	niște pijamale	pijamalele
	GD	unor pijamale	pijamalelor

Neuter nouns

- cons., plural *-e*

		Indefinite	Definite
Sg.	NA	un oraș	orașul
	GD	unui oraș	orașului
Pl.	NA	niște orașe	orașele
	GD	unor orașe	orașelor

- cons., plural *-uri*

		Indefinite	Definite
Sg.	NA	un timp	timpul
	GD	unui timp	timpului
Pl.	NA	niște timpuri	timpurile
	GD	unor timpuri	timpurilor

-u, plural *-e*

		Indefinite	Definite
Sg.	NA	un teatru	teatrul
	GD	unui teatru	teatrului
Pl.	NA	niște teatre	teatrele
	GD	unor teatre	teatrelor

-u, plural *-uri*

		Indefinite	Definite
Sg.	NA	un lucru	lucrul
	GD	unui lucru	lucrului
Pl.	NA	niște lucruri	lucrurile
	GD	unor lucruri	lucrurilor

-iu

		Indefinite	Definite
Sg.	NA	un exercițiu	exercițiul
	GD	unui exercițiu	exercițiului
Pl.	NA	niște exerciții	exercițiile
	GD	unor exerciții	exercițiilor

-e

		Indefinite	Definite
Sg.	NA	un nume	numele
	GD	unui nume	numelui
Pl.	NA	niște nume	numele
	GD	unor nume	numelor

Irregular nouns

un om, oameni m. 'human'

		Indefinite	Definite
Sg.	NA	un om	omul
	GD	unui om	omului
Pl.	NA	nişte oameni	oamenii
	GD	unor oameni	oamenilor

un ou, ouă n. 'egg'

		Indefinite	Definite
Sg.	NA	un ou	oul
	GD	unui ou	oului
Pl.	NA	nişte ouă	ouăle
	GD	unor ouă	ouălor

o soră, surori f. 'sister'

		Indefinite	Definite
Sg.	NA	o soră	sora
	GD	unei surori	surorii
Pl.	NA	nişte surori	surorile
	GD	unor surori	surorilor

o soră, surori f. 'nurse'

		Indefinite	Definite
Sg.	NA	o soră	sora
	GD	unei sore	sorei
Pl.	NA	nişte surori	surorile
	GD	unor surori	surorilor

o noră, nurori f. 'daughter-in-law'

		Indefinite	Definite
Sg.	NA	o noră	nora
	GD	unei nurori	nurorii
Pl.	NA	nişte nurori	nurorile
	GD	unor nurori	nurorilor

o piele, piei f. 'skin'

		Indefinite	Definite
Sg.	NA	o piele	pielea
	GD	unei pieli	pielii
Pl.	NA	nişte piei	pieile
	GD	unor piei	pieilor

o piele, piei f. 'leather'

		Indefinite	Definite
Sg.	NA	o piele	pielea
	GD	unei piei	pieii
Pl.	NA	nişte piei	pieile
	GD	unor piei	pieilor

o zi, zile f. 'day'

		Indefinite	Definite
Sg.	NA	o zi	ziua
	GD	unei zile	zilei
Pl.	NA	nişte zile	zilele
	GD	unor zile	zilelor

o luni, luni f. 'Monday'

		Indefinite	Definite
Sg.	NA	o luni	lunea
	GD	unei luni	(lunii)
Pl.	NA	niște luni	lunile
	GD	unor luni	lunilor

o șa, șei f. 'saddle'

		Indefinite	Definite
Sg.	NA	o șa	șaua
	GD	unei șei	șeii
Pl.	NA	niște șei	șeile
	GD	unor șei	șeilor

Genitive article

One of the special features of Romanian is the so-called genitive (or possessive) article, which is used in some cases in front of a possessive pronoun or a
genitive form of a noun or pronoun. The genitive article has the following
forms:

	Singular		Plural	
	m., n.	f.	m.	n., f.
NA	al	a	ai	ale
GD	-		alor	

In some dialects an invariable form *a* is used, but this is not accepted in the standard language.

The genitive and dative forms of the genitive article occur only before independently used possessive pronouns (see also p. 153):

ai mei	mine, my family, my friends
alor mei	to mine, my family, my friends

The singular genitive and dative forms (*alui, alei*) are old-fashioned and not used in modern language. They can be replaced with the demonstrative article (see p. 95).

When the genitive article is used as an attribute of a noun, it agrees with the
possessed noun in both gender and number, but not in case (only NA is used).
Notice, that if a possessive pronoun is used, it agrees with the possessed noun
also in case:

NA: o prietenă *a mea*	a friend of mine
GD: unei prietene *a mele*	to a friend of mine
NA: niște prietene *ale mele*	friends of mine
GD: unor prietene *ale mele*	to friends of mine

When several possessed nouns are mentioned, the genitive article usually
agrees with the closest one:

câini și *pisici ale* lui Ion	Ion's dogs and cats

The article can also agree with both nouns (see the agreement of the predicative, p. 120): *câini și pisici ai lui Ion.*

The genitive article must be used when:

- The possessed noun is not in the definite form (*-ul/-le/-a, -lui/-i, -i/-le, -lor*), i.e.:

  ➢ The noun is in the indefinite form:

o carte a mea	a book of mine
un prieten al meu	a friend of mine
niște prieteni ai mei	friends of mine

  ➢ The noun has no article at all:

această carte a mea	this book of mine
trei prieteni ai mei	three friends of mine
Ion al meu	my Ion

  ➢ The definite article suffix is not attached to the noun itself, but to a preceding adjective:

marile religii ale lumii	the great religions of the world
noua lege a pensiilor	the new pension law

  ➢ The possessed object is not a noun (but a pronoun or a numeral):

cel al lui Ion	the one belonging to Ion
al treilea al lui Ion	the third one belonging to Ion

- The possessive pronoun or the genitive form are not placed *directly* after the noun they modify. This happens when:

  ➢ There is an adjective or some other word between them:

cartea *aceasta* a mea	this book of mine
Oficiul *Poștal* al Moșului	Santa Clause's Post Office
Statele *Unite* ale Americii	the United States of America
prințesa *Letizia* a Spaniei	princess Letizia of Spain

  ➢ the possessive pronoun or the genitive form is placed before the possessed noun:

scriitoarea, a cărei carte	the writer whose book
a mea viață	my life (rare, poetic)

- The possessive pronoun or the genitive form is used independently, without the possessed noun. In this case the genitive article is actually a pronoun:

- A cui este această carte?	- Whose book is this?
- A mea. / A lui Ion. / A Mariei.	- Mine. / Ion's. / Maria's.

Cartea aceasta este a mea.	This book is mine.
Acele sunt ale lui Ion.	Those are Ion's.
Ale mele sunt aici.	Mine are here.

Unul este al meu, altul al tău.	One is mine, the other yours.

Le-am dat alor mei un cadou.	I have given a present to my children.

When an independent genitive article is used as a direct object, the preposition *pe* must always precede it (see p. 287):

O iubesc pe a mea.	I love my wife.

In a partitive structure the preposition *de* is used:

Este de-ai noştri.	He/she is one of us.
un prieten de-ai mei	one of my friends
(= de-al meu[51])	

Notice that if needed, also the genitive form *alor* of the genitive article might require a genitive article itself:

viaţa mea şi a alor mei	the life of me and my family

Thus the genitive article is not used if:

- The possessive pronoun or the genitive form of a noun or a pronoun is located directly after the noun it modifies *and* the noun is in the definite form:

cartea mea	my book
prietenilor lui Ion	to Ion's friends
Regatul Suediei	the Kingdom of Sweden
Maria mea	my Maria

- The possession is expressed with the preposition *a* (and not with genitive):

produsul vectorial a doi vectori	the vector product of two vectors (math.)

---

[51] This structure has recently been accepted, but traditionally it is not recommended.

When there are several genitive forms modifying a noun, each of them has (if needed by the rules mentioned) its own genitive article:

prietenii lui Ion și ai Mariei	Ion and Maria's friends
niște prieteni ai lui Ion și ai Mariei	some friends of Ion and Maria
Memorialul Victimelor Comunis-mului și al Rezistenței	Memorial of the Victims of Communism and Resistance

This is the traditional rule. However, in modern language the genitive article is not obligatory, if the coordinate nouns in genitive are seen as forming a single unit:

studiul limbii și culturii române	the study of Romanian language and culture
Regatul Unit al Marii Britanii și (al) Irlandei de Nord	the United Kingdom of Great Britain and North Ireland
Ministerul Educației, Cercetării, Tineretului și Sportului	Ministry of Education, Research, Youth and Sport

Notice that *ministerul educației și al cercetării* could also mean 'the ministry of education and the ministry of research', i.e. two different ministries (= *ministerul educației și cel al cercetării*).

The genitive article is also used to form ordinal numerals (see p. 132).

Demonstrative article

Romanian also has a so-called demonstrative (or adjective) article, which declines as follows:

	Singular		Plural	
	m., n.	f.	m.	n., f.
NA	cel	cea	cei	cele
GD	celui	celei	celor	

The demonstrative article is used:

* As a semi-independent pronoun replacing a definite noun that one does not want to repeat. *Cel* can be used directly in front of adjectives and cardinal numerals:

cel bun, cea bună	the good one
cei buni, cele bune	the good ones
cei trei, cele trei	the three

regiunea baltică și cea mediteraneană	the Baltic and Mediterranean regions

Compare:

elevul cel cuminte și silitor	the nice, hard working pupil (= one pupil)
elevul cel cuminte și cel silitor	the well-behaved pupil and the hard-working pupil (= two pupils)

Before adverbs, ordinal numerals and preposition structures the preposition *de* must be added:

cel de aici	the one over here
cei de acolo	the ones over there
cel de al treilea	the third one
cel de pe masă	the one over the table
cel de piatră[52]	the one of stone

Cel can occur also in front of a genitive form, even though it is not needed in NA (because of the genitive article):

(cel) al Mariei	Maria's one
celui al Mariei	to the Maria's one
președintele României și (cel) al Poloniei	the president of Romania and the president of Poland

The semi-independent *cel* is not recommended in front of a possessive pronoun (~~cel~~ *al meu* 'mine'). However, it can be used to replace the missing cases of the genitive article (*celui al, celei a*).

If a semi-independent *cel* is used as a direct object, the prepositions *pe* (see p. 287) must be used (even if *cel* refers to inanimate objects):

Următorul DVD conține biografia Evei Braun și *pe cea* a lui Jules Verne. (*Adevărul*)	The following DVD contains the biographies of Eva Braun and (that of) Jules Verne.

- *Cel* + adjective and *cel de* can also be used after a definite noun or a proper noun. This structure answers the question 'which one?'

NA studenta cea silitoare GD studentei celei silitoare	the hard working student (and not the lazy one)
NA podul cel de piatră GD podului celui de piatră	the stone bridge (not not the wooden one)
NA copiii cei cuminți GD copiilor celor cuminți	the well-behaved children

---

[52] *Cel de + de piatră → cel de piatră.*

If the GD is formed by the article *lui, cel* is used in the nominative form:

NA Alexandru cel Mare   Alexander the Great
GD lui Alexandru cel Mare

In freer style, especially in the masculine and neuter singular, *cel* is often not declined (*podu-lui cel de piatră*), but in standard language it must agree with the case of the noun.

- As a definite article when there is a numeral in front of the noun:

    cei trei bărbați   the three men
    cel de al treilea bărbat   the third man

- In the relative pronouns *cel care* (see p. 171) and *cel ce* (p. 172).

- In the superlative (see p. 123). Compare *cel* + comparative with the superlative form:

    cel mai bun decât mine   the one better than me (comparative)
    cel mai bun dintre noi   the best among us (superlative)

Compound nouns

Only the last part is declined in nouns like:

    un sud-european, niște sud-europeni   South European man
        sud-europeanul, sud-europenii
    o după-amiază, niște după-amiezi   afternoon
        după-amiaza, după-amiezile
        GD: unei după-amiezi, după-amiezii
    un prim-ministru, niște prim-miniștri   Prime Minister
        prim-ministrul, prim-miniștrii

In some words only the first part is declined:

    un an-lumină, niște ani-lumină   light year
        anul-lumină, anii-lumină
    un kilowatt-oră, niște kilowați-oră   kilowatt hour
        kilowattul-oră, kilowații-oră
    un bloc-turn, niște blocuri-turn   tower block
        blocul-turn, blocurile-turn
    o femeie-soldat, niște femei-soldat,   female soldier
        femeia-soldat, femeile-soldat
    o floarea-soarelui, niște florile-soarelui sunflower
        floarea-soarelui, florile-soarelui
        GD: unei florii-soarelui, florii-soarelui

Both parts are declined in words like:

un câine-lup, nişte câini-lupi	German shepherd
câinele-lup, câinii-lupi	
un redactor-şef, nişte redactori-şefi	editor-in-chief
redactorul-şef, redactorii-şefi	
o iarbă-neagră, nişte ierbi-negre	heather
iarba-neagră, ierbile-negre	
GD: unei ierbi-negre, ierbii-negre	

With these kinds of nouns the possessive pronouns are placed after the first element: *câinele meu lup* 'my German shepherd'.

Some compound nouns (especially those formed from verbs) are invariable, and the plural has the same form as the singular:

un zgârie-nori, nişte zgârie-nori	skyscraper
GD: unui zgârie-nori, unor zgârie-nori	
un vorbă-lungă, nişte vorbă-lungă	babbler
GD: unui/unor vorbă-lungă, lui vorbă-lungă	
un frige-linte, nişte frige-linte	scrooge
GD: unui/unor frige-linte, lui frige-linte	
o nu-mă-uita, nişte nu-mă-uita	forget-me-not (plant)

Proper nouns

The declension of proper nouns differs somewhat from the declension of common nouns.

Personal names

The masculine personal names (e.g. *Radu, Ion*) are used without a definite article[53], and the definite form cannot be formed. When they are used as the direct object, the preposition *pe* must be used (see p. 287). The genitive and dative forms are formed by *lui*.

The feminine personal names ending in -*a*-, -*ia*- and -*ea* (e.g. *Ana, Maria, Andreea*) are definite forms. Just like with masculine names, the preposition *pe* is required when feminine names are used as direct objects. After the preposition the definite form is used. The genitive and dative forms are formed by

---

[53] The names ending in -*u* are actually definite forms from which the final *l* has disappeared, and the u is now part of the stem.

the suffix *-ei* (*-a* → *-ei*, *-ia* → *-iei*, *-ea* → *-ei*[54]). Other feminine names (e.g. *Carmen, Jeni*) act like masculine names.

Thus the personal names are declined as follows:

N.	Radu	Ion	Carmen	Jeni	Ana	Maria	Andreea
A.	pe Radu	pe Ion	pe Carmen	pe Jeni	pe Ana	pe Maria	pe Andreea
GD.	lui Radu	lui Ion	lui Carmen	lui Jeni	Anei	Mariei	Andreei

Feminine personal names have no sound changes (*Floarea: Floarei*[55]).The genitive and dative forms of feminine names ending in *-ca-* and *-ga* are formed either with *-ăi* or (more rarely) *-ii*[56]: *Olga: Olgăi, Olghii, Monica: Monicăi, Monichii*.

In colloquial style also feminine personal names ending in *-a* can form the genitive and dative with *lui: lui Maria*. In standard language this is not accepted.

The classical Latin and Greek names should be declined according to the original stems: *Artemis: Artemidei, Dido: Didonei, Venus: Venerei*.

The masculine personal names ending in *-a* (*-ia, -ea*) can also form their genitive and dative with the feminine endings: *lui Toma / Tomei, lui Luca / Lucăi / Luchii, lui Badea / Badei*. The masculine names ending in *-i* [i̯] or *-u* [u, u̯] can have a genitive and dative ending in *-(u)lui: lui Mihai / Mihaiului, lui Alexandru / Alexandrului*. However, all of these forms are very rare in the modern language.

If both the first and last names are used, only the first name is declined:

fratele lui Ion Popescu	Ion Popescu's brother
fratele Monicăi Popescu	Monica Popescu's brother

The same is true of first names in two parts: *Ana Maria, GD Anei Maria*.

In some contexts, personal names can occur also in the indefinite form. Feminine names ending in *-a, -ia-* and *-ea* have indefinite forms ending in *-ă, -ie, -e*, although the definite forms can also be used:

NA: un Ion	NA: o Ană ~ o Ana
GD: unui Ion	GD: unei Ane
NA: o Marie ~ o Maria	NA: o Andree ~ o Andreea
GD: unei Marii	GD: unei Andrei
NA: o Carmen	
GD: unei Carmen	
Cunosc un Ion.	I know a John.
Îl cunosc pe un Ion.	

---

[54] Unlike the common nouns ending in *-e*, which have the genitive and dative definite ending *-ii*: *ideea, ideii*.

[55] Compare with *floarea: florii* 'flower'.

[56] Since there is no sound change, an *h* must be added in spelling.

Un Dali vândut cu 2 milioane de euro (*Adevărul*)	A Dali sold for 2 million euros

The plural forms are formed like normal nouns, both in their indefinite and definite forms:

Ion: Ioni, unor Ioni, Ionii, Ionilor
Ana: Ane, unor Ane, Anele, Anelor
Maria: Marii, unor Marii, Mariile, Mariilor

În România sunt mulți Ioni.	In Romania there are many Ions.
La mulți ani Ionilor!	Congratulations to Ions!

The last name *-escu* has an indefinite plural form ending in *-escu* or *-ești* and a definite form ending in *-eștii*, GD *-eștilor*:

doi Popescu / Popești	two Popescus
Popeștii	the Popescus
sfârșitul Ceaușeștilor	the end of the Ceaușescus

Personal names are often used in the vocative case (see p. 68).

Animal names

Animal names behave like personal names.

Îl iubesc pe Rex / pe Negruța.	I love Rex / Negruța (dogs).
zgarda lui Rex / Negruței.	Rex's / Negruța's collar

Astronomical names

The masculine and neuter astronomical names do not usually have on article, while the feminine names are in the definite form (*-a*). The genitive and dative forms are formed like with personal names (*lui, -ei*):

Jupiter, GD lui Jupiter	Jupiter
Uranus, GD lui Uranus	Uranus
Marte, GD lui Marte	Mars
Andromeda, GD Andromedei	Andromeda
Terra, GD Terrei	Terra

Geographical names

Geographical names are usually either feminine or neuter. Only some names used in the plural can be masculine.

In maps and encyclopaedias the masculine and neuter names are used without an article (*Cluj, Carpați, Vietnam*). However, with feminine names the definite form ending in -*a* is used (*Finlanda, România, Dobrogea*). Exceptions are very rare (e.g. the feminine names *Târgoviște, Orăștie, Oglinzi*).

These forms are also used:

- In definitions:

București este capitala Rômânei.	Bucharest is the capital of Romania. (we are told what Bucharest is)
Similarly: Capitala României este / se numește București.	The capital of Romania is (called) Bucharest.

- When the geographical name is preceded by a common noun (and the name itself functions as a appositive modifier):

râul Olt	the river Olt
orașul București	the city of Bucharest
munții Alpi	the Alps
statul Peru	the country of Peru
Republica România	the Republic of Romania
orașul Roma	the city of Rome
fluviul Sena	the river Seine
orașul Târgoviște	the city of Târgoviște

  This way, the declension of a geographical name can be avoided, since the apposition is not declined:

centrul orașului Helsinki = centrul Helsinkiului	the centre of Helsinki
președintele Republicii Chile	the president of the Republic of Chile

  Even the use of the genitive is possible (*Republica României*), although somewhat old-fashioned. The genitive is often used with kingdoms:

Regatul Spaniei	the Kingdom of Spain

- After prepositions that require the accusative case:

la București	in Bucharest
la Cluj	in Cluj
la Târgoviște	in Târgoviște
la Satu Mare	in Satu Mare
în Finlanda	in Finland
în România	in Romania

An exception is *Dunărea*, which is used without the article:

pe Dunăre   on the Danube

However, if the geographic name has a modifier, the definite form is used:

în Bucureştiul de azi	today's Bucharest
în Berlinul Răsăritean	in East Berlin
în Alpii Italieni	in the Italian Alps
pe Dunărea de Jos	the Lower Danube

Otherwise (as a subject, direct object or in the genitive or dative case) the definite form is used in all genders:

Carpaţii sunt foarte frumoşi.	The Carpathians are very beautiful.
Bucureştiul este capitala europeană cea mai expusă riscului seismic. (*Jurnalul de Vrancea*)	Bucharest is the European capital most exposed to seismic risk.
Iubesc Clujul / Carpaţii / România.	I love Cluj / the Carpathians / Romania.
centrul Bucureştiului populaţia României	the centre of Bucharest the population of Romania

Geographical names are declined like common nouns:

Finlanda, GD Finlandei	Finland
România, GD României	Romania
Germania, GD Germaniei	Germany
Irak: Irakul, GD Irakului	Iraq
Cipru: Ciprul, GD Ciprului	Cyprus
Vietnam: Vietnamul, GD Vietnamului	Vietnam
Constanţa, GD Constanţei	Constanţa
Turda, GD Turzii	Turda
Londra, GD Londrei	London
Cluj: Clujul, GD Clujului	Cluj
Paris: Parisul, GD Parisului	Paris
New York: New Yorkul, GD New Yorkului	New York
Sena, GD Senei	the Seine
Olt: Oltul, GD Oltului	the Olt
Nil: Nilul, GD Nilului	the Nile

The genitive and dative of names ending in *-ca-* and *-ga* are formed with the ending *-ăi*:

Jamaica, GD Jamaicăi	Jamaica
Volga, GD Volgăi	Volga

Ladoga, GD Ladogăi	Ladoga
Alaska, GD Alaskăi	Alaska

Exceptions:

America, GD Americii	America
Africa, GD Africii	Africa
Danemarca, GD Danemarcei / -cii	Denmark

Names ending in -*ea* have the genitive and dative ending in -*ei*:

Dobrogea, GD Dobrogei	Dobrogea
Tulcea, GD Tulcei	Tulcea
Târgovişte: Târgoviştea, GD Târgoviştei	Târgovişte
Coreea, GD Coreei	Korea
Guineea Ecuatorială, GD Guineei Ecuatoriale	Equatorial Guinea

Exceptions:

Dunărea, GD Dunării	the Danube
Oradea, GD Oradiei, (Orăzii)[57]	Oradea

Compound Romanian names are declined as follows:

noun + noun:	Târgu-Mureş: Târgu-Mureşul, Târgu-Mureşului
noun + adj.:	Satu Mare: Satul Mare, Satului Mare
	Valea Lungă: Văii Lungi
noun + gen.:	Vatra Dornei, Vetrei Dornei
noun + *de:*	Curtea de Argeş: Curţii de Argeş
single word:	Câmpulung: Câmpulungul, Câmpulungului

Neuter names ending in -*e* and -*o* are usually invariable and the base form is used instead of GD:

independenţa Kosovo	the independence of Kosovo
ambasada Chile	the embassy of Chile

However:

Congo: Congoul, GD Congoului	Congo

The plural forms are formed as with regular nouns:

Germania, Germanii, Germaniile	Germany
Vietnam: Vietnamul, Vietnamuri, Vietnamurile	Vietnam
cele două Germanii	the two Germanies

Some names (mostly mountains or archipelagos) are always plural:

Alpi: Alpii, GD Alpilor	the Alps
Carpaţi: Carpaţii, GD Carpaţilor	the Carpathians

---

[57] From the older form *Oradia*. The official city web page uses "municipiului Oradea".

Anzi: Anzii, GD Anzilor	the Andes
Filipine: Filipinele, GD Filipinelor	The Philippines
Azore: Azorele, GD Azorelor	The Azores
Statele Unite ale Americii	the United States of America

Some city and village names can also be plural. Feminine plural names are in the nominative and accusative either in the indefinite (e.g. *Oglinzi, Lespezi*) or the definite form (e.g. *Luncile, Odăile, Pietrele*). With plural masculine and neuter names the singular form has become more common in modern language:

București: Bucureștiul, GD Bucureștiului	Bucharest
(rare) Bucureștii, GD Bucureștilor	
Iași: Iașiul, GD Iașiului	Iași
(rare) Iașii, GD Iașilor	

An indefinite form can be formed from all the geographical names (the feminine endings -*a* → -*ă*, -*ia* → -*ie*, -*ea* → -*e*):

Vreau o Românie mai curată.	I want a cleaner Romania.
Vreau un Cipru unificat.	I want a united Cyprus.

The form without an article must also be used when the article is attached to a preceding adjective or when there is a pronoun that requires a form without an article:

Marea Britanie	Great Britain
GD: Marii Britanii	
Noua Zeelandă	New Zealand
GD: Noii Zeelande	
acest Irak	this Iraq
această Finlandă	this Finland
acești Carpați	these Carpathians

Commercial names

Commercial names (names of companies, brand names, etc.) are usually invariable and the NA form is also used for the genitive:

vânzările Nokia	the sales of Nokia
vânzările Sony	the sales of Sony
reclama Microsoft	the advertisement of Microsoft
reclama Peugeot / Dacia	the advertisement of Peugeot / Dacia
flota TAROM	the fleet of TAROM
fondatorul Facebook	the founder of Facebook

After a preposition, the NA form is also used for the dative:

potrivit Adevărul	according to *Adevărul*
potrivit The Times	according to The Times

Otherwise, in the dative the declined forms must be used, but this is usually avoided by adding a noun in front of the name:

(Nokiei) ~ companiei Nokia	to Nokia

The singular NA form is also used in the plural:

un Mercedes, două (mașini) Mercedes	a Mercedes Benz
un Nokia, două (telefoane) Nokia	a Nokia phone
o Dacia, două (mașini) Dacia	a Dacia

In freer style, also forms such as *Microsoftul, GD Microsoftului, Taromul, GD Taromului, Mercedesul, GD Mercedesului,* pl. *Mercedesuri, o Dacia / o Dacie, GD Daciei,* pl. *Dacii* occur.

Spelling of foreign words

If a foreign word ends in a letter which is pronounced the same as in Romanian, the suffixes are added directly to the noun:

trend [trend], trendul, trenduri
copyright ['kopirait], copyrightul
business ['biznis], businessul, businessuri
boom [bum], boomul, boomuri

However, if the foreign word ends in a letter which is not pronounced the same as in Romanian (e.g. -y [i], -sh [ʃ] or a silent letter), the suffix is added with the help of a hyphen:

show [ʃoṷ], show-ul
gay [gʲeĭ], gay-ul, pl. gay, gay-i
Bruxelles [bry'sel], Bruxelles-ul
flash [fleʃ], flash-ul, flash-uri

The above-mentioned spelling rules are quite recent and often not respected.

Adjectives

In Romanian, adjectives agree with the noun they refer to (or substitute) in gender, number and case.

Forms of adjectives

Declension of adjectives

All adjectives have the same form in the masculine and neuter nominative singular. Similarly, all adjectives have the same form in the feminine and neuter nominative plural. Thus, in the nominative the adjectives have four different forms: masculine and neuter singular, feminine singular, masculine plural, and feminine and neuter plural.

The accusative form of adjectives is always the same as the nominative form. The masculine and neuter genitive and dative forms are also the same as the nominative forms. The feminine genitive and dative singular and plural have the same form as the feminine nominative plural. For the formation of the vocative case, see p. 115.

The feminine form is usually formed by the suffix -*ă*. The adjectives are declined the same way as the nouns, so the masculine plural ending is -*i* and the feminine and neuter plural ending is usually -*e*. Most Romanian adjectives have these four different forms.

E.g. *bun, bună, buni, bune* 'good':

		M.	N.	F.
Sg.	NA	bun		bună
	GD			
Pl.	NA	buni	bune	
	GD			

Other examples:

alb, albă, albi, albe	white
regional, regională, regionali, regionale	regional
englez, engleză, englezi, engleze	English
român, română, români, române	Romanian

The adjectives ending in *-u* have four forms as well. The vowel *-u* is removed before the endings *-ă, -i, -e*:

dublu, dublă, dubli, duble	double
simplu, simplă, simpli, simple	simple
sacru, sacră, sacri, sacre	sacred

The same also happens with adjectives ending in *-uu*:

ambiguu [-u.u], ambiguă [-u.ə],	ambiguous
ambigui [-uį], ambigue [-u.e]	
continuu, continuă, continui, continue	continuous

The adjectives have the same sound changes as nouns. Consonant changes are more regular than vowel changes.

All the adjectives ending in *-t-, -d-, -s-, -x-, -st-, -xt-* and *-stru* have the following sound changes in the masculine plural:

t → ț

bogat, bogată, bogați, bogate	rich
suficient, suficientă, suficienți, suficiente	sufficient
înalt, înaltă, înalți, înalte	tall

d → z

nud, nudă, nuzi, nude	naked
surd, surdă, surzi, surde	deaf
timid, timidă, timizi, timide	shy

s → ș (x → cș)

gras, grasă, grași, grase	fat, greasy
noros, noroasă, noroși, noroase	cloudy
fix, fixă, ficși, fixe	fixed
ortodox, ortodoxă, ortodocși, ortodoxe	orthodox

st → șt (xt → cșt)

trist, tristă, triști, triste	sad
prost, proastă, proști, proaste	stupid
capitalist, capitalistă, capitaliști, capitaliste	capitalistic
mixt, mixtă, micști, mixte	mixed

str → ștr:

albastru, albastră, albaștri, albastre	blue
sinistru, sinistră, siniștri, sinistre	sinister
ilustru, ilustră, iluștri, ilustre	illustrious, famous

Adjectives ending in *-sc-, -c-* and *-g* have a regular sound change in the plural of all genders (and in the feminine genitive and dative singular):

sc → șt:

brusc, bruscă, bruști, bruște	sudden

[k] → [t͡ʃ]:

biologic, biologică, biologici, biologice	biological
puternic, puternică, puternici, puternice	strong
bosniac, bosniacă, bosniaci, bosniace	Bosniac

[g] → [d͡ʒʲ]:

analog, analo(a)gă, analogi, analo(a)ge	analogical
cronofag, cronofagă, cronofagi, cronofage	time consuming
centrifug, centrifugă, centrifugi, centrifuge	centrifugal

The consonant change *sc* → *șt* does not occur with following adjectives, which have the sound change *sc* → [st͡ʃ] instead:

basc, bască, basci, basce	Basque
monegasc, monegască, monegasci, monegasce	Monégasque (from Monaco)
etrusc, etruscă, etrusci, etrusce	Etruscan
morisc, moriscă, morisci, morisce	Moor
osc, oscă, osci, osce	Oscan (hist.)
volsc, volscă, volsci, volsce	Volscian (hist.)
flasc, flască, flasci, flasce	flaccid

The word *ambidextru* does not have the sound change *str* → *știr*:

ambidextru, ambidextră, ambidextri, ambidextre	ambidexter

Rarer consonant changes that occur only in a few words include *z* → *j* and the loss of *l*:

dârz, dârză, dârji, dârze	daring, bold
treaz, trează, treji, treze	awake ; sober
viteaz, vitează, viteji, viteze	brave

chel, cheală, chei, chele	bald
gol, goală, goi, goale	empty
sătul, sătulă, sătui, sătule	full, satiated

Most adjectives ending in -*z* or -*l* are regular:

francez, franceză, francezi, franceze	French
spaniol, spaniolă, spanioli, spaniole	Spanish

The vowel changes are best learnt individually with each word. The following vowel changes are quite common:

- *o* → *oa* in the feminine (singular and plural):

frumos, frumoasă, frumoși, frumoase	beautiful
ușor, ușoară, ușori, ușoare	easy ; light

- *e* → *ea* in the feminine nominative and accusative singular:

negru, neagră, negri, negre	black
drept, dreaptă, drepți, drepte	straight

- *ia* → *ie* in the plural (and feminine genitive and dative singular):

italian, italiană, italieni, italiene	Italian
austriac, austriacă, austrieci, austriece	Austrian

- the unstressed *ă* → *e* in the plural (and feminine genitive and dative singular):

proaspăt, proaspătă, proaspeți, proaspete	fresh
geamăn, geamănă, gemeni, gemene	twin

Rarer vowel changes include *e* → *a*, *â* → *i*:

deșert, deșartă, deșerți, deșarte	deserted
sfânt, sfântă, sfinți, sfinte	holy
tânăr, tânără, tineri, tinere	young
vânăt, vânătă, vineți, vinete	violet-blue, pale

Exceptions

- If the feminine plural (and the genitive and dative singular) is formed with *-i*, it is identical to the masculine plural. Thus these adjectives have only three different forms, e.g. *mic, mică, mici, mici* 'small':

		M.	N.	F.
Sg.	NA	mic		mică
	GD			
Pl.	NA	mici		
	GD			

All these adjectives have a stem ending in *-c* or *-g* and they have the sound change [k] → [t͡ʃ], [g] → [d͡ʒ] or [sk] → [ʃt]:

sec, seacă, seci, seci	dry
sărac, săracă, săraci, săraci	poor
larg, largă, largi, largi	wide, broad
lung, lungă, lungi, lungi	long

românesc, românească, românești, românești	Romanian
arăbesc, arăbească, arăbești, arăbești	Arabic

However, not all the adjectives ending in *-c* or *-g* belong to this group. As seen above, e.g. the adjectives ending in *-ic-*, *-iac-*, *-log-*, *-fag-* and *-fug* have four forms.

- Adjectives ending in *-e* have only one form for all genders in the nominative and accusative singular. The feminine genitive and dative singular and the plural of all genders are formed with the ending *-i*. Thus these adjectives have only two different forms, e.g. *mare, mare, mari, mari* 'big':

		M.	N.	F.
Sg.	NA	mare		
	GD			
Pl.	NA	mari		
	GD			

Other adjectives like this include:

rece, rece, reci, reci	cold
dulce, dulce, dulci, dulci	sweet
tare, tare, tari, tari	hard

Adjectives ending in *-de-* and *-te* have the consonant change *t → ț, d → z* in the plural (and in the feminine genitive and dative singular):

cuminte, cuminte, cuminți, cuminți	obedient
verde, verde, verzi, verzi	green

Only the following two adjectives have a vowel change:

moale, moale, moi, moi	soft
călare, călare, călări, călări	riding

Exceptions:

june, junā, juni, june (rare)	young
rapace, rapace, rapaci, rapace	rapacious
sagace, sagace, sagaci, sagace	sagacious
tenace, tenace, tenaci, tenace	tenacious
vorace, vorace, voraci, vorace	voracious

- Adjectives created by the suffix *-tor* have a feminine singular and plural form ending in *-toare*:

următor, următoare, următori, următoare	following, next
gânditor, gânditoare, gânditori, gânditoare	pensive, thoughtful

- In adjectives ending in *-iu*, the *-u* disappears in the other forms and the ending for the feminine singular NA is *-e* (*i + ă → ie*). The plural ending (and the ending for feminine GD singular) is *-i* in all genders:

propriu, proprie, proprii, proprii	own
obligatoriu, obligatorie, obligatorii, obligatorii	obligatory
azuriu, azurie, azurii, azurii	azure

- Adjectives ending in *-eu* make their feminine forms with *-e* (both in the singular and plural):

instantaneu, instantanee, instantanei, instantanee	instantaneous
ateu, atee, atei, atee	atheistic

- The following four adjectives have some irregular forms:

roşu, roşie, roşii, roşii	red
nou, nouă, noi, noi	new
greu, grea, grei, grele	difficult ; heavy
rău, rea, răi, rele	bad

- There are only a few adjectives ending in *-i*. The most frequent is *vechi*, which has a feminine nominative and accusative singular form ending in *-e,* while all the other forms (including the feminine GD singular) end in *-i*:

vechi, veche, vechi, vechi	old
străvechi, străveche, străvechi, străvechi	ancient

Adjectives ending in *-ui* have the feminine nominative and accusative singular form *-uie*. The plural ending (and the ending for feminine GD singular) is *-i* in all genders:

gălbui, gălbuie, gălbui, gălbui	yellowish
verzui, verzuie, verzui, verzui	greenish
haihui, haihuie, haihui, haihui	light-headed, giddy

Exceptions:

silhui, silhuie, silhui, silhuie	dense, thick
şui, şuie, şui, şuie	stupid (colloq.)

The feminine singular and plural ending of adjectives ending in *-ci* is *-ce*:

stângaci, stângace, stângaci, stângace	left-handed
fugaci, fugace, fugaci, fugace	fugacious, fleeting

The feminine singular and plural ending of other adjectives ending in *-i* is *-ie*:

bălai, bălaie, bălai, bălaie	fair (coloured)
rotofei, rotofeie, rotofei, rotofeie	fat, plump
vioi, vioaie, vioi, vioaie	lively

Exception:

lai, laie, lăi, lăi	blackish (non-standard)

- Adjectives formed with the diminutive ending *-el* are declined irregularly, since the feminine nominative-accusative singular is formed with the ending *-ică*:

frumuşel, frumuşică, frumuşei, frumuşele	pretty
singurel, singurică, singurei, singurele	alone
tinerel, tinerică, tinerei, tinerele	young

Regular feminine forms ending in *-ea* (*frumuşea, singurea, tinerea*) are possible, but rarer. However:

mişel, mişea, mişei, mişele	coward

Incomplete adjectives

Because of their meaning, some adjectives do not have all the forms:

- only masculine and neuter singular: *zahăr farin* 'brown sugar'
- only masculine singular and plural: *an bisect, ani bisecţi* 'leap year'
- only feminine singular and plural: *liră sterlină, lire sterline* 'pound sterling'

Invariable adjectives

Romanian also has some invariable adjectives. These are usually new, foreign words like the colours *bej* 'beige', *bleu* 'light blue', *gri* 'grey', *kaki* 'khaki', *lila* 'lilac', *mov* 'mauve', *oliv* 'olive', *roz* 'pink'. Some other new words include e.g. *eficace* 'efficient', *feroce* 'ferocious', *precoce* 'precocious', *vivace* 'lively', *forte* 'strong', *gay, latino, sexy, stereo* etc.

muzică latino	Latin music
muzică pop	pop music
căşti stereo	stereo headphones
fustă mini	mini-skirt
limbile bantu	the Bantu language
cultura maya	the Mayan culture
atacuri feroce	fierce attacks
asemenea lucru	a thing like that
mişcarea gay	the gay movement

Some older loanwords can also be invariable (e.g. *gata* 'ready'). Also some adjectives made from adverbs are invariable: *aşa* 'such', *asemenea* 'similar', *astfel de* 'like this', *altfel de* 'different'.

Adjectives with irregular genitive and dative

The adjectives *diferit* and *felurit* 'different' have special forms ending in *-or* for the genitive and dative plural: *diferitor, feluritor*. These forms are used before nouns, but they can also be replaced by the prepositions *a* and *la* + accusative:

diferitor oameni   to different people
= la diferiți oameni

If these adjectives are preceded by a declined pronoun or article (ending in *-or*), the regular plural forms *diferiți, diferite, feluriți, felurite* are used:

acestor diferiți oameni   to these different people

The definite genitive and dative forms of these adjectives are regular (*diferiților oameni*).

Definite forms of adjectives

The definite article is added to adjectives the same way as to the nouns (see p. 75-), e.g.:

Adjectives ending in a consonant:
bun: NA: bunul, buna, bunii, bunele
                        GD: bunului, bunei, bunilor, bunelor

Adjectives ending in -u:
albastru: NA: albastrul, albastra, albaștrii, albastrele
                        GD: albastrului, albastrei, albaștrilor, albastrelor

Adjectives ending in -e:
mare: NA: marele, marea, marii, marile
                        GD: marelui, marii, marilor, marilor

Adjectives ending in -iu:
propriu: NA: propriul, propria, propriii, propriile
                        GD: propriului, propriei, propriilor, propriilor

Others:
rău: NA: răul, reaua, răii, relele
                        GD: răului, relei, răilor, relelor

roșu: NA: roșul, roșia, roșiii, roșiile
                        GD: roșului, roșiei, roșiilor, roșiilor

nou: NA: noul, noua, noii, noile
                        GD: noului, noii, noilor, noilor

vechi: NA: vechiul, vechea, vechii, vechile
                        GD: vechiului, vechii, vechilor, vechilor

The definite form of the adjective is used when the adjective attribute is placed before the noun (see p. 116).

Invariable adjectives (see p. 112) do not usually have definite forms either. An exception is the adjectives ending in -*e,* which have all the definite forms, except the masculine plural:

ferocele tigru	the fierce tiger
ferocea presa de scandal	the fierce yellow press
eficacele sisteme	efficient systems

The names of the colours can also be used as nouns, in which case they do have a regular definite form:

Îmi place rozul.	I like pink.

Compound adjectives

In compound adjectives usually only the last part is declined:

greco-roman, greco-romană, greco-romani, greco-romane	Greco-Roman
marxist-leninist, marxist-leninistă, marxist-leniniști, marxist-leniniste	Marxist-Leninist
social-democrat, social-democrată, social-democrați, social-democrate	Social democratic
est-european, est-europeană, est-europeni, est-europene	East-European
sud-american, sud-americană, sud-americani, sud-americane	South American
nou-născut, nou-născută, nou-născuți, nou-născute	new-born
așa-numit, așa-numită, așa-numiți, așa-numite	so called
bine-cunoscut, bine-cunoscută, bine-cunoscuți, bine-cunoscute	well-known

In different shades of colour only the first element is declined:

verde-deschis, verzi-deschis	light green
verde-închis, verzi-închis	dark green
roșu-aprins, roșie-aprins, roșii-aprins, roșii-aprins	bright red
galben-pal, galbenă-pal, galbeni-pal, galbene-pal	pale yellow

However, these adjectives are often treated as invariable:

o rochie albastră-deschis ~ albastru-deschis[58]	a light blue dress

Some compound adjectives are totally invariable:

alb-negru	black and white
pursânge	full-blooded

Vocative

When an adjective is used as an attribute before or after a noun, the nominative form is usually used instead of the vocative:

iubit coleg! coleg iubit!	dear colleague!
frumoasă fată!	beautiful girl!

This is always the case with feminine and plural nouns:[59]:

dragă prietenă!, iubită prietenă!	dear friend!
dragi prieteni!, iubiți prieteni! (masc.)	dear friends!
dragi prietene!, iubite prietene! (fem.)	
colegi iubiți!	dear colleagues!

When an adjective precedes a masculine or neuter noun in the singular, the vocative can also be used. The vocative is especially common with adjectives like *drag / iubit* 'dear' and *stimat* 'esteemed'. The masculine vocative of adjectives is formed with the ending *-e*, except *drag*, which has the irregular masculine vocative form *dragă*.

dragă prietene!	dear friend!
dragă domnule!	dear Sir!
iubite prietene!	dear friend!
stimate domnule!	esteemed Sir!

The ending *-e* causes the same sound changes as the feminine plural ending *-e*. E. g.:

sfânte: sfinte Dumneazeule!	holy God!

A proper name can occur in the nominative even after an adjective in the vocative:

dragă Radule / dragă Radu!	dear Radu!

---

[58] According to Academia Română (GLR I, p. 153) the forms *albastru-deshisă* and *albastră-deschisă* are also possible. However, DOOM[2] does not mention these forms.
[59] Forms like *bătrinilor codri!* 'old forests!' belong only to poetry.

When the adjective is placed after a noun in the vocative, the nominative form is used:

    Statule român!   Country of Romania!

When an adjective is used independently, a special vocative form is used in all genders. The ending for masculine and neuter is usually -*ule* and for the feminine it is -*o* (exception: *drag: dragule, dragă*):

    iubitule! (masc.), iubito! (fem.)   dear!
    dragule! (masc.), dragă! (fem.)

The feminine vocative form has the same vowel changes as the nominative:

    frumos, frumoasă: frumoaso!   beauty!

The plural vocative ending is -*lor*, which is added to the plural form of the adjective:

    dragilor!   dear loved ones!

However, when an independent adjective is modified by a possessive pronoun, the vocative cannot be used and the definite nominative form is used instead:

    iubitul meu! iubita mea!   my love!
    dragii mei!   my love! (pl.)

Position of adjectives

Semantically, adjectives are used either as qualitative (descriptive) or categorical adjectives. The difference between qualitative and categorical adjectives is not restrictive, since many adjectives can be used both qualitatively and categorically.

Categorical adjectives express a category or a class to which the noun belongs. They are always placed after the noun they modify:

    Uniunea Europeană   the European Union
    un centru sportiv   a sports centre
    un student finlandez   a Finnish student

Categorical adjectives have a restrictive sense: the *European* Union, not the Soviet Union; a *sports* centre, not a shopping centre, etc. Categorical adjectives cannot be used in comparative or superlative forms.

Qualitative adjectives are also usually placed after the noun:

    o carte bună   a good book
    cartea bună   the good book

However, if a qualitative adjective is stylistically emphasized, it can also be placed before the noun. If this is the case, the indefinite and the definite articles are added to the adjective, not to the noun:

NA: *o* bună carte	a good book
GD: *unei* bune cărţi	
NA: bun*a* carte	the good book
GD: bun*ei* cărţi	

A qualitative adjective preceding the noun often expresses an inherent characteristic of the noun. Compare:

faimosul scriitor Victor Hugo	the famous writer Victor Hugo
El este un scriitor faimos.	He is a famous writer.
talentaţii actori ai teatrului	the talented actors of the theatre (all the actors are talented, non-restrictive)
actori talentaţii ai teatrului	the talented actors of the theatre (and not the untalented ones, restrictive)

If there are more than one adjective preceding the noun, the definite article must be repeated:

faimos*ul* şi talentat*ul* actor	the famous and talented actor

However, only one indefinite article is needed: *un faimos şi talentat actor* 'a famous and talented actor'.

In some fixed expressions the adjective is always placed before the noun:

un mic dejun	a breakfast
micul dejun	the breakfast
micul ecran	the small screen, the television

Some adjectives have different a meaning when they are placed before or after the noun, e.g.:

o nouă maşină	a new (= another) car
o maşina nouă	a new (= just made) car
o bună parte	a large part
o parte bună	a good part
un sărac om	a poor (= pitiable) man
un om sărac	a poor (= having no money) man
un simplu plan	just a plan
un plan simplu	a simple plan

un înalt oficial	a high official
un oficial înalt	a tall official
diferite opinii	different opinion
opinii diferite	differing opinions
în plină noapte	in the middle of the night
o noapte plină de surprize	a night full of surprises

When the adjective *întreg* 'whole' is placed in front of the noun, in the nominative and accusative the definite article can also be added to the noun:

întregul popor = întreg poporul	the whole nation
întreaga carte = întreagă cartea	the whole book

GD: întregului popor, întregii cărți

In some exclamations the article is added to the noun following the adjective:

Frumoasă fata!	What a beautiful girl!
Bună ziua!	Hello!, Good day!
Bună seara!	Good evening!
Bună dimineața!	Good morning!

But e.g.: *noaptea bună!* 'good night!', *Crăciun fericit!* 'merry Christmas!'.

Similarly the article is added to the noun in the expression *în plin centrul* + genitive 'right in the middle of (a town)':

A fost împușcat în plin centrul orașului.	He was shot right in the middle of the city.

Some structures can have two definite articles. When a noun is preceded by an adjective meaning 'poor, pitiable' (*biet, sărac, sărman, răposat, regretat*), the noun can be in the definite form (either with possessive meaning or if it has another modifier):

săraca bunica	my poor grandmother
săracul prietenul meu	my poor friend

Compare with *săraca bunică* 'the poor grandmother'.

The colloquial invariable adjectives *coșcogea(mite), ditai, ditamai* 'huge' always precede the noun. The noun is usually in the definite form, even after an indefinite article:

NA: un ditamai scandalul	a huge scandal
GD: unui ditamai scandalul, a/la ditamai scandalul	
NA: o ditamai bomba	a huge bomb
GD: unei ditamai bombe, a/la ditamai bomba	

If an adjective expressing an indefinite quantity is placed before an indefinite noun, the genitive and dative forms are replaced with prepositions (the genitive with *a*, the dative with *la*):

> la numeroşi oameni to numerous people
> la diverşi oameni to divers people

A similar thing happens when a noun is preceded by a numeral (see p. 126-), and this can also be done with quantitative indefinite pronouns (see p. 184-). The definite forms are regular: *numeroşilor oameni* 'to t154merous people'.

The prepositions are also used when an adverbial adjective (*aşa* 'such', *asemenea* 'similar', *astfel de* 'like this', *altfel de* 'different'...) is used in front of the noun and there is no article or other modifier:

> NA: (o) asemenea situaţie a similar situation
> GD: unei asemenea situaţii =
> a/la asemenea situaţie

Agreement of adjectives

Adjective as attribute

When an adjective modifies a noun, it must have the same gender, number and case as the noun:

> NA: un prieten bun a good friend (masc.)
> GD: unui prieten bun
>
> NA: o prietenă bună a good friend (fem.)
> GD: unei prietene bune

If the adjective attribute has several head nouns, it usually agrees with the closest one:

> limba şi literatura română Romanian language and literature

In formal language an adjective can agree also with both of the nouns, just like an adjective used as a predicative:

> lungimea şi lăţimea măsurată / măsurate[60] the measured length and width

When one noun has several attributes, they are all in the same form:

> NA: limba română şi finlandeză Romanian and Finnish language
> GD: limbii române şi finlandeze

---

[60] Example from *Enciclopedia limbii române*, p. 20.

The structure *limbile română și finlandeză* (= *limba română și limba finlandeză*) is possible, but not recommended. In the genitive and dative of this structure the adjectives remain in the nominative (*limbilor română și finlandeză*).

Adjective as predicative

When an adjective is used as a subject predicative, it must be in the same gender and number as the noun or pronoun it is referring to (i.e. the subject):

John este canadian.	John is Canadian.
Mary este canadiană.	Mary is Canadian.
Prietenii mei sunt canadieni.	My friends (masc.) are Canadian.
Prietenele mele sunt canadiene.	My friends (fem.) are Canadian.

If the predicative refers to several different nouns, it is put in the plural form:

John și Jack sunt canadieni.	John and Jack are Canadian.
Mary and Kate sunt canadiene.	Mary and Kate are Canadian.

If the nouns are of different genders, the following rules are followed:

- If the nouns are *animate* (persons or animals), the masculine plural is used:

John și Mary sunt canadieni.	John and Mary are Canadian.
Elena, Maria și Ion sunt români.	Elena, Maria and Ion are Romanian.

- If some of the nouns are animate and some are not, the adjective agrees with the gender of the animate noun(s) and comes in either the masculine or feminine plural form:

Radu și mașina lui sunt inseparabili.	Radu and his car are inseparable.

- It the nouns are not animate, the following rules are followed:

  ➤ Usually the feminine/neuter plural form of the adjective is used:

Para (perele) și mărul (merele) sunt proaspete.	The pear(s) and the apple(s) are fresh.
Para (perele) și morcovul sunt proaspete.	The pear(s) and the carrot are fresh.
Morcovul (morcovii) și para (perele) sunt proaspete.	The carrot(s) and the pear(s) are fresh.
Morcovul (morcovii) și merele sunt proaspete.	The carrot(s) and the apples are fresh.
Morcovul și mărul (merele) sunt proaspete.	The carrot and the apple(s) are fresh.
Mărul (merele) și morcovul sunt proaspete.	The apple(s) and the carrot are fresh.

| Mărul (merele) şi para (perele) sunt proaspete. | The apple(s) and the pear(s) are fresh. |

> If a masculine plural noun is closer to the adjective, the masculine plural is used:

| Para (perele) şi morcovii sunt proaspeţi. | The pear(s) and the carrots are fresh. |
| Mărul (merele) şi morcovii sunt proaspeţi. | The apple(s) and the carrots are fresh. |

> Masc. pl. + neuter sg. → masc. pl.

| Morcovii şi mărul sunt proaspeţi. | The carrots and the apple are fresh. |

Declension models

Adjective after the noun

Masculine

		Indefinite	Definite
Sg.	NA	un bărbat bun	bărbatul bun
	GD	unui bărbat bun	bărbatului bun
Pl.	NA	nişte bărbaţi buni	bărbaţii buni
	GD	unor bărbaţi buni	bărbaţilor buni

Feminine

		Indefinite	Definite
Sg.	NA	o femeie bună	femeia bună
	GD	unei femei bune	femeii bune
Pl.	NA	nişte femei bune	femeile bune
	GD	unor femei bune	femeilor bune

Neuter

		Indefinite	Definite
Sg.	NA	un animal bun	animalul bun
	GD	unui animal bun	animalului bun
Pl.	NA	nişte animale bune	animalele bune
	GD	unor animale bune	animalelor bune

Adjective before the noun

Masculine

		Indefinite	Definite
Sg.	NA	un bun bărbat	bunul bărbat
	GD	unui bun bărbat	bunului bărbat
Pl.	NA	nişte buni bărbaţi	bunii bărbaţi
	GD	unor buni bărbaţi	bunilor bărbaţi

Feminine

		Indefinite	Definite
Sg.	NA	o bună femeie	buna femeie
	GD	unei bune femei	bunei femei
Pl.	NA	nişte bune femei	bunele femei
	GD	unor bune femei	bunelor femei

Neuter

		Indefinite	Definite
Sg.	NA	un bun animal	bunul animal
	GD	unui bun animal	bunului animal
Pl.	NA	nişte bune animale	bunele animale
	GD	unor bune animale	bunelor animale

Comparison

Positive

Comparison with a noun is usually made with *ca* 'as'. When the adjective refers to size or quantity, even *cât* can be used. After *ca* and *cât*, the noun must have a determiner (an article, a pronoun, etc):

alb ca zăpada	white as snow
mare ca/cât un munte	big as a mountain

The comparison 'as – as' is constructed with the words *tot așa de / tot atât de / la fel de / deopotrivă de - ca / ca și / cât / cât și*:

Ion este *tot atât de* înalt *ca/cât* mine[61].	Ion is as tall as me.
Această carte este *tot așa de* interesantă *ca și* aceea.	this book is as interesting as that one.
Este zahărul *la fel de* toxic *ca* țigările?	Is sugar as toxic as cigarettes?

In the comparison 'not as – as' *nu așa de / atât de / astfel de - ca / cât* are used:

Ion nu este *atât de* înalt *ca/cât* Maria.	Ion is not as tall as Maria.

When two different qualities are compared, the words *tot atât de - cât și de* or *pe cât de - pe atât de* are used:

Este *tot atât de* interesant *cât și de* important.	It is as interesting as it is important.

The positive form can be intensified with the adverb *foarte* 'very' or with structures like *incredibil de* 'incredibly', *nemaiauzit de* 'unheard-of', *extrem de* 'extremely' etc.:

pantofi *foarte* ieftini	very cheap shoes
pantofi *incredibil de* scumpi	incredibly expensive shoes
Este un lucru *cât se poate de* normal.	It is a thing as normal as can be.

Comparative

The comparative forms are made by placing the adverb *mai* 'more' or *mai puțin* 'less' before the adjective:

mai bun, -ă, -i, -e	better
mai puțin bun, -ă, -i, -e	worse

---

[61] For the use of accusative after a comparison, see p. 279.

When the comparative form modifies a noun, it is placed after it:

salarii mai mari și condiții mai bune de lucru (*Adevărul*)	bigger salaries and better working conditions

The comparison is made with the adverbs *decât* or (less frequently) *ca* 'than':

Ea este mai tânără *decât* mine.	She is younger than me.
Această carte este mai bună *decât* aceea.	This book is better than that one.

When comparing an amount, *de* is used before a numeral:

mai mult de 10 persoane	more than 10 persons
mai mult de 3 metri	more than 3 meters

The comparison can be emphasized with the adverb *mult* 'much': *mult mai bun* 'much better'. Progressiveness is expressed with *din ce în ce, tot* or *mereu*:

din ce în ce mai bun	better and better

Comparison can also be made with expressions like *față de, în comparație cu, în raport cu* + accusative:

El este înalt *în comparație cu* Ion.	He is tall compared to Ion.

Superlative

The superlative is formed by adding the demonstrative article *cel* (see p. 95) in front of the comparative form:

NA:	cel mai bun, cea mai bună, cei mai buni, cele mai bune	the best
GD:	celui mai bun, celei mai bune, celor mai buni, celor mai bune	

The superlative form usually comes before the noun, and the noun has no article. However, the superlative can also come after the noun, in which case the noun must be in the definite form:

cea mai bună carte = cartea cea mai bună	the best book
cel mai puțin scump oraș	the cheapest city
Premiul Oscar pentru cel mai bun film	the Academy Award for the best picture
Cele mai dese boli profesionale (*Cotidianul*)	the most frequent professional diseases
Cele mai sexy actrițe române (*Cotidianul*)	the sexiest Romanian actresses

directorul celei mai mari firme	the director of the biggest firm

If two adjectives modify a noun, *cel mai* is not repeated:

cel mai bun și prietenos Linux (*videotutorial.ro*)	the best and the most user-friendly Linux

The group that something is compared to is expressed with the preposition *din* + a singular noun or *dintre* + a plural noun:

cel mai mic computer din lume	the smallest computer in the world
cel mai tânăr din grup	the youngest in the group
cel mai bătrân dintre profesori	the oldest of the teachers

Numerals

Cardinal numerals

0	zero
1	un / unu (m., n.), o / una (f.)
2	doi (m.), două (f., n.)
3	trei
4	patru
5	cinci
6	şase
7	şapte
8	opt
9	nouă
10	zece

11	unsprezece
12	doisprezece (m.), douăsprezece (f., n.)
13	treisprezece
14	paisprezece
15	cincisprezece ['tʃin(tʃ)sprezetʃe]
16	şaisprezece
17	şaptesprezece
18	optsprezece
19	nouăsprezece

20	douăzeci
21	douăzeci şi unu (m., n.), una (f.)
22	douăzeci şi doi (m.), două (n., f.)
29	douăzeci şi nouă

30	treizeci
40	patruzeci
50	cincizeci [tʃin(tʃ)'zetʃ]
60	şaizeci
70	şaptezeci
80	optzeci
90	nouăzeci

100	o sută
101	o sută unu (m., n.), o sută una (f.)
102	o sută doi (m.), o sută două (f., n.)
199	o sută nouăzeci şi nouă

200	două sute		600	șase sute
300	trei sute		700	șapte sute
400	patru sute		800	opt sute
500	cinci sute ['t͡ʃin(t͡ʃ)'sute]		900	nouă sute

1000	o mie
1001	o mie unu (m., n.), o mie una (f.)
1002	o mie doi (m.), o mie două (f., n.)
1999	o mie nouă sute nouăzeci și nouă

2000	două mii		6000	șase mii
3000	trei mii		7000	șapte mii
4000	patru mii		8000	opt mii
5000	cinci mii		9000	nouă mii

10 000	zece mii		100 000	o sută de mii
20 000	douăzeci de mii		200 000	două sute de mii

1 000 000 un milion
2 000 000 două milioane

Larger numbers include e.g. (the long scale is used in Romania):

un miliard, două miliarde	10^9
un bilion, două bilioane	10^{12}
un trilion, două trilioane	10^{18}
un cvadrilion, două cvadrilioane	10^{24}

Notice that in Romanian the comma is not used in large numbers like 2000 (English 2,000).

In the numerals 11-19 the ending -sprezece is often pronounced colloquially [ʃpe]: *unșpe, doișpe, treișpe, paișpe, cinșpe* etc.

The numbers 1-9 are added to the numbers 20-90 with the conjunction *și*:

31	treizeci și unu/una
93	nouăzeci și trei

Colloquially, the conjunction is also used after hundreds, thousands etc.:

1001	o mie (și) unu, o mie (și) una
7 000 200	șapte milioane (și) două sute

The numerals *sută, mie* and the plural form *zeci* 'tens' act like feminine nouns, while the larger numerals *milion, miliard, bilion* etc. are neuter:

o sută, două sute	a hundred, two hundred
un milion, două milioane	a million, two millions

Un/o or *unu/una*?

The forms *un, o* of the numeral 'one' are used as attributes before nouns (i.e. just like the indefinite article), while the forms *unu, una* are used independently:

un bărbat şi o femeie	one man and one women
Vreau numai unu / una.	I want only one.

However, in some sayings the form *unul* is used instead (see p. 175).

In larger numerals ending in 'one' (21, 31, 101, 121 etc.) the longer forms *unu, una* are always used:

o sută unu bărbaţi	101 men
o sută una femei	101 women

Gender

Apart from the number *unu,* the numerals *doi* and *doisprezece* also have different forms for different genders:

doi bărbaţi, două femei	2 men, women
doisprezece bărbaţi, douăsprezece femei	12 men, women
o sută doi bărbaţi, o sută două femei	102 men, women

Notice, that the numeral *unsprezece* has only one form:

unsprezece bărbaţi / femei	11 men, women

When a numeral comes after a noun, it is usually in the masculine form:

pagina unu	page 1
Formula Unu	Formula 1

An exception is expressions of the time of day, where 1 and 21 are masculine, but 2, 12 and 22 are feminine:

ora unu, douăzeci şi unu	1.00, 21.00
ora două, douăsprezece, douăzeci şi două	2.00, 12.00, 22.00

The dates 2, 12 and 22 can be in the masculine or the feminine:

2 [doi / două] iulie	July 2nd
12 [doisprezece / douăsprezece] iulie	July 12th
22 [douăzeci şi doi / două] iulie	July 22nd

Cardinal numerals as attributes

The numerals 0-19 and larger numerals ending in 01-19 (i.e. 101-119, 201-219 etc.) are used as attributes directly before a noun. After the number 1, the noun is in the singular, and after the other numbers, the plural is used:

zero grade	0 degrees
un grad	1 degree
cinci câini	5 dogs
cincisprezece câini	15 dogs
o sută cinci câini	105 dogs
o sută cincisprezece câini	115 dogs
cinci sute cinci câini	505 dogs
o mie cinci câini	1005 dogs
o mie cincisprezece câini	1015 dogs

For clarity, letters, numbers, etc. may be preceded by the preposition *de*:

cinci (de) *i*	five letters *i*
doi (de) *de*	two *de* prepositions
trei (de) *doi*	three twos

The other numerals (i.e. 20-99 and larger numerals ending in 20-99 or 00) require the use of the preposition *de* before the noun:

douăzeci de câini	20 dogs
douăzeci şi unu de câini	21 dogs
cincizeci de câini	50 dogs
o sută de câini	100 dogs
o sută douăzeci de câini	120 dogs
două sute de câini	200 dogs
două sute douăzeci de câini	220 dogs
o mie de câini	1 000 dogs
o mie douăzeci de câini	1 020 dogs
o mie două sute de câini	1 200 dogs

Since the larger numerals *mie, milion, miliard* etc. act like nouns, the preposition *de* is also used before them when needed:

15 000	cincisprezece mii	
20 000	douăzeci *de* mii	
50 *de* milioane *de* ani		50 million years

When the numeral is used as an attribute of an abbreviation, the preposition is not written, but it must be added in reading:

30 km	treizeci *de* kilometri

Mathematical expressions

In calculation (when one is not referring to concrete nouns), the masculine forms of 1, 2 and 12 are used:

$1 + 3 = 4$	unu plus trei egal / fac patru
$6 - 1 = 5$	şase minus unu egal cinci
$2 \times 4 = 8$	doi ori patru egal opt
$6 : 3 = 2$	şase împărţit la trei egal doi
$\sqrt{13}$	radical din treisprezece

For decimal fractions the comma (*virgulă*) is used:

2,53	doi virgulă cincizeci şi trei

Percentage

1 %	unu la sută = un procent
10 %	zece la sută = zece procente
20 %	douăzeci la sută = douăzeci de procente
1 ‰	unu la mie = o promilă
15 ‰	cincisprezece la mie = cincisprezece promile

Sunt sută la sută nevinovat. (*Adevărul*)	I am one hundred percent not guilty.

Declension of cardinal numerals

Only the numeral for 'one' is declined: NA: *un/unu, o/una,* GD: *unui/unuia, unei/uneia* (compare this with the declension of the pronoun *un(ul)* p. 175 and the indefinite article p. 71). The shorter forms are used adjectivally in front of a noun; otherwise the longer forms are required:

NA: un băiat, o fată	one boy, one girl
GD: unui băiat, unei fete	to one boy, to one girl
NA: numai unu, numai una	only one
GD: numai unuia, numai uneia	only to one

With other numerals the genitive is replaced with the preposition *a* + accusative, and the dative is replaced with *la* + accusative:

la doi, la două	to two
la două fete	to two girls
la zece fete	to 10 girls
la douăzeci de fete	to 20 girls
la douăzeci şi una de fete	to 21 girls
Am scris o scrisoare la trei prieteni.	I wrote a letter to three friends.
o mamă a doi copii	a mother of two children

A preposition is also used before the *un*, if it is coordinated with another numeral:

la unu sau (la) doi	to one or two

The genitive and dative of the numbers *o sută, o mie, un milion, un miliard,* etc. are replaced with prepositions as well:

la o suta de fete	to 100 girls
la un milion de fete	to a million girls
A fost înmormântat în prezența a o mie de oameni. (*Adevărul*)	He was buried in the presence of one thousand people.

However, if these numerals are used without *un/o*[62], they are declined regularly:

NA: prima sută de oameni	the first hundred people
GD: primei sute	
NA: primul milion de lei	the first million leus
GD: primului milion	

When these numerals are preceded by another numeral, the genitive and dative are always formed with a preposition:

la două sute de persoane	to 200 persons
la doi milioane de persoane	to 2 million persons

The definite form (starting from 2) is expressed by the demonstrative article *cel* (see p. 95), which can be fully declined:

NA: cele două fete	the two girls
GD: celor două fete	
NA: cei șapte frați	the seven brothers
NA: celor șapte frați	

Before larger numerals (*o sută, o mie,* etc.) *cel* and other pronouns agree with the noun, not with the numeral. When used in the genitive or dative, only the first element is declined:

NA: cei o sută de bărbați	the hundred men
GD: celor o sută de bărbați	
cei două sute de bărbați	the two hundred men

The numerals *o sută, o mie, un milion, un miliard,* etc. can also be used in the definite form (*suta, mia, milionul, miliardul*). The definite genitive and dative forms are regular (*sutei, miei, milionului, miliardului*):

Mia este de zece ori mai mare decât suta.	The number 1000 is ten times bigger than the number 100.

---

[62] The grammar of Academia Română from 1966 also gives the indefinite genitive and dative form (*unei sute*), but according to DOOM[2,] the indefinite form *o sută* is a invariable numeral.

milionul câştigat la loto	the million won in the lottery
câştigarea milionului (de dolari)	the winning of the million dollars
recordul sutei de metri	the record of 100 meters

The plural forms *zeci, sute, mii, miloane*, etc. used to express imprecise numbers are declined regularly both in the indefinite and definite forms. However, the genitive and dative forms can also be replaced with prepositions:

NA: sute de bărbaţi	hundreds of men
GD: unor sute de bărbaţi	to hundreds of men
= a/la sute de bărbaţi	
NA: sutele de bărbaţi	the hundreds of men
GD: sutelor de bărbaţi	to the hundreds of men
= a/la sutele de bărbaţi	
Au venit cu miile	They came in thousands.

In this case, possible modifiers agree with the numeral, not with the noun (the plural forms *zeci, sute, mii, milioane*, etc. are actually nouns):

câteva sute de bărbaţi	a couple of hundred men
câteva sute de femei	a couple of hundred women

The word *zero* is a neuter noun: *zero, zeroul*, pl. *zerouri, zerourile*:

Un milion are şase zerouri.	A million has six zeros.
Se pregăteşte tăierea zerourilor din coadă leului. (*Adevărul*)	The cutting of zeros from the end of the *leu* is being prepared.

Ordinal numerals

In Romanian, 'first' is either *întâi(ul)* or *prim(ul),* and 'last' is *ultim(ul).* The other ordinal numerals are formed with the article *al* (see p. 92) and the suffix *-lea* (m., n.), *-a* (f.). In longer numerals this suffix is added only to the last numeral.

1	întâi(ul), prim(ul)	6	al şaselea, a şasea
2	al doilea (m., n.), a doua (f.)	7	al şaptelea, a şaptea
3	al treilea, a treia	8	al optulea, a opta
4	al patrulea, a patra	9	al nouălea, a noua
5	al cincilea, a cincea	10	al zecelea, a zecea

11	al unsprezecelea, a unsprezecea
12	al doisprezecelea, a douăsprezecea
13	al treisprezecelea, a treisprezecea
14	al paisprezecelea, a paisprezecea
15	al cincisprezecelea, a cincisprezecea

16	al şaisprezecelea, a şaisprezecea
17	al şaptesprezecelea, a şaptesprezecea
18	al optsprezecelea, a optsprezecea
19	al nouăsprezecelea, a nouăsprezecea

20	al douăzecilea, a douăzecea
21	al douăzeci şi unulea, a douăzeci şi una
22	al douăzeci şi doilea, a douăzeci şi doua

30	al treizecilea, a treizecea
40	al patruzecilea, a patruzecea
50	al cincizecilea, a cincizecea
60	al şaizecilea, a şaizecea
70	al şaptezecilea, a şaptezecea
80	al optzecilea, a optzecea
90	al nouăzecilea, a nouăzecea

100	al o sutălea, a (o) suta
101	al o sută unulea, a (o) sută una
102	al o sută doilea, a (o) sută doua
199	al o sută nouăzeci şi nouălea, a (o) sută nouăzeci şi noua
200	al două sutelea, a două suta

1000	al o mielea, a (o) mia
2000	al două miilea, a două mia
10 000	al zece miilea, a zece mia
20 000	al douăzeci miilea, a douăzeci mia

1 000 000	al (un) milionulea, a milioana
2 000 000	al două milioanelea, a două milioana

1 000 000 000	al (un) miliardulea, a miliarda
2 000 000 000	al două miliardelea, a două miliarda

Unlike with the cardinal numerals, the preposition *de* is not used before the numerals *sută, mie, milion* etc.: *douăzeci de mii,* but: *al douăzeci miilea.*

Întâi and *prim* are declined both in the indefinite and definite forms. The word *întâi* has two alternative forms in the indefinite feminine singular (*întâi* and *întâia*)[63]:

NA:	întâi, întâi(a), întâi, întâi	prim, primă, primi, prime
GD:	întâi, întâi(a), întâi, întâi	prim, prime, primi, prime

NA:	întâiul, întâia, întâii, întâile	primul, prima, primii, primele
GD:	întâiului, întâii, întâilor, întâilor	primului, primei, primilor, primelor

---

[63] DOOM[2]. Previously, only the form *întâi* was accepted. Vintilă-Rădulescu (2009) accepts the longer form only in the nominative and accusative.

When used adjectivally, *prim* always comes before the noun[64] and the articles are attached to it:

un prim pas, GD: unui prim pas	a first step
primul pas, GD: primului pas	the first step
o primă dată, GD: unei prime date	a first time
prima dată, GD: primei date	the first time
primele cinci episoade	the first five episodes

In the modern language *întâi* is much rarer than *prim*. Before a noun the definite form *întâiul* is used:

NA: întâiul pas	the first step
GD: întâiului pas	
NA: întâia dată	the first time
GD: întâii date	
moartea întâilor născuţi	death of the first-born (Bible)

The definite forms are also used as independent pronouns:

Primul / Întâiul este din Bucu-	The first one is from Bucharest,
reşti, al doilea din Iaşi.	the second one from Iaşi.

The other ordinal numerals are indeclinable. They usually come before a noun without an article. Only the nominative and accusative are used:

al treilea copil	third child
a doua şansă	second change

Ordinal numerals can be used in the genitive and dative if they are preceded by the indefinite article or by any other conjugated modifier (ending in *-ui*, *-ei*):

NA: un al treilea copil	NA: o a doua şansă
GD: unui al treilea copil	GD: unei a doua şanse
succesul acestei a doua cărţi	the success of this second book

Ordinal numerals (except *prim*) can also be placed after a noun, in which case the noun has to be in the definite form or preceded by a demonstrative pronoun:

al doilea pas = pasul al doilea	the second step
a doua şansă = şansa a doua	the second chance
aceasta carte a doua	this second book

---

[64] When it means 'original', *prim* is placed after the noun: *număr prim* 'prime number', *materie prima* 'crude material'.

This is done especially in some fixed expressions like:

clasa I [=întâi(a)]	the first grade
capitolul II [= al doilea]	the second chapter

Sometimes the ordinal numeral has a more abstract meaning, in which case it is placed after the noun. Compare:

al doilea premiu	the second prize (in order of being received or given)
NA: premiul al doilea	the second prize, silver
GD: premiului al doilea	
a doua persoană	the second person (in order)
NA: persoana a doua	the second person (grammatical
GD: persoanei a doua	term)

After a noun the indefinite forms of *întâi* are used:

NA: premiul întâi	the first prize
GD: premiului întâi	
NA: persoana întâi(a)	the first person
GD: persoanei întâi(a)	

Ordinal numerals are written with Arabic or Roman numerals as follows:

al II-lea, a II-a	2nd
al 37-lea, a 37-a	37th

Ordinal numerals can also be preceded by the demonstrative article *cel* (see p. 95) + *de.* The preposition *de* merges with the numeral *întâi*, while it can be joined to the other numerals with a hyphen:

cel dintâi, cea dintâi[65]	the first one
cel de al doilea, cea de a doua	the second one
= cel de-al doilea, cea de-a doua	
Slovacia a devenit cea de a 16-a	Slovakia became the 16th country
ţară a Uniunii Europene care a	of the European Union to adopt the
adoptat euro. (*Adevărul*)	euro.

These constructions can also be declined:

NA: cel de-al doilea copil	NA: cea de-a doua şansă
GD: celui de-al doilea copil	GD: celei de-a doua şanse

The form *dintâi* occurs sometimes (old-fashioned, non-standard) directly after a noun: *dragostea dintâi* 'first love'.

---

[65] In the feminine, the shorter form is always used.

Ordinal numerals are used less in Romanian than in English. For example, in dates the first day is expressed with an ordinal numeral, while the others are expressed with a cardinal:

întâi ianuarie	January 1st
doi / două ianuarie	January 2nd
trei ianuarie	January 3rd

Colloquially, ordinal numerals are often replaced with cardinals:

etajul întâi = etajul unu	the first floor
volumul întâi = volumul unu	the first volume

However, ordinal numerals must be used in the names of kings and other rulers, the names of the world wars and with school grades:

Carol I [= întâi]	Charles I
Papa Benedict al XVI-lea	Pope Benedict XVI
Primul Război Mondial	the First World War
al Doilea Război Mondial	the Second World War
clasa a VI-a	the 6th grade

When an ordinal numeral is used independently as a direct object, it must be preceded by the preposition *pe* (see p. 287):

Am citit a treia carte.	I read the third book.
→ Am citit-o pe a treia.	I read the third one.

On some rare occasions the loanwords *secund* 'second' and *terț* 'third' are used:

vioară secundă	second violin
regizor secund	assistant director
terță persoană	third party (jur.)

Cvint 'fifth' is used only in *Carol Cvintul* 'Charles V'.

Partitive numerals

Fractions are formed with the suffix *-ime* (only 2-19, *sută*, *mie*, *milion*, etc.):

doime, treime, pătrime, cincime,	1/2, 1/3, 1/4, 1/5
șesime, șeptime, optime, noime,	1/6, 1/7, 1/8, 1/9
zecime, unsprezecime,	1/10, 1/11
doisprezecime, treisprezecime	1/12, 1/13
sutime, miime, milionime	1/100, 1/1000, 1/1 000 000

These forms are feminine and they are declined regularly (plural *-imi*):

o doime	1/2
două cincimi	2/5

trei optimi	3/8
cinci sutimi	0,05, 5/100
trei și două cincimi	$3\frac{2}{5}$

NA: o doime, doimea, doimi, doimile
GD: unei doimi, doimii, unor doimi, doimilor

'Half' is also *o jumătate*, pl. *jumătăți*, 'quoter' *un sfert*, pl. *sferturi*:

un sfert de litru	a quarter of a litre

These are used for expressing the time:

8:10	ora opt și zece	8:15	ora opt și un sfert
7:50	ora opt fără zece	8:30	ora opt și jumătate
		8:45	ora opt și trei sferturi

Colloquially, a part can also be expressed with an ordinal numeral + *parte*:

a cincea parte din populația României = o cincime din populația României	a fifth of the Romanian population

In mathematics, the prepositions *pe* or *supra* are used:

unu pe/supra patru	1/4
doi pe/supra cinci	2/5

It is also possible to use the feminine cardinal form of the numerator and the feminine ordinal form of the denominator:

una a patra	1/4
două a cincea	2/5

Multiplicative numerals

Multiplicative numerals are formed with the prefix *în-* (*îm-*) and the suffix *-it*. Formally, multiplicative numerals are actually participles. The most used are 2-4, 10, 100 and 1000:

îndoit, întreit, împătrit	twofold, threefold, fourfold
(încincit, înșesit, înșeptit)	fivefold, sixfold, sevenfold
înzecit	tenfold
însutit	hundredfold
înmiit	thousandfold

Multiplicative numerals are declined like adjectives: *îndoit, îndoită, îndoiți, în-doite*. Some multiplicative numerals have an adjective with the same mean-ing: *îndoit = dublu* 'double', *întreit = triplu* 'triple'. Rarer forms are *cvadruplu* 'quadruple', *cvintuplu* 'quintuple', *sextuplu* 'sextuple'.

Adverbial numerals

Numeral adverbs answer the question 'how many times?'. They are formed with the preposition *de* and the feminine noun *oară* (pl. *ori*):

de două ori	twice
de trei ori	three times
de sute de ori	hundreds of times

'Once' is *o dată*:

o dată pentru totdeauna	once and for all

With the ordinal numerals *oară* can also be used: *întâia dată/oară, prima dată/oară* 'first time'. In expressions like 'for the first time' the preposition *pentru* is usually used:

Madonna, pentru prima dată	Madonna for the first time in
în România! (*Cotidianul*)	Romania!

Collective numerals

'Both' is expressed in Romanian by *amândoi* or *ambii*. These are naturally plural forms and they are declined as follows:

	Plural	
	m.	n., f.
NA	amând**oi**	amând**ouă**
GD	amând**ur**or(a)	

	Plural	
	m.	n.,, f.
NA	**a**mbii	**a**mbele
GD	**a**mbilor	**a**mbelor

Amândoi can be used adjectivally before or after the noun. The headword must be in the definite form (or preceded by another determinant). In the genitive and dative the longer form is used after a noun or as an independent pronoun, while the shorter form is used before a noun:

amândoi studenții	both students (m.)
= studenții amândoi	
amândouă studentele	both students (fem.)
= studentele amândouă	
amândouă aceste probleme	both these problems
amânduror studenților	to both students (masc.)
= studenților amândurora	
amândurora	to both

When *ambii* is used as an adjective, it always precedes the noun and the noun does not have any article (since the definite article is attached to *ambii*):

NA: ambii studenţi, ambele studente   both students
GD: ambilor studenţi, ambelor studente

The dative forms of both *amândoi* and *ambi* can be replaced by the preposition *la* + accusative:

la amândoi studenţii = la ambii studenţi   to both students

However, the genetive forms can not be replaced with a preposition.

Other collective numerals are indeclinable. These numerals are formed with either *toţi/toate* or *câteşi* + a cardinal number.

toţi trei, toate trele	all three
= câteşitrei, câteşitrele	
toţi / toate patru = câteşipatru	all four
toţi / toate cinci = câteşicinci	all five
toţi / toate şase = câteşişase	all six
toţi / toate şapte = câteşişapte	all seven

Colloquially, the smaller numbers (1-10) also have the forms *tustrei* (m.) / *tustrele* (f., n.), *tuspatru*, *tuscinci* etc.

After these collective numerals the noun must come in the definite form:

toţi cinci studenţii   all five students
toţi cincizeci studenţii   all fifty students

The genitive of these collective numerals is replaced with the preposition *a,* and dative with the preposition *la*:

Le-am dat la toţi cinci cam 1,5   I gave all five of them only 1.5
litri de vin (*Ziarul de Iaşi*)   litres of wine.

However, the numeral 'all three' also has the rarer genitive and dative forms *tustreilor, tustrelelor, câteşitreilor, câteşitrelelor.*

When the collective numerals are used independently as a direct object, it must be preceded by the preposition *pe* (see p. 287):

Am citit amândouă cărţile.   I have read both the books.
→ Le-am citit pe amândouă.   I have read both (of them).

Distributive numerals

Distributive numerals are formed by placing the word *câte* before a cardinal or partitive numeral:

câte doi / două	two each
câte trei	three each
câte o treime	one third each
Ei stau în rând câte cinci.	They are standing in rows of five.
= stau în rânduri de câte cinci	
Vin în grupuri de câte patru.	They come in groups of four.
10 premii de/a câte 100 euro	10 prizes, 100 euros each
= 10 premii, fiecare de (câte) 100 euro	
Pacienţii stau şi câte doi în pat	At the County Hospital there can
la Spitalul Judeţean (*Adevărul*)	be even two patients in one bed.
Câte cinci ani de închisoare	Five years of prison for each of the
pentru trei hoţi	three thieves.

When a distributive numeral is used in front of a noun, the preposition *de* is used as with cardinal numerals:

câte 15 ani	15 years each
câte 20 de ani	20 years each

The genitive of these numerals is formed with the preposition *a*, and the dative with *la*:

o carte la câte doi studenţi	one book for every two students

Notice that *câte* can also express approximative amounts:

câte două, trei zile	2-3 days

Pronouns and pronominal adjectives

Personal pronouns

Personal pronouns are declined in all the cases. The nominative, genitive and vocative forms are always stressed, while the accusative and dative forms have two variants: stressed (1) and unstressed (2).

The forms of the personal pronouns are as follows:

	I	you (sg.)	he, it (m., n.)	she, it (f.)	we	you (pl.)	they (m.)	they (f., n.)
N	eu	tu	el	ea	noi	voi	ei	ele
A1	mine	tine	el	ea	noi	voi	ei	ele
A2	mă	te	îl	o	ne	vă	îi	le
G			lui	ei			lor	lor
D1	mie	ție	lui	ei	nouă	vouă	lor	lor
D2	îmi	îți	îi	îi	ne	vă	le	le
V		tu!				voi!		

The missing genitive forms are replaced by possessive pronouns (see p. 153).

Personal pronouns starting with *e* are pronounced irregularly: *eu* [jeu̯], *el* [jel], *ea* [ja], *ei* [jej], *ele* ['jele]. The pronoun *eu* also has a colloquial form *io*.

Notice that in Romanian there is no difference between the animate and inanimate third person (English *he/she - it*).

Stressed forms

Stressed forms of personal pronouns are used:

- After a preposition (accusative and dative):

cu tine	with you
pentru mine	for me
fără voi	without you
grație mie	thanks to me

- Independently (without a verb). When used as a direct object, the preposition *pe* must be used (see p. 287):

Cine este acolo?	- Eu!	Who is there?	- Me!
Pe cine iubești?	- Pe tine!	Who do you love?	- You!

- When the pronoun modifies an adjective or a noun:

util ție	useful for you
nepotul lui	his grandchild

- To emphasize an unstressed pronoun:

Pe tine te cunosc!	I know you!
Mie îmi plac limbile.	I like languages.

- Nominative forms are used as stressed subjects or predicates:

Eu sunt finlandez, iar el este român.	I am Finnish, while he is Romanian.

Since the unstressed subject is expressed by the verbal ending, there are no unstressed personal pronouns in the nominative. The stressed third person forms (*el, ea, ei, ele*) are mainly used for referring to persons only, whereas the demonstrative pronoun *acesta* can be used for both persons and inanimate subjects (for examples, see p. 163).

Possible modifiers (nouns, numerals, pronouns, etc.) are placed after the stressed personal pronouns. Nouns and adjectives are used in the definite form:

noi românii	we Romanians
noi toți	we all, all of us
voi doi	you two, the two of you
voi amândoi	you both, both of you

Însul

The third person also has the stressed forms *însul, însa, înșii, însele* (NA only). These forms are rare in modern language and are used mainly after the prepositions *în, prin, din* (as *într-, printr-, dintr-*). They usually refer to inanimate nouns:

un oraș fără oameni într-însul	a city without people in it
(*Octavian Bud*)	
cei mai mulți dintr-înșii	most of them

Unstressed accusative and dative forms

Unstressed accusative and dative forms are used when a pronoun is used as a complement (direct or indirect object) of the verb without a preposition:

îl cunosc bine.	I know him well.
Te iubesc.	I love you.
Îți dau o carte.	I will give you a book.

The unstressed feminine form *o* also has the neuter meaning 'that thing, it' and in refers to the whole previous clause or the subject one is talking about:

Am greşit şi o ştiu.	I made a mistake and I know it.
Unii o fac doar pentru bani.	Some people do it only for money.
(*Adevărul*)	

This pronoun is also used in some fixed colloquial expressions like the following:

Ia-o mai încet!	Take it easy!
a o păți, a o pune de mămăligă	to get into trouble
a o duce	to live, to pass one's life
a o tăia la fugă	to run away

The unstressed accusative and dative forms are also often used as redundant object and indirect object pronouns (see p. 290 and 294).

Placement of unstressed accusative and dative forms

The unstressed accusative and dative forms are usually placed directly before the verb or the auxiliary verb, after the negative adverb *nu*, the conjunction *să* or the infinitive marker *a*:

nu îl (= nu-l) văd	I do not see him
nu l-am văzut	I have not seen him
îl voi vedea	I will see him
să îl (= să-l) văd	I see him (conj.)
a îl (= a-l) vedea	to see him

With future forms formed with the conjunctive, the pronouns are placed before the conjunctive form and not before the auxiliary verb:

am să-l văd	I will see him

Only the semi-adverbs *mai, tot, cam, prea, şi* (see p. 274) can be placed between an unstressed accusative or dative pronoun and the verb:

îl mai văd	I still see him

When the auxiliary verb begins with a vowel, the feminine accusative third person singular form *o* is placed after the main verb:

am văzut-o	I have seen her
aş vedea-o	I would see her
aş fi văzut-o	I would have seen her
aş fi văzând-o	I might see her
oi vedea-o (colloq.) = o voi vedea	I will see her

When the verb is an affirmative imperative form or a gerund, all the unstressed pronouns are placed after the verb:

văzându-l	seeing him
vezi-l!	see it!

For more details, see p. 367.

Combined forms of the personal pronoun

The unstressed accusative and dative pronouns have slightly different forms in certain situations. The following changes occur:

- The vowel *î* disappears from the beginning of a pronoun when the pronoun is combined with a word starting or ending in a vowel.
- The vowel *ă* disappears from the end of a pronoun when the pronoun is combined with a word starting with a vowel.
- The dative pronouns *ne, vă, le* have the forms *ni, vi, li* in front of an accusative pronoun (except before *o*).
- Combined vowels are pronounced as diphthongs (e.g. *te-am* [tẹam], *mi-am* [mjam], *mi-i* [miị]). Before a consonant [ⁱ] is pronounced as [i] (e.g. *mi-l* [mil], *aşteptaţi-mă!* [-tsimə]).

Pronouns are combined with the preceding or the following word in the following cases (the first four are obligatory in standard language, the other combinations belong to more colloquial usage):

- Before the auxiliary verb *avea*, which occurs in the perfect indicative (*am, ai, a, am, aţi, au*), the present and perfect conditional (*aş, ai, ar, am, aţi, ar*) and in some presumptive forms. A hyphen is added between the pronoun and the auxiliary verb. However, the feminine accusative third person singular pronoun *o* is placed after the main verb.

The different possible combinations are:

Accusative

	am	ai	a	ați	au	aș	ar
mă	m-am	m-ai	m-a	m-ați	m-au	m-aș	m-ar
te	te-am	te-ai	te-a	te-ați	te-au	te-aș	te-ar
îl	l-am	l-ai	l-a	l-ați	l-au	l-aș	l-ar
o	after the main verb						
ne	ne-am	ne-ai	ne-a	ne-ați	ne-au	ne-aș	ne-ar
vă	v-am	v-ai	v-a	v-ați	v-au	v-aș	v-ar
îi	i-am	i-ai	i-a	i-ați	i-au	i-aș	i-ar
le	le-am	le-ai	le-a	le-ați	le-au	le-aș	le-ar

Dative

	am	ai	a	ați	au	aș	ar
îmi	mi-am	mi-ai	mi-a	mi-ați	mi-au	mi-aș	mi-ar
îți	ți-am	ți-ai	ți-a	ți-ați	ți-au	ți-aș	ți-ar
îi	i-am	i-ai	i-a	i-ați	i-au	i-aș	i-ar
ne	ne-am	ne-ai	ne-a	ne-ați	ne-au	ne-aș	ne-ar
vă	v-am	v-ai	v-a	v-ați	v-au	v-aș	v-ar
le	le-am	le-ai	le-a	le-ați	le-a	le-aș	le-ar

E.g.:

l-am văzut	I have seen him
l-ar vedea	I would see him
l-ar fi văzut	I would have seen him
l-ar fi văzând	I might see him

But in feminine:

am văzut-o	I have seen her
ar vedea-o	I would see her
ar fi văzut-o	I would have seen her
ar fi văzând-o	I might see her

mi-a spus	he/she said to me
mi-ar spus	he/she would say to me
mi-ar fi spus	he/she would have said to me
mi-ar fi spunând	he/she might say to me

- When there are two unstressed personal (or reflexive) pronouns, the one in the dative comes before the accusative. Before the accusative pronouns *îl, o* and *îi* a hyphen is used. The following combinations are possible:

	mă	te	îl	o	ne	vă	îi	le	se
îmi	-	mi te	mi-l	mi-o	-	-	mi-i	mi le	mi se
îți	-	-	ți-l	ți-o	-	-	ți-i	ți le	ți se
îi	-	i te	i-l	i-o	-	-	i-i	i le	i se
ne	-	ni te	ni-l	ne-o	-	-	ni-i	ni le	ni se
vă	-	-	vi-l	v-o	-	-	vi-i	vi le	vi se
le	-	li te	li-l	le-o	-	-	li-i	li le	li se

E.g.:

| Ți-o voi spune. | I will tell it to you. |
| Ni le va da. | He/she will give them to us. |

For the missing combinations the stressed dative forms are used:

| Vă recomandă mie. | He/she recommends you to me. |

Before the auxiliary verb *avea* the hyphen comes only after the accusative and the auxiliary verb: *mi te-, mi l-, mi i-, mi le-, mi s-*, etc.: *Ți l-am dat* 'I gave it to you'. The feminine accusative form *o* comes after the verb: *mi-a dat-o* 'he/she gave it to me', *mi-ar da-o* 'he/she would give it to me'.

- All unstressed accusative and dative forms are added to the gerund with a hyphen. A vowel *-u* is added at the end of the gerund (except before *o*), e.g. *deșteptând* 'waking someone up', *dând* 'giving':

Accusative	deșteptându-mă	deșteptându-ne
	deșteptându-te	deșteptându-vă
	deșteptându-l	deșteptându-i
	deșteptând-o	deșteptându-le
Dative	dându-mi	dându-ne
	dându-ți	dându-vă
	dându-i	dându-le

If the gerund is followed by two pronouns, both of them are added to the gerund with a hyphen: *dându-ți-le* 'giving them to you'.

- Also after the affirmative imperative all the unstressed accusative and dative pronouns are added to the verb with a hyphen. If the imperative form ends in the vowel -*ă*, it disappears before the pronoun *o*, e.g. *deşteaptă* 'wake someone up', *dă* 'give':

Accusative	deşteaptă-mă	deşteaptă-ne
	deşteaptă-te	deşteaptă-vă
	deşteaptă-l	deşteaptă-i
	deşteapt-o	deşteaptă-le
Dative	dă-mi	dă-ne
	dă-ţi	dă-vă
	dă-i	dă-le

A stressed *ă* does not disappear before *o*: *fă-o!* 'do it!'. Also an unstressed *u* can disappear: *ad-o / adu-o* 'bring it!'.

Pronouns are added the same way to the affirmative imperative plural: *deşteptaţi-mă!, deşteptaţi-o!, daţi-mi!, daţi-i!* and so on.

If the affirmative imperative is followed by two pronouns, both of them are added to the imperative form with a hyphen: *dă-mi-o!* 'give it to me!', *daţi-mi-o!* 'give (pl.) it to me!'.

However, in the negative imperative all the unstressed pronouns are placed before the verb: *nu-l da!, nu-l daţi!* (or: *nu îl da!, nu îl daţi!*).

- Forms starting with a vowel (except in the combination *a o*) can be combined with the negative adverb *nu*, the conjunction *să* and the infinitive marker *a*:

Accusative

	mă	te	îl	o	ne	vă	îi	le
nu	nu mă	nu te	nu-l	n-o	nu ne	nu vă	nu-i	nu le
să	să mă	să te	să-l	s-o	să ne	să vă	să-i	să le
a	a mă	a te	a-l	a o	a ne	a vă	a-i	a le

Dative

	îmi	îţi	îi	ne	vă	le
nu	nu-mi	nu-ţi	nu-i	nu ne	nu vă	nu le
să	să-mi	să-ţi	să-i	să ne	să vă	să le
a	a-mi	a-ţi	a-i	a ne	a vă	a le

However, before the auxiliary verb *avea* the pronoun is combined with the auxiliary verb: *nu m-a văzut, nu m-ar vedea, nu mi-a dat, nu mi-ar da* etc. If there are two pronouns, the pronouns are not combined with *nu, să, a*: *nu mi-l, nu mi le* etc.

- Pronouns starting with a vowel are sometimes combined with other pronouns and conjunctions ending in a vowel:

Ce-ți place să citești?	What do you like to read?
Știu că-ți place.	I know you like it.

- Pronouns can also be combined with a verb starting with a vowel. This is especially common with the verbs starting with *a* and with the verb *fi* :

M-așteaptă.	He/she is waiting for me.
Mi-e foame.	I am hungry.

After the words *nu, să, a* there are two possibilities:

nu-l aștept, nu l-aștept	I do not wait for him

However, the pronoun *o* cannot be combined with a verb starting with an *a*, but it can be combined with verbs starting with *î*:

o aștept	I am waiting for her
o-nvăț (= o învăț)	I am teaching her

Pronouns are also combined with the colloquial forms of the auxiliary verb *vrea* (*oi, îi (ăi, ei, oi), a (o), om, îți (ăți, eți, oți), or*), e.g.:

îl va vedea → l-o vedea	he/she will see him
îl va fi văzând → l-o fi văzând	he/she might see him

However, the accusative form *o* of the feminine third person singular is placed after the main verb:

o va vedea → o vedea-o	he/she will see her
o va fi văzând → o fi văzând-o	he/she might see her

Polite personal pronouns

Like other Romance languages (French *vous*, Spanish *usted*, Italian *Lei)*, Romanian has separate polite pronouns.

The polite forms are used very frequently in Romanian. In fact, the personal pronoun *tu* should only be used when speaking to very close friends or children.

The most used polite pronoun is *dumneavoastră*, which has the same form for all the genders and cases, both in the singular and plural:

	Singular	Plural
NA		
GD	dumneavoastră	
V		

Dumneavoastră vorbiți românește?	Do You (one or several people) speak Romanian?
numele dumneavoastră	Your name

When *dumneavoastră* is the subject of the phrase, the verb is always in the second person plural form. Predicative adjectives (and passive verb forms) agree with the natural gender and number of the person(s) one is talking to:

Dumneavoastră sunteți român / româncă?	Are you (singular) Romanian?
Dumneavoastră sunteți români / românce?	Are you (plural) Romanian?

The unstressed accusative and dative form of *dumneavoastră* is *vă*:

Dumnevoastră cum vă numiți?	What is your name?

When speaking to one person, the pronoun *dumneata* can also be used. However, it is not as polite as *dumneavoastră*. *Dumneata* is declined as follows:

	Singular
NA	dumneata
GD	dumitale
V	dumneata

When *dumneata* is the subject, the verb must be in the second person singular. The unstressed accusative and dative forms are *te* (acc.) and *îți* (dat.):

Dumneata vorbești românește?	Do you speak Romanian?
Dumneata cum te numești?	What is your name?

This pronoun also has the colloquial form *mata* (GD *matale*), which also has the indeclinable diminutive form *mătăluță*.

Thus in Romanian, while speaking to one person, three levels of politeness can be distinguished (*tu - dumneata - dumneavoastră*). While speaking to several people, there are only two levels of politeness (*voi - dumneavoastră*).

The third person polite pronoun is *dumnealui*:

	Singular		Plural	
	m.	f.	m.	f.
NA	dumnealu̱i	dumneae̱i	dumnealo̱r	
GD				

Dumnealui este român.	He is Romanian.
numele dumneaei	her name

In the singular there is also an old-fashioned non-standard form, *dumneasa, GD dumisale.*

In the third person the pronoun *dânsul* can also be used, but it is not as polite as *dumnealui. Dânsul* is declined as follows:

	Singular		Plural	
	m.	f.	m.	f.
NA	dâ̱nsul	dâ̱nsa	dâ̱nșii	dâ̱nsele
GD	dâ̱nsului	dâ̱nsei	dâ̱nșilor	dâ̱nselor

Thus in the third person there are three different levels of politeness (*el – dânsul – dumnealui*).

The polite pronouns are often abbreviated in writing: *dv. = dvs. = d-voastră, d-ta, d-tale, d-lui, d-ei, d-lor, d-sa, d-sale.*

In very polite style, the older forms written as two words are sometimes used (second person: *Domnia Voastră*, pl. *Domniile Voastre*, third person: *Domnia Sa*, pl. *Domniile Lor*). Other polite forms include e.g. *Maiestatea Ta / Voastră / Sa* 'Your Majesty, His/Her Majesty', *Alteța Voastră / Sa* 'Your Highness, His/Her Highness', *Sfinția Voastră / Sa* 'Your Holiness, His/Her Holiness' etc. When these forms are used as subject, the predicates agree either with the person expressed by the possessive pronoun (*Maiestatea Ta ești / Maiestatea Voastră sunteți foarte generos/generoasă* 'Your Majesty is very generous') or with the noun (*Maiestatea Ta / Voastră este generoasă*).

When polite pronouns are used as the direct object, they are always preceded by the preposition *pe* (see p. 287). The redundant object pronoun (see p. 290) must also be used:

Pe dumneavoastră v-am văzut ieri.	I saw you yesterday.
Pe dumneata te-am văzut ieri.	I saw you yesterday.
Pe dumneaei am văzut-o ieri.	I saw her yesterday.
Pe dânșii i-am văzut ieri.	I saw them yesterday.

Reflexive pronouns

Only the third person has its own reflexive pronoun; in all the other persons personal pronouns are used. Reflexive pronouns do not have nominative, genitive nor vocative forms. Like personal pronouns, reflexive pronouns have a stressed and an unstressed form in the accusative and dative.

The forms of the reflexive pronouns are:

	eu	tu	el, ea	noi	voi	ei, ele
A1	mine	tine	sine	noi	voi	-
A2	mă	te	se	ne	vă	se
D1	mie	ţie	sieşi, sie	nouă	vouă	-
D2	îmi	îţi	îşi	ne	vă	îşi

In modern Romanian, the stressed third person forms *sine, sie(şi)* are used only in the singular.

The accusative and the dative forms of the reflexive pronoun refer to the subject of the same sentence:

a îmbrăca	to dress
a se îmbrăca	to dress oneself, to get dressed
a deştepta	to wake someone up
a se deştepta	to wake up
a spăla	to wash someone / something
a se spăla	to wash oneself
a numi	to give a name
a se numi	to be called
a aminti	remind
a-şi aminti	remember

Compare:

Mama se îmbracă.	Mother is getting dressed.
Mama îl îmbracă pe copil.	Mother is dressing the child.

The reflexive pronoun *se/îşi* is combined with other words like *mă/îmi* (see p. 144): *s-, -se, şi-, -şi, şi*. Notice that *se* is combined with the following word in the form *s-* (unlike *te-, ne-*):

s-a spălat	he/she has washed himself/herself
are să se spele	he/she will wash himself/herself
spălându-se	washing himself/herself

și-a imaginat	he/she has imagined
are să-și imagineze	he/she will imagine (fut.)
și-o imaginează	he/she is imagining it

The stressed forms are used like stressed personal pronouns (see p. 141). The third person stressed forms are used quite rarely:

Se spală pe sine.	He/she is washing himself/herself.
Își mulțumește sieși.	He/she is thanking himself/herself.

Sine also occurs is some fixed expressions, and can sometimes also be used as a noun:

stima de sine	self-esteem
de la sine	by itself, without help
Faptele vorbesc de la sine.	The facts speak for themselves.
în sinea mea	inside me, in my heart

The stressed form *sine* is also used after a preposition, but the stressed forms of personal pronouns *el, ea, ei, ele* are also possible:

Este acasă la sine = la el / la ea.	He/she is at home.
Vorbește cu sine însuși	He/she is talking to himself/herself.
= cu el însuși / cu ea însăși.	

In the plural, the reflexive pronoun can also have the meaning 'each other' (*reflexivul reciproc*):

Maria și Mihai se văd rar.	Maria and Mihai meet each other rarely.
a se cunoaște	to know each other
a se saluta	to greet each other

With some verbs the reflexive pronoun may also have the meaning 'to have done' (*reflexivul factitiv*):

Ea se tunde la coafor.	She has her hair cut at the hairdresser's.
a-și tăia părul	to have one's hair cut

The dative form of the reflexive pronoun can also be used in a possessive structure (possessive dative, see p. 281):

Își zugrăvește casa.	He is painting his own house.
Compare with:	
Îi zugrăvește casa.	He is painting his (= someone else's) house.
Zugrăvește casa sa / lui.	He is painting his (= his own or someone else's) house.

Uniunea Europeană și-a lansat prima bibliotecă virtuală. (*Cotidianul*)	The European Union opened its first virtual library.
a-și pierde viața	to lose one's life

Reflexive pronouns are also used in certain passive constructions (see p. 268). For reflexive verbs, see also p. 269.

Possessive pronouns and adjectives

Romanian possessive pronouns can be used either independently as pronouns or as adjectives modifying a noun.

Adjectival use

The forms of the possessive adjectives in different persons are as follows (nominative-accusative):

	Singular		Plural	
	M., N.	F.	M.	N, F.
eu	m<u>e</u>u	me<u>a</u>	m<u>e</u>i	m<u>e</u>le
tu	t<u>ă</u>u	t<u>a</u>	t<u>ă</u>i	t<u>a</u>le
el, ea	s<u>ă</u>u	s<u>a</u>	s<u>ă</u>i	s<u>a</u>le
noi	n<u>o</u>stru	no<u>a</u>stră	n<u>o</u>ștri	no<u>a</u>stre
voi	v<u>o</u>stru	vo<u>a</u>stră	v<u>o</u>ștri	vo<u>a</u>stre
ei, ele	l<u>or</u>			

In the third person plural the missing possessive pronoun is replaced by the genitive form of the personal pronoun *lor*. That is why it is indeclinable.

Possessive adjectives are preceded by the genitive article when needed (see p. 92).

Possessive adjectives are declined like regular adjectives, i.e. the feminine singular genitive and dative forms are the same as the feminine plural form. All the other genitive and dative forms are the same as the nominative-accusative form.

The possessive adjective usually comes after the noun it modifies. Like any adjective, the possessive adjective must be in the same case, number and gender as the noun it modifies.

E.g. *prietenul meu* 'my friend', *cartea mea* 'my book', *numele meu* 'my name':

		Masculine	Feminine	Neuter
Sg.	NA	prietenul meu	cartea mea	numele meu
	GD	prietenului meu	cărţii mele	numelui meu
Pl.	NA	prietenii mei	cărţile mele	numele mele
	GD	prietenilor mei	cărţilor mele	numelor mele

If the noun has other modifiers, the possessive adjective can be placed before them, or (if more emphasized) after them:

NA: maşina mea albastră   my blue car
GD: maşinii mele albastre
NA: maşina albastră a mea   the blue car of mine
GD: maşinii albastre a mele

When especially stressed, or in poetic language the possessive adjective can be placed before the noun phrase (only in NA). Notice that the noun has no article:

al meu prieten   my friend
a mea albastră maşină   my blue car

If an adjective in the definite form precedes the noun, the possessive adjective may be placed after it:

noul său album   his/her new album

The third person possessive adjective *său* does not have any special reflexive meaning, and the genitive forms of the personal pronoun *lui* (m., n.), *ei* (f.) can always be used instead:

El vorbeşte cu prietenul său/lui.   He talks with his friend.

If a possessive pronoun modifies several nouns, it (and the possible genitive article) agrees with the closest noun:

fratele şi sora mea   my brother and sister
sora şi fratele meu   my sister and brother

In Romanian the possessive adjective can also modify an indefinite noun. In this case the genitive article is always needed:

NA: o prietenă a mea   a friend of mine
GD: unei prietene a mele

When talking about body parts, the possessive pronoun is not usually needed in Romanian:

Mă doare capul.	I have a headache.
Deschide ochii!	Open your eyes!

Similarly, some nouns referring to relatives (especially *tata* 'father', *mama* 'mother', *bunicul* 'grandfather', *bunica* 'grandmother') can be used in the definite form to refer to the relatives of the speaker or the hearer. These definite forms can also be used after a preposition:

tata = tatăl meu/nostru	my/our father
Am fost la bunica	I was at my/our grandmother's.
= bunica mea/noastră	

Colloquially, these form the genitive and dative with the article *lui: lui tata, lui mama* (in standard language *tatei / lui tata, mamei*).

Other nouns that can be used like this include *unchi* 'uncle', *mătuşă* 'aunt', *socru* 'father-in-law', *soacră* 'mother-in-law', etc.

However, the possessive adjective should be used with *soţ* 'husband', *soţie* 'wife', *frate* 'brother', *soră* 'sister', *văr/verişoară* 'cousin', *nepot* 'nephew, grandson', *nepoată* 'niece, grand-daughter'[66]:

fratele meu	my brother
verişoara mea	my cousin

In colloquial language, possessive pronouns *meu, tău, său* can be added directly to nouns referring to relatives (in singular only). The definite article is not used, but the vowel *-u* is added to the masculine nouns ending in a consonant. Eg.:

tată-meu, -tău, -său	father
taică-meu, -tău, -său	dad
mama-ta, -sa[67]	mother
maică-mea, -ta, -sa	mom
frate-meu, -tău, -să	my/your/his/her brother
soră-mea, -ta, -sa	my/your/his/her sister
bunicu-meu, -tău, -său	my/your/his/her grandfather
bunică-mea, -ta, -sa	my/your/his/her grandmother

The genitive-dative forms of the masculine nouns are formed with *lui*:

lui frate-tău	to your brother

The feminine genitive and dative forms are formed with *-mii, -tii, -sii* and the vocative with *-meo*. The head noun is not declined:

soră-mii = surorii mele	to my sister
soră-meo! = sora mea! = soro!	my sister!

An exception is *nevastă-mea/ta/sa*: GD *nevesti-mii/tii/sii* 'my, your, his wife'.

---

[66] Avram (2001:93).
[67] *mamă-mea is not used (DOOM²).

Possessive adjectives are very often replaced with the unstressed dative forms of personal or reflexive pronouns (possessive dative, see p. 281), which are added to the verb:

Am pierdut cartea mea.	I lost my book.
→ Mi-am pierdut cartea.	

In old-fashioned or poetic language the possessive dative pronoun may also be added to a noun:

Am pierdut cartea-mi.	I lost my book.

Pronominal use

Independent possessive pronouns are always preceded by the genitive article. Thus the different forms (NA) are:

	Singular		Plural	
	M., N.	F.	M.	N, F.
eu	al m<u>e</u>u	a me<u>a</u>	ai m<u>e</u>i	ale m<u>e</u>le
tu	al t<u>ă</u>u	a t<u>a</u>	ai t<u>ă</u>i	ale t<u>a</u>le
el, ea	al s<u>ă</u>u	a s<u>a</u>	ai s<u>ă</u>i	ale s<u>a</u>le
noi	al n<u>o</u>stru	a no<u>a</u>stră	ai n<u>o</u>ștri	ale no<u>a</u>stre
voi	al v<u>o</u>stru	a vo<u>a</u>stră	ai v<u>o</u>ștri	ale vo<u>a</u>stre
ei, ele	al lor	a lor	ai lor	ale lor

Independent possessive pronouns must have the same gender and number as the noun they substitute:

Aceasta carte este a mea.	This book is mine.
Aceste cărți sunt a mele.	These books are mine.

In the plural the independent possessive pronoun has the genitive and dative forms *alor mei, alor mele, alor tăi, alor tale* etc. Since the genitive article does not have singular genitive and dative forms, the demonstrative article must be used in the singular: *celui al meu* etc.

An independently used possessive pronoun can sometimes have a specific meaning:

a mea	my wife
al meu	my husband
ai mei, GD alor mei	my parents, my family, my children
ale mele, GD alor mele	my things

Emphatic reflexive pronominal adjective

The emphatic reflexive pronominal adjective declines in gender, number, case and person:

	Masc.	Fem.	
	NAGD	NA	GD
eu	însumi	însămi	însemi
tu	însuţi	însăţi	înseţi
el, ea	însuşi	însăşi	înseşi
noi	înşine	însene	
voi	înşivă	însevă	
ei, ele	înşişi	înseşi / însele	

There are two alternative forms in the feminine (and neuter) third person plural: *înseşi* and *însele*.

In colloquial speech the invariable form *însuşi* or *însăşi* (no gender difference) is sometimes used (*eu însuşi*, etc.). This is not accepted in the standard language.

The emphatic reflexive pronominal adjective emphasizes the noun or the pronoun[68] it modifies:

Am făcut-o eu însumi/însămi.	I did it myself.
Mă iubesc pe mine însumi/însămi.	I love myself.
un aspect al meu însumi/însămi	an aspect of myself
papa însuşi	the pope himself

In older language emphatic reflexive pronominal adjective could also be used as an independent subject pronoun (*însumi l-am făcut*). In modern language this is very rare.

The different forms are used with the personal, reflexive and polite pronouns as follows:

Masculine	Feminine
eu/mine însumi	eu/mine însămi
mie însumi	mie însemi
tu/tine/dumneata însuţi	tu/tine/dumneata însăţi
ţie/dumitale însuţi	ţie/dumitale înseţi

---

[68] A personal, reflexive, polite, possessive or demonstrative pronoun.

Masculine	Feminine
el/sine însuşi	ea/sine însăşi
lui/sie însuşi	ei/sie înseşi
noi înşine	noi însene
nouă înşine	nouă însene
voi/dumneavoastră înşivă	voi/dumneavoastră însevă
vouă/dumneavoastră înşivă	vouă/dumneavoastră însevă
ei înşişi	ele înseşi/însele
lor înşişi	lor înseşi/însele

In spoken language this pronoun is usually replaced with adverbs like *chiar,*
personal or the adjective *propriu*:

chiar eu	I myself
eu personal	I personally
propiul papă	the pope himself

When the headword is a pronoun, the emphatic pronominal adjective is usually placed after it. This is always the case when the pronoun is a personal
pronoun plural or when the pronoun is in the accusative, genitive or dative
case. However, when the head is a pronoun (other than *noi, voi, ei, ele*) and it is
in the nominative case, the emphatic pronominal adjective can also be placed
before it:

| eu însumi, însumi eu | I myself |

| însuşi el o foloseşte pentru a | Even [Freud] himself used it |
| alunga oboseala. (*Cotidianul*) | [=marijuana] to expel fatigue. |

When the headword is a noun in the nominative or accusative case, the emphatic pronominal adjective can be placed both before or after it. The noun
must be in the definite form (or preceded by another definite determiner):

bărbatul însuşi = însuşi bărbatul	the man himself
femeia însăşi = însăşi femeia	the woman herself
acest bărbat însuşi =	this man himself
însuşi acest bărbat	

| L-am văzut pe Elvis însuşi. = | I saw Elvis himself. |
| L-am văzut pe însuşi Elvis. | |

However, the form *însele* comes always after the head:

| fetele însele | the girls themselves |
| = fetele înseşi, înseşi fetele | |

In the genitive or dative case the pronominal adjective is always placed after the noun:

bărbatului însuşi	to the man himself
femeii înseşi	to the woman herself
fetelor înseşi/însele	to the girls themselves
lui Elvis însuşi	to Elvis himself

Demonstrative pronouns and adjectives

The Romanian demonstrative pronouns and adjectives are *acest(a)* 'this', *acel(a)* 'that', *acelaşi* 'the same', *celălalt* 'the other' and the old-fashioned *cestălalt* 'this one (of two)'.

ACEST(A) (adj.) 'this', ACESTA (pron.) 'this (one)'

The pronominal adjective *acest(a)* has two forms: a shorter form and a longer one ending in -*a*:

	Singular		Plural	
	m., n.	f.	m.	n., f.
NA	acest(a)	această, aceasta	aceşti(a)	aceste(a)
GD	acestui(a)	acestei(a)	acestor(a)	

The pronoun *acesta* always has the longer form:

	Singular		Plural	
	m., n.	f.	m.	n., f.
NA	acesta	aceasta	aceştia	acestea
GD	acestuia	acesteia	acestora	

Colloquially, the form *ăsta* is used for *aceasta* (pron., adj.):

	Singular		Plural	
	m., n.	f.	m.	n., f.
NA	ăsta	asta	ăştia	astea
GD	ăstuia	ăsteia	ăstora	

Only the feminine form *asta* (with a neutral meaning) is used in the standard language.

The shorter adjective forms (*ăst, astă, ăstui, ăstei, ăşti, aste, ăstor*) belong only to non-standard speech. There is also the form *cest(a)*, which is also non-standard.

ACEL(A) (adj.) 'that', ACELA (pron.) 'that (one)'

The pronominal adjective *acel(a)* has two forms: a shorter and a longer one ending in -*a*:

	Singular		Plural	
	m., n.	f.	m.	n., f.
NA	acel(a)	acea, aceea	acei(a)	acele(a)
GD	acelui(a)	acelei(a)	acelor(a)	

The pronoun *acela* always has the longer form:

	Singular		Plural	
	m., n.	f.	m.	n., f.
NA	acela	aceea	aceia	acelea
GD	aceluia	aceleia	acelora	

Colloquially, the form *ăla* is used for the *acela* (pron., adj.):

	Singular		Plural	
	m., n.	f.	m.	n., f.
NA	ăla	aia	ăia	alea
GD	ăluia	ăleia	ălora	

The adjectival forms (*ăl, a, ălui, ălei, ăi, ale, ălor*) belong only to non-standard speech. There is also the form *cel(a)*, which is also non-standard.

Use of *acest(a)* and *acel(a)*

When a demonstrative pronoun modifies a noun, it can be placed either before or (if emphasized) after the noun. Before the noun the short form is used and the noun has no article. If the demonstrative adjective is placed after the noun, the longer form ending in -*a* must be used and the noun must be in the definite form.

E.g. *acest/acel bărbat* 'this/that man', *această/acea femeie* 'this/that woman', *acest/acel animal* 'this/that animal':

Masculine

Sg.	NA	acest bărbat	bărbatul acesta
	GD	acestui bărbat	bărbatului acestuia
Pl.	NA	acești bărbați	bărbații aceștia
	GD	acestor bărbați	bărbaților acestora

Sg.	NA	acel bărbat	bărbatul acela
	GD	acelui bărbat	bărbatului aceluia
Pl.	NA	acei bărbați	bărbații aceia
	GD	acelor bărbați	bărbaților acelora

Feminine

Sg.	NA	această femeie	femeia aceasta
	GD	acestei femei	femeii acesteia
Pl.	NA	aceste femei	femeile acestea
	GD	acestor femei	femeilor acestora

Sg.	NA	acea femeie	femeia aceea
	GD	acelei femei	femeii aceleia
Pl.	NA	acele femei	femeile acelea
	GD	acelor femei	femeilor acelora

Neuter

Sg.	NA	acest animal	animalul acesta
	GD	acestui animal	animalului acestuia
Pl.	NA	aceste animale	animalele acestea
	GD	acestor animale	animalelor acestora

Sg.	NA	acel animal	animalul acela
	GD	acelui animal	animalului aceluia
Pl.	NA	acele animale	animalele acelea
	GD	acelor animale	animalelor acelora

Demonstrative adjectives come before any other modifiers:

aceste noi cărți	these new books
aceste două cărți	these two books
aceste cărți ale mele = cărțile acestea ale mele = (rare) aceste ale mele cărți	these books of mine

Demonstrative pronouns are used independently (without a noun) and they always have the longer form:

Acesta este un student.	This one is a student.
Aceasta este o problemă gravă.	This is a serious problem.

Compare the pronominal and adjectival use:

mașina aceasta (adj., = *această mașina*)	this car
mașina acestui bărbat (adj., *acest bărbat* in genitive)	the car of this man
mașina acestuia (pron. in genitive)	the car of this one (masc.), his car

The adjective form must have the same case, number and gender as the noun it modifies. The case of an independent pronoun is determined by its syntactic function in the sentence.

When an independent demonstrative pronoun is used as a direct object, the preposition *pe* (see p. 287) must always be used. The redundant object pronoun (see p. 290) must also be used:

Cunosc acest oraș.	I know this city.
→ Îl cunosc pe acesta.	I know this.

The feminine forms can also be used with a general neuter meaning 'this/that thing':

Asta e adevărul.	This is the truth.
Este țigan și se mândrește cu asta.	He is a Gypsy and proud of it.
Ce e aceasta?	What is this?
cu toate acestea	nevertheless, even so, even then
de aceea	that is why
acestea fiind zise	that being said

Adjectives referring to these neutral pronouns are in the neuter form:

Asta este greu.   This is difficult.

However, with *bun* 'good' the feminine form is usually used:

Asta e bună!   This is good!

When this kind of *asta* is used as a direct object, the preposition *pe* is not used (see p. 290).

In Romanian the demonstrative pronoun is often used instead of the third person of the personal pronoun (*el, ea, ei, ele*), both for animate and inanimate subjects:

Părinţii îşi pot da în judecată
copiii dacă *aceştia* nu îi vizitează
suficient de des. (*Adevărul*)

Parents can sue their children, if
they do not visit often enough.

locuitorii oraşului şi împreju-
rimilor acestuia

the inhabitants of the city and its
surroundings

ACELAŞI (adj., pron.) 'the same'

	Singular		Plural	
	m., n.	f.	m.	n., f.
NA	acelaşi	aceeaşi	aceiaşi	aceleaşi
GD	aceluiaşi	aceleiaşi	aceloraşi	

Acelaşi can be used both independently or as a pronominal adjective. When used as an adjective, it always precedes the noun it modifies and the noun has no article:

aceeaşi problemă   the same problem
aceleaşi două probleme   the same two problems
două aceleaşi probleme   two of the same problem

în acelaşi timp   at the same time
aceleaşi reguli   the same rules

cărţi ale aceluiaşi autor   books by the same author
potrivit aceluiaşi studiu   according to the study in question

NA: unul şi acelaşi   one and the same
GD: unuia şi aceluiaşi

When *acelaşi* is used as an independent direct object, the preposition *pe* (see p. 287) must always be used. The redundant object pronoun (see p. 290) must also be used:

Cunosc acelaşi oraş.	I know the same city.
→ Îl cunosc pe acelaşi.	I know the same one.

CELĂLALT (adj., pron.) 'the other'

	Singular		Plural	
	m., n.	f.	m.	n., f.
NA	celălalt	cealaltă	ceilalţi	celelalte
GD	celuilalt	celeilalte	celorlalţi	celorlalte

This pronoun can be used both as an independent pronoun and a pronominal adjective. It can either precede a noun without an article or (if emphasized) it can be placed after a definite noun:

celălalt student = studentul celălalt	the other student
Petrom şi celelalte companii	Petrom and the other companies
împotriva celorlalte echipe	against the other teams

If a numeral precedes the noun, *celălalt* comes before it:

ceilalţi doi studenţi	the other two students

When *celălalt* is used as an independent direct object, the preposition *pe* (see p. 287) must always be used. The redundant object pronoun (see p. 290) must also be used:

Pe celălalt l-a primit „The Chicago Tribune". (*Cotidianul*)	"The Chicago Tribune" got the other [award].

Notice, that in the indefinite meaning 'another' the indefinite pronoun *alt* (see p. 178) is used.

CESTĂLALT (adj., pron.) 'this one (of two)'

	Singular		Plural	
	m., n.	f.	m.	n., f.
NA	cestălalt	ceastălaltă	ceştilalţi	cestelalte
GD	cestuilalt	cesteilalte	cestorlalţi	cestorlalte

This pronoun is old-fashioned and not used in modern language. It also has shorter colloquial forms *ăstălalt, astalaltă, ăștielalți / ăștialalți, ăstelalte / ăstealalte*, which are not used in standard language either.

Interrogative pronouns and adjectives

The Romanian interrogative pronouns are *cine* 'who', *ce* 'what', *care* 'which', *cât* 'how much, how many' and *al câtelea* 'at which place (in an order)'. Besides these, there are also some interrogative adverbs (see p. 270).

CINE (pron.) 'who'

	Singular
NA	cine
GD	cui

Cine refers to humans or animals, and it cannot be used adjectivally. Morphologically, *cine* is always masculine and singular, and if it functions as a subject, the verb must be in the masculine third person singular:

| Cine a venit? | Who came? |
| Cine a fost arestat? | Who was arrested? |

Notice, that with the verb *fi* 'to be' (and other copula verbs) *cine* is the predicative, and therefore the verb can be conjugated in the plural and also in other persons:

Nu a precizat cine sunt ceilalți trei candidați. (*Adevărul*)	He did not specify who the other three candidates were.
Cine suntem?	Who are we?
Cine au fost vinovații?	Who were the guilty ones?

When *cine* is used as a direct object, the preposition *pe* must be used (see p. 287). However, the redundant object pronoun cannot be used (see p. 292):

| Pe cine ai văzut ieri? | Who did you see yesterday? |
| Pe cine urăști? | Who do you hate? |

On the other hand, the redundant indirect object pronoun (see p. 294) can be used:

| Cui (i-)ai dat flori? | To whom did you give flowers? |

The genitive form is usually preceded by the genitive article (see p. 92):

| A cui este această carte? | Whose book is this? |

CE (adj., pron.) 'what'

The pronoun *ce* is indeclinable and it can be used only in the nominative and accusative cases. As an independent pronoun, *ce* refers to lifeless things, but as a pronominal adjective it can also modify nouns that refer to humans and animals. When used as an adjective, it can modify both singular and plural nouns.

Ce ai citit?	What did you read?
Ce carte ai citit?	What book did you read?
Ce cărți ai citit?	What books have you read?
Ce femeie ar putea rezista tentației?	What woman could resist the temptation?
Din ce oraș sunteți?	Which city are you from?
Ce vor bărbații moderni de la femei? (*Cotidianul*)	What do modern men want from women?

When the pronoun *ce* functions as a subject, the verb must be in the third person singular:

Ce s-a întâmplat?	What has happened?

With the verb *fi* 'to be', *cine* is the predicative, and therefore the verb can also be conjugated in the plural:

Dar ce sunt acele stele? (*Vasile Alecsandri*)	But what are those stars?

The missing genitive case can be replaced with the preposition *a,* and the dative case with *la.* However, this is quite rare:

împotriva a ce?	against what?
util la ce?	useful for what?

This pronoun is also used for the questions *de ce* 'why' and *ce fel de* 'what kind of':

De ce studiezi limba română?	Why do you study Romanian?
Ce fel de muzică îți place?	What kind of music do you like?

Besides questions, *ce* is also used in exclamations (see p. 283).

CARE (adj., pron.) 'which'

	Singular		Plural	
	m., n.	f.	m.	n., f.
NA	care			
GD	cărui(a)	cărei(a)	căror(a)	

The pronoun *care* can be used both as an independent pronoun and as a pronominal adjective. When the independently used *care* functions as a subject, the verb must be in the third person (singular or plural):

| Care vine? | Which one will come? |
| Care vin? | Which ones will come? |

Colloquially, other persons are also possible:

| Care veniți? | Which ones of you will came? |

When *care* is used as an adjective, it always precedes the noun it modifies and the noun has no article. Before a noun the shorter forms of the genitive and dative are used:

| Care carte? | Which book? |
| Care cărți? | Which books? |

| Cărui student? Cărei studente? | To which student? |
| Căror studenți? | To which students? |

| A cărui student este această carte? | Which student's (m.) book is this? |
| A cărei studente este această carte? | Which student's (f.) book is this? |

| Capitala cărei țări este Praga? | The capital of which country is Prague? |

When the genitive and dative forms are used independently, the longer forms are used:

| Căruia dintre ei? | To which one of them? |
| Al căruia dintre ei? | Of which one of them? |

| A căruia este această carte? | Whose book is this? |

However, if the genitive form is used before a noun it modifies, the short form is used:

| cu a cărui mașină? | with whose car? |
| = cu mașina căruia? | |

When *care* is used as a direct object, the redundant object pronoun (see p. 290) must also be used:

Care carte ai citit-o?	Which book did you read?
Pe care fată o cunoști?	Which girl do you know?

When the independent form is used as a direct object, it is always preceded by the preposition *pe* (see p. 287). The redundant object pronoun (see p. 290) must also be used:

Pe care o vrei să citești?	Which one do you want to read?

When *care* functions as the indirect object, the redundant indirect object pronoun (see p. 294) must always be used as well:

Căror prieteni le-ai dat flori?	To which friend did you give flowers?
→ Cărora le-ai dat flori?	To which one did you give flowers?
Cărei țări îi aparțin insulele Åland?	To which country do the Åland islands belong?

CÂT (adj., pron.) 'how many, how much'

	Singular		Plural	
	m., n.	f.	m.	n., f.
NA	cât	câtă	câți	câte
GD	-		câtor(a)	

Cât can be used both as an independent pronoun and a pronominal adjective. When used adjectivally, it always precedes the noun it modifies:

Câți studenți sunt în clasă?	How many students are there in the class?
Câți sunteți în clasă?	How many of you are in the class?
Câtă apă avem?	How much water do we have?
Cât e ceasul?	What time is it?
Câți dintre noi?	How many of us?

In the genitive and dative the shorter form is used adjectivally before a noun, and the longer form is used as an independent pronoun:

Câtor studenți le place limba română?	How many students like Romanian?
→ Câtora le place limba română?	How many like Romanian?
Câtora dintre noi?	To how many of us?

However, if the independent genitive form comes before the noun it modifies, the short form is used:

al câtor apartament = apartamentul câtora	the apartment of how many people

The missing singular genitive form is replaced by the preposition *a*, and the dative with *la*. The plural form can be replaced by these prepositions as well:

câtora = la câți, la câte	to how many?
câtor studenți = la câți studenți	to how many students?

Adjectives and adverbs are added to *cât* with the help of the preposition *de*:

Cât de bolnav este?	How sick is he/she?
Cât de mulți oameni?	How many people?
cât de des	how often

When *cât* is used independently as a direct object, it can be preceded by the preposition *pe* (see p. 287):

Pe câți i-ai văzut? = Câți ai văzut?	How many did you see?

Cât is also used in exclamations (see p. 283).

AL CÂTELEA (adj., pron.)

Al câtelea is an interrogative pronoun for asking about the order of things, and an ordinal numeral is expected for the answer. The pronoun *al câtelea* has the feminine form *a câta*, but it does not have a plural form nor a genitive or dative. This pronoun can be used as an independent pronoun or as a pronominal adjective. When used adjectivally, it precedes the noun it modifies and the noun must be without an article.

Al câtelea sunt pe listă?	At which place am I on the list?
În a câta lună de sarcină ești?	How many months pregnant are you?
Al câtelea președinte finlandez este Halonen?	In chronological order, which Finnish president is Halonen?

Relative pronouns

There are two important differences between English and Romanian use of relative pronouns:

- Unlike in English, the relative pronouns can not usually be omitted in Romanian:

    cartea pe *care* o citesc   the book (*that*) I'm reading

- The prepositions must always precede the relative pronoun:

    studentul *cu* care am vorbit   the student (that) I talked *with*
    barul *în* care se afla   the bar he/she was *in*

CARE 'that, who'

The most frequently used relative pronoun is *care.* It is declined like the interrogative pronoun *care* (see p. 167). When *care* functions as the subject of the relative clause, the predicative agrees with the antecedent in number:

    studentul care locuiește la Iași   the student who lives in Iași
    studenți care locuiesc la Iași   the students who live in Iași

If the antecedent is in the 1st or 2nd person, the predicative can agree with the person:

    Sunt eu care l-a / l-am făcut.   It is I who did it.

When the pronoun *care* is used as the direct object of the relative clause, it must be preceded by the preposition *pe* (see p. 287). The redundant object pronoun (see p. 290) must also be used:

    cartea pe care o citesc   the book I am reading
    cartea pe care am citit–o   the book I have read

    100 de cărți pe care trebuie să le   the hundred books you must have in
    ai în bibliotecă (*Adevărul*)   your library

In the genitive case, the shorter forms are used before the possessed noun, and the longer forms are used after it:

    studentul a cărui carte   the student whose book

    studentul cu mama căruia   the student whose mother I talked
    am vorbit   with
    = studentul cu a cărui mamă

The genitive forms of the relative pronoun must agree with the gender and number of the *possessor*. When *care* precedes the possessed noun, the genitive article must be used (see p. 92). The genitive article agrees with the *possessed* noun. E.g. 'the man/men/woman/women whose dog(s)/cat(s)':

bărbatul al cărui câine	femeia al cărei câine
bărbatul ai cărui câini	femeia ai cărei câini
bărbatul a cărui pisică	femeia a cărei pisică
bărbatul ale cărui pisici	femeia ale cărei pisici
bărbații al căror câine	femeile al căror câine
bărbații ai căror câini	femeile ai căror câini
bărbații a căror pisică	femeile a căror pisică
bărbații ale căror pisici	femeile ale căror pisici

In the dative the longer forms ending in -*a* are always used:

teoria conform căreia   the theory according to which

When *care* functions as the indirect object, the redundant indirect object pronoun (see p. 294) must always be used:

băiatul căruia i-am dat flori   the boy to whom I gave flowers
băieții cărora le-am dat flori   the boys to whom I gave flowers
fata căreia i-am dat flori   the girl to whom I gave flowers
fetele cărora le-am dat flori   the girls to whom I gave flowers

CEL CARE 'the one that, the one who'

The relative pronoun *cel care* is formed by the demonstrative article (see p. 95) and the pronoun *care*:

	Singular		Plural	
	m., n.	f.	m.	n., f.
NA	cel care	cea care	cei care	cele care
GD	celui care	celei care	colors care

This structure is used when the relative pronoun does not have a head. *Cel* is in the case required by the main clause, while *care* must be in the case required by the relative clause:

Cel care a venit este fratele meu.   The one who came is my brother

Totalul celor care vor rămâne fără lucru va fi de 210. (*Adevărul*)   The total number of those losing their jobs will be ca 210.

Dânsul este cel care cunoaşte cel mai bine jucătorii. (*Adevărul*)	He is the one who best knows the players.

The pronoun *care* can also be declined in the genitive and dative:

cel a cărui maşină	the one whose car

The pronoun *cel care* can be preceded by the pronominal adjective *tot*:

toţi cei care	all who

Both the demonstrative article and the pronoun *care* can be preceded by a preposition:

pentru cel cu care	for the one with whom

Both the demonstrative article *cel* and the relative pronoun *care* are preceded by the preposition *pe* when they are used as direct objects (see p. 287):

Rusia îi ascunde pe cei care m-au otrăvit. (*Adevărul*)	Russia is hiding the people who poisoned me.
cei pe care îi iubesc	the ones I love
Merkel nu i-a numit pe cei pe care i-a criticat (*realitatea.net*)	Merkel did not mention by name the persons she criticised.

CEL CE 'the one that, the one who'

The relative pronoun *cel ce* means the same as *cel care.* The singular feminine form is not used in modern language. The pronoun *ce* is indeclinable (only nominative and accusative):

	Singular		Plural	
	m., n.	f.	m.	n., f.
NA	cel ce	-	cei ce	cele ce
GD	celui ce	celei ce	celor ce	

Din totalul celor ce s-au prezen-tat la urne, 20,1% au între 18 şi 34 de ani. (*Adevărul*)	Of those who voted, 20.1% were 18 -34 years old.
L-am dat celui ce a venit.	I gave it to the one who came.
o ţară din care toţi cei ce îşi pierd speranţa pleacă (*Cotidianul*)	a country which all those who lose hope leave

When the demonstrative article *cel* is used as a direct object, it is always preceded by the preposition *pe* (see p. 287):

Îi ignorăm pe cei ce ne adoră,	We ignore those who adore us
îi adorăm pe cei ce ne ignoră.	and adore those who ignore us.

CEEA CE 'what'

Ceea ce is an independent pronoun with a neuter meaning 'that thing that'. This pronoun is indeclinable (only nominative and accusative singular are used) and it cannot refer to any noun, since it never has a head.

Ceea ce ai spus este interesant.	What you said is interesting.
în ceea ce priveşte integrarea europeană a Republicii Moldova (*Adevărul*)	What comes to the European integration of the republic of Moldova

However, this pronoun can be preceded by the pronominal adjective *tot*: *tot ceea ce* 'everything that'.

The missing genitive is replaced by the preposition *a*, and the dative with *la*:

A votat împotriva a ceea ce a promis în campania electorală. (*Cotidianul*)	He voted against what he had promised during the electoral campaign.
El n-a venit din cauza a ceea ce i-ai spus tu.	He did not come because of what you said to him.
Dau crezare la ceea ce spui.	I trust in what you say.

CINE 'who' and CE 'what'

Cine (GD. *cui*) and *ce* (only NA) occur as relative pronouns usually without a headword. *Cine* refers to a human or animal, *ce* to inanimate objects. *Cine* and *ce* are used in the case required by the main cause:

Cine râde la urmă râde mai bine.	'He who laughs last, laughs longest.'
Ce ţie nu-ţi place altuia nu-i face.	What you do not like, do not do it to others.
Fă ce vrei!	Do what you want!
L-am dat cui l-a cerut.	I gave it to him/her who asked for it.

If *cine* is the direct object of the main clause, it is always preceded by the preposition *pe* (see p. 287). However, the redundant object pronoun cannot be used (see p. 292):

Iubesc pe cine nu trebuie. (the film *She's the Man*)	I love someone I should not.

The missing genitive form the pronoun *ce* can be replaced with the preposition *a* and the dative with the preposition *la*:

în ciuda a tot ce am spus	in spite of all I said
Dau crezare la ce spui.	I trust in what you say.

Ce is often preceded by *tot*:

Tot ce trebuie să cunoaşteţi despre gripa porcină (*Cotidianul*)	All you need to know about the swine flu

Only an indefinite pronoun can function as a head of *cine*:

Caut pe cineva cine să mă ajute.	I am looking for someone who could help me.
N-am pe nimeni cine să mă ajute.	I have no-one who could help me.

Ce can also occur with a headword (human, animal or inanimate), even though the use of the pronoun *care* is recommended:

numărul de animale ce pot fi vânate (*Adevărul*)	the number of animals that can be hunted
Ursul ce a devenit agresiv poate fi împuşcat de vânători. (*Adevărul*)	A bear that has become aggressive can be shot by hunters.

According to the literary norm, the pronoun *ce* can be used to refer to a headword only when one wishes to avoid repeating the word *care*.

CÂT 'the amount that'

The pronoun *cât* (see p. 168) can also sometimes be used as a relative pronoun:

Cumpără bere câtă vrei!	Buy as much beer you want! (= the amount you want)

ORICINE 'whoever', ORICE 'whatever', ORICARE 'whichever', ORICÂT 'any amount that'

The pronouns *oricine, orice, oricare* (see p. 181) and *oricât* (see p. 192) are also sometimes used as relative pronouns:

Vine oricine vrea.	Anyone who wants will come.
o carte utilă pentru oricine doreşte să cunoască istoria României	a useful book to anyone who wants to know about Romanian history

DE 'that'

In standard language the relative pronoun *de* is very rare. It is used colloquially, especially after the pronoun *ăl(a)*:

exemplu' ăla de l-ai dat tu *(forum.ubuntu.ro)*	that example you gave

Indefinite pronouns and adjectives

Most Romanian indefinite pronouns are formed from the words *un, cine, ce, care, cât* with the prefixes *fie-, ori-, oare-*.

Indefinite pronouns can be used both as independent pronouns (pron.) and as pronominal adjectives (adj.). The adjectival forms usually come before the noun they modify and they must agree with it in case, number and gender. Many pronouns have different forms for independent and adjectival use.

UN (adj.) 'some', UNUL (pron.) 'one'

	Singular		Plural		Singular		Plural	
	m., n.	f.	m.	n., f.	m., n.	f.	m.	n., f.
NA	un	o	unii	unele	unul	una	unii	unele
GD	unui	unei	unor		unuia	uneia	unora	

The indefinite adjective *un* differs from the indefinite article (see p. 71) only in the nominative and accusative plural. The adjective form can only be used before countable nouns[69]:

un profesor	some teacher
unii profesori	some teachers
în unele ţări africane	in some African countries

---

[69] For 'some water' etc. *ceva* (see p. 180) or *nişte* (p. 192) is used.

unii oameni dorm mai puțin (*Adevărul*)	some people sleep less

The pronoun *unul* is used to replace an indefinite noun[70]:

Această modificare va fi una benefică. (= o modificare benefică) (*Adevărul*)	This modification will be a beneficial one.
Decizia este una politică. (= o decizie politică)	The decision is a political one.

The plural form *unii* also has the meaning 'some people':

Unora nu le plac pisicile.	Some people do not like cats.

The pronoun *unul* is often used in the reciprocal structure *unul ... altul* (fem. *una ... alta*) 'one - another, each other'. Both the pronouns *unul* and *altul* must always be in the same case, gender and number:

Ion și Maria se ajută unul pe altul.	Ion and Maria help each other.
Maria și Elena se ajută una pe alta.	Maria and Elena help each other.
unul lângă altul	side by side
Obama și McCain se acuză unul pe altul de criza economiei americane. (*Ziarul Financiar*)	Obama and McCain blame each other for the American economic crisis.

When referring to plural nouns, the plural forms (*unii ... alții, unele ... altele*) can also be used:

Voi și Maria vă ajutați unul pe altul / unii pe alții.	You (masc. pl.) and Maria help each other.
Voi și Maria vă ajutați una pe alta / unele pe altele.	You (fem. pl.) and Maria help each other.

The feminine form *una* sometimes has a neutral meaning 'one thing, something':

A promis una și alta.	He/she promised this and that.
până una-alta	by the way

Notice the difference between *unul* and the numeral *unu*:

Am văzut unu, nu doi.	I saw one, not two.
Am văzut unul, nu altul.	I saw one, not the other.

However, in some fixed expressions the form *unul* is usually used instead of *unu*:

unul din patru	one out of four
unul din noi	one of us

---

[70] A definite noun can be replaced with *cel* (see p. 95).

Au murit până la unul.	They all died.
Eu unul nu îl cred.	I for one do not believe it.
de unul singur	alone
unul câte unul / una câte una	one by one

VREUN (adj.) 'any', VREUNUL (pron.) 'anyone'

Vreun(ul) is declined like *un(ul)*:

	Singular		Plural
	m., n.	f.	
NA	vreun	vreo	-
GD	vreunui	vreunei	vreunor

Singular		Plural	
m., n.	f.	m.	n., f.
vreunul	vreuna	vreunii	vreunele
vreunuia	vreuneia	vreunora	

This pronoun is mainly used in interrogative and negative sentences.

vreunul dintre voi	any one of you
vreunii dintre ei	any of them
Ai vreun piercing?	Do you have any piercings?
Are vreo importanţă?	Does it have any importance?
Nu sunt supuse vreunor restricţii.	They are not under any restrictions.
Nu a citit vreuna din cărţile lui J.K Rowling. (*Cotidianul*) → Nu a citit vreo carte a lui J.K.R.	He/She has not read any books by J. K. Rowling.
Nadal ajunge în semifinale fără să piardă vreun set! (*Adevărul*)	Nadal makes it to the semi-finals without losing a game!

Vreun(ul) can also be used in conditional clauses:

Dacă ai vreo problemă, dă-mi de ştire!	If you have any problems, let me know!

In negative sentences *vreun* has almost the same meaning as *niciun* (the latter is more categoric). Compare:

N-am citit vreuna din cărţile.	I have not read any of the books.
N-am citit niciuna din cărţile.	I have read none of the books.

In front of nouns and numerals that act as nouns *vreun* also expresses an undefined amount:

peste vreo lună	after about a month
vreun milion	about a million

However, in front of other numerals the adverb *vreo* is used:

vreo șase ani	about six years
vreo două milioane de euro	about two million euros

ALT (adj.), ALTUL (pron.) 'other'

	Singular		Plural		Singular		Plural	
	m., n.	f.	m.	n., f.	m., n.	f.	m.	n., f.
NA	alt	altă	alți	alte	altul	alta	alții	altele
GD	altui	altei	altor		altuia	alteia	altora	

The shorter form *alt* is used as an adjectival attribute, the longer form *altul* as an independent pronoun:

altă persoană	other person
alte două cazuri	other two cases
două alte cazuri	two other cases
alții doi, altele două	the other two
alții mulți, altele multe	many others
cine altul?	who else?
un milion de dolari pentru nevasta altuia (*Adevărul*)	a million dollars for the wife of another.
→ nevasta altui bărbat	wife of another man
Femeile preferă bărbații altor femei.	Women prefer other women's men.
→ bărbații altora	men of others
cetățeni ai altor țări	citizens of other countries

This pronoun is often preceded by the indefinite article (English 'another'):

un alt bărbat	another man
Un bărbat a fost ucis și un altul rănit.	One man was killed and another injured.

After the indefinite article or another declined modifier the genitive and dative forms are *alt, alte, alți, alte*:

unui alt bărbat	to another man
unei alte femei	to another woman
unor alți oameni	to other people
oricărui alt bărbat	to any other man

However, after a pronominal adjective denoting amount, *alt* is declined regularly:

multor altor oameni	to many other people
tuturor altor oameni	to all the other people

The independently used feminine form *alta* also has a general neuter meaning:

printre altele	among other things
nu de alta, dar...	not for any other reason but
nimic alta	nothing else

In the definite meaning the demonstrative pronoun *celălalt* 'the other' (see p. 164) is used.

CINEVA (pron.) 'someone', ALTCINEVA (pron.) 'someone else'

	Singular
NA	cinev<u>a</u>
GD	cuiv<u>a</u>

Cineva 'someone' refers to a human or an animal. The pronoun *altcineva* 'someone else' is declined in the same way. Both these pronouns only have singular forms.

Mai citeşte cineva cărţi?	Does anyone still read books?
L-a făcut altcineva!	Someone else did it!
A luat maşina altcuiva.	He/She took some one else's car.
L-am dat cuiva.	I gave it to someone.

When used independently as a direct object, *cineva* and *altcineva* are always preceded by the preposition *pe* (see p. 287). However, the redundant object pronoun cannot be used (see p. 292):

Nu pot iubi pe altcineva.	I cannot love any other.
Chiar ieri am trimis pe cineva să-mi cumpere nişte medicamente. (*Adevărul*)	Just yesterday I sent someone to buy me some medicine.

Colloquially, the pronoun *cineva* also has the meaning 'an important person':

Crede că este (un) cineva.	He/She thinks he/she's someone.

CEVA (adj., pron.) 'something, some', **ALTCEVA** (pron.) 'something else'

Both *ceva* and *altceva* refer to inanimate things. They are both indeclinable (only nominative and accusative).

Spune-mi ceva!	Tell me something!
S-a întâmplat ceva?	Has something happened?
ceva interesant	something interesting
Neanderthalienii au avut ceva în comun cu oamenii moderni. (*Cotidianul*)	Neanderthals had something in common with modern men.
Vreau şi altceva decât bani.	I want something else besides money.
Nu face altceva decât să doarmă.	He/She does not do anything else but sleep.

The missing genitive and dative forms are replaced by the prepositions *a* (genitive) and *la* (dative):

asupra a ceva	on something
util la ceva	useful to something

Ceva can also be used as a pronominal adjective before a noun:

ceva carte	some book
ceva cărţi	some books
ceva zahăr	some sugar

In contrast, the pronoun *altceva* can only be used independently.

CAREVA (adj., pron.) 'some, someone, something'

The pronoun *careva* is rarer and it means 'someone, something (of a group)'. As an independent pronoun it usually refers to a human or an animal (the direct object form is *pe careva*), as a pronominal adjective it can also modify an inanimate noun:

Mă poate ajuta careva?	Could someone help me?
Nimeni nu i-a putut oferi careva informaţii. (*Adevărul*)	No-one could give him any information.

In standard language the pronoun *careva* is indeclinable (only the NA is used). Dialectally there is also a pronoun *altcareva* 'someone else' (GD *altcăruiva*).

ORICINE (pron.) 'whoever', **ORICE** (adj., pron.) 'whatever', **ORICARE** (adj., pron.) 'whichever'

These indefinite pronouns are declined like *cine* (p. 165), *care* (p. 167) and *ce* (p. 166). The prefix *ori-* is pronounced as one syllable: [ori'ʧine, ori'ʧe, ori'kare]. The pronoun *oricine* can only be used as an independent pronoun; the others can also be used as pronominal adjectives, e.g.:

Oricine poate adopta un copil. (*Adevărul*)	Anyone can adopt a baby.
Uşa este deschisă oricui. (*Cotidianul*)	The door is open for anyone.
un program care citeşte orice format	a program that can read any file format
oricare carte = orice carte oricare student = orice student	any book any student
oricare femeie, GD oricărei femei oricare femei, GD oricăror femei	any woman any women
în orice moment orice altă maşină orice altceva	at any moment any other car whatever else
666 e un număr ca oricare altul. (*Cotidianul*)	666 is a number like any other.

When *oricine* is used as a direct object, it is always preceded by the preposition *pe* (see p. 287). However, the redundant object pronoun cannot be used (see p. 292):

o echipă capabilă să învingă pe oricine (*Cotidianul*)	a team able to beat anyone

When used independently as a direct object, *oricare* is always preceded by the preposition *pe* (see p. 287). The redundant object pronoun (see p. 290) can also be used:

Poţi citi oricare carte. → (O) poţi citi pe oricare.	You can read any book (you like).

These pronouns also have the longer forms *orişicine, orişice, orişicare.*

FIECARE (adj., pron.) 'every, each'

	Singular	
	m., n.	f.
NA	fiec**a**re	
GD	fiec**ă**rui(a)	fiec**ă**rei(a)

Fiecare is used only in the singular. When it is used adjectivally, it is placed before the noun:

fiecare copil	every child, each child
fiecărei fete	to every girl
în fiecare zi	every day
de fiecare dată	every time

The longer genitive and dative forms are used as independent pronouns, and the shorter ones as pronominal adjectives before nouns:

rezolvarea fiecăreia dintre aceste probleme	the resolution of each of these problems
dreptul la viață al fiecărui om → dreptul la viață al fiecăruia	every man's right to a life everyone's right to a life
100.000 de dolari fiecărui jucător (*Cotidianul*) → 100.000 de dolari fiecăruia	100,000 dollars to every player 100,000 dollars to everyone

When used independently as a direct object, *fiecare* is always preceded by the preposition *pe* (see p. 287):

Am citit fiecare carte.	I've read every book.
→ Am citit(-o) pe fiecare.	I've read every one.

The forms *fiecine* (GD *fiecui*), *fiece* are rare and old-fashioned:

în fiece zi (= în fiecare zi)	every day

In non-standard and old-fashioned speech these pronouns have also the forms *fieşicare, fieştecare, fitecare, fitecine, fitece.*

ANUMIT (adj.) 'certain, particular'

Anumit is declined like an adjective and it is used with nouns in the indefinite form, after the indefinite article. It also has the plural genitive and dative form *anumitor*, which is used in front of a noun without the indefinite article:

într-un anumit moment	at a certain moment
o anumită persoană	a certain person

Președintele recunoaște existența unor anumite probleme.	The President admits the existence of certain problems.
opiniile anumitor tineri = opiniile unor anumiți tineri	the opinions of certain young people

The indeclinable pronoun *anume* has the same meaning:

o anume carte	a certain book

OARECARE (adj.) 'some'

The opposite of the word *anumit* is *oarec̦re*, which is invariable and always an adjective. It is used with a noun in the indefinite form:

o oarecare problemă	some problem
un oarecare Popescu	some Joe Bloggs (Br.), some John Doe (Am.)

After a noun *oarecare* has the meaning 'whoever/whatever, any':

niște cărți oarecare	whatever books
un maghiar oarecare, János Kovács, să spunem (*Cotidianul*)	any Hungarian, let us call him János Kovács[71]

The independent pronouns *oarecare* (GD *oarecăruia, oarecăreia, oarecărora*) and *oarecine* (GD *oarecui*) are old-fashioned or dialectal. The pronoun *oarece* is used in non-standard speech. These pronouns also have the longer forms *oareșicare, oareșicine, oareșice*.

CUTARE (adj., pron.) 'so-and-so'

	Singular		Plural
	m., n.	f.	
NA		cutare	
GD	cutărui(a)	cutărei(a)	cutăror(a)

The pronoun *cutare* is used when one wishes not to name a person or a thing. The shorter genitive and dative forms are used as adjectives before a noun, the longer ones as independent pronouns.

la ora cutare = la cutare oră	at so-and-so o'clock
cutărei femei → cutăreia	to that woman

---

[71] Hungarian Joe Bloggs (Br.), John Doe (Am.).

Din taxele dvs. în valoare de 500 de euro, o sută s-au dat la spitalul cutare şi s-a făcut cutare lucru, 250 la şcoala cutare şi aşa mai departe. (*Cotidianul*)	From your taxes worth 500 euros 100 euros has been given to some hospital and something has been done with it, 250 euros to some school and so on.

When *cutare* is used independently as a subject, the verb comes in the third person singular:

Cutare a zis aşa.	So and so said so.

There is also the family name *Cutărescu*[72], GD *lui Cutărescu*.

ATARE (adj.) 'like that, such'

The pronominal adjective *atare* is declined regularly (pl. and f. GD *atari*)[73]. It is always used before a noun:

o atare problemă	a problem like that

ALDE (adj.) 'likes of'

The pronoun *alde* is colloquial and non-standard. It always has a plural meaning. In front of a name it means 'family, friends of', etc.:

alde Ion	Ion's people

After the preposition *de*, *alde* means 'people like':

de alde voi	people like you

Quantitative indefinite pronouns and adjectives

Quantitative indefinite pronouns have several features in common:

- They are usually placed before a noun.
- They do not have singular genitive or dative forms, which are replaced by the prepositions *a* (genitive) and *la* (dative).
- The plural genitive and dative form can also be replaced with prepositions (as is also done after the quantitative adjectives, see p. 119).
- When a quantitative indefinite pronoun is preceded by a demonstrative pronoun or a demonstrative article, the indefinite pronoun is declined like an adjective.

---

[72] Other forms also occur: *Să zicem ca acesta este Cutărescu, care l-a sunat pe Cutărache în legătura cu un anume interes al lui Cutăreanu, care Cutăreanu are afaceri cu Cutăriţă, iar despre Cutăriţă ştim noi foarte bine ce învârte dat fiind că soţia lui e cumnata lui Cutăraru, fosta consilieră a lui Cutărică. (*Cotidianul*).*

[73] DOOM[2].

TOT (adj., pron.) 'whole, all'

	Singular		Plural	
	m., n.	f.	m.	n., f.
NA	tot	toată	toți	toate
GD		-	tuturor(a)	

The shorter genitive and dative form *tuturor* can be used both adjectivally and as a pronoun, while the less frequent longer form *tuturora* can only be used pronominally[74]:

tuturor românilor	to all Romanians
Bună ziua tuturor(a)!	Good day to all!
nouă tuturor(a)	to us all

When *tot* is used as a pronominal adjective, it usually precedes the noun. In old-fashioned style, however, it can also be placed after it. In both cases the noun must be in the definite form:

toată lumea = lumea toată	all people
Am citit toate cărțile.	I've read all the books.
toate știrile	all the news
toate ultimele știri	all the latest news

However, the definite article is not used when the noun is preceded by some other pronoun requiring the noun to be without article. Both pronouns are declined in GD:

toate aceste știri	all this news
tuturor acestor oameni	to all these people
toți alți bărbați	all the other men
tuturor altor bărbați	to all the other men

When *tot* modifies an independently used adjective, the demonstrative article is used (see p. 95):

toți cei albaștri	all the blue ones
tuturor celor interesați	to everyone who is interested

For the use of *tot* before numerals (*toți trei bărbații* 'all three men'), see collective numerals (p. 139).

---

[74] DOOM². Vintilă-Rădulescu (2009) uses the long form when an adjectival *tot* is placed after the noun (*oamenilor tuturora* 'to all the people').

The missing singular genitive and dative forms are replaced by the prepositions *a* (genitive) and *la* (dative). The plural genitive and dative form can also
be replaced by these prepositions:

la toată lumea	to all people
tuturor(a) = la toți, la toate	to everyone
la toți studenții,	to all students
la toate studentele	

The independent neuter forms can be used with the meaning 'everything'. As
a subject, the definite form *totul* is used. *Totul* can also be used as a direct object:

Totul este pierdut.	All is lost.
Totul a început în 1983.	All began in 1983.
A făcut tot(ul).	He/She did all (he/she could).
Eu știu tot(ul) despre el.	I know all about him.
înainte de toate	most of all, above all

The definite form is also used in expressions *cu toții / toatele, cu totul*:

au venit cu toții	they all came
O să murim cu toții!	We are all going to die!
o cu totul altă poveste	a whole other story
cinci cu totul	five in total

The neuter pronoun is also used in the expression *tot (ceea) ce* 'everything
that':

Am făcut tot ce trebuia.	I did everything that was needed.

When an independent *tot* replaces a noun, the direct object is formed with
the preposition *pe* (see p. 287). The redundant object pronoun (see p. 290)
must also be used:

Am citit toate cărțile.	I read all the books.
→ Le-am citit pe toate.	I read them all.
I-am mâncat pe toți.	I ate them all.
L-am mâncat pe tot.	I ate all of it.
Vreau să vă cunosc pe toți.	I want to know you all.

MULT (adj., pron.) 'much, many'

	Singular		Plural	
	m., n.	f.	m.	n., f.
NA	mult	multă	mulți	multe
GD	-		multor(a)	

The longer genitive and dative form ending in -a is used as an independent pronoun, and the shorter one as a pronominal adjective before a noun:

În clasă sunt mulți studenți.	In the class there are many students.
Ion are multe cărți.	Ion has many books.
NA: mulți alții, multe altele	many others
GD: multor altor	
dispariția multor specii	the disappearance of many species
→ dispariția multora	the disappearance of many
Multora le este frică de gripa porcină.	Many people are afraid of swine flu.
Pe mulți i-au luat cu mașina. (*Cotidianul*)	They took many people by car.
La Paris i-a cunoscut pe mulți dintre scriitorii importanți. (*Cotidianul*)	In Paris he got to know many of the important writers.

The missing singular genitive and dative forms are replaced by the prepositions *a* (genitive) and *la* (dative). The plural genitive and dative form can also be replaced by these prepositions:

la multă lume	to many people
multora = la mulți, la multe	to many
la mulți oameni	to many people

Mult is sometimes used as a regular adjective (GD *mult, multe, mulți, multe*). This happens in the following cases:

- When *mult* is preceded by a demonstrative pronoun or a demonstrative article:

acestor mulți oameni	to these many people
puterea celor puțini asupra celor mulți	the power of the few over the many

- When *mult* is placed before a definite noun. Notice that the definite article is attached to *mult*:

multele cărți pe care le-am citit	the many books I have read
mulților oameni	to the many people

- When *mult* is placed (for emphasis) after the noun (or pronoun) is modifies:

cărți multe	many books
cărțile multe pe care le am citit	the many book I have read

alții mulți, GD altor mulți	many others
oamenilor mulți	to the many people

Mult can also be used in the comparative and superlative:

tot mai mulți tineri	more and more young people
părerea tot mai multor tineri	the opinion of more and more young people
NA: cei mai mulți oameni	most people
GD: celor mai mulți oameni	

An independently used neuter plural *multe* has the meaning 'many things':

Am multe de spus despre asta.	I have much to say about this.

The masculine/neuter singular form can also be used as an adverb:

El mănâncă mult.	He eats a lot.
o persoană mult admirată	a much admired person
cel mai mult	most

PUȚIN (adj., pron.) 'little, few'

	Singular		Plural	
	m., n.	f.	m.	n., f.
NA	puțin	puțină	puțini	puține
GD	-		puținor(a)	

Puțin is used like *mult*. The longer genitive and dative form ending in -*a* is used as an independent pronoun, and the shorter one as a pronominal adjective before a noun:

Am puțini bani.	I have little money.
Ei au puține cărți.	They have few books.
Foarte puținor oameni le-a plăcut filmul acela.	Only a few people liked that film.
→ foarte puținora le-a plăcut	
Numai pe puțini îi interesează.	Only a few people find it interesting.

The missing singular genitive and dative forms are replaced by the prepositions *a* (genitive) and *la* (dative). The plural genitive and dative form can also be replaced by these prepositions:

la puțină lume	to few people
puținora = la puțini, la puține	to few
la puțini studenți	to few students

Just like *mult*, *puțin* is used as a regular adjective (GD *puțin, puține, puțini, puține*) in the following cases:

- When *puțin* is preceded by a demonstrative pronoun or a demonstrative article:

acestor puțini oameni	to these few people
privilegiu celor puțini	privilege of the few

- When *puțin* is placed before a definite noun. Notice that the definite article is attached to *puțin*:

puținele cărți pe care le-am citit	the few books I have read
puținilor oameni	to the few people

- When *puțin* is placed for emphasis) after the noun (or pronoun) is modifies:

cărți puține	few books
cărțile puține pe care le-am citit	the few books I have read
oamenilor puțini	to the few people

Puțin can also be used in the comparative and superlative:

tot mai puțini tineri	fewer and fewer young people
părerea tot mai puținor tineri	the opinion fewer and fewer young people
țara cu cei mai puțini șomeri	the country with the least
(GD: celor mai puțini șomeri)	unemployed people

The masculine/neuter singular form can also be used as an adverb:

El mănâncă puțin.	He eats little.
o problemă puțin cunoscută	a little-known problem
cel puțin doi	at least two
cel mai puțin	least

DESTUL (adj., pron.) 'enough, quite a lot, quite many'

		Singular		Plural	
		m., n.	f.	m.	n., f.
NA		dest<u>u</u>l	dest<u>u</u>lă	dest<u>u</u>i	dest<u>u</u>le
GD		-		dest<u>u</u>lor(a)	

destulă lume	enough people
destui oameni	enough people
Destul!	Enough!
Ai făcut destule!	You have done enough!

The longer genitive and dative form ending in -*a* is used as an independent pronoun, and the shorter one as a pronominal adjective before a noun. The genitive and dative forms can also be replaced by prepositions *a* (genitive) and *la* (dative):

sprijinul destulor oameni	the support of enough people
= sprijinul a destui oameni	
sprijinul destulora	
= sprijinul a destui	

If, in the plural GD, the pronoun *destul* is preceded by a demonstrative pronoun or a demonstrative article, *destul* is declined like an adjective (GD *destul, destule, destui, destule*):

acestor destui oameni	to these enough many peoply

The masculine/neuter singular form can also be used as an adverb:

A mâncat destul.	He/She has eaten enough.

CÂTVA (adj., pron.) 'some, couple of'

	Singular		Plural	
	m., n.	f.	m.	n., f.
NA	câtva	câtăva	câțiva	câteva
GD	-	-	câtorva	

The pronoun *câtva* can be used both as an independent pronoun and a pronominal adjective. When it is used adjectivally, it precedes the noun it modifies:

câțiva dintre noi	some of us
acum câtva timp	some time ago
după câtăva vreme	after some time
câțiva ani	a couple of years
câteva luni	a couple of months
câteva considerații	some considerations
la câțiva metri	at the distance of a few metres
opinia câtorva membri	the opinion of some members
de-a lungul câtorva luni	during some months

The missing singular genitive and dative forms are replaced by the prepositions *a* (genitive) and *la* (dative). The plural genitive and dative form can also be replaced by these prepositions:

câtorva = la câțiva, la câteva	to some people
câtorva studenți	to a couple of students
= la câțiva studenți	

If, in the plural GD, the pronoun *câtva* is preceded by a demonstrative pronoun or a demonstrative article, *câtva* is declined like an adjective (GD *câtva, câteva, câțiva, câteva*):

acestor câțiva oameni   to these few people

ATÂT(A) (adj.) and ATÂTA (pron.) 'so much, so many'

	Singular		Plural		Singular		Plural	
	m., n.	f.	m.	n., f.	m., n.	f.	m.	n., f.
NA	atât(a)	atâta	atâți(a)	atâtea	atâta	atâta	atâția	atâtea
GD	-		atâtor		-		atâtora	

Even when used as a pronominal adjective, the longer form is usually used in the nominative and accusative. In the genitive and dative only the shorter form can be used as an adjective:

atât(a) zgomot	so much noise
atât(a) timp	so much time
atâta energie	so much energy
atâți(a) ani	so many years
atâtea femei	so many women
de atâtea ori	so many times
de-a lungul atâtor ani	during so many years
prezența atâtor lideri străini	the presence of so many foreign
(*Cotidianul*)	leaders
→ prezența atâtora	the presence of so many

The missing singular genitive and dative forms are replaced by the prepositions *a* (genitive) and *la* (dative). The plural genitive and dative form can also be replaced by these prepositions:

atâtora = la atâți(a), la atâtea	to so many
atâtor studenți	to so many students
= la atâți(a) studenți	

As an adverb the shorter form *atât* is normally used, but the longer form *atâta* is also possible:

Am mâncat atât(a).   I ate so much.

However, in the following three structures the shorter form must be used:

atât eu, cât și tu	both me and you
atât de frumos	so beautiful
cu atât mai frumos	so much more beautiful

ORICÂT (adj., pron.) 'no matter how much, no matter how many'

	Singular		Plural	
	m., n.	f.	m.	n., f.
NA	oricât	oricâtă	oricâți	oricâte
GD	-		oricâtor(a)	

In the plural genitive and dative the longer form *oricâtora* is used as an independent pronoun and the shorter form *oricât* as an adjective pronoun. The adjective pronoun *oricât* always precedes the noun:

oricât timp	no matter how long
oricâtă apă	no matter how much water
oricâte stele	no matter how many stars
oricâtor persoane → oricâtora	to no matter how many people

The missing singular genitive and dative forms are replaced by the prepositions *a* (genitive) and *la* (dative). The plural genitive and dative form can also be replaced by these prepositions:

oricâtora = la oricâți, la oricâte	to no matter how many
oricâtor studenți	to no matter how many students
= la oricâți studenți	

In non-standard speech this pronoun also has the form *orișicât*.

NIȘTE (adj.) 'some'

The adjective pronoun *niște* is only used in the nominative and accusative singular before a mass noun. It expresses an unspecified quantity:

Am băut niște vin.	I drank some wine.
Am cumpărat niște pește.	I bought some fish.

In the plural the indefinite article with the same form is used (see p. 71-).

NISCAI(VA) (adj.) 'some'

The pronouns *niscai* and *niscaiva* are non-standard and they are used only as adjectives:

niscaiva întrebări	some questions
niscaiva apă	some water

In standard language the form *niște* is used, which in the singular is an indefinite pronoun (see p. 192) and in the plural an indefinite article (see p. 71).

Negative indefinite pronouns and adjectives

The negative indefinite pronouns are *nimeni* 'nobody', *nimic* 'nothing' and *niciun(ul)* 'not any'.

When a negative pronoun functions as a subject or as a complement of a verb (direct or indirect object, prepositional complement), the verb must always be in the negative form (*nu, ne-, fără*).

NIMENI (pron.) 'nobody'

	Singular
NA	nimeni
GD	nimănui

The pronoun *nimeni* can only be used independently and it always refers to humans. Grammatically, it is always masculine singular.

Nimeni nu este perfect.	Nobody is perfect.
N-am făcut rău nimănui.	I have not hurt anyone.
Nimănui nu îi place cartea mea.	No-one likes my book.
Nu a venit nimeni.	Nobody came.
N-am vorbit cu nimeni.	I have not talked with anyone.
Nimeni altul n-o poate face.	No-one else can do it.
nevenind nimeni	because/if no-one comes
fără să vină nimeni	without anyone coming

When used as a direct object, *nimeni* is always preceded by the preposition *pe* (see p. 287). However, the redundant object pronoun cannot be used (see p. 292):

Nu cunosc pe nimeni.   I do not know anybody.

Colloquially, this pronoun also has the meaning 'a meaningless person':

Ești (un) nimeni!   You are a nobody!

Colloquially, the dative form can be replaced with *la nimeni*. There are also the colloquial forms *nimenea*, GD *nimănuia*.

NIMIC (pron.) 'nothing'

The pronoun *nimic* can only be used independently. It is indeclinable and can be used only in the nominative or accusative. It refers to inanimate things and is grammatically always neuter singular.

Nimic n-a fost făcut.	Nothing was done.
Nu vreau nimic.	I do not want anything.
Nimic nou sub soare.	Nothing new under the sun.
totul sau nimic	all or nothing
nefăcând nimic	doing nothing
fără să fac nimic	without doing anything
Nu m-a întrebat nimeni nimic. (*EVZ*)	No-one asked me anything.
Nu vrem să impunem nimic, nimănui. (*Cotidianul*)	We do not want to impose anything to anyone.

Colloquially, this pronoun also has the form *nimica*.

NICIUN (adj.), NICIUNUL (pron.) 'no, none'

	Singular		Plural	Singular		Plural	
	m., n.	f.		m., n.	f.	m.	n., f.
NA	niciun	nicio	-	niciunul	niciuna	niciunii	niciunele
GD	niciunui	niciunei	niciunor	niciunuia	niciuneia	niciunora	

Previously, *niciun(ul)* was written as two words: *nici un(ul)*, but now it is spelled as one word. *Niciun(ul)* is declined as *un(ul)* (see p. 175). The shorter forms are used adjectivally before a noun and the longer forms as independent pronouns. The adjective genitive and dative forms can also be pronounced as *niciunui, niciunei*. The adjectival form does not have nominative-accusative plural forms.

Niciun(ul) can refer to both humans and inanimate things:

Nu are nicio dovadă.	He/She has no proof.
Nu are niciun efect.	It has no effect.
Nu atingeți niciunul din aceste cabluri.	Touch none of these cables. Do not touch any of these cables.
Nu este candidatul niciunui partid.	He is not a candidate of any party.
nefăcând niciun compromis	by making no compromise
fără să fac niciun compromis	without making any compromise

Nu mai vreau să dau votul meu
niciunuia dintre candidați. (*EVZ*)

I do not want anymore to give my
vote to any of the candidates.

Departamentul de Stat nu a luat
nicio decizie asupra niciunei
inițiative precise. (*Cotidianul*)

The U.S. State Department has
made no decisions on any precise
initiatives.

The independent pronoun *niciunul* referring to a human or an animal used as
a direct object is preceded by the preposition *pe* (see p. 287). However, the redundant object pronoun cannot be used (see p. 292):

N-am cunosc pe niciunul dintre ei.   I know none of them.

The pronoun *niciun(ul)* must not be confused with the conjunction *nici* and
the pronoun *unul, una*, the numeral *un(u), una/o* or the indefinite article *un, o*.
These are written as two separate words:

nici unul, nici altul   neither one
N-am nici o pisică, nici două.   I do not have one cat, or two.

Prepositions

In Romanian, prepositions require a noun or a preposition in the accusative, genitive or dative case.

Prepositions requiring the accusative case

Most Romanian prepositions require a noun or a pronoun in the accusative case. The stressed forms of personal and reflexive pronouns are used (*mine, tine, el, sine* etc.).

After a preposition the indefinite article can be used, but the definite article is normally omitted (except with the prepositions *cu* and *de-a*). Compare:

după + un dulap → după un dulap	behind a cupboard
după + dulapul → după dulap	behind the cupboard

The definite form can only be used if the noun has some other modifier, like an adjective, a genitive attribute, a relative clause or a preposition phrase:

în dulapul mare	in the big cupboard
în dulapul lui Radu	in Radu's cupboard
în dulapul care este acolo	in the cupboard that is over there
în dulapul din bucătărie	in the kitchen cupboard

Some nouns referring to relatives can be used in the definite form with a possessive meaning (see p. 155):

la bunica	at *my* grandmother's

The definite forms of proper nouns ending in *-a, -ia, -ea* are also used after prepositions. The definite form is also used if it is part of the name:

cu Maria	with Maria
în Finlanda	in Finland
pentru Cotidianul	for *Cotidianul* (newspaper)
la Steaua	in *Steaua* (football team)

Similarly: *despre dracul/Domnul* 'about the Devil/the Lord'.

Notice also that some pronouns and numerals always include the article, even after a preposition:

pe altul / alții	the other, the others
pe unul / unii	the one, the ones
pe primul / ultimul	the first, the last

The pronouns requiring the accusative case are:

ÎN   *in, into, to*

în România	in Romania, to Romania
în Cluj	in/to Cluj
în centru	in/to the centre
în centrul orașului	in/to the city centre
în patru zile	in four days
în fiecare zi	every day
în iunie	in June
în 1995	in 1995
Venim în / pe 5 ianuarie.	We will come on January 5th.

In front of the indefinite article, the pronoun *însul* and adverbs beginning with a vowel the form *într-* (from *întru*) is used:

într-o casă	in/to a house
într-un restaurant	in/to a restaurant
într-acolo	to that direction

In front of the genitive article, the numeral *unul/una* and pronouns and adjectives beginning with a vowel both forms can be used:

în al meu / intr-al meu	in/to mine
în altul / într-altul	in/to the other one

The form *întru* occurs in some set phrases like:

întru totul	fully
intru cât	somewhat

DIN   *from*

din România	from Romania
din Cluj	from Cluj
din ianuarie	from January
din nou	again
din întâmplare	by chance

In front of the indefinite article, the pronoun *însul* and adverbs beginning with a vowel the form *dintr-* (from *dintru*) is used:

dintr-o casă	from a house
dintr-însul	in it

In front of the genitive article, the numeral *unul/una* and pronouns and adjectives beginning with a vowel both forms can be used.

LA   *at, to*

la teatru	at/to the theatre
la Teatrul Ion Creangă	at/to the Ion Creangă theatre
la şcoală	at/to school
la ţară	in/to the country
la vară	next summer
la ora 10	at 10 o'clock
la / pe / în 1 ianuarie	on January 1st
S-a născut la 5 ianuarie 1848[75].	He/she was born on January 5th 1848.
la stânga / la dreapta[76]	on/to the left / on/to the right
la uşă	at/to the door
la tine	at/to your place
la telefon	on the phone
la doctor	at/to the doctor's
la revedere!	See you!
cinci la sută	5%
la 23 de ani	at the age of 23

With city names *la* is more frequent than *în*[77]:

la Bucureşti ~ în Bucureşti	in / to Bucharest

This preposition is also used in certain cases (e.g. with numerals) to replace the missing dative forms:

la trei studenţi	to three students

Colloquially, *la* also has the meaning 'a lot of':

Are la bani.	He/she has loads of money.

DE LA   *from*

de la teatru	from the theatre
de la Helsinki	from Helsinki
De la Pământ la Lună (*Jules Verne*)	From the Earth to the Moon
de la începutul lui ianuarie	from the beginning of January
de la / de pe / din 1 ianuarie	from the January 1st
de la 5 (până) la 10 martie	March 5th – 10th

---

[75] In historical dates the preposition *la* is usually used. However, the practice varies greatly.

[76] Notice the definite form: *stânga = mâna stângă* 'left hand', *dreapta = mâna dreaptă* 'right hand'.

[77] In principle, the preposition *în* is used when the speaker is in the same city. However, the use of *la* has become more frequent in this case as well.

CĂTRE   towards

trenul către București	the train to Bucharest
către cititori	to the readers
către ora trei	at three-ish

DE CĂTRE agent of an action in a passive sentence (see p. also p. 267):

Cinci medici acuzați de discriminare de către organizațiile seropozitivilor. (*Adevărul*)	Five doctors accused of discrimination by the AIDS organisations.

CU   with

After this preposition, both the indefinite and definite article can be used:

cu un prieten	with a friend
cu prietenul	with the friend
cu mine	with me
cu 2 milioane de dolari	with two million dollars
un pahar cu apă	a glass of water
cu mulți ani în urmă	many years ago
cu doi ani mai mare	two years older

In colloquial style *cu un* can be also spelled *c-un*: *c-un prieten*.

When the noun expresses an instrument, the definite form is used:

un desen cu creionul	a pencil drawing
o călătorie cu trenul	a train trip
pedeapsa cu moartea	the death penalty

However, with mass nouns and abstract nouns the definite article is not used:

spălarea cu săpun	washing with soap
cu grijă	with care

The article is also not used in phrases expressing accumulation or reciprocity:

pas cu pas	step by step

The preposition *cu* can also be used after the conjunction *și*:

tu și cu mine = tu și eu	you and I

FĂRĂ   without

fără tine	without you
fără viză	without a visa

Este opt făra cinci.	It's 5 to 8.
o crimă fără precedent	a crime without precedent

The final -*ă* can be elided in colloquial style:

patru făr-sfert	quarter to four

DE   *De* is used to combine nouns. It can often be translated by *of*:

pastă de dinți	toothpaste
un pahar de apă	a water glass, a glass of water
un inel de aur	a gold ring
un manual de limba română	a manual of Romanian language

The preposition *de* is often used to add an adverb or another prepositional phrase to a noun or pronoun:

un actor de la Teatrul Național	an actor of the National Theatre
câinele de sub masă	the dog under the table
cartea de pe masă	the book on the table
ziarul de azi	today's paper
lecția de ieri	yesterday's lesson
cursul de la ora 10	the course held at 10 o'clock
Franța de peste mări	Overseas territories of France
reduceri de până la 70 %	discounts up to 70%

In this case *de* + *în(-)* → *din(-)*:

hainele din dulap	the clothes in the cupboard
industria forestieră din Finlanda	the forestry industry of Finland
timpul dinainte revoluției	the time before the revolution
gradina dinapoia casei	the garden behind the house
trenul dinspre România	the train to Romania

The preposition *de* is also used after nouns denoting amount, and also after some numerals (see p. 129):

un litru de apă	one litre of water
un kilogram de aur	one kilogram of gold
25 de cărți	25 books

The preposition *de* also expresses material:

Inelul este de aur.	The ring is made of gold.

De also expresses the agent of an action in a passive sentence (see also p. 267):

făcut de mine	made by me

The preposition *de* is also used to form the supine (see p. 264) and adverbial numerals (see p. 138).

DESPRE about

a vorbi despre ceva	to talk about something
Totul despre sex	all about sex, "Sex in the City" (TV)
nimic despre politică	nothing about politics

DUPĂ behind, after, according to

după dulap	behind the cupboard
după gratii	behind bars
după război	after the war
după lege	according to the law
după mine	in my opinion
bunica după mama (coll.)	grandma on my mother's side

The final *-ă* can be elided in colloquial style:

dup-o oră	after an hour, an hour later

The preposition *după* also has the meaning '(to go) after something':

merge după cumpărături	to go shopping
Polițistul fuge după hoț.	The policeman runs after the thief.
nostalgia după comunism	nostalgia for communism

DE DUPĂ from behind

de după colț	from behind the corner

ÎNTRE between

între dulap și perete	between the cupboard and the wall
între prieteni	between friends
între 3 și 5 kg	3 – 5 kg
între iunie și iulie	in June - July

DINTRE from (a group)

Peste 32% dintre români	over 32% of Romanians
Unul dintre motoarele avionului a luat foc.	One of the motors of the airplane caught fire.
unul dintre cele mai frumoase orașe din România	one of the most beautiful cities in Romania.

PRINTRE among

Cultiva marijuana printre roșii și salată. (*Adevărul*)	He was growing marijuana among tomatoes and salad.
printre altele	among other things
un trădător printre noi	a traitor in our midst

LÂNGĂ   beside, next to

Lângă casă este un pom.   There is a tree next to the house.
lângă tine   by your side

The final -*ă* can be elided in colloquial style:

lâng-un parc   next to the park

DE LÂNGĂ from the side of

Vine de lângă Cluj.   He/she is from around Cluj.
De ce ai plecat de lângă mine?   Why did you leave my side?

PÂNĂ   until. *Până* can be used only before an adverb or another preposition.

până aici   until here
până acum   until now
până luni   until Monday
până la martie   until Mars
până la Cluj   until Cluj

PE   on

pe masă   on the table
pe stradă   on the street
pe perete   on the wall
pe Internet   on the Internet
pe prima pagină   on the front page
a merge   pe jos   to go on foot
un spațiu de 5 pe 5 metri   a space of 5 m x 5 m

o dată pe săptămână   once a week
Suntem pe / în 5 ianuarie.   It is January 5th.
pe noapte   at night

The preposition *pe* is also used in some cases to mark the direct object (see p. 287).

Pe can also be added to some other prepositions or adverbs to express approximation:

a trece pe sub pomi   to walk under the trees
pe la nord   towards the north
pe la noi   at our house
pe la amiază   around midday
pe după casă   somewhere behind the house
Am trecut pe lângă casa ta.   I went past your house.
pe de altă parte   on the other hand
Pe unde ești?   Where are you?

In this case *pe + în, între → prin, printre:*

prin ianuarie	(sometimes) in January
prin oraş	around the city
o plimbare prin Cluj	a walk around Cluj
printre nori	among the clouds

DE PE from top of

de pe masă	from the table

PENTRU for

Aceste flori sunt pentru tine.	These flowers are for you.
L-a făcut pentru mine.	He/She did it for me.
tratament pentru această boală	treatment for this disease
vândut pentru 2 milioane	sold for two million
arestat pentru luare de mită	arrested for taking bribes
pentru că	because

PESTE above, over, across

peste noi	over us
peste tot	everywhere
peste pod	over the bridge
teritoriul de peste Nistru	the territory on the other side of the river Nistru
peste 800.000 de euro	over 800.000 euros
peste două milioane de şomeri	over two million unemployed persons
A durat peste 5 ore.	It lasted over five hours.
Va deveni mamă peste trei luni.	She will be a mother in 3 months.
peste noapte	overnight

PRIN through

a privi prin geam	to watch through the window
prin ochi de copil	through children's eyes
prin e-mail	by e-mail

In front of the indefinite article, the pronoun *însul* and adverbs beginning with a vowel the form *printr-* (from *printru*) is used:

printr-un parc	through a park

In front of the genitive article, the numeral *unul/una* and pronouns and adjectives beginning with a vowel both forms can be used.

SPRE towards

spre staţie	towards the station
spre Universitate	towards the university
trenul spre Iaşi	the train towards Iaşi
drumul spre succes	the road to success

| | noaptea spre miercuri | the night between Tuesday and Wednesday |
| | are spre 30 ani | he/she is under 30 |

ÎNSPRE   in the direction of

| | înspre Cluj | towards Cluj |

DINSPRE from the direction of

| | dinspre nord | from the north |
| | bunica dinspre mama | grandmother on the mother's side |

SUB   under

| | sub masă | under the table |
| | sub influența alcoolului | under the influence of alcohol |

DE SUB   from under

| | de sub masă | from under the table |

A   *A* is used before the infinitive (see p. 255):

| | a face | to do |
| | a cânta | to sing |

The preposition *a* is also used in certain cases (e.g. with numerals) to replace missing genitive forms:

| | prinderea a trei hoți | the capture of three thieves |

A is also used in expressions 'to look/smell etc. like':

| | miroase a primăvară | it smells like spring |
| | seamănă a bărbat | he/she looks like a man |

DE-A   This preposition is only used in some fixed expressions. The noun must be in the definite from:

	Copiii se joacă de-a pompierii. (*realitatea.net*)	The children are playing firemen.
	jocul de-a șoarecele și pisica	cat-and-mouse game
	de-a surda	in vain
	de-a dreptul	downright
	de-a binelea	fully, entirely

Prepositions are often added to adverbs and nouns to form new prepositions. These include:

în afară de   apart from

| | în afară de mine | apart from me |

alături de	next to, alongside, beside	
	alături de tine	next to you
aproape de	near	
	Oxfordul este aproape de Londra.	Oxford is near London.
în comparație cu	compared with	
	în comparație cu mine	compared with me
în curs de	in the course of	
	în curs de 5 zile	in five days
	în curs de apariție	about to be published
	țările în curs de dezvoltare	the developing countries
departe de	long way from	
	Bucureștiul este departe de Londra.	Bucharest is a long way from London.
	Criza financiară, departe de sfârșit (*Adevărul*)	The financial crisis is far from ending
dincolo de	on the other side	
	dincolo de nori	on the other side of the clouds
de dincolo de	from the other side	
	de dincolo de moarte	from beyond the grave
față de	towards, against	
	atitudine pozitivă față de sex (*Cotidianul*)	positive attitude towards sex
	Euro s-a apreciat față de dolar. (*Cotidianul*)	The euro strengthened against the dollar.
	Margaret Atwood protestează față de cenzura din Dubai. (*Cotidianul*)	Margaret Atwood is protesting against the censorship in Dubai.
înainte de	before	
	înainte de plecare	before leaving
	cu două luni înainte de naștere	two months before the birth
în loc de	instead of	
	În loc de carne am cumpărat pește.	Instead of meat I bought fish.
relativ la	related to	
	un document relativ la transport	a document on transport

în timp de	during

în timp de război	during the war

în urmă cu	ago

în urmă cu 5 minute = cu 5 minute în urmă	five minutes ago

vizavi de	opposite

vizavi de biserică	opposite the church

Prepositions requiring the genitive case

Unlike with prepositions requiring the accusative, the indefinite and definite forms can be used after prepositions requiring the genitive case:

în fața unei case	in front of a house
în fața casei	in front of the house

Formally, these prepositions are in the definite form (they end in -*a*, -*ul*/-*le*). The genitive article (see p. 92) must be used when needed:

în fața casei și *a* pomului	in front of the house and the tree

The genitive forms of personal pronouns are replaced with the possessive pronouns, which agree with the gender and number of the noun forming the preposition:

împotriva ta, împotriva noastră	against you, against us
în spatele tău, în spatele nostru	behind you, behind us

When these prepositions are used before a numeral or a pronoun not having a genitive from, the preposition *a* is added:

în spatele *a* doi prieteni	behind two friends
în spatele *a* ceva	behind something

Prepositions requiring the genitive case include:

asupra	on

comentarii asupra unui articol	comments on an article
violența asupra femeii	violence against women

deasupra	over

deasupra casei	over the house

dedesubtul	under

dedesubtul mesei	under the table

împotriva, contra   against

lupta împotriva terorismului	fight against terrorism
contra Guvernului	against the government
România va juca împotriva Spaniei.	Romania will play against Spain.
împotriva mea, contra mea	against me
împotriva a doi colegi	against two colleagues

However, in the meaning 'in exchange for something' the accusative case is used with *contra*:

contra un cost de 10 lei	against the payment of 10 lei
contra cost	for a fee

The accusative case is also used in some expressions:

fiu contra tată	son against father

înaintea   in front of, before

înaintea mea	in front of me, before me
înaintea casei	in front of the house
înaintea războiului	before the war

dinaintea   from in front of

înapoia, îndărătul behind

înapoia mea, îndărătul meu	behind me

dinapoia, dindărătul from behind

înăuntrul   inside

înăuntrul casei	inside the house

dinăuntrul   from inside

împrejurul   around

împrejurul bisericii	around the church

dimprejurul   from around

The genitive is also used after longer prepositional phrases formed with nouns. These include:

în fața   in front of ; compared with

omul din fața Mariei	the man in front of Maria
în fața bibliotecii	in front of the library
în fața a ceva	in front of something

În faţa yenului, euro s-a depreciat cu 0,1%. (*Cotidianul*)	The euro weakened 0.1% against the yen.
în faţa legii	before the law
în faţa ta	in front of you

din faţa   from the front of

din faţa clădirii	from the front of the building

în spatele   behind

Ion este în spatele lui Radu	Ion is behind Radu.
în spatele meu	behind me

din spatele   from behind

din spatele clădirii	from behind the building

în centrul   in the centre of

în centrul galaxiei	in the centre of the galaxy
în centrul atenţiei	at the centre of attention

din centrul   from the centre of

în mijlocul   in the middle of

în mijlocul străzii	in the middle of the street
în mijlocul naturii	in the midst of nature
în mijlocul lunii ianuarie	in the middle of January

din mijlocul   from the middle of

în jurul   around

în jurul oraşului	around the city
în jurul orei 15.00	around three o'clock
în jurul lumii	around the world
în jurul tău	around you

din jurul   from around

în dreapta, în stânga on/to the right, on/to the left

în stânga mea	on/to my left side
în dreapta drumului	on/to the right side of the street

din dreapta, din stânga from the right, from the left

în favoarea   in favour of

o sentinţă în favoarea prizonierului	a judgement in favour of the prisoner

în defavoarea	in disfavour of

> Mercedes a ales Polona în defavoarea României (*Curierul Național*)

> Mercedes chose Poland instead of Romania.

în numele	in the name of

> Vorbesc în numele colegilor.

> I am speaking in the name of my colleagues.

în vremea	in time of

> în vremea noastră

> in our time

în timpul	during

> în timpul cursului
> în timpul războiului rece

> during the course
> during the cold war

> Militar mort în timpul unui exercițiu (*Adevărul*)

> A soldier killed during an exercise

de-a lungul	during, along

> de-a lungul veacurilor
> de-a lungul anului
> de-a lungul carierei sale
> de-a lungul râului

> during the centuries
> during the year
> during his/her career
> along the river

din cauza	because of

> Trenuri întârziate din cauza unui accident (*EuropaFM*)

> Trains late because of an accident

în urma	after, according to

> în urma exploziei
> în urma investigațiilor

> after the explosion
> according to the investigations

în ciuda	despite

> în ciuda caniculei
> în ciuda problemelor financiare

> despite the heat
> despite the financial problems

Prepositions requiring the dative case

Just as with prepositions requiring the genitive case, the indefinite and definite forms of nouns can be used after a preposition requiring the dative case:

> grație unui prieten
> grație prietenului

> thanks to a friend
> thanks to the friend

There are only a few prepositions that require the use of the dative case:

datorită, grație, mulțumită   owing to, thanks to

grație ajutorului	thanks to the help
datorită acestui contract	owing to this contract
mulțumită ție	thanks to you

Apart from these prepositions there are some adverbs requiring the dative:

contrar   contrary to

contrar așteptărilor	contrary to expectations

conform, potrivit   according to

conform estimărilor	according to the estimations
potrivit cotidianului	according to the daily paper
potrivit ție	according to you
potrivit studiului	according to the study

However, when modifying a noun, the adjectives *contrar, conform* and *potrivit* are used instead:

o hotărâre contrară legii	a decision contrary to the law

If a preposition requiring the dative case is used before a numeral or a pronoun without a dative form, the preposition *a* is added (and not *la*, as is usually done in dative):

grație a doi colegi	thanks to two colleagues
datorită a ceea ce ai făcut	thanks to what you have done
contrar a ceva	contrary to something

Verbs

Romanian verbs are conjugated in mood, tense, person and number. There are five finite moods: indicative, conjunctive, conditional, presumptive and imperative. The number of tenses varies in each mood. There are three persons: first, second and third, and two numbers: singular and plural. The nominal forms are four: infinitive, participle, gerund and supine.

Conjugations

Romanian verbs are traditionally divided into four conjugations according to the ending of the infinite form:

I	II	III	IV
-A	-EA	-E	-I, -Î

The fourth conjugation is further divided into two groups: those ending in -*i* and those ending in -*î*.

The verbs in the first and fourth conjugations are also divided into two subgroups (called *a* and *b* in this grammar) according to whether the long or short personal endings are used in the indicative and conjunctive present. This difference must be learnt individually with every verb, and therefore the form of the present first person singular is usually given in dictionaries. About 65% of the verbs in the first conjugation and about 90% of those in the fourth conjugation belong to the subgroup *b*.

For the regular conjugations of verbs the following verbs are used as examples in this book:

Ia:	jura	*to swear*
Ib:	lucra	*to work*
II:	vedea	*to see*
III:	face	*to do*
IVa:	fugi	*to run, to flee*
IVb:	citi	*to read*
IVa (-î):	coborî	*to take down*
IVb (-î):	hotărî	*to decide*

The conjugation models for different conjugations can be found in the appendix 2 (see p. 320).

According to the dictionary *Dicționar invers al limbii române*, most Romanian verbs belong to the first conjugation (ca. 4700 verbs). Only 27 verbs belong to the second conjugations, and 294 to the third. The fourth conjugation has 2118 verbs. There are only 34 verbs ending in -î.

According to grammatical tradition, there are only a few irregular nouns:

- auxiliary verbs *fi* 'to be', *avea* 'to have', *vrea* 'to want'
- verbs *bea* 'to drink', *da* 'to give', *la* 'to wash (non-standard)', *lua* 'to take', *mânca* 'to eat', *sta* 'to stand', *usca* 'to dry'.

For the conjugation of these verbs see appendix 3, p. 350.

However, the very frequent consonant and vowel changes in the stems make the Romanian conjugation system quite complicated. The consonant changes are usually regular (see p. 35), but the vowel changes must be learnt individually.

Personal forms

The Romanian verbs are conjugated in three persons, both in singular and plural (I, you (sg.), he/she/it, we, you (pl.), they):

sunt	suntem	I am	we are
ești	sunteți	you are (sg.)	you are (pl.)
este	sunt	he/she/it is	they are

For details of subject–predicate agreement, see p. 284.

Unipersonal verbs

In Romanian there are some unipersonal verbs that can only be used in the third person, usually in the singular but sometimes also in the plural. These include verbs referring to natural phenomena:

Plouă.	It is raining.
Ninge.	It is snowing.

Because of their meaning, some nouns cannot have a human as a subject, and therefore they are used only in the third person (singular and plural):

oua	to lay eggs
măcăi	to quack

Some other verbs and structures occur only in the third person as well, e.g.:

Mă cheamă[78] Ion.	My name is Ion.
Trebuiau[79] să plece.	They had to go.
Ce înseamnă asta?	What does this mean?
Nu-mi pasă!	I do not care!
Ce s-a întâmplat?	What has happened?

Negative forms

Negative forms are usually formed by placing *nu* before the verb and possible auxiliary verbs:

nu sunt (present)	I am not
nu am fost (perf.)	I have not been
nu voi fi (fut.)	I will not be

Only the imperative second person singular has different verb forms for the affirmative and the negative:

lucrează!	work!
nu lucra!	do not work!

In the infinitive, the conjunctive, and in certain forms of the presumptive the negative adverb *nu* is placed after *a* and *să*:

a nu fi	to not be
să nu fiu	I am not
să nu fi fiind	I might not be
să nu fi fost	I might have not been

With future forms formed with the conjunctive, the negative adverb is placed before the auxiliary verb:

nu am să fiu (fut.)	I will not be
= nu o să fiu (fut.)	

Before a verb starting with an *a* the form *n-* can be used. This is done especially before the verb *avea*:

N-am fost niciodată în România.	I have never been to Romania.
N-ajunge (*Voltaj*)	It is not enough.

N- can also occur before future forms starting with *o*:

N-o să jur.	I will not swear.

The negative adverb *nu* can also be attached to verbs starting with *î*:

Nu-nțeleg. = Nu înțeleg.	I do not understand.

---

[78] Compare with the reflexive verb *a se numi: mă numesc.*
[79] For the use of *trebui* see p. 357.

Between the negative adverb and the verb, it is only possible to place an un-stressed personal or reflexive pronoun or one of the adverbs *mai, tot, cam, și, prea* (see p. 274). Otherwise, the negative adverb *nu* cannot be separated from the verb:

Nu-l mai iubesc.   I do not love him anymore.

The negative forms of the participle and gerund are formed with the prefix *ne-* (see p. 258 and p. 261):

nefăcut   not done
nefăcând   by not doing

In Romanian the negative form is used after verbs and structures meaning fear (*a-i fi frică / teamă, a se teme*), when one fears something that might possibly happen:

România se teme să *nu* lase   Romania fears that Moldova
Moldova fără români.   will be (because of emigration)
(*Cotidianul*)   left without Romanians.

Și mie mi-e frică să *nu* mă   Even I am afraid to be arrested.
aresteze. (*Cotidianul*)

Compare with a fact:

Una din șase fete se teme să   One of six girls is afraid to go
meargă acasă. (*Cotidianul*)   home.

Auxiliary verbs and compound verb forms

Some Romanian tenses and moods are formed as compound verb forms using the auxiliary verbs *avea, vrea* and *fi*. When used as auxiliary verbs, these verbs are often conjugated irregularly.

Between the auxiliary verb and the main verb it is only possible to place one of the adverbs *mai, tot, cam, și, prea* (see p. 274). Otherwise, the auxiliary verb cannot be separated from the main verb.

For more details on the word order of the verbal structure, see the appendix 6 (p. 367).

Indicative mood

The indicative mood has eight different tenses in Romanian:

- present
- imperfect
- perfect
- simple perfect
- pluperfect
- future
- future perfect
- past future

The present, imperfect, simple perfect and pluperfect are formed with suffixes, the others are compound forms.

Present indicative

The regular conjugation models for the present indicative are:

	1st p. sg.	2nd p. sg.	3rd p. sg.	1st p. pl.	2nd p. pl.	3rd p. pl.
Ia: -A	jur-	jur-i	jur-ă	jur-ăm	jur-ați	jur-ă
Ib: -A	lucr-ez	lucr-ezi	lucr-ează	lucr-ăm	lucr-ați	lucr-ează
II: -EA	văd-	vez-i	ved-e	ved-em	ved-eți	văd-
III: -E	fac-	fac-i	fac-e	fac-em	fac-eți	fac-
IVa: -I	fug-	fug-i	fug-e	fug-im	fug-iți	fug-
IVb: -I	cit-esc	cit-ești	cit-ește	cit-im	cit-iți	cit-esc
IVa: -Î	cobor-	cobor-i	coboar-ă	cobor-âm	cobor-âți	coboar-ă
IVb: -Î	hotăr-ăsc	hotăr-ăști	hotăr-ăște	hotăr-âm	hotăr-âți	hotăr-ăsc

Conjugation Ia

The regular personal endings of the first conjugations are -, -i, -ă, ăm, -ați, -ă:

	1st p. sg.	2nd p. sg.	3rd p. sg.	1st p. pl.	2nd p. pl.	3rd p. pl.
jura	jur-	jur-i	jur-ă	jur-ăm	jur-ați	jur-ă

Thus the third person singular and third person plural forms are identical. The first person singular has no ending at all.

The stress is usually on the last syllable of the stem. Only in the first and second person plural is the stress always on the ending.

In some longer verbs the stress in the singular and in the third person plural is on the penultimate syllable of the stem. However, the plural endings -*ăm* and -*aţi* are always stressed, e.g.:

termina:	țermin, țermini, țermină	*to finish*
	terminắm, terminaţi, țermină	

To this group belong e.g. the verbs ending in –*fica,* such as *falsifica* 'to falsify', *clasifica* 'to classify', *modifica* 'to modify' etc.

The following verbs have irregular personal endings:

- Verbs which have a stem ending in a consonant + *l/r* have the ending -*u* in the first person singular, e.g.:

intra:	intru, intri, intră,	*to come in*
	intrăm, intraţi, intră	

Similarly conjugated are e.g. *afla* 'to find out', *consacra* 'to dedicate', *contempla* 'to contemplate', *sufla* 'to blow', *umbla* 'to walk', *umfla* 'to fill', *urla* 'to roar'.

- The verb *continua* is conjugated as follows:[80]:

continua [-uˈʷa]:	contịnui, contịnui, contịnuă,	*to continue*
	[-uị, -uị, -uʷə]	
	continuắm, continuaţi, contịnuă	
	[-uʷəm, -uʷatsʲ, -uʷə]	

- Verbs ending in a vowel + -*ia* have no ending in the second person singular. In the third person singular and plural as well as the first person plural the vowel *ă* of the ending is changed into *e*[81]. E.g.:

încuia [-uˈja]:	încụi, încụi, încụie,	*to lock*
	[-uị, -uị, -uje]	
	încuiẹm, încuiaţi, încụie	
	[-uˈjem, -uˈjatsʲ, -uje]	

In this group belong e.g. the verbs *descuia* 'to unlock', *încheia* 'to close', *descheia* 'to open'.

---

[80] The normative form for the first person singular used to be *continuu.* In 2007 (DOOM²) the normative form was changed to *continui.* However, DEX (2009) gives both forms.
[81] Because there is no diphthong [jə] in Romanian.

- Verbs ending in a consonant + *-ia* have the ending *ii* [-ii̯] in the first and second person singular. In the third person singular and plural as well as the first person plural the vowel *ă* of the ending is changed into *e*. E.g.:

întârzia [-iʲi̯a]:	întârzii, întârzii, întârzie	to be late
	[-ii̯, -ii̯, -i̯ʲe]	
	întârzie̯m, întârzia̯ți, întârzie	
	[-iʲi̯em, iʲi̯atsʲ, -i̯ʲe]	

This group includes e.g. *a se apropia* 'to come closer', *infuria* 'to infuriate'.

- The verb *deochea*[82] has irregular endings:

| deochea | deochi, deochi, deoache, | to cast an evil eye |
| | deochem, deocheați, deoache | |

Consonant changes of the first conjugation

The regular consonant changes occur only in the second person singular:

d	→ z
t	→ ț
s	→ ș
st, sc, șc	→ șt
[k]	→ [t͡ʃ]
[g]	→ [d͡ʒʲ]

These changes occur in every verb in this conjugation that ends in *-da, -ta, -sa, -sta, -sca* or *–șca*, e.g.:

$d \to z$	uda:	ud, uzi, udă, udăm, udați, udă	to wet
$t \to ț$	ajuta:	ajut, ajuți, ajută, ajutăm, ajutați, ajută	to help
$s \to ș$	lăsa:	las, lași, lasă, lăsăm, lăsați, lasă	to leave
$st \to șt$	asista:	asist, asiști, asistă, asistăm, asistați, asistă	to assist
$sc \to șt$	risca:	risc, riști, riscă, riscăm, riscați, riscă	to risk
$șc \to șt$	mișca:	mișc, miști, mișcă, mișcăm, mișcați, mișcă	to move

Notice that the consonants [k] and [g] change into [t͡ʃ] and [d͡ʒʲ], but the spelling does not change (both sounds are spelled with 'c' and 'g'), e.g.:

| pleca: | plec, pleci, pleacă, plecăm, plecați, pleacă | to leave |

---

[82] This verb belongs to the first conjugation, and not to the second, like most verbs in *-ea*.

ruga:	rog, rogi, roagă,	*to pray*
	rugăm, rugați, roagă	

The consonant change *str → ștr* occurs only in the verb *mustra* 'to reprimand':

mustra:	mustru, muștri, mustră	*to reprimand*
	mustrăm, mustrați, mustră	

Vowel changes of the first conjugation

In the first conjugation, vowel changes are very frequent. Since these changes are not regular, they must be learnt individually with every verb.

The vowel changes can occur both in the stressed syllable and in the following syllable. Since the regular consonant changes also occur in these verbs, some verbs may have three different sound changes!

A. Verbs with the stress on the last syllable of the stem in the singular and in the third person plural

In these verbs the vowel changes occur only in the stressed syllables. Thus the first and second person plural are always regular, i. e. they have the same vowel as the infinitive.

	Inf.	1st p. sg.	2nd p. sg.	3rd p. sg.	1st p. pl.	2nd p. pl.	3rd p. pl.
1.	întreba	întreb	întrebi	întreabă	întrebăm	întrebați	întreabă
2.	ierta	iert	ierți	iartă	iertăm	iertați	iartă
3.	așeza	așez	așezi	așază	așezăm	așezați	așază
4.	prezenta	prezint	prezinți	prezintă	prezentăm	prezentați	prezintă
5.	lăsa	las	lași	lasă	lăsăm	lăsați	lasă
6.	arăta	arăt	arăți	arată	arătăm	arătați	arată
7.	spăla	spăl	speli	spală	spălăm	spălați	spală
8.	înota	înot	înoți	înoată	înotăm	înotați	înoată
9.	juca	joc	joci	joacă	jucăm	jucați	joacă

1. 'to ask'. Change *e → ea* in the third person singular and plural. Similarly conjugated verbs include:[83] *alerga* 'to run', *apleca* 'to bend, to incline', *aștepta (tu aștepți)* 'to wait', *boteza* 'to baptise', *certa (tu cerți)* 'to quarrel', *chema* 'to call', *cuteza* 'to dare', *delega* 'to delegate', *deseca* 'to dry', *deștepta (tu deștepți)* 'to wake up', *dezgheța* 'to melt', *dezlega* 'to untie', *freca* 'to rub', *încerca* 'to try', *îneca* 'to drown', *îngheța* 'to freeze', *însemna*[84] 'to

---

[83] For more detailed lists of verbs see appendix 2 (p. 320).
[84] In the meaning 'to write down' this is conjugated according to the conjugation Ib (-ez).

mean', *lega*[85] 'to tie', *nega* 'to deny', *pleca* 'to leave', *râncheza* 'to neigh', *rechema* 'to call back', *renega* 'to disown, to deny' and *seca* 'to dry'.

2. 'to forgive'. Change *ie* → *ia* in the third person singular and plural. Similarly: *dezmierda* (*tu dezmierzi*) 'to caress' and *zbiera* 'to roar, to yell'.

3. 'to seat'. Change *e* → *a* in the third person singular and plural after ș. Similarly: *deșela* 'to work to death', *înșela* 'to deceive' and *reașeza* 'to put sth. back'.

4. 'to present'. Change *e* → *i* when stressed. Similarly: *reprezenta* 'to represent'.

5. 'to leave'. Change *ă* → *a* when stressed. Similarly: *băga* 'to put in', *călca* 'to step on', *căra* 'to carry', *căsca* (*tu caști*) 'to open (mouth)', *descălța* 'to take off one's shoes', *descărca* 'to unload', *dezbrăca* 'to undress', *îmbrăca* 'to dress', *împăca* 'to reconcile', *înălța* 'to raise', *încălca* 'to invade, to infringe', *încălța* 'to put on one's shoes', *încărca* 'to load', *îngrășa* 'to fatten', *lătra* (*eu latru*) 'to bark', *păpa* 'to peck, to eat', *prăda* (*tu prazi*) 'to rob', *răbda* (*tu rabzi*) 'to endure', *sălta* (*tu salți*) 'to jump', *săpa* 'to dig', *scălda* (*tu scalzi*) 'to bathe', *scăpa* 'to escape' and *tăia* (a verb ending in -ia: tai, tai, taie, tăiem, tăiați, taie) 'to cut'.

6. 'to show'. Chang *ă* → *a* only in the third person of the singular and plural. Similarly: *adăpa* 'to give sth. to drink', *agăța* 'to hang' and *crăpa* 'to split'.

7. 'to wash'. Change *ă* → *ă, e, a, ă, ă, a*. There is always a labial consonant (*p, b, f, v*) before the vowel. Similarly: *apăsa* (*tu apeși*) 'to push', *dezvăța* 'to get out of a habit', *făta* 'to cub, to calve', *îmbăta* (*tu îmbeți*) 'to make someone drunk', *înfășa* 'to swaddle', *înfăța* 'to change the sheets', *învăța* 'to learn, to teach', *răsfăța* 'to pamper, to spoil' and *vărsa* (*tu verși*) 'to pour'.

8. 'to swim'. Change *o* → *oa* in the third person singular and plural. Similarly: *convoca* 'to summon', *dezghioca* 'to husk', *dezgropa* 'to dig up, to exhume', *deznoda* (*tu deznozi*) 'to unknot', *împroșca* (*tu împroști*) 'to splash, to spatter', *îngropa* 'to bury', *îngroșa* 'to make thick', *înnoda* (*tu înnozi*) 'to knot', *provoca* 'to provoke', *toca* 'to hack, to knock' and the verbs in -oia (with the personal endings -oi, -oi, -oaie, -oiem, -oiați, -oaie) *încovoia* 'to bend', *înfoia* 'to swell'.

9. 'to play'. Change *u* → *o, o, oa, u, u, oa*. Similarly: *desfășura* 'to unfold', *împresura* 'to encircle', *înfășura* 'to wrap', *însura* 'to marry', *măsura* 'to measure', *purta* (*tu porți*) 'to carry', *răsturna* 'to overturn', *ruga* 'to beg, to pray', *scula* 'to wake up', *turna*[86] 'to pour', *zbura* 'to fly' and the verbs in -uia-(with the personal endings -oi, -oi, -oaie, -uiem, uiați, -oaie) *despuia* 'to strip', *înmuia* 'to soak', *muia* 'to wet' .

---

[85] In the meaning 'to leave in a will' this is conjugated according to the conjugation Ib (-*ez*).
[86] In the meaning 'to shoot a film' this is conjugated according to the conjugation Ib (-*ez*).

B. Verbs with the stress on the penultimate syllable of the stem in the singular and in the third person plural

B1.Vowel change only in the stressed syllable of the stem

The following verb types have a vowel change only in the stressed syllable:

	Inf.	1st p. sg.	2nd p. sg.	3rd p. sg.	1st p. pl.	2nd p. pl.	3rd p. pl.
1.	căuta	caut	cauţi	caută	căutăm	căutaţi	caută
2.	fermeca	farmec	farmeci	farmecă	fermecăm	fermecaţi	farmecă
3.	mieuna	miaun	miauni	miaună	mieunăm	mieunaţi	miaună
4.	scheuna	scheaun	scheauni	scheaună	scheunăm	scheunaţi	scheaună
5.	rezema	reazem	rezemi	reazemă	rezemăm	rezemaţi	reazemă
6.	forfeca	foarfec	foarfeci	foarfecă	forfecăm	forfecaţi	foarfecă

1. 'to search'. Change *ă* → *a*. Similarly: *adăuga* 'to add', *căţăra* 'to climb', *clătina* 'to shake', *descăleca* 'to dismount a horse', *încăleca* 'to mount a horse', *lăuda* (*tu lauzi*) 'to praise', *măcina* 'to grind, to mill', *sătura* 'to satisfy' and *scărpina* 'to scrach'.

2. 'to enchant'. Change *e* → *a* when stressed.

3. 'to miaou'. Change *ie* → *ia* when stressed.

4. 'to yelp'. Change *e* → *ea*. Similarly: *fremăta* (*tu freamăţi*) 'to rustle' and *zgrepţăna* 'to scratch (non-standard)'.

5. 'to lean'. Change *e* → *ea* when stressed, except in the second person singular.

6. 'to cut with scissors'. Change *o* → *oa* when stressed.

B2. Vowel changes (also) in the last, unstressed, syllable of the stem

These verbs have a vowel change in the last syllable of the stem. Some of these verbs also have a vowel change in the stressed syllable.

	Inf.	1st p. sg.	2nd p. sg.	3rd p. sg.	1st p. pl.	2nd p. pl.	3rd p. pl.
1.	cumpăra	cumpăr	cumperi	cumpără	cumpărăm	cumpăraţi	cumpără
2.	scăpăra	scapăr	scaperi	scapără	scăpărăm	scăpăraţi	scapără
3.	semăna	semăn	semeni	seamănă	semănăm	semănaţi	seamănă
4.	pieptăna	pieptăn	piepteni	piaptănă	pieptănăm	pieptănaţi	piaptănă
5.	şchiopăta	şchiopăt	şchiopeţi	şchioapătă	şchiopătăm	şchiopătaţi	şchioapătă
6.	enumera	enumăr	enumeri	enumără	enumerăm	enumeraţi	enumără

1. 'to buy'. Vowel change *ă* → *e* in an unstressed syllable in the second person singular. Similarly conjugated verbs are: *apăra* 'to defend', *astâmpăra* 'to calm down', *curăţa* 'to clean', *numără* 'to count', *răscumpăra* 'to redeem' and *supăra* 'to irritate'.

2. 'to sparkle'. Vowel change *ă* → *e* in the unstressed syllable and *ă* → *a* in the stressed. Similarly conjugated verbs are: *căpăta* (*tu capeţi*) 'to receive, to acquire', *dărăpăna* 'to go to ruin', *scăpăta* (*tu scapeţi*) 'to decline' and *scărmăna* 'to card (wool)'.

3. 'to sow'. Vowel change *ă* → *e* in the unstressed syllable and *e* → *ea* in the stressed. Similarly conjugated verbs are: *a se asemăna* 'to resemble', *depăna* 'to reel up', *legăna* 'to swing', *lepăda* (*tu lepezi*) 'to throw away' and *trepăda* (*tu trepezi*) 'to trot'.

4. 'to comb'. Vowel change *ă* → *e* in the unstressed syllable and *ie* → *ia* in the stressed.

5. 'to limp'. Vowel change *ă* → *e* in the unstressed syllable and *o* → *oa* when stressed. Can also be conjugated according to the conjugation Ib: *şchiopătez* etc.

6. 'to enumerate'. Vowel change *e* → *ă* in the unstressed syllable only in the first person singular.

Conjugation Ib

In this group the stress is always on the ending. The regular personal endings are *-ez, -ezi, -ează, -ăm, -aţi, -ează*:

	1st p. sg.	2nd p. sg.	3rd p. sg.	1st p. pl.	2nd p. pl.	3rd p. pl.
lucra	lucr-ez	lucr-ezi	lucr-ează	lucr-ăm	lucr-aţi	lucr-ează

However, after *i* and *che/ghe* the endings are slightly different:

-IA: studia [-iʲa]:   studiez, studiezi, studiază,   *to study*
                        [-iʲez, -iʲezʲ, -iʲazə]
                        studiem, studiaţi, studiază
                        [-iʲem, -iʲatsʲ, -iʲazə]

-CHEA: urechea [-'kʲa]   urechez, urechezi, urechează,   *to pull one's ear*
                         [-'kʲez, -'kʲezʲ, -'kʲazə]
                         urechem, urecheaţi, urechează
                         [-'kʲem, -'kʲatsʲ, -'kʲazə]

-GHEA: veghea [-'gʲa]:   veghez, veghezi, veghează,   *to be awake*
                         [-'gʲez, -'gʲezʲ, -'gʲazə]   *to oversee*
                         veghem, vegheaţi, veghează
                         [-'gʲem, -'gʲatsʲ, -'gʲazə]

If the verb stem ends in *c* or *g*, an *h* is added before an *e* so that the pronunciation does *not* change, e.g.:

-CA: parca: parchez, parchezi, parchează,   *to park*
                parcăm, parcaţi, parchează

-GA: dialoga: dialoghez, dialoghezi, dialoghează,   *to have a*
                                dialogăm, dialogați, dialoghează   *dialogue*

The conjugation Ib also includes some verbs which have a stem ending in the vowel *e* (and thus the infinitive ends in *-ea* [e.'a]. These verbs must not be confused with the second conjugation, which has the infinitive ending *-ea* [ea]. Such verbs include: *agrea* 'to like', *crea* 'to create', *procrea* 'to procreate', *recrea* 'to recreate', *grea* 'to rig (a ship)', *suplea* 'to substitute'. These verbs are conjugated completely regularly:

crea: creez, creezi, creează,   *to create*
                    creăm, creați, creează

Some verbs can be conjugated according to both the conjugation I and Ib, e.g.:

inventa: inventez ~ invent   to invent
anticipa: anticip ~ anticipez   to anticipate

Some verbs have a different meaning in the two conjugation types, e.g.:

acorda: acord   to grant, to give
acorda: acordez   to tune (an instrument)

însemna: înseamnă (3. p.)   to mean
însemna: însemnez   to write down

manifesta: manifest   to show, to manifest
manifesta: manifestez   to demonstrate an opinion (by a
                            rally or march)

ordona: ordon   to command
ordona: ordonez   to put in order, to arrange

turna: torn   to pour
turna: turnez   to shoot (a film)

Conjugation II

Regular personal endings in the second conjugation are -, *-i*, *-e*, *-em*, *-eți*, -. The first person singular and the third person plural are identical. The stress is on the last syllable of the stem, except in the first and second person plural, where the stress is on the ending.

All the verbs in this conjugation have one of the following sound changes:

	Inf.	1st p. sg.	2nd p. sg.	3rd p. sg.	1st p. pl.	2nd p. pl.	3rd p. pl.
1.	părea	par	pari	pare	părem	păreți	par
2.	tăcea	tac	taci	tace	tăcem	tăceți	tac

	Inf.	1st p. sg.	2nd p. sg.	3rd p. sg.	1st p. pl.	2nd p. pl.	3rd p. pl.
3.	cădea	cad	cazi	cade	cădem	cădeți	cad
4.	putea	pot	poți	poate	putem	puteți	pot
5.	durea			doare			dor
6.	şedea	şed	şezi	şade	şedem	şedeți	şed
7.	vedea	văd	vezi	vede	vedem	vedeți	văd

1. 'to show, to seem'. Change ă → a when stressed. Similarly: *apărea* 'appear', *compărea* 'to appear before a judge', *dispărea* 'disappear', *reapărea* 'reappear', *redispărea* 'to disappear again' and *transpărea* 'to be transparent (rare)' and *încăpea* 'to fit in'.

2. 'to be silent, to shut up'. Change ă → a when stressed and change [t͡ʃ] → [k] in the first person singular and the third person plural (spelled always as 'c'). Similarly: *plăcea* 'to please', *complăcea* 'to please', *displăcea* 'to be displeasing' and *zăcea* 'to lie (down)'.

3. 'to fall'. Change ă → a when stressed and change d → z in the second person singular. Similarly conjugated are *decădea* 'to decay' and *scădea* 'to decline'.

4. 'can, to be able to'. Vowel change u → o, o, oa and consonant change t → ț in second person singular.

5. 'to hurt'. Vowel change as in the previous type. Other persons may occur in poetical language.

6. 'to sit'. Vowel change e → a in the third person singular.

7. 'to see'. Vowel change e → ă in the first person singular and the third person plural. Consonant change d → z in second person singular. The derivations of this verb are conjugated similarly (*întrevedea* 'to envision', *prevedea* 'to foresee', *revedea* 'to see again; to review' and *străvedea* 'see through (rare)').

The non-standard verb *mânea* 'to spend the night' has other irregularities:

mânea:	mân/mâi, mâi, mâne,	to spend the night
	mânem, mâneți, mân	(non-standard)

Conjugation III

The regular personal endings in the third conjugation are -, -*i*, -*e*, -*em*, -*eți*, - :

	1st p. sg.	2nd p. sg.	3rd p. sg.	1st p. pl.	2nd p. pl.	3rd p. pl.
face	fac-	fac-i	fac-e	fac-em	fac-eți	fac-

Just as in the second conjugation, the first person singular and the third person plural are identical. However, in this conjugation the stress always falls on the last syllable of the stem, even in the first and second person plural.

Most of the sound changes in this conjugation follow these rules:

- The vowel *o* in the stem changes to *oa,* when the ending begins with an *e* (this also happens in the infinitive!).
- The consonants *d, s* and *t* change to *z, ş, ţ* in the second person singular.
- The consonant group *sc* changes to *şt,* when the ending begins with an *e* or *i* (this also happens in the infinitive!)
- The consonants *c* [k] and *g* [g] change into [ʧ] and [ʤ], when the ending begins with an *e* or *i* (this also happens in the infinitive!). However, this does not effect the spelling (always 'c' and 'g').

Thus, the regular sound changes in the third conjugation are:

oa	→ o, o, oa	oa, oa, o
d	→ d, z, d	d, d, d
t	→ t, ţ, t	t, t, t
s	→ s, ş, s	s, s, s
şt	→ sc, şt, şt	şt, şt, sc
[ʧ]	→ [k, ʧ, ʧ]	ʧ, ʧ, k]
[ʤ]	→ [g, ʤ, ʤ]	ʤ, ʤ, g]

E.g.:

d → z	crede:	cred, crezi, crede, credem, credeţi, cred	*to believe*
t → ţ	admite:	admit, admiţi, admite, admitem, admiteţi, admit	*to admit*
s → ş	ţese	ţes, ţeşi, ţese, ţesem, ţeseţi, ţes	*to weave*
şt → sc	naşte	nasc, naşti, naşte, naştem, naşteţi, nasc	*to give birth*
[ʧ]→[k]	face	fac, faci, face, facem, faceţi, fac	*to do*
[ʤ]→[g]	merge	merg, mergi, merge, mergem, mergeţi, merg	*to go*

Some verbs have both a consonant and a vowel change, e.g.:

roade:	rod, rozi, roade, roadem, roadeţi, rod	*to gnaw*
cunoaşte:	cunosc, cunoşti, cunoaşte, cunoaştem, cunoaşteţi, cunosc	*to know*
coase:	cos, coşi, coase, coasem, coaseţi, cos	*to sew*
toarce:	torc, torci, toarce, toarcem, toarceţi, torc	*to spin*

The consonant *n* in the verbs *pune*, *rămâne* and *ține* disappears in the second person singular:

pune:	pun, pui, pune,	*to put*
	punem, puneți, pun	
rămâne:	rămân, rămâi, rămâne,	*to remain*
	rămânem, rămâneți, rămân	
ține	țin, ții, ține, ținem, țineți, țin	*to hold*

The verbs *scrie* and *umple* have the irregular ending -*u* in the first person singular and in the third person plural:

scrie:	scriu, scrii, scrie,	*to write*
	scriem, scrieți, scriu	
umple:	umplu, umpli, umple,	*to fill*
	umplem, umpleți, umplu	

The verb *vinde* has a vowel change *i* → *â* in the first person singular and in the third person plural:

vinde:	vând, vinzi, vinde,	*to sell*
	vindem, vindeți, vând	

The derivations of these verbs are conjugated similarly.

Conjugation IVa (-i)

The regular personal endings in this conjugation are -, -*i*, -*e*, -*im*, -*iți*, -:

	1st p. sg.	2nd p. sg.	3rd p. sg.	1st p. pl.	2nd p. pl.	3rd p. pl.
fugi	fug-	fug-i	fug-e	fug-im	fug-iți	fug-

The first person singular and the third person plural are identical. In the singular and in the third person plural, the stress is usually on the last syllable of the stem, in some cases on the penultimate syllable of the stem. The first and second person plural endings are always stressed.

Sound changes of the fourth conjugation

The regular sound changes in the fourth conjugation are:

- The vowel *o* changes to *oa* in the third person singular (because the ending begins with an *e*).
- The vowel *ă* changes to *a* when stressed.
- The consonants *d, s* and *t* change to *z, ș, ț* before an *i* (this happens also in the infinitive!)

• The consonant *g* [g] changes into [ʤʲ] before an *i* (this also happens in the infinitive!)[87]. However, this does not effect the spelling (always 'g').

Thus the sound changes in the fourth conjugation are:

o	→ o, o, oa	o, o, o
ă	→ a, a, a	ă, ă, a
ţ	→ t, ţ, t	ţ, ţ, t
ş	→ s, ş, s	ş, ş, s
z	→ d, z, d	z, z, d
[ʤʲ]	→ [g, ʤʲ, ʤʲ	ʤʲ, ʤʲ, g]

E.g.:

o → oa	dormi:	dorm, dormi, doarme, dormim, dormiţi, dorm	*to sleep*
ă → a	sări:	sar, sari, sare, sărim, săriţi, sar	*to jump*
ţ → t	minţi:	mint, minţi, minte, minţim, minţiţi, mint	*to tell a lie*
ş → s	ieşi:	ies, ieşi, iese, ieşim, ieşiţi, ies	*to leave*
z → d	auzi:	aud, auzi, aude, auzim, auziţi, aud	*to hear*
ă → a, ţ → t	împărţi:	împart, împarţi, împarte, împărţim, împărţiţi, împart	*to divide*
[ʤʲ] → [g]	fugi:	fug, fugi, fuge, fugim, fugiţi, fug	*to run, to flee*

However, the -ă and -e verbs (see p. 227 and 228) do not usually have any vowel changes.

The verb *mirosi* has a consonant change only in the second person singular (but not in the infinitive):

mirosi:	miros, miroşi, miroase, mirosim, mirosiţi, miros	*to smell*

The verb *muri* has the sound change *u → o, oa*:

muri:	mor, mori, moare, murim, muriţi, mor	*to die*

The verb *veni* has the sound change *e → i*. The consonant *n* disappears in the second person singular:

veni:	vin, vii, vine, venim, veniţi, vin	*to come*

The derivations of this verb are conjugated similarly.

---

[87] There is no verbs ending in [ʧ] in this conjugation.

Verbs with a stem ending in a vowel

The verbs with a stem ending in a vowel have an *i* in all forms. In the third person singular and plural the ending is -*ie*, e.g.:

sui [-uʲi̯]:	sui, sui, suie, [-ui̯, -ui̯, -uje] suim , suiți, suie [-uʲim, -uʲitsʲ, '-uje]	*to climb up*

These verbs have the word stress on the penultimate syllable of the steam in the singular and in the third person plural, e.g.:

distribui̯:	distribui, distribui, distribuie, distribuim, distribuiți, distribuie	*to distribute*

However, the verbs *îndoi* 'to bend', *dezdoi* 'to straighten' and *jupui* 'to skin' are stressed on the last syllable of the stem. The first two also have the sound change *o → oa*:

îndoi̯:	îndoi, îndoi, îndoaie, îndoim, îndoiți, îndoaie	*to bend, to fold*

The verb *jupui* has the sound change *u → o, oa*:

jupui̯:	jupoi, jupoi, jupoaie, jupuim, jupuiți, jupoaie	*to skin, to bark*

-Ă verbs of the fourth conjugation

A few verbs in the fourth conjugation have the ending -*ă* in the third person singular and plural. These verbs include:

- The verbs *oferi* 'to offer', *conferi* 'to confer', *deferi* 'to submit to a court', *diferi* 'to differ', *referi* 'to report' and *absolvi* 'to acquit, to absolve; to finish one's studies':

oferi:	ofer, oferi, oferă, oferim, oferiți, oferă	*to offer*
absolvi:	absolv, absolvi, absolvă, absolvim, absolviți, absolvă	*to acquit, to absolve*

- The verbs *înăbuși* 'to suffocate' and *sprijini* 'to support', which have the word stress on the penultimate syllable of the steam in the singular and in the third person plural:

înăbuși:	înăbuș, înăbuși, înăbușă, înăbușim, înăbușiți, înăbușă	*to suffocate*
sprijini:	sprijin, sprijini, sprijină, sprijinim, sprijiniți, sprijină	*to support*

- The verbs *acoperi* 'to cover', *descoperi* 'to discover' and *suferi* 'to suffer'. These verbs have a vowel change in the first person singular. The stress is on the penultimate syllable of the steam in the singular and in the third person plural:

acoperi:	acopăr, acoperi, acoperă,	*to cover*
	acoperim, acoperiți, acoperă	

-E verbs of the fourth conjugation

Apart from the verbs with a vowel stem, some verbs with a consonant stem also have the third person singular and plural ending *-e*. These verbs have the word stress on the penultimate syllable of the steam in the singular and in the third person plural. Most of these verbs can also be conjugated according to the conjugation IVb.

Most of these verbs end in *-ăni*, e.g. *ciocăni* (usually *-esc*) 'to hammer, to knock', *clănțăni* (usually *-esc*) 'to clanc', *cloncăni* (or *-esc*) 'to chuck', *măcăni* 'to quack', *țăcăni* (or *-esc*) 'to rattle':

ciocăni:	ciocăn, ciocăni, ciocăne,	*to knock*
	ciocănim, ciocăniți, ciocăne	
măcăni:	măcăne	*to quack*

The verb *băuni* 'to roar (dial.)' can also have a vowel change:

băuni:	băun, băuni, băune, băunim, băuniți, băune	*to roar (dial.)*
	baun, bauni, baune, băunim, băuniți, baune	

Other irregularities of the fourth conjugation

The verb *şti* has an irregular ending *-u* in the first person singular and in the third person plural:

şti:	ştiu, ştii, ştie, ştim, ştiți, ştiu	*to know*

The verb *azvârli* has an irregular ending *-ă* in the third person plural:

azvârli:	azvârl, azvârli [-i], azvârle,	*to throw*
	azvârlim, azvârliți, azvârlă	

The non-standard form of this verb *zvârli* can also be conjugated regularly (third person plural *zvârlă* or *zvârl*).

Conjugation IVb (-i)

Most of the verbs in the fourth conjugation are conjugated like this. There are no sound changes and the word stress is always on the ending. The regular endings are -*esc*, -*ești*, -*ește*, -*im*, -*iți*, -*esc*:

	1st p. sg.	2nd p. sg.	3rd p. sg.	1st p. pl.	2nd p. pl.	3rd p. pl.
citi	cit-esc	cit-ești	cit-ește	cit-im	cit-iți	cit-esc

If the verb stem ends in a vowel, an *i* is written before *e*, e.g.:

trăi [-əʲi]:	trăiesc, trăiești, trăiește, [-əˈjesk, -əˈjeʃtʲ, - əˈjeʃte] trăim, trăiți, trăiesc [-əʲim, -əʲitsʲ, -əˈjesk]	*to live*

Similarly conjugated verbs include *locui* 'to live, to dwell', *construi* 'to build, to construct' etc.

If the stem ends in *i*, only one *i* is used before *e*:

pustii [-iʲi]:	pustiesc, pustiești, pustiește, [-iʲesk, -iʲeʃtʲ, - iʲeʃte] pustiim, pustiiți, pustiesc [-iʲim, -ʲitsʲ, -iʲesk]	*to devastate*

Some verbs can be conjugated according to both the conjugations IVa and IVb. These include:

cheltui: cheltui, cheltuiesc	*to spend*
drăcui: drăcui, drăcuiesc	*to curse*
zgândări: zgândăr, zgândăresc[88]	*to irritate, to anger*

Conjugation IVa (-î)

These verbs, unlike most of the verbs of the fourth conjugation, have the same form in the third person singular and plural. The endings are -, -*i*, -*ă*, -*âm*, -*âți*, -*ă*:

	1st p. sg.	2nd p. sg.	3rd p. sg.	1st p. pl.	2nd p. pl.	3rd p. pl.
coborî	cobor-	cobor-i	coboar-ă	cobor-âm	cobor-âți	coboar-ă

The endings of the first and second person plural are always stressed, while in other persons the stress usually lies on the last syllable of the stem.

---

[88] DOOM². DEX (2009) gives only *zgândăresc*.

There are only a few verbs belonging to this conjugation. All the verbs with an *o* in the last syllable of the stem (e.g. *doborî* 'to throw down' and *omorî* 'to murder, to kill') are conjugated like *coborî*, i.e. with the sound change *o* → *oa* in the third person singular and plural.

The verb *vârî* 'to push, to shove into' is the only verb with no sound changes.

The verb *tăbărî* has the word stress on the penultimate syllable of the stem in the singular and in the third person plural. The stressed syllable has the vowel change *ă* → *a*, while the unstressed has the change *ă* → *e* in the second person singular:

tăbărî:	tabăr, taberi, tabără,	*to camp; to attack*
	tăbărâm, tăbărâți, tabără	

Conjugation IVb (-î)

The personal endings in this conjugation are *-ăsc, -ăști, -ăște, -âm, -âți, -ăsc*:

	1st p. sg.	2nd p. sg.	3rd p. sg.	1st p. pl.	2nd p. pl.	3rd p. pl.
hotorî	hotăr-ăsc	hotăr-ăști	hotăr-ăște	hotăr-âm	hotăr-âți	hotăr-ăsc

The endings are always stressed. Only a handful of verbs belongs to this group and they are all conjugated regularly, e.g. *amărî* 'to embitter', *chiorî* 'to lose one eye', *deszăvorî* 'to unbolt', *hotărî* 'to decide', *izvorî* 'to spring', *mohorî* 'to darken', *pârî* 'to sneak, to tell on', *posomorî* 'to sadden', *târî* 'to drag', *urî* 'to hate', *zădărî* 'to irritate' and *zăvorî* 'to bolt'.

Irregular verbs

The present forms of the irregular verbs are:

avea:	am, ați, are, avem, aveți, au	*to have*
bea:	beau, bei, bea, bem, beți, beau	*to drink*
da:	dau, dai, dă, dăm, dați, dau	*to give*
fi:	sunt, ești [jeſtⁱ], este ['jeste] (*unstressed:* e [je], *colloq.* -i [i̯]), suntem, sunteți, sunt[89]	*to be*
la:	lau, lai, lă, lăm, lați, lau	*to wash (non-standard)*
lua:	iau, iei, ia, luăm, luați, iau	*to take*
mânca:	mănânc, mănânci, mănâncă, mâncăm, mâncați, mănâncă	*to eat*

---

[89] Before the orthographic reform of 1993, the forms *sînt, eşti, este, sîntem, sînteți, sînt* were used. In the first and second person plural the stress could also be on the ending: *suntem, sunteți*.

sta:	stau, stai, stă, stăm, stați, stau	to stand
usca:	usuc, usuci, usucă,	to dry
	uscăm, uscați, usucă	
vrea:	vreau, vrei, vrea, vrem, vreți, vor	to want

The derivations of these verbs are conjugated similarly.

Use of the present tense

Just as in English, the present tense is used for general truths and to describe a settled state of affairs:

Marte este al patrulea corp ceresc al sistemului solar.	Mars is the fourth planet of the Solar System.
doi plus doi fac patru	2 + 2 = 4
Astăzi este ziua mea.	Today is my birthday.

The present is also used for regular or habitual actions:

Studiez limba română.	I study Romanian.
Lucrez în Londra.	I work in London.
Citesc ziarul în fiecare zi.	I read the newspaper every day.

The Romanian present is also used for taking about something that is happening right know. In English the present continuous is used:

| - Ce faci? | - What are you doing? |
| - Citesc. | - I'm reading. |

The Romanian present can also refer to the future, especially when a temporal adverb is used:

| Mâine merg la plajă. | Tomorrow I am going to the beach. |

When telling a story, the Romanian present can also be used as a historical or narrative present:

| Jurnalistul și scriitorul Jack London se naște la San Francisco, pe 12 ianuarie 1876. (*Adevărul*) | The journalist and writer Jack London was born in San Francisco on January 12th 1876. |

In subordinate sentences the Romanian present often refers to the same time as the main sentence:

| A spus că are 21 de ani. | He said he *was* 21 years old. |

For more details on the use of tenses in subordinate clauses, see p. 297.

Imperfect indicative

The imperfect tense can be formed from the infinitive: *-a, -î* → *-am; -ea, -e, -i* →
-eam. The personal endings are the same in all the conjugations: *-am, -ai, -a,*
-am, -ați, -au. The stress is always on the ending.

	1st p. sg.	2nd p. sg.	3rd p. sg.	1st p. pl.	2nd p. pl.	3rd p. pl.
Ia: -A	jur-am	jur-ai	jur-a	jur-am	jur-ați	jur-au
Ib: -A	lucr-am	lucr-ai	lucr-a	lucr-am	lucr-ați	lucr-au
II: -EA	ved-eam	ved-eai	ved-ea	ved-eam	ved-eați	ved-eau
III: -E	făc-eam	făc-eai	făc-ea	făc-eam	făc-eați	făc-eau
IVa: -I	fug-eam	fug-eai	fug-ea	fug-eam	fug-eați	fug-eau
IVb: -I	cit-eam	cit-eai	cit-ea	cit-eam	cit-eați	cit-eau
IVa: -î	cobor-am	cobor-ai	cobor-a	cobor-am	cobor-ați	cobor-au
IVb: -î	hotăr-am	hotăr-ai	hotăr-a	hotăr-am	hotăr-ați	hotăr-au

Irregular endings

In the fourth conjugation, if the stem ends in a vowel, the imperfect personal
endings are *-iam, -iai* etc. If the stem ends in *i*, only one *i* is used, e.g.:

locui [-uˈʲi]:	locuiam [-ˈjam], locuiai, locuia,	*to live*
	locuiam, locuiați, locuiau	
pustii [-iˈʲi]:	pustiam [-i.ˈjam], pustiai, pustia,	*to devastate*
	pustiam, pustiați, pustiau	

Regular sound changes

Vowel changes occur only with those verbs in the third conjugation that have
a stressed *a* or *oa* in the infinitive. Since the stress is moved to the ending,
these vowels change to *ă* and *o*, e.g.:

a → *ă*	bate:	băteam	*to hit*
	face:	făceam	*to do*
oa → *o*	cunoaște:	cunoșteam	*to know*
	coase:	coseam	*to sew*

Exception: the verb *arde* 'burn' does not change: *ardeam, ardeai,* etc.

No consonant changes occur in the imperfect tense, not even in the fourth
conjugation: *auzi* 'to hear' → *auzeam, minți* 'to tell a lie' → *mințeam*.

Irregular verbs

The following verbs have an irregular stem in the imperfect:

şti :	ştiam, ştiai, ştia,	*to know*
	[ʃtiˈʲam, ʃtiˈʲaị, ʃtiˈʲa]	
	ştiam, ştiaţi, ştiau	
	[ʃtiˈʲam, ʃtiˈʲatsʲ, ʃtiˈʲaụ]	
scrie:	scriam, scriai, scria,	*to write*
	[skriˈʲam, skriˈʲaị skriˈʲa]	
	scriam, scriaţi, scriau	
	[skriˈʲam, skriˈʲatsʲ, skriˈʲaụ]	
fi:	eram, erai, era, eram, eraţi, erau	*to be*
	[jeˈram, jeˈraj, jeˈra, jeˈram, jeˈratsʲ, jeˈraụ]	
da:	dădeam, dădeai, dădea,	*to give*
	dădeam, dădeaţi, dădeau	
sta:	stăteam, stăteai, stătea,	*to stand*
	stăteam, stăteaţi, stăteau	

The derivations of the verb *scrie* and the verbs *răzda* 'to give much (rare)', *reda* 'to give back, return' are conjugated similarly.

The imperfect forms of the verb *vrea* are very rare. In particular, the second person singular and the first and second person plural are almost never used. The imperfect forms are usually replaced with the verb *voi*:

voi:	voiam, voiai, voia,	*to be able, can*
	voiam, voiaţi, voiau	

Use of the imperfect tense

The imperfect tense is used for durative or repetitive actions in the past. In English, the durative action is often expressed by the imperfect continuous and the repetitive action with expressions like 'used to':

Citeam o carte.	I was reading a book.
Citeam ziarul în fiecare zi.	I used to read the newspaper every day.

In conditional clauses the imperfect has the same hypothetical meaning as the perfect conditional (see p. 304). In the language of children the imperfect tense can also be used to express imaginary roles while playing:

Eu eram poliţistul şi tu erai hoţul.	I am the policeman and you are the thief.

Perfect indicative

The perfect tense is formed by the auxiliary verb *avea* and the participle (see p. 258). In the perfect tense the participle is invariable.

	Auxiliary verb	Participle
1st p. sg.	am	
2nd p. sg.	ai	
3rd p. sg.	a	jurat, lucrat, văzut, făcut, fugit, citit, coborât, hotărât
1st p. pl.	am	
2nd p. pl	aţi	
3rd p. pl	au	

In poetical language the auxiliary verb can also be placed after the main verb. If there is an accusative or dative personal pronoun before the auxiliary verb, a vowel -u is added to the participle (*văzutu-l-am* = *l-am văzut*). However, in modern language this is extremely rare.

The difference between the Romanian perfect and imperfect forms is the same as in French, Spanish and Italian. Unlike the imperfect, the perfect describes an action that has been fully finished in the past tense and that is not repetitive.

Thus the differences between these tenses are:

Imperfect	**Perfect**
imperfective	perfective
durative	finished
repetitive	unrepeated

E.g.:

Citeam o carte.	I was reading a book. (durative, unfinished action)
Am citit o carte.	I read a book. (and finished it.)
Lunea *mergeam* la teatru.	I used to go to the theatre on Mondays (a repetitive, habitual action)
Luni *am mers* la teatru.	On Monday I went to the theatre. (one finished action)
Când *am venit* acasă, televizorul *mergea*.	When I came home (finished action), the TV was on. (durative action, the TV was on while I came home)

Locomotiva care *venea* de la
Budapesta spre Bucureşti *a luat*
foc între localităţile Floreşti
şi Câmpina. (*Adevărul*)

The train coming from Budapest
to Bucharest, caught fire
between Floreşti and Câmpina.

Simple perfect indicative

The term 'simple' means that this tense is formed with one word, and not
with two words like the normal perfect indicative.

	1st p. sg.	2nd p. sg.	3rd p. sg.	1st p. pl.	2nd p. pl.	3rd p. pl.
Ia: -A	jur-ai	jur-aşi	jur-ă	jur-arăm	jur-arăţi	jur-ară
Ib: -A	lucr-ai	lucr-aşi	lucr-ă	lucr-arăm	lucr-arăţi	lucr-ară
II: -EA	văz-ui	văz-uşi	văz-u	văz-urăm	văz-urăţi	văz-ură
III: -E	făc-ui	făc-uşi	făc-u	făc-urăm	făc-urăţi	făc-ură
IVa: -I	fug-ii	fug-işi	fug-i	fug-irăm	fug-irăţi	fug-iră
IVb: -I	cit-ii	cit-işi	cit-i	cit-irăm	cit-irăţi	cit-iră
IVa: -Î	cobor-âi	cobor-âşi	cobor-î	cobor-ârăm	cobor-ârăţi	cobor-âră
IVb: -Î	hotăr-âi	hotăr-âşi	hotăr-î	hotăr-ârăm	hotăr-ârăţi	hotăr-âră

The endings are usually regular, except in the third person singular of the
first conjugation verbs ending in a *-ia, -chea, -ghea*. The stress is usually on the
ending. The simple perfect can be formed starting from the participle (see p.
258):

1st conjugation	-at	-ai, -aşi, -ă, -arăm, -arăţi, -ară
	-iat	-iai, -iaşi, -ie, -iarăm, -iarăţi, -iară
	-cheat	-cheai, -cheaişi, -che, -chearăm, -chearăţi, -cheară
	-gheat	-gheai, -gheaişi, -ghe, -ghearăm, -ghearăţi, -gheară
2nd conjugation	-ut	-ui, -uşi, -u, -urăm, -urăţi, -ură
3rd conjugation	-ut	-ui, -uşi, -u, -urăm, -urăţi, -ură
	-s	-sei, -seşi, -se, -serăm, -serăţi, -seră
	-t	-sei, -seşi, -se, -serăm, -serăţi, -seră
4th conjugation	-it	-ii, -işi, -i, -irăm, -irăţi, -iră
	-ât	-âi, -âşi, -î, -ârăm, -ârăţi, -âră

As you can see above, some verbs of the third person use an extra syllable *-se-*
in the simple perfect. In these verbs the stress is on the ending in the first
and second person singular, while in all the other persons it is on the last syllable of the verbal stem, e.g.:

zice: zis   zisei, ziseşi, zise,   *to say*
                 ziserăm, ziserăţi, ziseră

| rupe: rupt | rupsei, rupseși, rupse, | to break |
| | rupserăm, rupserăți, rupseră | |

In the first and second person plural of these verbs the stress can also be on the -se-: *rupserăm, rupserăți*. However, the stress pattern explained above is recommended.

In the simple perfect, vowel changes occur only with verbs with the extra -se-syllable. When unstressed, the vowel *a* changes to *ă* and when stressed, the vowel *o* changes to *oa*, e.g.:

coace: copt	copsei, copseși, coapse,	to cook
	coapserăm, coapserăți, coapseră	
rade: ras	răsei, răseși, rase,	to shave
	raserăm, raserăți, raseră	
roade: ros	rosei, roseși, roase,	to gnaw
	roaserăm, roaserăți, roaseră	
rămâne: rămas	rămăsei, rămăseși, rămase,	to remain
	rămaserăm, rămaserăți, rămaseră	
toarce: tors	torsei, torseși, toarse,	to spin
	toarserăm, toarserăți, toarseră	
trage: tras	trăsei, trăseși, trase,	to pull
	traserăm, traserăți, traseră	

If, in the first and second person plural, the stress is placed on the syllable -se-, the stem vowels will be *o* and *ă*: e.g. *torserăm, torserăți, rămăserăm, rămăserăți*.

The vowel change does not occur in the verb *arde* (*arsei, arseși*, etc.) 'to burn'.

In the second conjugation, the non-standard verb *mânea: mas* 'spend the night' has the vowel change *a → ă: măsei, măseși, mase* etc.

The following verbs have an irregular simple perfect:

fi:	fui, fuși, fu,	to be
	furăm, furăți, fură	
	or	
	fusei, fuseși, fuse,	
	fuserăm, fuserăți, fuseră	
avea:	avui, avuși, avu,	to have
	avurăm, avurăți, avură	
	or	
	avusei, avuseși, avuse,	
	avuserăm, avuserăți, avuseră	
da:	dădui, dăduși, dădu,	to give
	dădurăm, dădurăți, dădură	
sta:	stătui, stătuși, stătu,	to stand
	stăturăm, stăturăți, stătură	

The verbs *răzda* 'to give much (rare)' and *reda* 'to give back, to return' are conjugated similarly.

The simple perfect is used for finished past actions, like the perfect tense. In writing, the simple perfect is mostly used in fiction as a narrative tense. In spoken language, the simple past is replaced by the perfect tense. However, in Oltenia, South-Western Romania, the simple perfect is used in speech to describe actions that happened close to the present moment, usually during the last 24 hours.

Pluperfect indicative

	1st p. sg.	2nd p. sg.	3rd p. sg.	1st p. pl.	2nd p. pl.	3rd p. pl.
Ia: -A	jur-asem	jur-aseşi	jur-ase	jur-aserăm	jur-aserăţi	jur-aseră
Ib: -A	lucr-asem	lucr-aseşi	lucr-ase	lucr-aserăm	lucr-aserăţi	lucr-aseră
II: -EA	văz-usem	văz-useşi	văz-use	văz-userăm	văz-userăţi	văz-useră
III: -E	făc-usem	făc-useşi	făc-use	făc-userăm	făc-userăţi	făc-useră
IVa: -I	fug-isem	fug-iseşi	fug-ise	fug-iserăm	fug-iserăţi	fug-iseră
IVb: -I	cit-isem	cit-iseşi	cit-ise	cit-iserăm	cit-iserăţi	cit-iseră
IVa: -î	cobor-âsem	cobor-âseşi	cobor-âse	cobor-âserăm	cobor-âserăţi	cobor-âseră
IVb: -î	hotăr-âsem	hotăr-âseşi	hotăr-âse	hotăr-âserăm	hotăr-âserăţi	hotăr-âseră

Like the simple past, the pluperfect can also be formed from the stem of the participle:

1st conjugation	-at	-asem, -aseşi, -ase, -aserăm, -aserăţi, -aseră
2nd conjugation	-ut	-usem, -useşi, -use, -userăm, -userăţi, -useră
3rd conjugation	-ut	-usem, -useşi, -use, -userăm, -userăţi, -useră
	-s	-sesem, -seseşi, -sese, -seserăm, -seserăţi, -seseră
	-t	-sesem, -seseşi, -sese, -seserăm, -seserăţi, -seseră
4th conjugation	-it	-isem, -iseşi, -ise, -iserăm, -iserăţi, -iseră
	-ât	-âsem, -âseşi, -âse, -âserăm, -âserăţi, -âseră

The third conjugation verbs that have the extra -se- syllable always have the stress on the first -se-, e.g.:

zice: zis	zisesem, ziseseşi, zisese,	*to say*
	ziseserăm, ziseserăţi, ziseseră	
rupe: rupt	rupsesem, rupseseşi, rupsese	*to brake*
	rupseserăm, rupseserăţi, rupseseră	

These verbs have the sound change a → ă in all the persons:

rade: ras	răsesem, răseseşi, răsese,	*to shave*
	răseserăm, răseserăţi, răseseră	
rămâne: rămas	rămăsesem, rămăseseşi, rămăsese	*to stay*
	rămăseserăm, rămăseserăţi, rămăseseră	

| trage: tras | trăsesem, trăseseşi, trăsese, | *to pull* |
| | trăseserăm, trăseserăţi, trăseseră | |

The non-standard verb *mânea : mas* 'to spend the night' has the same sound change: *măsesem* etc.

However, the vowel change does not occur in the verb *arde (arsesem, arseseşi,* etc.) 'to burn'.

The following verbs have irregular pluperfect forms:

fi:	fusesem, fuseseşi, fusese,	*to be*
	fuseserăm, fuseserăţi, fuseseră	
avea:	avusesem, avuseseşi, avusese,	*to have*
	avuseserăm, avuseserăţi, avuseseră	
da:	dădusem, dăduseşi, dăduse,	*to give*
	dăduserăm, dăduserăţi, dăduseră	
sta:	stătusem, stătuseşi, stătuse,	*to stand*
	stătuserăm, stătuserăţi, stătuseră	

Similarly conjugated are the verbs *răzda* 'to give much (rare)' and *reda* 'to give back'.

The pluperfect refers to something that occurred before something else that happened in the past. It can be translated with the English past perfect or past perfect continuous:

Li se stricase o maşină de îngheţată şi eu am reparat-o. (*Adevărul*)	An ice-cream machine of theirs had broken down and I fixed it.
Suspectul fusese eliberat din penitenciar pe motive medicale. (*Adevărul*)	The suspect had been released from the penitentiary on medical grounds.
Şoferul consumase băuturi alcoolice.	The driver had been consuming alcoholic beverages.

In narration the Romanian pluperfect has the implicit meaning "before the other thing happened":

| Ministerul Educaţiei hotărâse, la începutul săptămânii, să elimine singura oră de istorie la clasele a XII-a de la liceele cu profil tehnic. (*EVZ*) | At the beginning of the week, the Minister of Education had decided to remove the only history class from the 12th class of the technical secondary school. (i.e. before he cancelled the decision later that week) |
| Numărul studenţilor „rusofili" scăzuse dramatic după 1989. (*Adevărul*) | The number of students taking Russian had fallen dramatically after 1989. (i.e. before the number rose back again) |

In Romanian the pluperfect is more common in the literary language than in speech, where it is often replaced by the perfect form.

Future indicative

The future indicative can be formed in three different ways:

- The auxiliary verb *vrea* + infinitive

	Auxiliary verb	Infinitive
1st p. sg.	voi	
2nd p. sg.	vei	
3rd p. sg.	va	jura, lucra, vedea, face, fugi, citi, coborî, hotărî
1st p. pl.	vom	
2nd p. pl	veți	
3rd p. pl	vor	

The auxiliary verb *vrea* has the colloquial forms *oi, ăi (ei, îi, oi), o (a), om, ăți (eți, îți, oți), or*, which are not used in the standard language. However, they occur in fiction.

In written language (mainly in poetry) the auxiliary verb and the pronouns attached to it can be placed after the main verb (*jura-voi = voi jura, vedea-te-voi = te voi vedea*). However, in modern language this is extremely rare.

- The auxiliary verb *avea* + *să* + present conjunctive (see p. 245)

am să jur	avem să jurăm
ai să juri	aveți să jurați
are să jure	au să jure

- The auxiliary verb *o* + *să* + present conjunctive

o să jur	o să jurăm
o să juri	o să jurați
o să jure	o să jure

In the third person plural the form *or* can also be used: *or să jure.*

The first future form given here (*voi jura*) is the one that is most used in literary language, while the last one (*o să jur*) is the most colloquial.

As in English, the future is used to refer to something that is expected to happen in the future:

Mâine o să mergem la Timişoara. = avem să mergem, vom merge	Tomorrow we will go to Timişoara.
România nu va adopta euro până în anul 2015 (*Adevărul*)	Romania will not adopt the euro until 2015.
Astăzi plouă, vineri va ninge. (*EVZ*)	Today it is raining, on Friday it will be snowing.

If the main clause is in the past tense, the future used in a subordinate clause can also refer to something that has already happened (past future):

Credeam că nu vei veni.	I thought you would not come.
A spus că va veni.	He/She said he/she would come.

Notice that the colloquial form *oi jura* is also used for the present presumptive (see p. 253).

Future perfect indicative

The future perfect is formed with the auxiliary verb *vrea* + *fi* + participle (see p. 258):

	Auxiliary verbs		Participle
1st p. sg.	voi		
2nd p. sg.	vei		
3rd p. sg.	va	fi	jurat, lucrat, văzut, făcut, fugit, citit, coborât, hotărât
1st p. pl.	vom		
2nd p. pl	veţi		
3rd p. pl	vor		

The auxiliary verb *vrea* also has the colloquial forms *oi, ăi (ei, îi, oi), o (a), om, ăţi (eţi, îţi, oţi), or*. However, the future perfect form is very rarely used in colloquial speech.

The future perfect refers to something that will have happened in the future :

Când vei veni acasă, eu voi fi placat deja la plajă.	When you come home, I will have already left for the beach.

In Romanian the future perfect mainly belongs to the language of writing. In speech it is usually replaced with the perfect (*eu am plecat deja la plajă*). Notice that the same verb form is also used for the perfect presumptive (see p. 254).

Past future indicative

The past future tense is formed with the imperfect form of the auxiliary verb *avea* and the present of conjunctive:

aveam să jur	aveam să jurăm
aveai să juri	aveați să jurați
avea să jure	aveau să jure

The past future is used to describe something that was going to happen in the past:

El avea să fie primul care avea să moară. (*Ioana Scoruș*)	He was going to be / He would be the first one to die.

The imperfect form of the verb *urma* can also be used as the auxiliary verb (*urma să moară*).

In Romanian grammar books this form is usually not included as an independent tense.

Imperative mood

The imperative second person singular usually has the same form as the indicative third person singular. However, the intransitive verbs of the conjugations II, III and IVa have an imperative form identical to the indicative second person singular. The negative imperative is formed with *nu* + infinitive. The imperative second person plural is identical to the indicative form.

Thus the different regular endings for the imperative mood are:

	Ia: -A	Ib: -A	II: -EA	III: -E	IVa: -I:	IVb: -I:	IVa: -î:	IVb: -î:
2nd p. sg. affirmative	-ă	-ează	intr. -i, trans. -e		-ește		-ă	-ăște
2nd p. sg. negative	nu -a		nu -ea	nu -e	nu -i		nu -î	
2nd p. pl.	(nu) -ați		(nu) -eți	(nu) -eți	(nu) -iți		(nu) -âți	

First conjugation

In the first conjugation the imperative singular is always identical to the third person singular and thus the ending is usually *-ă* or *-ează*. In verbs with a stem ending in *i* (and *deochea*) the endings are *-e, -iază*:

cânta:	cântă!	sing!
lucra:	lucrează!	work!
întârzia:	întârzie!	be late!
studia:	studiază!	study!

This is also true with the irregular verbs:

da:	dă!	give!
la:	lă!	wash! (non-standard)
lua:	ia!	take!
mânca:	mănâncă!	eat!
usca:	usucă!	dry!

Exception: *sta: stai!* 'stay!'.

Conjugations II, III and IVa (-i)

In these conjugations the imperative form of the intransitive verbs is identical to the indicative present second person singular and thus the ending is always *-i*:

tăcea:	taci!	be quiet!
şedea:	şezi!	sit!
merge:	mergi!	go!
rămâne:	rămâi!	stay!
fugi:	fugi!	run!
dormi:	dormi!	sleep!

The transitive verbs have an imperative identical to the indicative present third person singular, and the ending is always *-e*:

cere:	cere!	ask!
bate:	bate!	hit!
scrie:	scrie!	write!
simţi:	simte!	feel!
mirosi:	miroase!	smell!

The irregular verb *bea* 'to drink' also has an imperative with the same form as the third person singular: *bea!* 'drink!'.

Since some verbs can be used both as intransitive or transitive verbs, they have two different imperative forms. These verbs include e.g. *adormi* 'to fall asleep / to put asleep', *ajunge* 'arrive/reach', *arde* 'to be on fire, to burn/to put on fire, to burn something', *creşte* 'to get bigger, to grow/to grow something', *minţi* 'to lie/to deceive', *plânge* 'to cry/to weep for someone', *scădea* 'to become smaller, to decrease/to make smaller, to decrease something', *trece* 'to pass/to cross':

adormi!	Get to sleep!
adoarme-l!	Put him to bed!
plângi!	Cry!
plânge-l!	Weep for him!
minţi!	Lie!
minţe-l!	Deceive him!

Exceptions

Even though the following verbs are transitive, they form their imperative with the ending -*i*:

avea:	ai!	*to have*	auzi:	auzi!	*to hear*
vedea:	vezi!	*to see*	şti:	ştii!	*to know*

In the fourth conjugation all the verbs that have a stem ending in a vowel, form their imperative with the ending -*e*:

sui:	suie!	climb up!
distribui:	distribuie!	distribute!

-Ă and -e verbs of the fourth conjugation

The imperatives of the -*ă* and -*e* verbs of the fourth conjugations have the same form as the third person singular of the indicative present:

oferi:	oferă!	offer!
suferi:	suferă!	suffer!
ciocăni:	ciocăne!	knock!

Conjugation IVb and the -î-verbs

The imperatives of all the -*esc* and -*î* verbs have the same form as the third person singular (endings -*eşte*, -*ă* and -*ăşte*):

citi:	citeşte!	read!
coborî:	coboară!	take down!
hotărî:	hotărăşte!	decide!

Some verbs have an alternative shorter form: *a o tuli: tuleşte-o / tule-o* 'get lost!', *ghici: ghiceşte / ghici* 'guess!'.

Irregular imperative forms

The following verbs have irregular imperative forms:

face:	fă!	do!
fi:	fii!	be!
duce:	du!	take!
pieri:	piei!	perish!
veni:	vino!	come!
zice:	zi!	say!

The derivations of these verbs are conjugated similarly. However, the verb *aduce* has the word stress on the first syllable: *ạdu!* 'bring!'.

Negative imperative

The negative second person singular is formed regularly with all verbs (*nu* + infinitive):

nu cânta!	do not sing!
nu bea!	do not drink!
nu face!	do not do!
nu vine!	do not come!
nu fugi!	do not run away!
nu fi!	do not be!

Imperative plural

The imperative second person plural is identical to the indicative form, both in the affirmative and negative forms:

cântați!	sing!
nu cântați!	do not sing!
mergeți!	go!
nu mergeți!	do not go!

The only exception is the verb *fi* 'to be':

fiți!	be!
nu fiți!	do not be!

Conjunctive mood

The conjunctive mood has only two tenses: present and perfect.

Present conjunctive

The conjunctive present differs from the present indicative only in the third person singular and plural (except the verb *fi*, which has its own conjunctive forms in every person).

The third person singular and plural forms are also always identical to each other. The stress is on the same syllable as in the indicative.

	1st p. sg.	2nd p. sg.	3rd p. sg.	1st p. pl.	2nd p. pl.	3rd p. pl.
Ia: -A	jur-	jur-i	jur-e	jur-ăm	jur-ați	jur-e
Ib: -A	lucr-ez	lucr-ezi	lucr-eze	lucr-ăm	lucr-ați	lucr-eze
2: -EA	văd-	vez-i	vad-ă	ved-em	ved-eți	vad-ă
3: -E	fac-	fac-i	fac-ă	fac-em	fac-eți	fac-ă
IVa: -I	fug-	fug-i	fug-ă	fug-im	fug-iți	fug-ă
IVb: -I	cit-esc	cit-ești	cit-ească	cit-im	cit-iți	cit-ească
IVa: -Î	cobor-	cobor-i	coboar-e	cobor-âm	cobor-âți	coboar-e
IVb: -Î	hotăr-ăsc	hotăr-ăști	hotăr-ască	hotăr-âm	hotăr-âți	hotăr-ască

If the third person singular ending of the indicative mood is *-ă*, the ending of the conjunctive third person is *-e*. This is the case in the following verb categories:

Ia-conjugation:	cânt-ă	să cânt-e	*to sing*
Ib-conjugation:	lucr-eaz-ă	să lucr-ez-e	*to work*
IVa-conjugation -ă-verbs:	ofer-ă	să ofer-e	*to offer*
IVa î-verbs:	coboar-ă	să coboar-e	*to take down*

If the indicative third person singular ends in *-e*, the conjunctive has the ending *-ă*:

II-conjugation	ved-e	să vad-ă	*to see*
III-conjugation	fac-e	să fac-ă	*to do*
IV-conjugation:	aud-e	să aud-ă	*to hear*
IVb-conjugation:	cit-eșt-e	să cit-easc-ă	*to read*
IVb î-verbs:	hotăr-ășt-e	să hotăr-asc-ă	*to decide*

Exceptions

The conjunctive third person form is identical to the indicative singular third person in the following cases:

- Those verbs of the first conjugation that have an indicative form ending in -*e* (i.e. verbs with a stem ending in *i* and the verb *deochea*), e.g.:

tăia:	taie	să taie	*to cut*
întârzia:	întârzie	să întârzie	*to be late*
deochea:	deoache	să deoache	*to cast an evil eye*

- The verbs *ploua* and *oua*[90]:

ploua:	plouă	să plouă	*to rain*
oua:	ouă	să ouă	*to lay an egg*

- The verbs *scrie* and *umple* (and their derivations):

scrie:	scrie	să scrie	*to write*
umple:	umple	să umple	*to fill*

- Fourth conjugation verbs with a stem ending in a vowel[91], e.g.:

sui:	suie	să suie	*to climb up*
contribui:	contribuie	să contribuie	*to contribute*

- The -*e*-verbs of the fourth conjugation:

ciocăni:	ciocăne	să ciocăne	*to knock*

- The verbs *şti, (a)zvârli, zgândări*[92]:

şti:	ştie	să ştie	*to know*
azvârli:	azvârle	să azvârle	*to throw*
zgândări:	zgândăre	să zgândăre	*to irritate, to anger*
	zgândăreşte	să zgândărească	

The following two verbs have the same ending in the conjunctive as in the indicative, but only the conjunctive form has a vowel change:

succeda:	succedă	să succedă	*to succeed*
preceda:	precedă	să preceadă	*to precede*

The following irregular verbs (and their derivations) have a conjunctive ending in -*ea*:

bea:	bea	să bea	*to drink*
da:	dă	să dea	*to give*

---

[90] Because the diphthong [we] does not occur in native Romanian words.
[91] Because there is no diphthong [jə] in Romanian.
[92] DOOM². DEX (2009) gives only *zgândăresc*.

sta:	stă	să stea	*to stand*
la:	lă	să lea	*to wash (non-standard)*
lua:	ia	să ia (← i + ea)	*to take*
vrea:	vrea	să vrea	*to want*

The conjunctive form of the verb *avea* is totally irregular:

avea:	are	să aibă	*to have*

The verb *trebui* has a conjunctive formed with the ending of the conjugation IVb:

trebui:	trebuie	să trebuiască	*to have to*

The verb *fi* has an irregular conjunctive in *all* the persons:

fi:	fiu, fii, fie, fim fiți, fie	*to be*

Consonant changes

Regular consonant changes occur with all verbs with stems ending in *-sc*, *-șt*, -[k], -[g], -[tʃ], -[dʒʲ].

Compared with the indicative, the ending *-e* causes the regular consonant change *sc/șc → șt, e.g.:*

risca:	riscă	să riște	*to risk*
mișca:	mișcă	să miște	*to move*

On the other hand, the ending *-ă* causes the regular consonant change *șt → sc, e.g.:*

cunoaște:	cunoaște	să cunoască	*to know*
naște:	naște	să nască	*to give birth*

This change also occurs with all verbs belonging to the conjugation IVb, e.g.:

citi:	citește	să citească	*to read*

The consonant change [k, g] ↔ [tʃ, dʒʲ] does not cause changes in spelling, since both sounds are written with 'c' and 'g', e.g.:

pleca:	pleacă	să plece	*to leave*
ruga:	roagă	să roage	*to pray*
face:	face	să facă	*to do*
merge:	merge	să meargă	*to go*

The verbs having the sound changes *n → 0* in the second person singular have a colloquial conjunctive third person form with *-ie*:

spune:	tu spui	să spuie	*to say*

The standard form is regular: *spună*.

Vowel changes

As in the indicative, vowel changes are more complicated than the consonant changes.

In the first conjugation, if the verb stem has a vowel change involving an *e* (*e* → *ea*, *ie* → *ia*, *e* → *a*, *e* → *i* , *ă* → *ă, e, a*), the conjunctive 3rd person has the same vowel(s) as the indicative 2nd person singular:

întreba:	întrebi	să întrebe	*to ask*
ierta:	ierți	să ierte	*to forgive*
aşeza:	aşezi	să aşeze	*to sit*
prezenta:	prezinți	să prezinte	*to present*
spăla:	speli	să spele	*to wash*
fermeca:	farmeci	să farmece	*to enchant*
mieuna:	miauni	să miaune	*to meow*
scheuna:	scheauni	să scheaune[93]	*to yelp*
rezema:	rezemi	să rezeme	*to lean*
cumpăra:	cumperi	să cumpere	*to buy*
scăpăra:	scaperi	să scapere	*to sparkle*
semăna:	semeni	să semene	*to sow*
pieptăna:	piepteni	să pieptene	*to comb*
şchiopăta[94]:	şchiopeți	să şchiopete	*to limp*
enumera:	enumeri	să enumere	*to enumerate*

With the other verbs the conjunctive has the same vowel as the indicative 3rd person singular (*ă* → *a, ă* → *ă, ă, a, o* → *oa, u* → *oa*):

lăsa:	lasă	să lase	*to leave*
arăta:	arată	să arate	*to show*
înota:	înoată	să înoate	*to swim*
juca:	joacă	să joace	*to play*
căuta:	caută	să caute	*to search*
forfeca:	foarfecă	să foarfece	*to cut*

Notice the difference between *spăla: să spele* and *arăta: să arate*.

In the conjugation Ib the ending is always *-eze*. The ending is added to verbs ending in *-chea/-ghea* and *-ca/-ga* the same way as in the indicative (see p. 221):

lucra:	lucrează	să lucreze	*to work*
studia:	studiază	să studieze	*to study*
urechea:	urechează	să urecheze	*to pull one's ear*
parca:	parchează	să parcheze	*to park*

---

[93] But: *zgrepţăna: să zgrepţene*.
[94] Or *-ez*: *şchiopătează, să şchiopăteze*.

The verbs of the second conjugation have the same vowel changes as in the indicative mood, except the verb *vedea* (and its derivations):

tăcea:	tace	să tacă	*to be quiet*
putea:	poate	să poată	*to be able, can*
şedea:	şade	să şadă	*to sit*
vedea:	vede	să vadă	*to see*

In the third and fourth conjugations the ending -*ă* causes the changes *e → ea, ie → ia, o → oa*, e.g.:

crede:	crede	să creadă	*to believe*
fierbe:	fierbe	să fiarbă	*to boil*
cunoaşte:	cunoaşte	să cunoască	*to know*
repezi:	repede	să repeadă	*to hurry*
ieşi:	iese	să iasă	*to go out*
dormi:	doarme	să doarmă	*to sleep*
citi:	citeşte	să citească	*to read*

The following verbs and their derivations have other vowel changes:

vinde:	vinde	să vândă	*to sell*
muri:	moare	să moară	*to die*
veni:	vine	să vină	*to come*

Perfect conjunctive

The perfect conjunctive is formed by the auxiliary verb *fi* + participle (see p. 258). This form is the same in all the different persons:

	Auxiliary verb	Participle
1st p. sg.		
2nd p. sg.		
3rd p. sg.	fi	jurat, lucrat, văzut, făcut, fugit, citit, coborât, hotărât
1st p. pl.		
2nd p. pl		
3rd p. pl		

The perfect form refers to something that has happened before the time frame of the main sentence:

Trebuia să fi zis ceva.	He/She had to have said something.
Este posibil să fi vândut produse expirate. (*Mediafax.ro*)	It is possible that expired products have been sold.

Notice that the same verb form is also used for the perfect presumptive (see p. 254).

Use of the conjunctive mood

The conjunctive mood is very frequent in Romanian - much more frequent than in other Romance languages. This is because in Romanian the infinitive form is quite rarely used and it is usually replaced with the conjunctive mood.

A verb in the conjunctive mood is usually preceded by the conjunction *să* '(so) that'. On the other hand, this conjunction is always followed by the conjunctive mood. If the verb is preceded by some word or structure that does not belong to the verbal structure[95] (e.g. a noun), the conjunction *ca ... să* must be used:

să mergem	that we will go
ca noi *să* mergem	that we will go
ca mâine *să* mergem	that we will go tomorrow

The conjunction *să* can be left out only in a few fixed expressions:

facă-se voia ta	thy will be done
ferească Dumnezeu!	God forbid!
trăiască România!	Long live Romania!
fie x = 10	let the value of x be 10

The conjunctive mood is used in a main sentence to express:

- an order or a recommendation. Thus the conjunctive can be used, for example, to replace the missing personal forms of the imperative mood:

Să mergem acasă!	Let's go home!
Să fiți cuminți!	Be nice!
să zicem	let us say
Să fie lumină!	Let there be light!

- Uncertainty or possibility in interrogative sentences:

Cât să fie ceasul?	What might the time be?
Ce să facem acum?	What can we do now?
Care să fie problema?	What might be the problem?

---

[95] That is, any other word than the negative adverb *nu*, an auxiliary verb, unstressed accusative or dative pronoun or any of the semi-adverbs *mai, tot, cam, prea, și.*

De ce să fi crezut eu altceva?! (*www.click.ro*)	Why would I have believed anything else?
Să râd sau să plâng?	Shall I laugh or cry?

The conjunctive mood is also used in many different kinds of subordinate clauses (p. 296).

Conditional mood

The conditional mood has two tenses: present and perfect.

Present conditional

The present conditional is formed with the auxiliary verb *avea* and the infinitive:

	Auxiliary verb	Infinitive
1st p. sg.	aş	
2nd p. sg.	ai	
3rd p. sg.	ar	jura, lucra, vedea, face, fugi,
1st p. pl.	am	citi, coborî, hotărî
2nd p. pl	aţi	
3rd p. pl	ar	

The auxiliary verb (and the possible unstressed personal pronouns) can also be placed after the main verb, but in modern language this is very rare. It occurs mostly in some more or less fixed structures like *Mânca-te-ar viermii!* 'May the worms eat you!'. If the auxiliary verb is not preceded by a pronoun, the long infinitive (see p. 255) can also be used: *fir-ar* (= *fire-ar*) *al naibii* 'damn!'

Perfect conditional

The perfect conditional is formed with the conditional form of the auxiliary verb *fi* and the participle (see p. 258):

	Auxiliary verbs		Participle
1st p. sg.	aș		
2nd p. sg.	ai		
3rd p. sg.	ar	fi	jurat, lucrat, văzut, făcut, fugit, citit, coborât, hotărât
1st p. pl.	am		
2nd p. pl	ați		
3rd p. pl	ar		

Notice that the same verb form is also used for the perfect presumptive (see p. 254).

Use of the conditional mood

The conditional mood is used in Romanian:

- in conditional clauses (see also p. 304):

Dacă aș avea bani, aș cumpăra o mașină.	If I had money, I would buy a car.
Dacă aș fi avut bani, aș fi cumpărat o mașină.	If I had had money, I would have bought a car.

- in hypothetical sentences:

Ar fi o surpriză plăcută.	It would be a nice surprise.
Ar fi fost o surpriză plăcută.	It would have been a nice surprise.
Ar fi putut fi evita cel de-a Doilea Război Mondial? (*Adevărul*)	Could the Second World War have been avoided?
Mâine ar fi împlinit 18 de ani.	Tomorrow he/she would have been 18 years old.

- as a contrafactual expression after *ca și cum, ca și când, (de) parcă* 'as if':

Ion se poartă ca și cum ar avea mulți bani.	Ion acts as if he had lots of money.

- to express wish or intention:

Aş vrea un pahar de apă.	I would like a glass of water.
De-ar ploua puţin!	I wish it was raining a little!
Australia ar trebui să devină republică. (*Cotidianul*)	Australia should become a republic.

- to express uncertainty:

Nu ştiu dacă ar veni.	I do not know if he is coming.
Care ar fi problema?	What might be the problem?
Sute de milioane de oameni ar putea să rămână fără internet (*Adevărul*)	Hundreds of millions could remain without internet
Pandemia de gripă porcină ar fi putut fi cauzată de un accident de laborator (*Adevărul*)	The swine flu might have been caused by a laboratory accident.

- to express a possibility, especially in exclamations and questions:

Cine ar face aşa?	Who could do so?
Cine ar fi făcut aşa?	Who could have done so?

Presumptive mood

The presumptive mood has two tenses: present and perfect.

Present presumptive

The present presumptive is formed with the future form of the auxiliary verb *fi* and the gerund (see p. 261):

	Auxiliary verbs		Participle
1st p. sg.	voi		
2nd p. sg.	vei		
3rd p. sg.	va	fi	jurând, lucrând, văzând, făcând, fugind, citind, coborând, hotărând
1st p. pl.	vom		
2nd p. pl	veţi		
3rd p. pl	vor		

The auxiliary verb *vrea* has the more colloquial forms *oi, ăi (ei, îi, oi), o (a), om, ăţi (eţi, îţi, oţi), or.*

The colloquial forms of the future (*oi jura, ăi jura, o jura,* etc., see p. 239) are also often used for the presumptive present. In addition, the standard future forms (*voi jura, vei jura, va jura,* etc.) can also be used for the presumptive, but this is rarely done.

Apart from these forms, the present presumptive can also be formed with the present conditional of the auxiliary verb *fi* and the gerund (*aş fi jurând, ai fi jurând, ar fi jurând,* etc.) or with *să fi* + gerund (*să fi jurând*), which has the same form in all persons. However, these forms are rare in the modern language.

Perfect presumptive

The perfect presumptive is formed with the auxiliary verb *vrea* + *fi* + participle (see p. 258):

	Auxiliary verbs	Participle
1st p. sg.	voi	
2nd p. sg.	vei	
3rd p. sg.	va	jurat, lucrat, văzut, făcut, fugit, citit, coborât, hotărât
1st p. pl.	vom	fi
2nd p. pl	veţi	
3rd p. pl	vor	

Thus the presumptive perfect has the same form as the indicative perfect future. The auxiliary verb *vrea* also has the more colloquial forms *oi, ăi (ei, îi, oi), o (a), om, ăţi (eţi, îţi, oţi), or.*

Apart from this form, forms identical to the perfect conditional (*aş fi jurat*) and the perfect subjunctive (*să fi jurat*) can also be used with the same meaning.

Use of the presumptive mood

The presumptive mood expresses uncertainty and possibility. It is used more frequently in colloquial speech (and in fiction) than in written language:

Unde va fi fiind Ion?	Where might Ion be?
Unde va fi fost Ion?	Where might Ion have been?

ce-o mai fi însemnând şi asta   whatever that might mean
(*Cotidianul*)

Care o fi problema? — What might be the problem?
Cât o fi ceasul? — What time might it be?

Oi fi eu stupid, dar nu sunt idiot. (*eva.ro*) — I might be stupid, but I am not an idiot.

Nominal forms

Infinitive

The Romanian infinitive is usually preceded by the preposition *a*, just like the English *to*. The Romanian infinitive has two tenses: present and perfect. The perfect tense is formed by *a + fi + participle*:

	I -A:	II -EA:	III -E	IV -I:	IV: -î
Pres.	a jura, a lucra	a vedea	a face	a fugi	a coborî, a hotărî
Perf.	a fi jurat, a fi lucrat	a fi văzut	a fi făcut	a fi fugit	a fi coborât, a fi hotărât

The ending of the third conjugation is unstressed, while all the other conjugations have stressed infinite endings. The negative form of the infinitive is formed with the adverb *nu*, which is placed after the preposition *a*:

a nu jura — to not swear
a nu-l vedea — to not see him
a fi sau a nu fi? — to be or not to be

If the whole verbal phrase is denied, the adverb *nu* is placed before the preposition *a*:

nu a scrie, ci a citi — not to write, but to read

The Romanian infinitive also has a longer form created by adding the suffix *-re* to the short infinitive:

1st conj.:	-a → -are	jura:	jurare	*to swear*
	-ia → -iere	studia:	studiere	*to study*
	-ea → -ere	veghea:	veghere	*to be awake*
2nd conj.:	-ea → -ere	vedea:	vedere	*to see*
3rd conj.:	-e → -ere	face:	facere	*to do*
4th conj.:	-i → -ire	citi:	citire	*to read*
	-î → -âre	hotărî:	hotărâre	*to decide*

The long infinitive can only be used in the formation of the conditional mood (see p. 251).

The suffix *-re* is also used for creating deverbal feminine nouns. These nouns also have the plural forms (*jurări, studieri, vegheri, vederi, faceri, citiri, hotărâri*):

construirea unei case	the construction of a house
stingerea incendiului	the extinction of the fire
Vremea este în răcire.	The weather is getting colder.
Trezirea!	Wake up!

Use of the infinitive

Because the conjunctive mood is usually used instead of the infinitive (see p. 298-), the infinite is less frequent in Romanian than in other Romance languages or in English. The infinitive can be used in Romanian:

- As a subject:

A greși este omenește.	To err is human.
Era imposibil a dormi.	It was impossible to sleep.

- As a direct object (rarely; usually the conjunctive is used):

Continuă a lucra.	He/She continues to work.
Am început a citi.	I started to read.

- As a secondary object:

M-a învățat a citi.	He/She taught me to read.

- As a predicative, with or without the preposition *de*:

Scopul este (de) a supraviețui.	The goal is to survive.

- As a prepositional compliment of a verb:

Se teme de a spune adevărul.	He/she is afraid to tell the truth.

- As a modifier of the adjectives *apt* 'suitable, able', *capabil* 'capable', *dator* 'indepted', *demn* 'worthy', *gata* 'ready', usually with the preposition *de*:

gata (de) a merge	ready to go
apt (de) a lucra	able to work

- As a modifier of a noun (or a pronoun), preceded by a preposition (usually by *de*, but other prepositions also occur):

dorința de a studia	the desire to study
dreptul de a se căsători	the right to marry
posibilitatea de a fi greșit medicul	the possibility that the doctor had made a mistake
UE are mijloacele de a pedepsi Ungaria. (*Adevărul*)	The EU has the means to punish Hungary.

Vulcanul Cleveland este pe punctul de a erupe. (*gandul.info*)	The volcano Cleveland is about to erupt.
N-am nimic de a face cu asta.	I have nothing to do with this.
Este timpul de a pleca.	It is time to go.
probleme în a învăța	learning difficulties

- After the adverbs *departe, aproape* preceded by the preposition *de*:

| A fost aproape de a muri. | He/she was close to death. |
| Criza este departe de a se termina. | The crisis is far from ending. |

- After the verb *putea*, without the preposition *a* (only the present infinitive):

| Pot vorbi românește. | I can speak Romanian. |

Unstressed personal and reflexive pronouns are added to the verb *putea*:

| Îmi poți da cartea? | Can you give the book to me? |
| (= Poți să-mi dai cartea?) | |

- After a relative pronoun or an adverb without the preposition *a* (only the present infinitive):

| N-are ce pierde. | He/She has nothing to lose. |
| N-am pe cine iubi. | I do not have anyone to love. |

- In non-finite clauses after the prepositions *până, înainte de, fără, pentru, spre, în loc de a, în afară de*:

până a începe să plouă	until it starts to rain
înainte de a pleca	before leaving
fără a spune nimic	without saying anything
pentru / spre a învăța românește	in order to learn Romanian
în loc de a face	instead of making
în afară de a face	besides making

In all the structures mentioned above, the conjunctive mood could also be used (if there is no subject, the impersonal *tu*[96] is used):

să greșești este	pot să vorbesc
continuă să lucreze	n-are ce să piardă
scopul este să supraviețuiești	până să înceapă să plouă
m-a învățat să citesc	înainte să plece
se teme să spună	fără să spună nimic
gata să meargă	pentru ca să învețe
dorința să studieze	în loc să facă
aproape să moară	în afară să facă

---

[96] See p. 268.

The present infinitive is also used in general orders, prohibitions and warnings:

A nu se fuma! No smoking!

The infinitive is also used in the formation of some verbal forms (future, conditional, negative imperative). In these cases the infinitive is never preceded by the infinitive marker *a*.

Participle

The participle can be formed from the infinitive: *-a* → *-at; -ea, -e* → *-ut; -i* → *-it; -î* → *-ât*. The word stress is on the ending.

-A: jura, lucra	-EA: vedea	-E: face	-I: fugi, citi	-Î: coborî, hotărî
jur-at, lucr-at	văz-ut	făc-ut	fug-it, cit-it	cobor-ât, hotăr-ât

The participles are declined like adjectives: *jurat, jurată, jurați, jurate*. The negative form is formed with the prefix *ne-: necântat, nevăzut*. The adverb *mai* (see p. 274) can be added after the prefix: *nemaivăzut* 'never seen'.

All the verbs of the first conjugation have a regular participle form and there are no sound changes.

In the second conjugation the verbs ending in *-dea* have the sound change *d* → *z* . The verb *vedea* has also a vowel change. E.g:

cădea:	căzut	*to fall*
şedea:	şezut	*to sit*
vedea:	văzut	*to see*

The derivations of these verbs are conjugated similarly. Notice also the sound change [tʃ] → [k] (always written as 'c'), e.g.:

tăcea:	tăcut	*to be silent*

The non-standard verb *mânea* 'to spend the night' is irregular: *mânea: mas*.

In the third conjugations the following regular sound changes occur: *a* → *ă*, *oa* → *o, şt* → *sc*, [tʃ] → [k], e.g.:

bate:	bătut	*to hit*
face:	făcut	*to do*
cunoaşte:	cunoscut	*to know*
naşte:	născut	*to give birth*

However, some of the verbs of the third conjugation have a participle ending in -s. These include the following verbs and their derivations (notice also the vowel changes):

Verbs in -*ge*, -*de*, e.g.:

merge:	mers, mearsă, merşi, merse	*to go*
arde:	ars, arsă, arşi, arse	*to burn*
roade:	ros, roasă, roşi, roase	*to gnaw*

Verbs in -*mite*[97], E.g.:

admite:	admis, admisă, admişi, admise	*to admit*
duce:	dus, dusă, duşi, duse	*to carry, to lead*
pune:	pus, pusă, puşi, puse	*to put*
rămâne:	rămas, rămasă, rămaşi, rămase	*to remain*
scoate:	scos, scoasă, scoşi, scoase	*to take out*
scrie:	scris, scrisă, scrişi, scrise	*to write*
sumete:	sumes, sumeasă, sumeşi, sumese	*to roll up (sleeves)*
toarce:	tors, toarsă, torşi, toarse	*to spin*
zice:	zis, zisă, zişi, zise	*to say*

The following verbs have a participle ending in -*t*:

coace:	copt, coaptă, copţi, coapte	*to bake, to cook*
fierbe:	fiert, fiartă, fierţi, fierte	*to boil*
frige:	fript, friptă, fripţi, fripte	*to roast*
frânge:	frânt, frântă, frânţi, frânte	*to break*
înfige:	înfipt, înfiptă, înfipţi, înfipte	*to stick*
rupe:	rupt, ruptă, rupţi, rupte	*to tear, to break*
sparge:	spart, spartă, sparţi, sparte	*to break, to crash*
suge:	supt, suptă, supţi, supte	*to suck*

In addition, the following verbs of the third conjugation have irregular participles:

coase:	cusut	(*oa* → *u*)	*to sew*
crede:	crezut	(ending -*ut*, *d* → *z*)	*to believe*
înveşte:	învăscut	(*e* → *ă*)	*to dress (dial.)*
pierde:	pierdut	(ending -*ut*)	*to lose*
vinde:	vândut	(ending -*ut*, *i* → *â*)	*to sell*

The verbs *accede* 'to accede' and *concede* 'to admit' do not have a participle at all[98].

In the fourth conjugation there is just one irregular participle:

şti:	ştiut [ʃtiˈʷut], ştiută, ştiuţi, ştiute	*to know*

---

[97] *Ad-, co-, compro-, de-, e-, o-, per-, pro-, re-, read-, retrans-, retri-, trans-* and *trimite*.
[98] But *purcede* 'to proceed' is regular: *purces*.

The irregular verbs *bea* and *fi* have irregular participles. Notice that there is no vowel change in the feminine forms of the participle of *fi*:

bea:	băut [bə'ʷut], băută, băuți, băute	*to drink*
fi:	fost, fostă, foști, foste	*to be*

The other irregular verbs have a regular participle form (*-a* → *-at*, *-ea* → *-ut*).

Use of the participle

The participle is used in forming the perfect forms of the indicative, subjunctive and presumptive. In these compound verb forms the participle is always invariable.

The participle is also used to form the passive voice (see p. 266).

The participle of transitive verbs can also be used as a verbal adjective with a passive meaning. Both affirmative and negative forms can be used:

fumatul interzis	smoking not allowed
un succes neașteptat	unexpected success
statele necorupte	the uncorrupted countries
Cartea aceasta este foarte cunoscută.	This book is very well known.

Some transitive verbs may have also a participle with an active meaning. Compare:

apa băută	the water that has been drunk
un om băut	a man that has been drinking
o carte citită	a book that has been read
un om citit	a well-read man

The participle of intransitive and reflexive verbs has an active meaning:

trenul ajuns la gară	the train (that has) arrived at the station
lucrul întâmplat	the thing that happened

The participle can also be used in the comparative and the superlative forms:

Danemarca este cea mai puțin coruptă țară din lume. (*Adevărul*)	Denmark is the least corrupt country of the world.
cele mai ascultate hituri (*Cotidianul*)	most listened hits

The participle of the verb *fi* also has the meaning 'ex-, former':

foștii comuniști	ex-communists
fostul și actualul ministru	the former and the present minister

The participle is also added to some verbs like *trebui, merita, a se cuveni, a lăsa*:

Copiii trebuie înscrişi la şcoală până la 1 mai 2009 (*Adevărul*)	The children must be registered in the school before 1st of May 2009.
Cartea aceasta merită citită. ~ Cartea aceasta se cuvine citită.	This book is worth reading.
Nu s-a lăsat fotografiat.	He did not allow himself to be photographed.

The participle is also used in temporal non-finite clauses to express finished actions (in the past, present or future):

ajuns trenul	when the train has/had arrived
ajunsă acasă	when she has/had arrived home
întorşi din Ungaria	having returned from Hungary, they...
Rugată să comenteze a spus că...	When asked to comment, she said that...

Gerund

The gerund is formed from the infinitive: *-a, -ea, -e, î* → *-ând; -i* → *-ind*. The stress is always on the ending:

-A: jura, lucra	-EA: vedea	-E: face	-I: fugi, citi	-Î: coborî, hotărî
jur-ând, lucr-ând	văz-ând	făc-ând	fug-ind, cit-ind	cobor-ând, hotăr-ând

The negative form is made with the prefix *ne-* ('by not ... -ing'):

nejurând	by not swearing
nelucrând	by not working

The adverbs *mai* and *prea* (see p. 274) can be added after the negative prefix: *nemaifăcând, nepreafăcând ~ ne prea făcând*.

Using the negative adverb *nu* will deny the whole constituent, and not just the verb itself ('not by -ing'):

nu scriind, ci citind	not by writing, but by reading

When an unstressed personal or reflexive pronoun in the accusative or dative (except *o*) is attached to a gerund, the vowel *u* is added to the end of the gerund form (see p. 146):

văzându-l	seeing him/it
văzând-o	seeing her/it

Irregular endings and sound changes

The verbs in the first conjugation ending in a palatal sound (-*ia*, -*chea*, -*ghea*) form their gerund with the ending -*ind*:

-Cia → -iind	apropia: apropiind [-iˈʲind]	*to come closer*
-Via → -Vind	tăia: tăind [-əˈʲind]	*to cut*
-chea → -chind	deochea: deochind	*to cast an evil eye*
-ghea → -ghind	veghea: veghind	*to be awake*

In the first conjugation there are no sound changes. Notice especially that unlike in the second and third conjugations, *t* and *d* do not change:

ajuta:	ajutând	*to help*
uda:	udând	*to wet*

In the second conjugation there is a consonant change *d* → *z*. The verb *vedea* also has a vowel change, *e.g.*:

cădea:	căzând	*to fall*
şedea:	şezând	*to sit*
vedea:	văzând	*to see*

Notice also the sound change [ʧ] → [k] (always written as 'c'):

tăcea:	tăcând	*to be silent*

The verbs of the third conjugation have the following sound changes:

- vowel changes: *a* → *ă*, *oa* → *o*
- consonant changes: *d* → *z*, *şt* → *sc*, [ʧ, ʤʲ] → [k, g]

These sound changes occur regularly in all the verbs of the third conjugation. Notice that many verbs have both a vowel and a consonant change, e.g.

crede:	crezând	*to believe*
pierde:	pierzând	*to lose*
decide:	decizând	*to decide*
rade:	răzând	*to shave*
cunoaşte:	cunoscând	*to know*
naşte:	născând	*to give birth*
creşte:	crescând	*to grow*
face:	făcând	*to do*
merge:	mergând	*to go*
coace:	cocând	*to bake, to cook*
coase:	cosând	*to sew*
roade:	rozând	*to gnaw*

However, the change *d* → *z* does not occur in the following two verbs[99]:

accede:	accedând	*to accede*
concede:	concedând	*to admit*

The change *t* → *ţ* occurs with verbs ending in *-mite* and the verb *scoate* (i.e. verbs that have a participle ending in *-s*):

admite:	admiţând	*to admit*
scoate:	scoţând	*to take out*

Other verbs ending in *-te* do not have this change:

bate:	bătând	*to hit*

The following verbs have other irregularities:

arde:	arzând (no vowel change)	*to burn*
scrie:	scriind (ending *-ind*)	*to write*
ucide:	ucigând (*d* → *g*)	*to kill*
sinucide:	sinucigând (*d* → *g*)	*to commit suicide*
vinde:	vânzând (*i* → *â*)	*to sell*

The only irregular gerund form in the fourth conjugation is:

şti:	ştiind	*to know*

The gerund of the verb *fi* is formed similarly:

fi:	fiind	*to be*

The other irregular verbs have a regular gerund (*-a* → *-ând*, *-ea* → *-ând*).

Use of the gerund

The gerund is mostly used as a modal, temporal (simultaneous), or causal non-finite clauses:

plouând	since it rains, when it rains
fiind foarte bogat	since he is rich, being rich
Nu vorbi mâncând!	Do not speak while eating!
începând cu anul viitor	starting from next year
Venind cu trenul a ajuns mai repede.	Since he came by train, he arrived faster.
Venind cu trenul ar ajunge mai repede.	If he came by train, he would arrive faster.

---

[99] But *purcede* 'to proceed' is regular: *purcezând*.

Venind cu trenul ar fi ajuns mai repede.	If he had come by train, he would have arrived faster.
Neavând dovezi, nu ai ce să faci. (*Cotidianul*)	Since there is no evidence, there is nothing you can do.
Vrând-nevrând, trebuie să lucrez.	I have to work, whether I want to or not.
acestea fiind zise	that being said

With verbs denoting seeing, hearing etc., the gerund can also modify the direct object:

L-am văzut dormind.	I saw him sleeping.
Te-am auzit cântând.	I heard you singing.

The Romanian gerund can also modify a noun. The gerund does not agree with the noun:

medicamentele conținând dextropropoxifenă	the medicines containing dextropropoxyphene
trei avioane aparținând Tarom (*Adevărul*)	three airplanes belonging to Tarom

However, a few gerunds have changed into full adjectives and they are also declined regularly:

crescând, crescândă, crescânzi, crescânde	growing
opoziția crescândă o rană sângerândă o mână tremurândă persoanele suferinde de insomnie	growing opposition a bleeding wound a shaking hand people suffering from insomnia

The gerund is also used in the forms of the presumptive present (see p. 253).

Supine

The supine is formed with *de* + participle (see p. 258):

-A: jura, lucra	-EA: vedea	-E: face	-I: fugi, citi	-Î: coborî, hotărî
de jur-<u>at</u>, lucr-<u>at</u>	de văz-<u>ut</u>	de făc-<u>ut</u>	de fug-<u>it</u>, cit-<u>it</u>	de cobor-<u>ât</u>, hotăr-<u>ât</u>

The participle is always in the masculine/neuter singular form. In the negative form, the negative participle with *ne-* is used (e.g. *de nejurat*). Usually the supine indicates purpose:

Am multe de făcut.	I have got lots to do.
Dă-mi de băut!	Give me something to drink!
Rămâne de văzut.	That remains to be seen.
prea scump de cumpărat	too expensive to be bought
Uşor de zis, greu de făcut!	Easy to say, difficult to do!
uşor de învăţat	easy to learn
maşini de închiriat	cars for rent
o greşeală de neiertat	unforgivable mistake
Această greşeală este de neiertat.	This mistake is unforgivable.
aşa cum era de aşteptat	as was expected

The supine is used with many impersonal structures like *e bine* 'it is good', *e greu/dificil* 'it is difficult', *e uşor* 'it is easy', *e necesar* 'it is necessary', *e posibil* 'it is possible', *e interesant* 'it is interesting'. However, the infinitive or conjunctive are also possible:

E uşor de citit.	It is easy to read.
= e uşor a citi / e uşor să citeşti[100]	

Words meaning 'to finish' are also used with the supine or conjunctive:

Am terminat de citit cartea.	I have finished reading the book.
= am terminat să citesc	

The supine is also used in many compound words:

maşină de scris	typewriter ('machine for writing')
maşină de spălat	washing machine ('machine for washing')
aparat de ras	razor ('machine for shaving')
apă de băut	drinking water ('water for drinking)

The verb of a sentence can also be emphasized by repeating it in the supine form at the beginning of the sentence. In this structure, only the affirmative supine form can be used:

De fumat, eu nu fumez.	As for smoking, I do not smoke.

A copula verb cannot be repeated by a supine, and the predicative is used instead:

De frumoasă, este frumoasă.	She is beautiful.

The supine can also be used in the comparative and superlative:

cel mai de temut terorist	the most feared terrorist

---

[100] Impersonal *tu*, see p. 268.

With some verbs the supine can be preceded by some other preposition E.g.:

a se pune pe citit / pe mâncat	to start to read / to eat
a pune la uscat	to put (clothes) out to dry
a lua de la uscat	to take (clothes) down from drying

In this case the line between a verb and a noun is not very clear since there are also some nouns created from supine forms like *mâncat* 'eating, food', *pescuit* 'fishing, fishery', *ras* 'shaving, shave' etc.

Passive voice

Formation of the passive

The passive voice is formed with the auxiliary verb *fi* and the participle perfect of the main verb. The participle agrees with the grammatical subject in gender and number, e.g. *a fi iubit* 'to be loved':

sunt iubit / iubită	suntem iubiți / iubite
ești iubit / iubită	sunteți iubiți / iubite
este iubit / iubită	sunt iubiți / iubite

All the tenses and moods are formed similarly (see also the annex 5, p. 364):

imperfect:	eram iubit(ă), erai iubit(ă) ...
perfect:	am fost iubit(ă), ai fost iubit(ă) ...
simple perfect:	fusei iubit(ă), fuseși iubit(ă) ...
pluperfect:	fusesem iubit(ă), fuseseși iubit(ă) ...
future:	voi fi iubit(ă), vei fi iubit(ă) ...
	am să fiu iubit(ă), ai să fii iubit(ă) ...
	o să fiu iubit(ă), o să fii iubit(ă) ...
future perfect:	voi fi fost iubit(ă), vei fi fost iubit(ă) ...
conjunctive:	să fiu iubit(ă), să fii iubit(ă) ...
conjunctive perfect:	să fi fost iubit, iubită, iubiți, iubite
conditional:	aș fi iubit(ă), ai fi iubit(ă) ...
conditional perfect:	aș fi fost iubit(ă), ai fi fost iubit(ă) ...
presumptive:	voi fi fiind iubit(ă), vei fi fiind iubit(ă) ...
presumptive perfect:	voi fi fost iubit(ă), vei fi fost iubit(ă) ...
imperative:	fii iubit(ă), nu fi iubit(ă)
	fiți iubiți/iubite, nu fiți iubiți/iubite
infinitive:	a fi iubit/iubită/iubiți/iubite
infinitive perfect:	a fi fost iubit/iubită/iubiți/iubite
gerund:	fiind iubit, iubită, iubiți, iubite

E.g.:

Incendiul a fost stins.	The fire has been extinguished.
Patru români au fost arestați. (*Adevărul*)	Four Romanians have been arrested.
Liderul talibanilor pakistanezi ar fi fost ucis. (*Cotidianul*)	The leader of the Pakistani Taliban may have been killed.
Suspecții de gripă porcină vor fi opriți să urce în avion. (*Adevărul*)	Those who are suspected to have swine flu are stopped from getting on the airplane.
Aceeași casă de bijuterii mai fusese spartă în anul 2003. (*Adevărul*)	The same jewellery store had also been robbed in 2003.
în paranteză fiind spus	said in parenthesis

Notice that many masculine and neuter forms are ambiguous:

voi fi iubit	active future perfect indicative
	passive future indicative
aș fi iubit	active perfect conditional
	passive present conditional
a fi iubit	active perfect infinitive
	passive present infinitive

The passive form agrees with a multiple subject in the same way as an adjective used as a predicative (see p. 120):

Elena și Maria sunt iubite.	Elena and Maria are loved.
Ion și Elena sunt iubiți.	Ion and Elena are loved.

The agent of a passive sentence can be expressed with the prepositions *de* or *de către*. The latter is more literate and can only be used with humans:

Volumul va putea fi achiziționat și direct de la editură *de către* cititori. (*Adevărul*)	The readers can also buy the book directly from the editor.
Semnalul de alarmă a fost dat *de către* vecinii din zonă. (*Adevărul*)	The alarm was given by the neighbours in the area.
Ei au fost prinși datorită ajutorului dat *de către* patru polițiști români. (*Cotidianul*)	They were caught because of the help given by four Romanian policemen.
un videoclip făcut *de (către)* mine	a video clip made by me
o școală administrată *de* ONU	a school administered by the UN

Turiștii au fost mușcați *de* vipere.
(*Adevărul*)

The tourists have been bitten by adders.

Passive and impersonal *se*

The passive can also be expressed with the accusative form of the reflexive pronoun (*se*) in all tenses:

Cum se spune „house" în limba
română?

How do you say "house" in Romanian?

Nu se știe cine a făcut-o.

It is not known who did it.

Se dorește să îi atragă pe turiști.
(*Adevărul*)

It is hoped to attract tourists.

A nu se fuma!

No smoking!

Opoziției nu i s-a dat nici o șansă.
(*Cotidianul*)

The opposition was not given any change.

The verb agrees with the formal subject (i.e. the logical object):

Unde se văd meciurile?
Unde se vede meciul?

Where can the matches be seen?
Where can the match be seen?

Li se promiseseră salarii mai mari.

They were promised higher salaries.

If there is no formal subject (so called impersonal *se*), the verb is in the third person singular:

Se vorbește mult despre el.

People talk much about him.

Impersonal *tu*

Like the English pronoun *you*, the Romanian *tu* can be used in a general, impersonal meaning:

Merită să faci sex la serviciu?
(*Adevărul*)

Is it worthwhile having sex at work?

Pleci în concediu, îți poți pierde
locul de muncă. (*Adevărul*)

If you go on holiday, you can loose your job.

În Occident, în momentul în care
ai făcut o greșeală gravă la locul
de muncă, ești chemat și ți se spune
să-ți strângi lucrurile și să pleci.
(*Adevărul*)

In the West, when you have made a serious mistake at work, you are called to a meeting and ordered to to collect your things and leave.

Reflexive verbs

In Romanian, reflexive pronouns (see p. 151) are added to the verb either in the accusative or (less frequently) in the dative case. For the declension of these forms, see the appendix 4 (p. 362), e.g.:

a se deştepta, a se trezi, a se scula	to wake up
a se culca	to go to bed
a se bărbieri, a se rade	to shave
a se pieptăna	to comb one's hair
a se căsători	to get married
a-şi aminti, a-şi aduce aminte	to remember
a-şi face iluzii	to have false hopes
a-şi da seama	to realise

Some verbs always require a reflexive pronoun:

a se odihni	to rest
a se întâmpla	to happen
a se bucura	to be glad
a se teme	to fear

With some verbs the reflexive pronoun can totally change the meaning of the verb:

a afla	to find out
a se afla	to be located
a comporta	to entail
a se comporta	to behave
a duce	to take
a se duce	to go
a uita	to forget
a se uita	to watch

E.g.:

Mă uit la televizor.	I am watching television.
Am uitat parola.	I have forgotten my password.
Duc cărţile la bibliotecă.	I am taking the books back to the library.
Mă duc acasă.	I am going home.
Aceasta decizie comportă probleme.	this decision brings problems.
Nu s-a comportat bine.	He/she did not behave well.
Am aflat adevărul.	I found out the truth.
Madridul se află în Spania.	Madrid is located in Spain.

Adverbs

Lexical adverbs

There are many different kinds of lexical adverbs, e.g:

Interrogative and relative adverbs

unde	where, to where
de unde	from where
încotro	to where
dincotro	from where
când	when
de când	since when
cum	how

Unde este Radu?	Where is Radu?
Când ajunge trenul?	When will the train arrive?
Cum te numeşti?	What is your name? (lit. How do you call yourself?)

Merg unde vreau.	I go where I want
Fă cum vrei!	Do what you want!

See also the relative clauses (p. 303).

Adverbs of place

aici	here
acolo	there
încoace	here (movement)
încolo	there (movement)
dincoace	on this side
dincolo	on the other side
sus, deasupra	above
jos, dedesubt	below
afară	outside
înăuntru	inside
departe	far away
aproape	close, near
oriunde	wherever
niciunde, nicăieri	nowhere
undeva	somewhere

Adverbs of time

acum, acuma	now
acum doi ani	two years ago
înainte cu doi ani	two years earlier
atunci	at that time, then
apoi	after that, then
imediat, numaidecât, (de) îndată	immediately
astăzi, azi	today
ieri	yesterday
alaltăieri	the day before yesterday
mâine	tomorrow
poimâine	the day after tomorrow
odată	once
mereu, (în)totdeauna	always
niciodată, nicicând	never
dimineaţa	in the morning, every morning
azi-dimineaţă	this morning
ieri-dimineaţă	yesterday morning
seara	in the evening, every evening
deseară, astă-seară	tonight
aseară, ieri-seară	last night
noaptea	at night, every night
la noapte	tonight
azi-noapte, astă-noapte, ieri-noapte	last night
oricând	whenever
des	often
rareori, rar	rarely
târziu	late
devreme	early
luni	on Monday
lunea	on Mondays
lunea trecută	last Monday
uneori, câteodată	sometimes
vara	in summer
(în) vara asta	this summer
astă-vară	last summer
la vară	next summer
zi şi noapte, ziua şi noaptea	day and night, always

Adverbs of manner

aşa, astfel	like this
altfel	differently
mult	much
puţin	a little bit
atât	so much

destul	enough
repede, iute	fast
încet, alene, agale	slowly
împreuna, laolaltă	together

Adverbs of probability

desigur	surely
bineînțeles	of course
probabil	probably
poate	maybe

Adverbs of negation and affirmation

- *nu*   no

- Sunteți român?	- Are you Romanian?
- Nu, sunt finlandez.	- No, I am Finnish.

Nu is used for the negative verb forms (see p. 213). Notice that *nu* can also be used for the negation of other elements than verbs. Compare:

Ion nu a venit azi.	Ion did not came today.
Nu Ion a venit azi.	It is not Ion who came today (but someone else did).
Ion a venit nu azi, ci ieri.	Ion came not today, but yesterday.

- Other adverbs used for negative response include *deloc, nicidecum* 'not at all'.

- *da*   yes

- Sunteți român?	- Are you Romanian?
- Da.	- Yes, I am.

- *ba da*   yes, an affirmative response to a negative question

- Nu sunteți finlandez?	- Are you not Finnish?
- Ba da.	- Yes, I am.

- Other adverbs used for affirmative response include *desigur* 'certainly', *sigur* 'sure', *evident* 'evidently', *bineînțeles* 'of course', *firește* 'of course', *natural* 'naturally', *adevărat* 'true', *exact* 'exact', *corect* 'correct', etc.

Derivation of adverb from adjectives

The singular masculine and neuter forms of adjectives can usually be used as adverbs:

Ea cântă *frumos*.	She sings beautifully.
Să trăim *sănătos*!	Let's live healthy!
Comisia Europeană va critica *oficial* Ungaria (*Adevărul*)	The European Commission will officially criticise Hungary.

However, the adjective *bun* has its own adverbial form *bine*:

Ce mai faci? - Bine.	How are you? - Fine.

The adverbial form of adjectives ending in *-esc* is formed with the ending *-ește*:

a trăi regește	to live like a king

These forms are also used with some names of languages:

Vorbesc românește.	I speak Romanian.
Știu englezește / franțuzește.	I can speak English / French.
Nu înțeleg rusește / italienește.	I do not understand Russian / Italian.

Adverbial phrases can also be made with structures like *în mod / într-un mod / în modul*:

în mod absurd / într-un mod absurd	in an absurd manner
într-un mod/fel/chip/stil original	in an eccentric manner

Comparison of adverbs

The comparison of adverbs denoting manner, place or time is formed the same way as the comparison of adjectives (see p. 123), i.e. the comparative is formed with the adverbs *mai* or *mai puțin*, and the superlative with *cel mai* or *cel mai puțin*:

mai bine	better
cel mai bine	best
mai puțin bine	worse
cel mai puțin bine	worst
mai bine târziu decât niciodată	better late than never
cel mai bine vândut album	the most sold album
cel mai devreme	earliest

Maşina mea merge cel mai repede.	My car goes the fastest.
În ianuarie, românii beau mai puţin. (*Adevărul*)	In January the Romanians drink less.
Vino mai aproape!	Come closer!

Semi-adverbs

Semi-adverbs are adverbs that always modify another word, i.e. they cannot be used independently, e.g.:

numai eu	just me
şi el	even he
circa / vreo / aproximativ 10	about 10
doar iubire	only love

The semi-adverbs *mai* 'once more, still', *tot* 'still, anyhow', *cam* 'hardly', *(nu) prea* 'not really' and *şi* 'also' differ from other adverbs also in that when they modify a verb, they are always placed inside the verbal structure. These adverbs come after *să, a, de,* the negative adverb *nu,* unstressed personal pronouns, and the auxiliary verbs *avea* and *vrea,* right in front of the main verb. If the auxiliary verb is *fi,* the adverbs are placed in front of it (except the adverb *şi,* which is always placed in front of the main verb). However, the adverb *tot* can also be placed outside the verbal structure.

E.g.:

L-am tot văzut = Tot l-am văzut.	Anyhow I saw him.
Îl tot văd.	I still see him.
Nu-l prea cunosc.	I do not really know him.
Îl cam cunosc.	I hardly know him.
Am şi studiat.	I have also studied.
NASA nu mai are bani pentru a-şi trimite astronauţii pe Lună (*Adevărul*)	NASA no longer has the money to send astronauts to the Moon.
Lumea nu va mai fi aceeaşi după această criză. (*Adevărul*)	The world will not be the same after this crisis.
Românii nu prea cred în criză. (*Adevărul*)	The Romanians do not really believe in the crisis.

For more details on the word order of the verbal structure, see appendix 6 (p. 367).

Conjunctions

Coordinating conjunctions

Copulative conjunctions

- *şi* 'and'

câini şi pisici	dogs and cats
eu şi el	he and I
lupta dintre David şi Goliat	the fight between David and Goliath
Lucrez şi studiez în acelaşi timp.	I am working and studying at the same time.

  Between subjects, *şi cu* + accusative can be used:

John *şi cu* mine studiem limba română.	John and I are studying Romanian.

- *cât şi, cum şi, precum şi, ca şi* 'as well as'

Printre invitaţi au fost Ion, Maria, precum şi Gheorghe.	Among the guests were Ion, Maria, and Gheorghe as well.

- *şi – şi* 'both – and'

şi tu *şi* eu	both you and me
Eu *şi* lucrez *şi* studiez în acelaşi timp.	I am both working and studying at the same time
Cel puţin 200 de specii marine trăiesc *şi* la Polul Nord, *şi* la Polul Sud. (*Cotidianul*)	At least 200 marine species live both at the North and the South Poles.

- *nici – nici, nu + verb – nici* 'neither – nor'. The predicative verb must be in the negative form.

Nici tu *nici* eu nu suntem români.	Neither you nor I are Romanian.
România nu acuză *nici* Ucraina, *nici* Rusia pentru criza gazelor. (*Adevărul*)	Romania does not blame Ukraine nor Russia for the gas crisis.
Nu mănânc acum, *nici* nu beau.	I will neither eat nor drink now.
Nu mănânc carne, *nici* peşte.	I do not eat either meat or fish.

- *nu numai / nu doar – ci şi / dar şi* 'not only – but too'

nu numai audio, *dar şi* video	not only audio, but also video
Michael Moore *nu numai* la Cannes, *ci şi* la Cluj (*Adevărul*)	Michael Moore not only in Cannes but also in Cluj

  Between two clauses *nu numai că / nu doar că – ci şi / dar şi* is used:

Nu numai că studiez, *ci şi* lucrez.	Not only am I studying, but I am working too.

- *atât – cât şi / precum şi* 'both – and'

atât bărbaţii, *cât şi* femeile	both men and women
atât pentru acest an, *cât şi* pentru 2009	both for this year and for 2009

Adversative conjunctions

- *dar, însă* 'but'

Am încercat să o scot, *dar* nu am putut. (*Adevărul*)	I tried to take it out, but I could not.

- *iar* 'whereas, while'

Eu sunt finlandez, *iar* ea este română.	I am Finnish, while she is Romanian.

- *nu – ci* 'no – but' introduces a correction:

Nu lucrez acolo, *ci* studiez.	I do not work there, I study there.
nu în mare, *ci* pe uscat	not on the sea, but on dry land

Disjunctive conjunctions

- *sau, ori* 'or'

Cine este mai infidel: bărbatul *sau* femeia? (*Adevărul*)	Who is more unfaithful: man or woman?

- *sau – sau, ori – ori, fie – fie, ba – ba, acum – acum, când – când* 'either – or'

fie azi *fie* mâine	either today or tomorrow
ba rece *ba* cald	either cold or hot

Conclusive conjunctions

- *deci, așa că, de aceea, așadar, atunci, ca atare, de aceea, prin urmare, în conse-cință,* 'thus'

Peste 70 la sută dintre ei muncesc, *deci* au venit aici pentru muncă. (*Adevărul*)	Over 70% of them are working, so they have come here for work.
Cuget *deci* exist.	I think, therefore I am.

- *vasăzică, carevasăzică* 'that is (to say)'

Subordinating conjunctions

The most frequently used subordinating conjunctions *că, să, ca să, dacă* and *de* can be used to introducing several kinds of subordinate clauses:

că	nominal, causal, consecutive, concessive clauses
să (ca ... să)	nominal, final, conditional, concessive, consecutive clauses
ca să	final, consecutive, oppositional clauses
dacă	conditional clauses, indirect questions
de (col.)	conditional, concessive, consecutive, causal, final clauses

The interrogative adverbs are sometimes used as conjunctions as well:

cum	relative, modal, temporal, causal clauses
unde	relative, causal, oppositional clauses
când	relative, temporal, conditional, adversative clauses

All of these are naturally also used in indirect questions.

Other conjunctions have more specific meanings:

Causal conjunctions:	*căci, deoarece, fiindcă, întrucât, din cauză că, din pricină că, de vreme ce, din moment ce, pentru că*
Concessive conjunctions:	*deși, cu toate că, chiar dacă, chiar de, măcar că*
Consecutive conjunction:	*încât*
Temporal conjunctions:	*imediat ce, îndată ce, abia ce, (ori) de câte ori*
Adversative conjunction:	*în loc să*
Cumulative conjunctions:	*după ce că, pe lângă că, plus că, lasă că*

For examples, see the subordinate clauses, p. 296-.

Syntax

Case usage

In Romanian the nouns, pronouns and adjectives have five cases: nominative, accusative, genitive, dative and vocative.

Nominative

The nominative case is used in Romanian when a noun functions:

- As a subject (see p. 283):

Maria locuieşte în România.	Maria lives in Romania.

- As a predicative (see p. 295):

  ➤ Subject predicative:

Sunt *student*.	I am a student.
Ion devine / va ieşi / va ajunge / va fi / se face *profesor*.	Ion will be a teacher.
Ion pare *bolnav*.	Ion seems ill.

  ➤ Object predicative:

Mă numesc *Ion*.	My name is Ion.
L-au ales *preşedinte*.	They elected him president.

- As a supplementary apposition:

  ➤ An attributive apposition (an apposition describing the head) is always in the nominative without an article:

Pier Paolo Pasolini, *scriitor, actor, regizor şi scenarist*, s-a născut la 05 martie 1922. (CineMagia.ro)	P.P. Pasolini, writer, actor, director, scenarist, was born on March 5th 1922.

  ➤ An identifying apposition (an apposition allowing the insertion of *that is to say, in other words*) is also usually in the nominative case:

Ion, *soţul meu*, este român. (= Soţul meu, *Ion*, este român.)	John, (that is to say) my husband, is Romanian.

Other cases are also possible, although rarer:

L-am dat lui Ion, *soțul meu*. (~ *soțului meu*)	I gave it to Ion, my husband.

- As an integrated appositive modifier, i.e. after a noun describing a category:

domnul *Popescu*	Mr. Popescu
domnului *Popescu*	to Mr. Popescu
domnule *ministru*!	Mr. Minister!
orașul *Iași*	the city of Iași
Muntele *Everest*	Mount Everest
anul *2005*	the year 2005
adverbul „*nu*"	the adverb 'nu'

Accusative

The accusative case is used:

- With direct objects of transitive verbs (see p. 287):

Cunosc *un român*.	I know a Romanian man.

However, the direct object is often expressed with the preposition *pe* (see p. 287).

- With secondary objects (see p. 293):

Mă învață *limba română*.	He/She is teaching me Romanian.

- As an adverb of time or quantity:

Ce ai făcut *săptămână trecută*?	What did you do last week?
Costă *3 lei*.	It costs 3 leu.

- With certain prepositions (see p. 196):

la *Iași*	in Iași

- Instead of the nominative when the comparative adverbs *decât, ca, cât* precede a noun or a pronoun (and not a subordinate clause):

Este mai înalt decât *mine*. (= decât *eu* sunt)	He is taller than me.
Ion este tot atât de înalt ca *mine*. (= ca *eu* sunt)	Ion is as tall as me.

The other cases do not change:

mai util ție decât *mie*	more useful for you than for me

Genitive

The genitive case is used as an attribute of a noun. It is usually translated in English by the clitic *'s* or with the preposition *of*. The Romanian genitive can express various things:

- Possession:

maşina *bunicului*	grandfather's car
casa *lui Ion*	Ion's house

- Relationships:

căpitanul *navei*	the ship's captain
membrii *partidului*	the members of the party

- The whole in relation to the part:

coperta *cărţii*	the cover of the book
începutul *săptămânii*	the beginning of the week
în estul *României*	in East Romania

- Agent or patient:

poezia *lui Eminescu*	Eminescu's poetry
naufragiul *vasului* de croazieră	the wreck of the cruise ship
pierderea *suveranităţii*	the loss of sovereignty
câştigătorul *războiului*	the winner of the war

- Classification:

luna *lui ianuarie*	the month of January
greva *foamei*	hunger strike
drepturile *omului*	human rights

- Comparison (superlative genitive):

problema problemelor	the problem of all problems, the biggest problem

As can be seen from the examples, the genitive is normally placed after the noun it modifies. A genitive form can also be used independently, in which case it is preceded by the genitive article (see p. 92):

Aceasta maşină este *a fratelui meu.*   this car is my brother's

The genitive is also used with certain prepositions (see p. 206).

Dative

The dative case in used:

- With indirect objects (see p. 293). It usually answers the question 'to whom?', 'to what?':

  (see p. 293)

I-am dat *unei prieten* o carte.	I gave a book to a friend.

- As an attribute of some adjectives:

tipic *comunismului*	typical to communism
util *mie*	useful to me
drag *tuturor*	dear to everyone
fidel *regelui*	loyal to the king
un cutremur similar *celui* din 1977	an earthquake similar to the one in 1977

  In some cases a preposition can also be used: *util pentru mine, similar cu cel din 1977*, etc.

- With few injections:

Bravo *ție!*	Good for you!

- The dative is also used with some prepositions (see p. 209).

  (see p. 209)

- As an expression of possession with personal and reflexive pronouns (possessive dative). The dative expresses the possessor of the subject, object or some other complement of the verb:

Mi-a murit *bunica.*	My grandmother died.
Care *vă* este *părerea?*	What is your opinion?
Ți-am văzut *mașina* ieri pe stradă.	I saw your car on the street yesterday.
Mi-am pierdut *pixul.*	I have lost my pen.
Mi-am înșelat *nevasta.*	I have cheated on my wife.

  In older or poetic language a possessive dative (only the pronouns *-mi, -ți, -i, -și*) can be used with nouns and some prepositions made from nouns. The nouns are usually in the definite form (the ending *-u* is used instead of *-ul*), except the nouns ending in *-ă* and *-e* that can be used in the singular also without an article:

prietenu-*mi*	my friend
în juru-*mi*	around me
asupra-*mi* / asupră-*mi*	above me
înaintea-*mi* / înainte-*mi*	before me

If an adjective in the definite form precedes the noun, these pronouns are added to the adjective:

frumoasa-mi fată	my beautiful girl

Vocative

The vocative case is used for addressing someone, and therefore it can only be used with nouns denoting things one can talk to, i.e. persons, animals or (more rarely) personified things (e.g. *dragă jurnalule* 'dear diary').

For examples, see p. 68 (nouns) and p. 115 (adjectives).

Sentence types

Apart from the basic declarative sentences, there are interrogative, exclamative and imperative sentences.

Interrogative sentence

In interrogative sentences the interrogative pronoun (see p. 165) or adverb (see p. 270) is usually placed at the beginning of the sentence. When the pronoun is not the subject of the sentence, the word order is reversed (the subject is placed after the verb):

Cu cine a vorbit Ion?	With whom did Ion speak?

If the interrogative pronoun is especially stressed, it can be placed in the same place as in a declarative sentence:

Ion a vorbit cu cine?!	Ion has spoken with who?!

A stressed subject (e.g. a stressed personal pronoun) or some other stressed element(s) may precede the interrogative pronoun:

Tu ce aștepți?	What are you waiting for?
Mâine ce faci?	What are you doing tomorrow?

Yes/no questions are formed with a rising intonation (see p. 23). The predicate verb is often placed at the beginning of the sentence, but the word order can also be the same as in a declarative sentence:

Ți-e foame?	Are you hungry?
A citit Ion cartea asta?	Has Ion read this book?
Dumneavoastră sunteți român?	Are you Romanian?

Alternative questions are formed with the conjunction *sau*:

| Vine Ion sau Maria? | Is Ion or Mary coming? |

Exclamative sentence

Exclamations are formed with the interrogative pronouns *ce* (see p. 166) and *cât* (see p. 168):

Ce frumoasă eşti!	How beautiful you are!
Ce pisică frumoasă!	What a beautiful cat!
Ce interesant!	How interesting!
Ce de lume!	What a lot of people!
Cât de frumoasă eşti!	How beautiful you are!
Câte probleme am!	How many problems I have!

Imperative sentence

In imperative sentences the verb is usually in the imperative (see p. 241) or in the conjunctive mood (see p. 250). In general orders also the infinitive can be used (see p. 258). A special form of conditional (see p. 251) is used in some curses.

Taci din gură!	Shut up!
Să taci din gură!	
Să fie lumină!	Let there be light!
A nu călca iarba!	Do not step on the grass!
Mânca-te-ar viermii!	May the worms eat you!

Syntactic functions

Subject

When a noun or a pronoun is used as a subject, the nominative case must be used:

| *Maria* citeşte. | Maria is reading. |

Unlike in English, the subject of a verbless clause is also in the nominative:

| Cine a făcut-o? - *Eu.* | Who did it? -Me. |

Since the personal ending of the predicate is enough to tell who is the subject, the personal pronouns are not usually used as subjects (unless one wishes to emphasise the subject):

Te iubesc.	I love you.
Eu te iubesc.	It is me who loves you.

A personal pronoun is not needed even if the subject is modified by a noun, a pronoun or an adjective:

Toți suntem oameni.	We are all humans.
Câți români suntem în Spania?	How many of us Romanians are there in Spain?

In some relative clauses the subject is not in the nominative, but in the case required by the main clause:

L-am dat *cui* l-a vrea.	I gave it to the person who wanted it.

Notice that Romanian has no impersonal subject like the English *it*:

Plouă.	It is raining.

Thus in structures like 'it is X', 'there is a X', 'X' is the subject in Romanian:

Sunt *eu*. / Suntem *noi*.	It is me. / It is us.
Este *ora* două.	It is two o'clock.
Pe masă este *o carte*.	There is a book on the table.

Subject-predicate agreement

A predicative verb agrees with the subject in number and person, whether the subject is explicitly mentioned or not:

Te iubesc. (subject: *eu*)	I love you.

However, if the subject is a geographical name in plural referring to a city, a village etc., the predicate is usually in the singular:

Pietrele *este* un sat în județul Giurgiu.	Pietrele is a village in Girgiu County.
Bucureștii Noi *este* un cartier din București.	Bucureștii Noi is a district in Bucharest.

Plural agreement is used with geographical names referring to mountains, archipelagos, etc.:

Alpii *sunt* un lanț muntos din Europa. (*Wikipedia*)	The Alps are a mountain range in Europe.

In the passive voice the predicate also agrees with the subject in gender. The participle agrees with the subject in the same way as an adjective used as a predicative (see p. 120):

Ea este *iubită*.　　　　　　　　　　　She is loved.

If the verb has no subject at all, the third person singular is used:

Plouă.　　　　　　　　　　　　　　　　It is raining.

The third person singular is also used when the subject is a nominal verb form or a subordinate clause:

A greși *este* omenește.　　　　　　　　To err is human.

Se *presupune* că făceau parte　　　　　It is assumed that they were part
dintr-o bandă. (*Adevărul*)　　　　　　of a crime ring.

When the subject is a collective noun denoting a group, the verb can be in the plural form:

un grup de cercetători a / au　　　　　a group of researchers has / have
descoperit că...　　　　　　　　　　　found out that...
O mulțime a / au venit.　　　　　　　　A large group came.
O mulțime ați venit.　　　　　　　　　Many of you came.

This is sometimes done also with nouns denoting a part of a group. However, the grammatical agreement is recommended:

O parte din studenți a / (au) venit.　　Some of the students came.
Majoritatea studenților a / (au) venit.　Most of the students came.
Fiecare dintre noi a / (am) citit cartea.　Everyone of us has read the book.

If the noun by itself tells what the group consists of, grammatical agreement is always used:

Studențimea are o problemă.　　　　　The students have a problem.

Armata ține la secret moartea　　　　　The army is keeping the death of
unui om. (*Adevărul*)　　　　　　　　one person secret.

Multiple subjects

With multiple subjects coordinated with the conjunction *și* or *și cu* + accusative 'and', the predicative comes in plural form:

Ion și Radu *sunt* români.　　　　　　Ion and Radu are Romanian.

However, the singular is used:

- if both nouns refer to the same person or thing:

Limba și literatura româna *este*　　　Romanian language and literature
o disciplină la școală.　　　　　　　　is a school subject.

Punctul și virgula *este* un semn de punctuație.	The semicolon is a punctuation mark.

- if the subjects are infinitives or supines:

Pentru mine a citi și a scrie *este* un privilegiu. (*www.9am.ro*)	For me, reading and writing is a privilege.

Multiple singular subjects coordinated with an adversative (*sau, fie, ori*) or a disjunctive (*nu - ci*) conjunction require the use of the singular:

Ion sau Radu *vine*.	Either Ion or Radu is coming.
Nu Ion, ci Radu *vine*.	Not Ion, but Radu is coming.

The plural form can be used if the coordination is not meant to be restrictive:

Ion sau Radu pot veni.	Ion or Radu (or both of them) can come.

With the conjunction *nici* both singular and plural are possible:

Nici Ion, nici Radu nu *vine* / *vin*.	Neither Ion nor Radu is coming.

If the nouns are placed after the verb, the agreement can also be with the closest noun:

Îi *place* muzica și dansul.	He/she likes music and dancing.
A *fost* odată un rege și o regină.	Once upon a time there was a king and a queen

The different persons are combined as follows:

eu și tu/voi suntem	you and I are
eu și el/ei suntem	he/they and I are
tu și noi suntem	you and we are
tu și el/ei sunteți	you and he/they are

Relative pronoun as the subject

If the subject is a relative pronoun, the verb is usually in the third person and agrees with the antecedent only in number (and gender):

băiatul care citește	the boy who is reading
băieții care citesc	the boys who are reading

However, if the antecedent is a personal or polite pronoun, agreement in person is also accepted:

Sunt eu care l-a făcut / l-am făcut.	It was I who did it.

Compare with the following sentence where the antecedent is *omul*:

Eu sunt omul care l-a făcut.	I am the person who did it.

Direct object

When a noun or a pronoun is used as a direct object, the accusative case must be used:

Te iubesc.   I love you.

Direct object with the preposition pe

With certain types of direct objects the preposition *pe* is required. The general rule is that the preposition *pe* is used when the direct object is a noun or a pronoun referring to a specific human being or a personified animal or thing (like pets or toys). However, the preposition is also used before certain pronouns and other structures when they refer to inanimate objects.

The use of the preposition *pe* is obligatory in the following cases:

- With the following nouns, noun phrases and pronouns referring to humans and personified animals or things:

    ➢ Names:

    L-aștept pe Ion.   I am waiting for Ion.
    O aștept pe Maria.   I am waiting for Maria.

    Îl iubesc pe Rex.   I love Rex (a personified dog).
    Kapetanos a salvat-o iar pe   Kapetanos saved the *Steaua*
    Steaua. (*EVZ*)   (a personified sports club)

    ➢ Nouns in definite form used with a modifier (pronoun, adjective, genitive attribute, etc.):

    pe vecinul meu   my neighbour
    pe profesorul acesta   this teacher
    pe prietenii lui Ion   Ion's friends
    pe copiii bolnavi   the sick children
    pe domnul Popescu   Mr. Popescu

    O iubesc pe păpușa mea.   I love my doll. (a personified thing).

    ➢ Nouns referring to relatives used in the definite form with a possessive meaning:

    O aștept pe mama.   I'm waiting for my mother.

- ➢ Nouns preceded by any of the demonstrative pronouns or by the pronouns *fiecare, tot, care, unii*:

pe acest student	this student
pe fiecare student	every student
pe toți prietenii	all the friends
pe care vecin?	which neighbour?
pe unii oameni	certain people

- ➢ independent pronouns *pe (ori)cine, pe (alt)cineva, pe careva, pe nimeni* and *pe niciunul* (the latter when it refers to humans or personified animals or things):

Nu cunosc pe nimeni.	I do not know anybody.

- With the following pronouns and other structures, even when they do not refer to humans or personified animals or things:

  - ➢ All stressed personal, reflexive and polite pronouns:

pe mine, pe tine, pe noi, pe voi	me, you, us, you
pe el, pe ei	him / it, they
pe dumneavoastră	You

  - ➢ All independent demonstrative pronouns, except the feminine forms with a general neuter meaning:

pe acesta, pe cealaltă, pe același	this one, the other, the same

  - ➢ Independent pronouns *(ori)care* (interrogative or relative) and *fiecare*:

pe care	whom, which
pe oricare	anybody, anyone
pe fiecare	everybody, every one

  - ➢ Structures substantivised with *cel* and *al*:

pe cei trei	those three
pe ai mei	mine

  - ➢ Ordinal numerals, collective numerals and the independent pronoun *tot* (except when it has a general neuter meaning[101]):

pe a treia	the third one
pe primul	the first one
pe ultimul	the last one
pe amândoi	both
pe toți	all

---

[101] E.g.. *știu tot* 'I know everything'.

➤ Cardinal numeral *before* the verb:

> Pe doi i-am văzut.   I saw two (of them).

In the following situations the use of a preposition is possible, but not compulsory. The use of *pe* more clearly identifies the noun:

- When a noun referring to a specific human (or personified animal or thing) is in definite form and does not have any modifier. However, the use of the preposition *pe* is recommended. Notice, that if the preposition is used, the noun loses its definite article (for the use of definite form after a preposition, see p. 196):

> L-aștept pe profesor / pe medic.   I am waiting for the teacher / the
> (= Aștept profesorul / medicul.)   doctor.

- When a noun referring to a human (or personified animal or thing) is preceded by the indefinite article, any of the indefinite pronouns *vreun, alt, mulți, puțini, câțiva, atâți, câți* or when these pronouns are used independently (except in general neuter meaning):

> Caut un student.   I am looking for a student.
> Îl caut pe un student.   I am looking for a certain student.
> Îl cunoști pe vreun (dintre ei)?   Do you know any of them?
> Cunoști vreunul ca el?   Do you know anyone else like him?
>
> Caută altul mai bun!   Look for another that is better!
> Caută pe altul!   Look for the other one!
>
> Câți ai văzut?   How many did you see?
> Pe câți ai văzut?   How many (of them) did you see?
>
> Pe mulți îi cunosc.   I know many (of them).
> cunosc mulți care...   I know many people who...

- An independent cardinal numeral after the verb:

> Am văzut doi.   I saw two.
> I-am văzut pe doi.   I saw two of them.

- When the noun is not referring to the person but to his works:

> (îl) citesc pe Eminescu.   I am reading Eminescu.
> = Citesc Eminescu.

- The preposition can also be used in other cases if it is needed for clarity:

> Scrie-l pe cinci / pe B!   Write the number "5" / letter "B"!
> mână pe mână spală   one hand washes the other

Pe is often needed in comparisons. Compare:

Îl iubeşte ca un frate.	He loves him like a brother (loves).
Îl iubeşte ca pe un frate.	He loves him like a brother is loved.

This can be done even if the noun does not refer to a person:

Te citesc ca pe o carte.	I can read you like a book.

The preposition *pe* cannot be used in the following cases:

- When the direct object is an inanimate noun or a regular animal:

Iubesc România!	I love Romania!
Am văzut o pisică.	I saw a cat.

- When the direct object is an independent pronoun *ce, (alt)ceva, orice, nimic* or *niciunul* (when it is not referring to persons or personified animals) or a feminine pronoun with a general neuter meaning (*asta, aia, alta*)[102]:

Nu ştiu nimic.	I do not know anything.
Vreau altceva.	I want something else.
Cine a făcut asta?	Who did this?
Nu face aia!	Do not do that!

- When the noun does not refer to any specific person, but to a group in general:

Căutăm secretară.	We are looking for a secretary.
Aştept prieteni.	I am waiting for (some) friends.

- When there is a *possessive dative* (see p. 281):

Îşi iubeşte părinţii.	He/She loves his/her parents.

- When the direct object is an unstressed personal or reflexive pronoun:

Te iubesc.	I love you.

Redundant direct object

In Romania the unstressed accusative form of the personal pronoun is often used even if the direct object occurs in the same sentence (clitic doubling).

These redundant direct object pronouns must be used in the following cases:

---

[102] However, Avram (2001: 369) accepts both *asta* and *pe asta*.

- When the direct object is placed before the verb and the object is in the definite form or preceded by a demonstrative pronoun or by *fiecare, care* or *cel*:

Cartea aceasta am citit-o.	I have read this book.
= Această carte am citit-o	
Fiecare carte am citit-o	I have read every book.
Cele două cărți le-am citit.	I have read those two books.
Care carte ai citit-o?	Which book did you read?
Bucureștiul l-am vizitat.	I have been to Bucharest.

The redundant pronoun is also possible when the object is placed before the verb in the indefinite form with an indefinite article. However, usually it is not used:

o carte am citit(-o)	I have read a book.

Similarly, the redundant pronoun is possible when a feminine demonstrative pronoun with a general neuter meaning precedes the verb. However, the redundant pronoun is usually not used:

Asta (o) vreau.	I want this.

- Usually when the direct object is expressed with the preposition *pe* (see p. 287-), both before and after the verb:

Îl cunosc pe Ion.	I know Ion.
= Pe Ion îl cunosc.	
Le cunosc pe Ana și Maria.	I know Ana and Maria.
Te cunosc pe tine.	I know you.
Îl vreau pe acesta.	I want this one.
Îi cunosc pe cei din Cluj.	I know the ones from Cluj.
cartea pe care o cunosc	the book I know
Îi cunosc pe toți.	I know them all.
Vă cunosc pe toți.	I know you all.

However, the redundant direct object pronoun is never used with the pronouns *pe (ori)cine, pe (alt)cineva* and *pe nimeni*.

The use of the redundant object pronoun is non-compulsory, when:

- The object is *pe* + indefinite pronoun (except *tot*):

(îl) cunosc pe fiecare.	I know (them) all.

However, in these cases the accusative pronoun is usually used.

- The object is *pe* + numeral placed after the verb:

(îi) cunosc pe trei.	I know the three (of them).
(îl) cunosc pe al patrulea.	I know the fourth one (of them).
(îi) cunosc pe amândoi.	I know (them) both.

In this case as well, the accusative pronoun is usually used.

- When the object is a subordinate declarative clause (see p. 298) or a subordinate interrogative clause (see p. 302) preceding the main clause. The redundant direct object pronoun is the neutral pronoun *o* or *asta*:

  Că el este român, (o) / asta (o)[103] știu.   I know that he is Romanian.
  Când vine (asta) nu (o) știu.   I do not know when he/she comes.

  With *dacă* clauses only the pronoun *o* can be used:

  Dacă el vine, nu (o) știu.   I do not know, if he comes.

In the following cases the redundant direct object pronouns cannot be used:

- When the object is placed after the verb and the preposition *pe* is not used:

  Beau apă.   I am drinking water.
  Nu am vizitat România.   I have never visited Romania.

- When the object is a noun without an article placed before the verb and the preposition *pe* is not used. The noun may also be preceded by *asemenea, așa, atare, atâta, ce, (ori)cât, niciun* or *vreun*:

  Cărți am citit.   I have read books.
  Câte cărți ai citit?   How many books have you read?
  Nicio carte n-am citit.   I have not read any books.

- With the dative possessive (see p. 281):

  Îi cunosc părinții.   I know his parents.

- When the object is *pe (ori)cine, pe (alt)cineva, pe nimeni, pe niciunul*:

  Pe cine nu cunoști?   Who do you not know?
  Nu cunosc pe nimeni.   I do not know anybody.
  Iubesc pe altcineva.   I love another.

- When the object is *(ori)ce, (alt)ceva* or *nimic*:

  Ce ai făcut?   What did you do?
  Nu știu nimic.   I do not know anything.

  However, when the pronoun *ce* is used as a relative pronoun (colloq.), the redundant direct object pronoun can be used:

  femeia ce o iubesc   the women I love

---

[103] In *că el este român, asta o știu* the pronoun *asta* is the redundant pronoun for *că el este român* and *o* is the redundant pronoun for *asta*.

Secondary object

In Romania some verbs can have two objects: a primary and a secondary object:

Mă învață *limba română.*	He/she is teaching me Romanian.
M-a întrebat *ceva.*	He/she asked me something.
M-a rugat *să plec.*	He/she asked me to leave.
M-a anunțat *că este însărcinată.*	She told me that she is pregnant.

The secondary object is never preceded by the preposition *pe*, and the redundant direct object pronoun can never be used.

Indirect object

The noun or the pronoun that functions as an indirect object must be in the dative case. The indirect object occurs with verbs denoting giving and saying:

I-am dat *Mariei* o carte.	I gave a book *to Maria.*
Profesorul le explică *studenților.*	The teacher explains *to the students.*

Notice, that in English the preposition 'to' is not always needed (*I gave Maria a book*). However, in Romanian the dative case must always be used.

In Romanian the indirect object is also used with verbs denoting asking, telling or forbidding. The direct object is expressed with a *să*-clause:

Mi-a cerut să plec.	He/She asked *me* to leave.
Mi-a interzis să plec.	He/She forbid *me* from leaving.

Compare with:

M-a cerut de nevastă.	He asked me to be his wife.

The dative is even used with some verbs that in English require the use of a direct object:

Cum supraviețuim *crizei?*	How do we survive the crisis?
Zahărul dăunează *sănătății.*	Sugar damages health.
Grecia a furat *Turciei* 16 insule.	Greece has stolen 16 islands
(*Adevărul*)	form Turkey.
a mulțumi *cuiva* pentru ceva	to thank someone for something

The indirect object also occurs in several impersonal expression, such as:

Mi-e foame / frig.	I am hungry / cold.
Îmi plac limbile.	I like languages.
Îmi trebuie bani.	I need money.

Redundant indirect object

Also the unstressed dative form of the personal pronoun is often used even if the indirect object occurs in the same sentence (clitic doubling). The redundant indirect object pronoun is used in the following cases:

- When the indirect object is placed before the verb:

Lui Ion *i-*am dat bani.	I gave money to Ion.
La trei dintre ei *le-*am dat bani.	I gave money to three of them.
Acestora *le* plac limbile.	These people like languages.
Mie *îmi* place limba română.	I like the Romanian language.

  However, the redundant pronoun is not obligatory with the pronouns *(ori)cine* and *(ori)cât*:

Cui (i-)ai dat cartea?	To whom did you give the book?
La câți (le-)ai dat bani?	To how many did you give money?

- When the indirect object is a stressed personal pronoun, a polite personal pronoun or a demonstrative pronoun placed after the verb:

Mi l-a dat numai mie.	He/she gave it only to me.
Li l-a dat acestuia.	He/she gave it to this one.

  With other pronouns the redundant pronoun is not compulsory.

- Usually when a noun referring to a human being is placed after the verb:

I-am dat bani lui Ion.	I gave money to Ion.

  However, this is not obligatory in modern language.

- The redundant pronoun can be used when the indirect object (placed after the verb) is a noun referring to an animal:

(I)-am dat câinelui meu apă.	I gave water to my dog.

The redundant pronoun is not usually used when an inanimate indirect object is placed after the verb:

Decizia contravine legii.	The decision is against the law.

The redundant pronoun is only used if the inanimate indirect object can be confused with the genitive form.

Predicative

A predicative is a complement that supplements the subject or (more rarely) the object.

Subject predicative

The subject predicative (or subject complement) is used with copula verbs (linking verbs), such as *a fi* 'to be', *a se face, a ajunge, a ieși, a devine* 'to become', *a părea* 'to seem', *a rămâne* 'to remain', etc. The subject predicative is expressed usually with a noun, a pronoun, an adjective or a numeral in the nominative case:

Sunt *Ion*.	I am Ion.
Cine este el?	Who is he?
Mașina este *roșie*.	The car is red.
Suntem *patru*.	We are four.
Ion devine / va ieși / va ajunge / va fi / se face *profesor*.	Ion will be a teacher.
Ion pare *bolnav*.	Ion seems ill.
A rămas *șocat*.	He/she was left shocked.

An adjective used as a subject predicative agrees with the subject in gender and number (see p. 120).

The subject predicative can also be expressed by a genitive structure or a possessive pronoun preceded by the genitive article (see p. 92):

Aceasta mașină este *a lui Ion / a mea*.	This car is Ion's / mine.

When there is no subject or the subject is a subordinate clause or a nominal verb form, an adverb is used as subject predicate instead of an adjective:

E *bine / important* să știi limbi străine.	It is good / important to know foreign languages.
Este *greu* să te lași de fumat.	It is difficult to stop smoking.
A greși este *omenește*.	To err is human.

Notice that the adverb usually has the same form as the neuter singular (see p. 273).

The subject predicative can also be expressed with an infinitive (usually preceded by the preposition *de*), a supine or a prepositional phrase:

Scopul este *(de) a supraviețui*.	The goal is to survive.
Această greșeală este *de neiertat*.	This mistake is unforgivable.

Asta este *contra legii*.	This is against the law.
Moneda aceasta este *de argint*.	This coin is made of silver.

Sometimes a predicative is used without a copula verb (as a supplementary predicative) to describe the subject:

Doarmă *liniștită*.	She is sleeping peacefully.
(= Ea este liniștită și doarmă.)	
A plecat de acasă *tânără*.	She left home young.
(= când era tânără.)	
Se știa *bolnav*.	He knew he was ill.
(= Știa că este bolnav.)	

Object predicative

The object predicative (or object complement) is always in the nominative-accusative case, and it is never preceded by the preposition *pe*. If the object predicative is a noun, it has no article:

Mă cheamă *Ion*.	My name is Ion.
Îmi spune/zice *Ion*.	
L-au ales *președinte*.	They elected him president / He was elected president.
L-au numit *ministru*.	They named him minister.
L-au angajat *profesor*.	They hired him as a teacher.
Cine te crezi (că ești)?	Who do you think you are?

If the object predicative is an adjective, it agrees with the object in gender and number:

Mă faci *gelos / geloasă*.	You make me jealous.
Ne faci *geloși / geloase*.	You make us jealous.

The rules of agreement are the same as for subject predicatives (see p. 120).

Subordinate clauses

Use of moods in subordinate clauses

In subordinate clauses the indicative, conditional and presumptive moods are used as in main clauses. If the subordinate clause starts with the conjunction *să (ca ... să)*[104], the conjunctive must always be used.

---

[104] See p. 250.

Use of tenses in subordinate clauses

When the main verb is in the present, in the subordinate clause the present is used for simultaneous, the future for later, and the perfect, imperfect and pluperfect for earlier actions[105]:

Știu că	plouă.	I know	it is raining.
	va plouă.		it is going to rain.
	a plouat.		it has rained.
	ieri la 5 ploua.		that yesterday at 5 o'clock it was raining.
	ieri, înainte de sosirea lui, plouase.		that yesterday, before he arrived, it had rained.

When the main verb is in a past tense, the same tenses are used in the subordinate clause:

Știam că	plouă.	I knew	it was raining.
	va ploua.		it was going to rain.
	a plouat.		it had rained.

However, the past tenses can also be used:

Știam că	ploua
	avea să plouă.
	plouase.

The meaning is not always the same. Compare:

I-am spus că Dan e bolnav.	I told him Dan was sick (he might still be sick).
I-am spus că Dan era bolnav.	I told him Dan was sick (he is not sick now).

For general truths only the present is possible:

Știam că unghiul drept are 90°.	I knew a right angle was 90°.

When the main verb is in the future, in the subordinate clause the present or future is used for simultaneous, the perfect for earlier, and the future for later actions:

Vei crede că plouă / va ploua.	You will think it is raining.
că a plouat.	You will think is has rained.
că va ploua.	You will think it will rain.

---

[105] The examples in this section are from *Enciclopedia limbii române*, p. 117-118.

If the verb of the subordinate clause is in the conjunctive, conditional or pre-sumptive, the present tense is used for simultaneous or posterior actions. Thus, if the main verb is in the past tense, the present can also refer to actions that have already occurred:

Vreau să plec.	I want to go.
Voiam să plec.	I wanted to go.
Lucruri pe care trebuie să le faci înainte să mori	things you have to do before you die
El a băut alcool înainte să moară.	He had drunk alcohol before he died.
Știu că ar veni.	I know he would come.
Știam că ar veni.	I knew he would come.

The conjunctive, conditional and presumptive perfect is used for actions that happened before the main verb:

Nu știu să fi venit cineva.	I do not know if anyone has come.
Nu știam să fi venit cineva.	I did not know if anyone had come.
Știu că ar fi venit.	I know he would have come.
Știam că ar fi venit.	I knew he would have come.

Subordinate declarative clauses

Subordinate declarative clauses (*that*-clauses) are used as subjects, direct objects, predicatives or attributes. In Romanian either the conjunction *că* + indicative (conditional, presumptive) or *să (ca ... să)* + conjunctive is used.

The conjunction *că* is used when the subordinate clause is seen as representing a fact. The main clause has a verb such as *admite* 'to admit', *adăuga* 'to add', *afirma* 'to afirm', *atesta / certifica* 'to testify', *constata* 'to state', *critica* 'to criticize', *demonstra* 'to demonstrate', *explica* 'to explain', *menționa* 'to mention', *raporta*, 'to tell, to report', *povesti* 'to tell a story', *spune / zice* 'to say', *ști* 'to know', *înțelege* 'to understand', an adverb such as *sigur* 'sure', *chiar* 'clear' or a noun such as *fapt* 'a fact', *adevăr* 'truth':

Spune/Afirmă/Știe că Ion este român.	He/she says/affirms/knows that Ion is Romanian.
Despre semințele de schinduf se știe că sunt bogate în fibre. (*Adevărul*)	It is known that thyme seeds are rich in fibre.
Este sigur că	It is sure that
Este adevărat că	It is true that
Este chiar că	It is clear that

faptul că...	the fact that
faptul este că...	the fact is that
adevărul este că...	the truth is that
Președintele italian neagă faptul că ar fi aprobat decretul. (*realitatea.net*)	The Italian president denies that the law would have been approved.
Regret că te am cunoscut.	I regret knowing you.

The conjunction *că* is also used when the subordinate clause is seen as certainly untrue (*contrafactiv*). In the main clause, verbs like *inventa* 'to make up', *minți, fabula* 'to lie', *a-și imagina* 'to imagine', *simula* 'to pretend' or nouns like *minciună* 'a lie' are used:

A mințit că a fost bătut.	He/she lied about having been beaten.
Este o minciună că...	It is a lie that
Au simulat că sunt bolnav. (*Adevărul*)	They pretended to be sick.

The conjunction *că* is also used with verbs and nouns denoting belief, such as *presupune* 'to presume', *crede* 'to believe', *opina* 'to think', *considera* 'to consider', *a se parea* 'to seem'. In these cases one does not say whether the sentence is true or not (*nonfactiv*):

Crede că Ion este român. Crede că ar fi posibil.	He/she believes Ion is Romanian. He/she believes that it would be possible.
credința că...	the belief that
Este acuzat că a furat un telefon mobil.	He is accused of stealing a mobile phone.
Se pare că nu aveți succes nici în afaceri. (*Cotidianul*)	It seems like you do not succeed even in business.
Se presupune că făceau parte dintr-o bandă. (*Adevărul*)	It is assumed that they were part of a crime ring.
Se crede că ar fi fost victima piraților. (*Cotidianul*)	It is believed that [the ship] has been the victim of pirates.

The conjunction *să (ca ... să)* + conjunctive is used when the action of the subordinate clause is seen as possible, uncertain, theoretical. The subordinate clause does not express a fact, but just a thought or an idea.

Thus, in the following example *să plece* 'he leaves' does not mean that he actually leaves, it just expresses the idea of him leaving:

Tata i-a permis lui Ion să plece.	Father gave Ion permission to leave.

This happens especially when one tries to make the subject of the subordinate clause do something, since we do not know whether the subject of the subordinate clause really does it or not:

Vreau ca tu să vii.	I want you to come.

In the main sentence, structures are used that denote e.g:

- a wish (*vrea, dori, spera*)
- a possibility (*putea*)
- an evaluation (*este dificil, este posibil, merita*)
- a request (*ruga, cere, pofti*)
- a piece of advice (*sugera, recomanda*)
- permission (*permite, lăsa, accepta, aproba*)
- a prohibition (*interzice*)
- an order, a demand (*comanda, ordona*)
- an obligation (*obliga, forţa, trebuie*)
- an attempt (*încerca, căuta*)
- helping (*ajuta*)

E.g:

Sper să fiu un preşedinte cu succes. (*Cotidianul*)	I hope to be a successful president.
Voi accepta să fiu candidat. (*Cotidianul*)	I will accept the candidacy.
Nu a fost lăsat să dea telefon. (*Adevărul*)	He was not allowed to phone.
Sosirea unor musafiri va obliga să vă schimbaţi planurile pentru azi. (*Cotidianul*)	The arrival of guests forces you to change your plans for the day.
Vinul te ajută să trăieşti mai mult. (*Cotidianul*)	Wine helps you to live longer.
Sper ca reacţia Rusiei să fie una pozitivă. (*Cotidianul*)	I hope that the reaction of Russia will be positive.
Toată lumea aşteaptă ca în această ţară să aibă loc o schimbare. (*Adevărul*)	Everybody hopes that there will be a change in this country.
Se doreşte să îi atragă pe turişti. (*Adevărul*)	It is hoped to attract tourists.
Ţi se spune să-ţi strângi lucrurile şi să pleci. (*Adevărul*)	You are ordered to collect your things and go
Este posibil să fi fugit cu un bărbat de 20 de ani. (*Adevărul*)	It is possible that she has run away with a 20-year-old man.

Era să murim.	We almost died.
Nu este uşor să treci printr-o astfel de pregătire. (*Adevărul*)	It is not easy to go through such training.
Nu este obligatoriu să comanzi de fiecare dată BigMac şi cartofi prăjiți. (*Adevărul*)	You do not have to order a Big Mac and fries every time.
Trebuie *ca* Radu *să* plece.	Radu has to go.
Merită să faci sex la serviciu? (*Adevărul*)	Is it worth having sex in the workplace?
Am nevoie să vorbesc cu cineva. N-am posibilitate să plec. Este timpul să plec.	I need to speak with someone. It is not possible for me to leave. It is time I leave.
Crăciunescu a dat ordin ca toți oficialii Universității să învețe spaniola. (*www.ziua.ro*)	Crăciunescu gave the order that all university officials must learn Spanish.
Am dorința ca viitorul premier să fie de la PD-L. (*realitatea.net*)	I hope that the next prime minister will be from PD-L.

As can be seen from the examples, in Romania the conjunctive mood is used even if the verb of the subordinate clause has the same subject as the main clause. In such cases English uses the infinite:

Vreau să vin.	I want to come.

However, with the verb *putea* the conjunctive mood can be replaced by the infinitive form without the prepositions *a*:

Pot veni. = Pot să vin.	I can come.
Mi-l poți da? = Poți să mi-l dai?	Can you give it to me?

A conjunctive is also used with verbs meaning 'to start, to continue, to stop':

A început să plouă.	It started to rain.
Continuă să plouă.	It keeps on raining.
A terminat să plouă.	It has stopped raining.

Some structures can be used both with the indicative and the conjunctive mood. In these cases the indicative expresses a fact, while the conjunctive expresses a possibility, a wish, an order, an idea etc. Compare e.g.:

Spune că pleacă.	He says he is leaving.
Spune să plece.	He tells him to leave.
Nu cred că vine.	I cannot believe he is coming. (He is coming, but I do not believe it.)
Nu cred să vină.	I do not believe he is coming. (I believe he is not coming.)

mă tem că aţi greşit	I am afraid you made a mistake (= I am sorry, but)
mă tem să fac ceva	I am afraid to do something
idea ca Pământul este rotund	the idea that the Earth is round.
Mi-a venit idea să scriu o carte.	I got the idea to write a book.
Nu ştie că bunica lui a murit.	He does not know his grandmother died. (It is a fact that his grandmother died.)
Nu ştiu să utilizez computerul.	He does not know how to use a computer.
Îmi place că eşti aici.	I am happy that you are here. (It is a fact that you are here.)
Îmi place să fii aici.	I would like you to be here. (I wish you were here.)
Este important că te văd.	It is important that I will meet you. (The fact that I will meet you is important)
Este important să te văd.	It is important that I meet you. (I wish to meet you.)
A învăţat ca Marte este o planetă.	He/she learnt that Mars is a planet. (a fact)
A învăţat să scrie.	He/she learnt how to write.
Este interesant că studiezi limbi străine.	It is interesting that you are studying foreign languages.
Este interesant să studiezi[106] limbi străine.	It is interesting to study foreign languages.

Subordinate interrogative, imperative and exclamative clauses

The subordinate interrogative and exclamative clauses start with an interrogative pronoun (see p. 165) or with an interrogative adverb (p. 270):

M-a întrebat *unde* trăiesc.	He/she asked me where I lived.
Nu ştie *ce* vorbeşte!	He does not know what he is talking about!
Ştiu *cui* i-a telefonat.	I know who he/she phoned.
Ştiu *ce* frumoasă este!	I know how beautiful she is!
Încă nu se ştie *cine* va fi la putere şi *cine* în opoziţie. (*Adevărul*)	It is not known yet who will be in power and who in the opposition.

---

[106] Impersonal *tu*, see p. 268.

| Nu contează *cine* și *cum* votează, ci doar *cine* numără voturile. (*Cotidianul*) | It does not matter who votes and how, but who counts the votes. |

If there is no interrogative pronoun or adverb, the conjunctions *dacă* or *de* (rare, colloq.) are used with the subordinate interrogative clauses and the conjunction *să* + conjunctive with the exclamative clauses:

| Nu știu *dacă/de* este român. (Este român?) | I do not know if he/she is Romanian. |
| Mi-a spus *să* plec. (Pleci!) | He/she told me to leave. |

In the subordinate interrogative clauses the conjunctive mood can be used for expressing uncertainty:

| Nu știu *ce* să facem acum. | I do not know what we should do now. |
| Nu știu *dacă* să râd sau să plâng. | I do not know whether to laugh or cry. |

Relative clauses

Relative clauses start either with relative pronouns (for examples, see p. 170), or with relative adverbs (p. 270):

orașul *unde* locuiesc	the city where I live
orașul *de unde* am venit	the city where I have come from
momentul *când* am venit	the moment I arrived
modul *cum* ai făcut-o	the way you did it
în timpul *cât* era căsătorit	during the time he was married

As can be seen from the examples above, in Romanian the relative pronoun or adverb must usually be used, whereas in English it is not always needed. Also, unlike in English, the prepositions are always placed before the relative pronoun or adverb.

The conjunctive mood is used in the relative clause if the relative pronoun is not referring to any specific person or a thing:

Nu există locuitor care să nu fi fost lătrat de maidanezi. (*Adevărul*)	There is no inhabitant at whom stray dogs have not barked.
Se caută secretară care să vorbească limba spaniolă.	A secretary with knowledge of Spanish is needed.
Compare: Caut secretara care vorbește limba spaniolă.	I am looking for the secretary who speaks Spanish.

If the conjunctive mood is used and the headword is a negative pronoun or an indefinite pronoun, the relative pronoun can be left out:

> Nu cunosc pe nimeni (care) să mă   I do not know anyone who could help me.
> poată ajuta.

Conditional clauses

Notice that in Romanian the conditional mood can be used in both the main clause (apodosis) and in the subordinate clause (protasis).

- if: *dacă* + indicative/conditional, *de* (colloq., poetic.), *să (ca ... să)* + conjunctive:

> Vin, *dacă* pot.   I will come, if I can.
> Aş veni, *dacă* aş putea.   I would come, if I could.
> Aş fi venit, *dacă* aş fi putut.   I would have come, if I had been able to.

> *Dacă* fotbal nu e, nimic nu e.   If there is no football, there is
> (*Cotidianul*)   nothing

> *Dacă* vei avea o nevastă bună,   If you get a good wife, you will happy;
> vei fi fericit; *dacă* nu, vei deveni   if not, you will be a philosopher.
> filosof. (*Sokrates*)

> Juanes ar fi votat pentru Obama,   Juanes would have voted for Obama
> *dacă* ar fi fost cetăţean american.   if he had been an American citizen.
> (*Mediafax.ro*)

> *De*-aş fi Peter Pan (film)   If I were Peter Pan

The conditional perfect can be replaced with the indicative imperfect both in the main cause and in the conditional clause:

> Veneam, dacă puteam.   I would have come if I had been able to.

Usually the same verb form (perfect conditional or imperfect indicative) is used both in the main and the subordinate clause, but other combinations are also possible (*veneam, dacă aş fi putut / aş fi venit, dacă puteam*).

The conjunction *să (ca ... să)* + conjunctive can also be used in the protasis, though mainly in colloquial style:

> Aş veni, *să* pot.   I would come if I could.
> Aş fi venit / veneam, *să* fi putut.   I would have come, if I had been able to.

- only if: *doar dacă*

Vom utiliza banii de la FMI *doar dacă* va fi nevoie. (*Adevărul*)	We will use the money from the IMF only if we have to.

- unless: *decât dacă*

Nu vom utiliza banii *decât dacă* va fi nevoie.	We will not use the money unless we need to.

- in the case that: *în caz că/dacă/când*

în caz că nu ştiaţi	in the case that you do not know
în caz că nu ar fi reuşit	in the case that he/she would not have succeeded

- on the condition that: *cu condiţia să (ca ... să)* + conjunctive

cu condiţia să plăteşti tu	on the condition that you will pay

Temporal clauses

Temporal subordinate clauses express time. Usually the indicative mood is used, but in some clause types referring to the future ('before', 'until') the conjunctive is required.

- when: *când*

Când eram tânăr, iernile erau mai reci.	When I was young, the winters were colder.
Vino *când* vrei!	Come when you want!

  Notice that in Romanian the future tense can be used in temporal clauses:

Când voi fi mare, voi fi arhitect.	When I grow up, I will be an architect.

- before: *înainte să (ca ... să)* + conjunctive

înainte ca România *să* intre în UE	before Romania enters the EU

- while: *în timp ce, în vreme ce, pe când*

o jurnalistă împuşcată *în timp ce* transmitea în direct (*EVZ*)	a journalist was shot while she was on the air

- until: *până (când/ce)* or *până (când) să (ca ... să)* + conjunctive (no difference in meaning), *când să (ca ... să)* + conjunctive

până când simptomele gripei vor dispărea (*Adevărul*)	until the symptoms of the flu disappear
Am citit *până ce* s-a terminat ora.	We were reading until the end of the class.

Va dura mult *până să* dispară gaura din stratul de ozon.	It will take a long time until the hole in the ozone layer disappears.

The negative *până nu* means 'as long as':

Beau *până nu* mai pot. (*Mr Juve*)	I will drink until I cannot any more. (= as long as I can)

Până nu is especially used after a negative main clause:

Nu cred *până nu* văd.	I do not believe until I see. (= I do not believe as long as I do not see).
Româncele nu pot pleca în concediu *până nu*-şi găsesc înlocuitoare. (*Adevărul*)	Romanian women cannot take leave of absence, until they find a substitute.
Nu se poate aprecia înălţimea valurilor *până nu* se identifică locul exact al epicentrului. (*Adevărul*)	The height of the waves cannot be estimated until the exact location of the epicentre is identified.

- since: *de când*

Sunt fericit *de când* te-am întâlnit.	I have been happy since I met you.

- as long as: *cât timp, câtă vreme, (atât) cât*

Câtă vreme sunt aici, poţi să faci ceea ce vrei.	As long as I am here, you can do what you want.
Trupele vor rămâne în Afganistan *atât cât* trebuie.	The troops will stay in Afghanistan as long as needed.

- whenever: *ori de câte ori, oricând, orişicând*

Comitetul se reuneşte *ori de câte ori* este necesar.	The committee assembles whenever needed.
Vino *oricând* vrei!	Come whenever you want!

- after: *după ce*

Doi tineri au murit, *după ce* maşina lor a luat foc. (*realitatea.net*)	Two young people died when their car caught fire.
Jurnalist în stare gravă *după ce* a fost bătut (*Adevărul*)	Journalist in severe state after being beaten up

- immediately when, once: *imediat ce, (de) îndată ce, o dată ce, (de) cum*

Ştiri *imediat ce* se întâmplă (*Hunedoreanul*)	News immediately as it happens.

Macedonia va fi invitată să adere la NATO *de îndată ce* va rezolva problema numelui statului în negocierile cu Grecia. (*Cotidianul*)

Macedonia will be invited to join NATO once the problem concerning the name of the state is resolved in negotiations with Greece.

Acest lucru va fi discutat la Națiunile Unite, *o dată ce* rolul ONU va fi clarificat. (*Adevărul*)

This will be discussed at the UN once the role of the UN has been clarified.

De cum vine zăpada, ursul își caută un bârlog sub o stâncă. (*animale-salbatice.ro*)

Once the snow arrives, the bear searches for a den under a rock.

Causal clauses

Causal clauses express a reason ('because'). Causal conjunctions include *pentru că, căci, deoarece, fiindcă, întrucât, că, cum, din cauză că, din pricină că, pe motiv că, pentru motivul că.*

Lupu a plecat din partid *pentru că* nu a fost propus președinte. (*Adevărul*)

Lupu left the party because he was not selected as a candidate for the presidency.

Israel a câștigat *deoarece* este o echipa mai valoroasă. (*Protv.md*)

Israel won because it is a more talented team.

Rusia ar trebui să respecte deciziile altor state, *întrucât* este dreptul acestora de a alege cu cine să se alieze. (*Cotidianul*)

Russia should respect the decisions of other countries, because it is their right to choose who they want to ally with.

Nu pot veni, *că* sunt bolnav.

I cannot come because I am sick.

Aceasta se întâmplă *din pricină că* facem prea puține lucruri care ne fac cu adevărat plăcere. (*Adevărul*)

This happens because we do too few things we really like.

Sute de candidați au fost scoși din sală *pe motiv că* diplomele lor sunt ilegale. (*Adevărul*)

Hundreds of candidates were removed from the lecture room because their diplomas were illegal.

Cum can be used only before the main clause, while *căci* is only used after it:

Cum sunt bolnav, nu pot veni.
Nu pot veni, *căci* sunt bolnav.

Since I am sick, I cannot come.
I cannot come, because I am sick.

Final clauses

Final clauses express purpose ('in order that, so that'). The conjunctive mood is usually used. The final conjunctions are *ca să, pentru ca să, pentru ca ... să, să (ca ... să)*:

Mâncăm *ca să* trăim, nu trăim *ca să* mâncăm.	We eat to live, we do not live to eat.
A plătit 10.000 de euro *ca să* joace tenis cu Ilie Năstase. (*Cotidianul*)	He paid 10.000 Euros in order to play tennis with Ilie Năstase.
Clinton va lupta *pentru ca* Obama *să* fie ales președinte. (*Mediafax.ro*)	Clinton will fight so that Obama will be elected president.
Merge *să* studieze în România.	He/she is going to Romania to study.
Românii sunt dispuși *să* accepte salarii mai mici. (*Adevărul*)	Romanians are ready to accept lower salaries.
N-am timp *să* studiez. Este timpul *să* studiezi.	I do not have time to study. It is time for you to study.

Colloquially, the conjunction *de* can also be used. The tense and mood used is the same as in the main clause:

S-a dus *de* s-a culcat. Du-te *de* te culcă!	He/she went to bed. Go to bed!

Concessive clauses

Concessive subordinate clauses express concession (even though something else happens).

- even though, although ; even if: *deși, cu toate că, chiar dacă/de/să*[107], *și dacă/de/să, indiferent dacă/că, în ciuda faptului că, chit că* (colloq.), *măcar că/dacă/de/să* (colloq.)

Eu vin, *chiar dacă* plouă! Eu vin, *chiar dacă* ar ploua!	I will come even though it is raining! I would come even if it rained!
Georgia este bombardată, *deși* Rusia a anunțat încetarea ofensivei. (*EVZ*)	Georgia is being bombarded, even though Russia has announced that they will stop the attack.
Procentajul de ocupare a hotelurilor din Spania a scăzut cu 10 %, *în ciuda faptului că* prețurile au fost reduse. (*Adevărul*)	The occupancy rate of Spanish hotels has dropped 10% even though the prices have been reduced.

---

[107] See conditional clauses, p. 304.

- not even if: *nici (chiar) dacă/de/să*

Fructele nu trebuie să lipsească din alimentaţia ta, *nici dacă* eşti perfect sănătos. (*Adevărul*)	Fruit should not be missing from your diet, not even if you are perfectly healthy.

Consecutive clauses

Consecutive clauses express a result. The conjunctive mood is used if the consequence is hypothetical. A consecutive clause is always placed after the main clause. The consecutive conjunctions are *aşa/astfel/atât - încât/că, aşa/astfel/atât - (încât) să (ca ... să), ca să, de* (colloq.).

Sunt bolnav, *aşa că* astăzi nu pot Sunt *aşa de* bolnav, *încât / că* nu pot să lucrez.	I am sick, so today I cannot work. I am so sick that today I cannot work.
Temperaturile vor creşte de la o zi la alta, *astfel încât* vineri şi sâmbătă vor depăşi 38 de grade. (*Adevărul*)	The temperatures will rise daily and will be over 38 degrees on Friday and Saturday.
Apa nu are un conţinut suficient de clor, *astfel încât să* fie potabilă. (*Adevărul*)	There is not enough chlorine in the water for it to be drinkable.
Sună prea frumos *ca să* fie adevărat. Am râs *de* am plâns.	Sounds too good to be true. I laughed so that I cried.

Modal clauses

Modal clauses express manner.

- as, like: *(aşa/astfel) cum, după cum, la fel cum, precum* (old-fashioned)

Am făcut (*aşa*) *cum* a spus el. Fă *cum* vrei!	I did as he told me. Do as you wish!

- as much as: *(atât) cât*

Vânzările de automobile n-au crescut *cât* era estimat. (*Ziarul Financiar*)	The car sales have not grown as much as estimated.

- as if: *ca şi cum, ca şi când, (de) parcă*

Se uită la mine *ca şi cum* nu m-ar cunoaşte.	He/she looks at me as if he/she does not know me.

De parcă nu ar fi avut un an întreg să se pregătească. (*Cotidianul*)	As if they did not have a whole year to prepare themselves.

- without: *fără să (ca ... să)* + conjunctive

Oamenii au aplicat pentru o slujbă *fără să* întrebe despre ce e vorba. (*Adevărul*)	People applied for the job without knowing what it was about.

Comparative clauses

- as + adj. + as: *la fel de / tot aşa de / tot atât de / deopotrivă de – (pre)cum / cât / după cum / aşa cum / întocmai cum*

Ion este *la fel de* înalt *cât* (este) şi ea.	Ion is as tall as she (is).

- so + adj. + as: *aşa de / atât de / astfel de – (pre)cum / cât*

Nu era *atât de* greu *precum* credeam.	It was not so difficult as I thought.

- Two different qualities are compared with *tot atât de – pe cât este de* or *pe cât este de - pe atât este de*:

Pe cât este de important, *pe atât* este de interesant.	It is as important as it is interesting.

- the more – the more: *cu cât (mai) – cu atât (mai), de ce – de ce / de aceea*

Cu cât mănânci mai multă ciocolată, *cu atât* eşti mai deprimat. (*Libertatea.ro*)	The more you eat chocolate, the more depressed you will be.

- than: *decât*

Ion este mai înalt *decât* este ea.	Ion is taller than she is.
Este mai interesant *decât* pare.	It is more interesting than it appears.
Oamenii au prostul obicei să mănânce mai mult *decât* au nevoie. (*Adevărul*)	People have the bad habit of eating more than they need.

The main clause can also requires the use of the conjunctive:

Prefer să stau acasă *decât* să merg în club.	I prefer staying at home to going to a club.
Mai bine mor *decât* să mă întorc în România. (*hotnews.ro*) (= este mai bine să mor *decât* să mă întorc)	I would rather die than return to Romania.

Adversative clauses

- instead of: *în loc să (ca ... să)* + conjunctive

Noi preferăm să ne uităm la tele-vizor *în loc să* facem mişcare. (*Adevărul*)	We would rather watch television, instead of doing sports.

- while: *(pe) când, (pe) câtă vreme, în timp/vreme ce*

Noi am avut o politică fiscală mai strictă, *în timp ce* a României a fost mai relaxată. (*dailybusiness.ro*)	We [in Bulgaria] have had a more strict fiscal policy while the one in Romania has been more relaxed.

Cumulative clauses

- apart from: *după ce (că) / pe lângă că / (în) afară că - (mai) şi*

Pe lângă că este frumoasă, este şi inteligentă.	Apart from being beautiful, she is also intelligent.

- not only – but also: *nu numai că - şi*

Nu numai că este frumoasă, este şi inteligentă.	She is not only beautiful, but intelligent too.

- also other things that: *şi altceva decât să*, also otherwise than: *şi altfel decât să*

Fac şi altceva *decât să* studiez.	I also do other things apart from study.

Şi altceva/altfel decât may also precede other subordinate clauses:

Vreau să fac şi altceva *decât ce* face toate lumea.	I also want to do something different to what everybody else does.

Exception clauses

- except that, besides: *(în) afară că*

Voi n-aveţi nimic de oferit *în afară că* sunteţi foarte frumoşi. (*Cotidianul*)	You have nothing to offer except that you are really beautiful.

- nothing else but: *decât să (ca ... să), decât (că), decât* + a subordinate clause

Nu fac altceva *decât să* studiez. (= *decât (că)* studiez)	I do nothing but study.

Decât can also be used in front of another subordinate clause:

Nu a spus *decât că*...	He only said that....
Nu vreau *decât să* studiez.	All I want is to study.
Nu face *decât ce* vrea.	He only does what he wants.
Nu vreau să fiu altceva *decât (ce)* sunt.	I do not want to be anything else than I am.

In this case, the mood in the subordinate exception clause is the same as in normal subordinate clauses (*a spus că, vreau să* etc.).

- (all) but: *mai puțin să*

Belgradul va face totul *mai puțin să* trimită tancuri. (*ziare.com*)	Belgrade will do everything except send tanks.

Mai puțin can also be used in front of another subordinate clause:

Știu tot *mai puțin ce* vrei tu.	I know everything, except what you want.

Word order

The Romanian word order is quite free. Neutral word order in declarative clauses is subject – predicate – direct object / indirect object / predicative - adverb:

Ion citește o carte la bibliotecă.	Ion is reading a book at the library.
Ion este român.	Ion is Romanian.

For emphasis, any element can be moved to the left:

Ion, *la bibliotecă*, citește o carte. *La bibliotecă*, Ion citește o carte.	*At the library*, Ion is reading a book.
Ion *o carte* citește la bibliotecă. *O carte* citește Ion la bibliotecă.	It is *a book* Ion is reading at the library.
O carte Ion citește la bibliotecă.	It is *a book Ion* is reading at the library. It is *Ion* who is reading *a book* at the library.
Citește Ion o carte la bibliotecă.	Ion is *reading* a book at the library.

An emphasized subject can be placed after the verb:

Citește *Ion* o carte la bibliotecă.	It is Ion who is reading a book at the library.

The subject is usually placed after the verb in following cases:

- When an interrogative pronoun or adverb is placed at the beginning of the sentence (unless the interrogative pronoun itself is the subject):

Unde este *Ion?*	Where is Ion?
Ce frumoasă este *Ioana!*	How beautiful Ioana is!
Cine a făcut asta?	Who has done this?
Cine ești *tu?*	Who are you?

- The same happens in indirect questions and relative sentences:

Nu știu unde este *Ion.*	I do not know where Ion is.
persoana cu care a vorbit *Ion*	the person Ion talked with

- When the verb is the focus of the sentence (answering the question 'what is happening/what happened'):

Sună *telefonul.*	The phone is ringing.
S-a întâmplat *un miracol!*	A miracle has happened!
A murit *Neil Armstrong.*	Neil Armstrong has died.

  This happens often in questions:

E bună *înghețata* pentru sănătate? (*Adevărul*)	Is ice-cream good for the health?
A fost sau n-a fost *Lupu* la Moscova? (*Adevărul*)	Has Lupu been to Moscow or not?

- In structures like:

Îmi trebuie *un plic.*	I need a pen.
Îmi place *muzică.*	I like music.
Mă doare *capul.*	I have a headache.
Îmi curge *nasul.*	My nose is running.
Este *frig.*	It is cold.
Mi-e *frig.*	I am cold.

- When the verb is an infinitive:

înainte de a sosi *invitații*	before the guests arrive(d), before the arrival of the guests

- When the subject is an infinitive or a sentence:

E dificil *a studia* limba română.	It is difficult to study Romanian
Despre semințele de schinduf se știe *că sunt bogate în fibre.* (*Adevărul*)	It is known that thyme seeds are rich in fibre.

- With an existential verb ('there is'):

Este *o problemă*.	There is a problem.
Nu există *soluții*.	There are no solutions.

- After quoted speech:

„Bună ziua", spuse *Ion*.	"Hello", said Ion.

In theses cases, the subject comes before the verb if emphasised:

Capul mă doare.	I have a *headache*.
Ceea ce ai spus este incredibil!	What you said is incredible!

The indirect object is placed like the direct object. When the verb has both a direct and an indirect object, the first object is more stressed:

I-am dat o carte lui Ion.	I gave Ion a book.
I-am dat lui Ion o carte.	

When the direct object is in the definite form, it usually comes after the indirect object in order to avoid ambiguity:

I-am dat lui Ion cartea.	I gave Ion the book.

I-am dat cartea lui Ion is also possible, but is avoided in writing because it can also mean 'I gave him/her Ion's book.'

For the position of adjective attributes, see p. 116.

Bibliography

Angelescu, Gabriel: *Dicționar practic al limbii române explicativ și morfologic*, ed. a 3-a, București: Editura C. N. I. Coresi, 2006.

Avram, Mioara: *Gramatica pentru toți*, ed. a 3-a, București: Humanitas, 2001.

Avram, Mioara: *Ortografie pentru toți : 30 de dificultăți*, București: Editura Academiei Române, 1990.

Barbu, Ana-Maria: *Conjugarea verbelor românești : 7500 de verbe românești grupate pe clase de conjugare*, București: Editura Coresi, 2006.

Beldescu, G.: *Punctuația în limba română*, ed. a 3-a, București: Gramar, 2004.

Buia, Mihaela: *Ortoepia limbii române și relațiile ei cu ortografia în procesul comunicării verbale actuale*, București: Editura Bren, 2006.

Calotă, Ion & Vlădulescu, Ștefanin: *Lexicon ortografic, ortoepic și morfologic școlar al limbii române (LOOMS)*, Craiova: Scrisul Românesc, 2003.

Canepari, Luciano: *Natural phonetics and tonetics*, Muenchen: Lincom Europa, 2007.

Chitoran, Ioana: *The phonology of Romanian: a constraint-based approach*, Berlin: Mouton de Gruyter, 2002.

Cojocaru, Dana: *Romanian grammar*, Slavic and East European Language Research Cente, 2003, http://www.seelrc.org:8080/grammar/pdf/stand_alone_Romanian.pdf.

Comșulea, Elena & Șerban, Valentina & Teiuș, Sabina: *Dicționar explicativ al limbii române de azi*, ed. a 2-a, București: Litera Internațional, 2007.

Comșulea, Elena & Șerban, Valentina & Teiuș, Sabina: *Dicționar uzual al limbii române*, Pitești: Paralela 45, 2008.

Constantinescu-Dobridor, Gh.: *Gramatica esențială a limbii române*, București: Vestala, 2005.

Constantinescu-Dobridor, Gh.: *Îndreptar ortografic, ortoepic, morfologic și de punctuație al limbii române*, ed. a 3-a, București: Lucman, 2009.

Coteanu, Ion: *Gramatica de bază a limbii române*, București: Albatros, 1982.

Cruceru, Constantin & Teodorescu, Vasile: *Gramatica limbii române*, București: Gramar, 2008.

Cychnerski, Tomasz: *Fleksja werbalna w języku rumu'nskim = Flexiunea verbală în limba română = Verbal inflection in Romanian*, Pozna'n: Uniwersytet im. Adama Mickiewicza w Poznaniu, 1999.

Dicționar invers al limbii române & CD-ROM, coordonator Cecilia Căpățînă, București: Niculescu, 2007.

Dicționar ortografic al limbii române : 74 500 de cuvinte, Academia de Știinţe a Republicii Moldova, Chișinău: Litera, 2001.

Dicționar ortografic, ortoepic și morfologic al limbii române DOOM, Academia Română, ed. a 2-a, București: Univers Enciclopedic, 2007.

Dicționarul explicativ al limbii române DEX, Academia Română, ed. a 2-a revăzută și adăugită, București: Univers Enciclopedic, 2009.

Dicționar explicativ ilustrat al limbii române DEXI, Chișinău: Arc, 2007.

Dimitriu, Corneliu: *Tratat de gramatică a limbii române*, Iași: Institutul European, 1999.

Dobrovie-Sorin, Carmen & Giurgea, Ion (eds.): *A reference grammar of Romanian. Volume 1: The noun phrase*, Amsterdam: Benjamins, 2013.

Doca, Gheorghe: *Learn Romanian: course for English speakers*, București: Niculescu, 2008.

Enciclopedia limbii române, Academia Română, București: Univers Enciclopedic, 2006.

Felecan, Daiana: *Complementele în limba română actuală : elemente de sintaxă și funționare discursivă*, București: Tritonic, 2010.

Forăscu, Narcisa: *Dificultăți gramaticale ale limbii române*, București, Universitatea din București, 2002, http://ebooks.unibuc.ro/ filologie/ Nforascu-DGLR.

Gönczöl-Davies, Ramona: *Romanian: an essential grammar*, London: Routledge, 2008.

Goga, Mircea: *Gramatica limbii române*, ed. a 2-a, București: Niculescu, 2008.

Gramatica de bază a limbii române, Academia Română, București: Univers Enciclopedic Gold, 2010.

Gramatica limbii române, ed. a 2-a, București: Academia Republicii Socialiste România, 1966.

Gramatica limbii române, I: Cuvântul, II: Enunțul, tiraj nou, revizuit, București: Academia Română, 2008.

Gramatica uzuală a limbii române, Academia de Științe a Moldovei, Chișinău: Litera, 2000.

Grammaire du romain = Romanian grammar = Gramatica limbii române, coordonnateurs Liana Pop, Victoria Moldovan, Cluj: Echinox, 1997. An updated version can be found at http://granturi.ubbcluj. ro/autodidact/ro/files/gramatica_ro.pdf

Iliescu, Ada: *Gramatica practică a limbii române actuale*, ed. a 2-a, București: Corint, 2008.

Iordan, Iorgu & Robu, Vladimir: *Limba română contemporană*, București, Editura Didactică și Pedagogică, 1978.

Irimia, Dumitru: *Structura gramaticală a limbii române : Verbul*, Iași: Junimea, 1976.

Irimia, Dumitru: *Gramatica limbii române*, ed. a 3-a, Iași: Polirom, 2008.

Îndreptar ortografic, ortoepic și de punctuație, Academia Română, ed. a 5-a, București: Univers Enciclopedic, 2001.

Limba română contemporană : fonetica, fonologia, morfologia, București: Editura Didactică și Pedagogică, 1985.

Lombard, Alf: "La prononciation du roumain", in *Uppsala universitets årskrift* 1936 (10), p. 103-176.

Lombard, Alf: *Rumänsk grammatik*, Lund: Gleerup, 1973.

Lombard, Alf & Gâdei, Constantin: *Dictionnaire morphologique de la langue roumaine*, Lund: Gleerup, 1981.

Marele dicționar ortografic al limbii române, București: Litera Internațional, 2008.

Mic dicționar academic MDA, Academia Română, București: Univers Enciclopedic Gold, 2010.

Moldovan, Victoria & Pop, Liana & Uricaru, Lucia: *Nivel prag : pentru învățarea limbii române ca limbă străină*, Consiliul Europei, Strasbourg, 2001, http://www.ilr.ro/files/nivel_prag.pdf.

Nagy, Rodica: *Sintaxa limbii române actuale : unități, raporturi și funcții*, Iași: Institutul European, 2005.

Noul dicționar universal al limbii române, ed. a 3-a, București: Litera, 2009.

Pană Dindelegan (ed.): *The grammar of Romanian*, Oxford: Oxford University Press, 2013.

Roach, Peter: "British English: received pronunciation", in *Journal of the International Phonetic Association*, 2004 (34):2, p. 239-245.

Sandfeld, Kr. & Olsen, Hedvig: *Syntax roumaine, I: Emploi des mots à flexion*, Paris: Droz, 1936.

Sandfeld, Kr. & Olsen, Hedvig: *Syntax roumaine, II: Les groupes de mots*, Copenhague: Munksgaard, 1960.

Sandfeld, Kr. & Olsen, Hedvig: *Syntax roumaine, III: Structure de la proposition*, Copenhague: Munksgaard, 1962.

Spinu, Laura: "Perceptual properties of palatalization in Romanian", in *Romance linguistics 2006*, Amsterdam: Benjamins, 2007, p. 303-307.

Tătaru, Ana: *Dicționar de pronunțare a limbii române*, ed. a 2-a, Cluj-Napoca: Clusium, 1999.

Tomescu, Domnița: *Gramatica numelor proprii în limba română*, București: All Educational, 1998.

Turculeț, Adrian: *Introducere în fonetica generală și românească*, Iași: Demiurg, 1999.

Turculeț, Adrian: "Statul fonematic al consoanelor palatale [k', g'] și unele aspecte conexe", *Philologica Jassyensia*, 2010 (6):1, p. 141-147, http://www.philologicajassyensia.ro/upload/VI_1_Turculet.pdf.

Vasiliu, Emanuel: *Fonologia limbii române*, București: Editura Științifică, 1965.

Vintilă-Rădulescu: *Dicționar normativ al limbii române ortografic DIN ortoepic, morfologic și practic*, București: Corint, 2009.

Sources of examples

Adevărul	http://www.adevarul.ro
Cotidianul	http://www.cotidianul.ro
Curierul Național	http://www.curierulnational.ro
EuropaFM	http://www.europafm.ro
EVZ (Evenimentul Zilei)	http://www.evz.ro

Appendix 1: The personal and temporal endings of the verbs

Present indicative

Ia -a	Ia -ia	Ib -a	Ib -ia	II -ea	III -e	IV -i	IV -i (-ă)	IV -Vi	IVb -i	IVb -Vi	IV -î	IVb -î
-,-u[108]	-i,-ii[109]	-ez	-iez	-	-	-	-	-i	-esc	-iesc	-	-ăsc
-i	-i, -ii	-ezi	-iezi	-i	-i	-i	-i	-i	-ești	-iești	-i	-ăști
-ă	-ie	-ează	-iază	-e	-e	-e	-ă	-ie	-ește	-iește	-ă	-ăște
-ăm	-em	-ăm	-iem	-em	-em	-im	-im	-im	-im	-im	-âm	-âm
-ați	-iați	-ați	-iați	-eți	-eți	-iți	-iți	-iți	-iți	-iți	-âți	-âți
-ă	-ie	-ează	-iază	-	-	-	-ă	-ie	-esc	-iesc	-ă	-ăsc

Present conjunctive, third person

Ia -a	Ia -ia	Ib -a	Ib -ia	II -ea	III -e	IV -i	IV -i (-ă)	IV -Vi	IVb -i	IVb -Vi	IV -î	IVb -î
-e	-ie	-eze	-ieze	-ă	-ă	-ă	-e	-ie	-ească	-iască	-e	-ască

Imperative

	Ia: -A	Ib: -A	II: -EA	III: -E	IVa: -I:	IVb: -I:	IVa: -î:	IVb: -î:
2nd pers. sg. affirmative	-ă	-ează[110]	intr. -i, trans. -e[111]		-ește		-ă	-ăște
2nd pers. sg. negative	nu -a		nu -ea	nu -e	nu -i		nu -î	
2nd pers. pl.	(nu) -ați		(nu) -eți	(nu) -eți	(nu) -iți		(nu) -âți	

---

[108] Verbs with stems ending in cons. +*l/r*.
[109] After a consonant.
[110] Verbs with stems in -*i* have the ending -*iază*.
[111] -Ă verbs have the ending -*ă*.

Imperfect

-A, -Î	-EA	-E	-I	vok.-I
-am	-eam			-iam
-ai	-eai			-iai
-a	-ea			-ia
-am	-eam			-iam
-aţi	-eaţi			-iaţi
-au	-eau			-iau

Simple perfect

-A (part. -at)	-EA (-ut)	-E (-ut)	E (-s, -t)	-I (-it)	-Î (-ât)
-ai	-ui		-sei	-ii	-âi
-aşi	-uşi		-seşi	-işi	-âşi
-ă, -e[112]	-u		-se	-i	-î
-arăm	-urăm		-serăm	-irăm	-ârăm
-arăţi	-urăţi		-serăţi	-irăţi	-ârăţi
-ară	-ură		-seră	-iră	-âră

Pluperfect

-A (part. -at)	-EA (-ut)	-E (-ut)	E (-s, -t)	-I (-it)	-Î (-ât)
-asem	-usem		-sesem	-isem	-âsem
-aseşi	-useşi		-seseşi	-iseşi	-âseşi
-ase	-use		-sese	-ise	-âse
-aserăm	-userăm		-seserăm	-iserăm	-âserăm
-aserăţi	-userăţi		-seserăţi	-iserăţi	-âserăţi
-aseră	-useră		-seseră	-iseră	-âseră

---

[112] *-i+ă → -ie.*

Appendix 2: Conjugation models

This appendix includes conjugation models of Romanian verbs, with all the sound changes and other irregularities. The following verbs are listed:

- all the verbs of the 1st conjugations having a vowel change.
- all the verbs of the 2nd and 3rd conjugations.
- all the verbs of the 4th conjugation conjugated like *fugi*.
- all the -*ă* and -*e* verbs of the 4th conjugations.
- all the -*î* verbs of the 4th conjugations.

An alphabetical list of all these verbs is given at the end of the book. Since the verb lists are meant to be as complete as possible, they also include some dialectal, old-fashioned or otherwise rare verbs.

For the following verb types only a regular model is given:

- the verbs of the 1st conjugations having no sound changes.
- the verbs of the 1st conjugation having a consonant change.
- the -*ez* verbs of the 1st conjugations.
- the 4th conjugation verbs with a vowel stem.
- the -*esc* verbs of the 4th conjugation.

Most Romanian verbs belong to these groups.

In this appendix the following verbal forms are given:

- The *infinitive*, which is used for the formation of the future, conditional and negative imperative.
- The *present indicative*, which is used for the first and second person of the conjunctive and for the imperative.
- The *third person of the present conjunctive*.
- The *first person singular of the imperfect, simple perfect* and *pluperfect*, from which the other persons can be formed. The simple perfect third person singular is also given when necessary.
- The *participle*, which is used for the perfect and the future perfect indicative, the perfect conjunctive, the perfect conditional and the perfect presumptive, the supine, and all the passive forms. The feminine form of the participle is given when needed.
- The *gerund*, which is used for the present presumptive.
- The second person singular of the *imperative* when needed.

Ia: JURA

Indicative

Present	Imperfect	Perfect	Simple perf.	Pluperfect
jur	juram	am jurat	jurai	jurasem
juri	jurai	ai jurat	jurași	juraseși
jură	jura	a jurat	jură	jurase
jurăm	juram	am jurat	jurarăm	juraserăm
jurați	jurați	ați jurat	jurarăți	juraserăți
jură	jurau	au jurat	jurară	jurasără

Future	Future Perfect
voi jura	voi fi jurat
vei jura	vei fi jurat
va jura	va fi jurat
vom jura	vom fi jurat
veți jura	veți fi jurat
vor jura	vor fi jurat

Conjunctive

Present	Perfect	Conditional Present	Perfect
să jur	să fi jurat	aș jura	aș fi jurat
să juri	să fi jurat	ai jura	ai fi jurat
să jure	să fi jurat	ar jura	ar fi jurat
să jurăm	să fi jurat	am jura	am fi jurat
să jurați	să fi jurat	ați jura	ați fi jurat
să jure	să fi jurat	ar jura	ar fi jurat

Presumptive

Present	Perfect	Imperative Affirmative	Negative
voi fi jurând	voi fi jurat		
vei fi jurând	vei fi jurat	jură	nu jura
va fi jurând	va fi jurat		
vom fi jurând	vom fi jurat		
veți fi jurând	veți fi jurat	jurați	nu jurați
vor fi jurând	vor fi jurat		

Infinitive

Present	Perfect
a jura	a fi jurat

Gerund	Participle	Supine
jurând	jurat, jurată, jurați, jurate	de jurat

Regular models

Verbs with the stem stress on the ultimate syllable of the stem

jura   jur, juri, jură, jurăm, jurați, jură, să jure,
        jurăm, jurai, jurasem, jurat, jurând

Verbs with the stem stress on the penultimate syllable of the stem

termina   termin, termini, termină, terminăm, terminați, termină, să termine
           terminăm, terminai, terminasem, terminat, terminând

Regular consonant changes

d → z
acorda[113]   acord, acorzi, acordă, acordăm, acordați, acordă, să acorde,
               acordăm, acordai, acordasem, acordat, acordând

aplauda   aplaud, aplauzi, aplaudăm, aplaudăm, aplaudați, aplaudă, să aplaude,
           aplaudăm, aplaudai, aplaudasem, aplaudat, aplaudând

t → ț
ajuta   ajut, ajuți, ajută, ajutăm, ajutați, ajută, să ajute,
         ajutăm, ajutai, ajutasem, ajutat, ajutând

solicita   solicit, soliciți, solicită, solicităm, solicitați, solicită, să solicite,
            solicitam, solicitai, solicitasem, solicitat, solicitând

s → ș
lăsa   las, lași, lasă, lăsăm, lăsați, lasă, să lase,
        lăsăm, lăsai, lăsasem, lăsat, lăsând

st → șt
asista   asist, asiști, asistă, asistăm, asistați, asistă, să asiste,
          asistăm, asistai, asistasem, asistat, asistând

sc → șt
risca   risc, riști, riscă, riscăm, riscați, riscă, să riște,
         riscăm, riscai, riscasem, riscat, riscând

șc → șt
mișca   mișc, miști, mișcă, mișcăm, mișcați, mișcă, să miște,
         mișcăm, mișcai, mișcasem, mișcat, mișcând

[k] → [tʃ]
arunca   arunc, arunci, aruncă, aruncăm, aruncați, aruncă, să arunce,
          aruncăm, aruncai, aruncasem, aruncat, aruncând

critica   critic, critici, critică, criticăm, criticați, critică, să critice,
           criticăm, criticai, criticasem, criticat, criticând

---

[113] In the meaning 'to tune an instrument' *acorda* is conjugated according to the Ib-conjugation (*-ez*).

[g] → [dʒʲ]

obliga   oblig, obligi, obligă, obligăm, obligați, obligă, să oblige,
          obligam, obligai, obligasem, obligat, obligând

rumega   rumeg, rumegi, rumegă, rumegăm, rumegați, rumegă, să rumege,
          rumegam, rumegai, rumegasem, rumegat, rumegând

Vowel changes

These verbs also have regular consonant changes in the second person singular of the present indicative and the second and third person singular and the third person plural of the present conjunctive.

Verbs with the stem stress on the ultimate syllable of the stem

e → ea

întreba   întreb, întrebi, întreabă, întrebăm, întrebați, întreabă, să întrebe,
          întrebam, întrebai, întrebasem, întrebat, întrebând

          Similarly: *abnega, alega (= a se ține de capul cuiva, -ez = invoca), alerga, apleca, aseca, aștepta (tu aștepți), boteza, cerca, certa (tu cerți), chema, cuteza, delega, denega, deseca, deștepta (tu deștepți), dezgheța, dezlega, freca, încerca, închega, îndemna, îndesa (tu îndeși), îndrepta (tu îndrepți), îneca, înghața, înjgheba (or -ez), însemna (= a reprezenta, -ez = a nota), înțepa, înțesa (tu înțeși), lega (= a uni, -ez = a lăsa prin testament), necheza, nega, pleca, râncheza, reboteza, rechema, redeștepta (tu redeștepți), reînchega, renega, reteza and seca.*

ie → ia

ierta   iert, ierți, iartă, iertăm, iertați, iartă, să ierte,
          iertam, iertai, iertasem, iertat, iertând

          Similarly: *aiepta (tu aiepți), dezmierda (tu dezmierzi) and zbiera.*

e → a

așeza   așez, așezi, așază, așezăm, așezați, așază, să așeze,
          așezam, așezai, așezasem, așezat, așezând

          Similarly: *deșela, deșerta (tu deșerți), înșela and reașeza.*

e → i

prezenta prezint, prezinți, prezintă, prezentăm, prezentați, prezintă, să prezinte,
          prezentam, prezentai, prezentasem, prezentat, prezentând

          Similarly: *reprezenta.*

ă → a

lăsa   las, lași, lasă, lăsăm, lăsați, lasă, să lase,
          lăsam, lăsai, lăsasem, lăsat, lăsând

          Similarly: *băga, căca, călca, căra, căsca (tu caști, să caște), delăsa (tu delași), descălca, descălța, descărca, deshăma, destrăma, dezbăra (tai dezbăr, dezbări, dezbară), dezbrăca, îmbrăca, împăca, înălța, încălca, încălța, încărca, îngrășa, înhăma, înhăța, însfăca, întărca, păpa, prăda (tu prazi), presăra, răbda (tu rabzi), reînălța, reîncărca, sălta (tu salți), săpa, scălda (tu scalzi), scăpa, supraîncărca, tresălta (tu tresalți), țesăla (or țesăl, țesăli, țesală, să țesăle) and văita (tu vaiți).*

ă → ă, ă, a
arăta

arăt, arăți, arată, arătăm, arătați, arată, să arate,
arătam, arătai, arătasem, arătat, arătând

Similarly: *adăpa, adăsta, agăța, crăpa and îngăima (or: îngaim, îngaimi).*

ă → ă, e, a
spăla

spăl, speli, spală, spălăm, spălați, spală, să spele
spălam, spălai, spălasem, spălat, spălând

Similarly: *apăsa (tu apeși), desfășa, desfăta (tu desfeți), desfăța, dezbăta (tu dezbeți), dezmăța, dezvăța, făta, îmbăta (tu îmbeți), înfășa, înfăța, învăța, păsa (tu peși), răsfăța, revărsa (tu reverși) and vărsa (tu verși).*

o → oa
înota

înot, înoți, înoată, înotăm, înotați, înoată, să înoate,
înotam, înotai, înotasem, înotat, înotând

Similarly: *cocoța, convoca, dezghioca, dezgropa, deznoda (tu deznozi), împroșca (tu împroști, să împroaște), îndopa, înfiora, înfoca, întroloca/întruloca, îngropa, îngroșa, înnoda (tu înnozi), provoca, reconvoca, reînnoda (tu reînnozi) and toca.*

u → o, o, oa
juca

joc, joci, joacă, jucăm, jucați, joacă, să joace,
jucam, jucai, jucasem, jucat, jucând

Similarly: *dejuca, desfășura, despresura, împresura, înconjura, înfășura, însura, înturna, măsura, purta (tu porți), răscula, răsturna, reînfășura, reînturna, repurta (= a-și îndrepta gândurile spre trecut, -ez = a obține un succes), returna (= a turna din nou, -ez = a returna un film), ruga, scula, strecura, turna (= a vărsa, a denunța, -ez = a realiza un film), zbura.*

Verbs with the stem stress on the penultimate syllable of the stem

ă → a
căuta

caut, cauți, caută, căutăm, căutați, caută, să caute,
căutam, căutai, căutasem, căutat, căutând

Similarly: *adăuga, bălega/băliga, cățăra, clătina, dezbăiera, descăleca, îmbăiera, încăiera, încăleca, lăuda (tu lauzi), măcina, răgila, răscrăcăra/răscrăcăna, sătura, scărpina, văiera, vătăma and zmăcina.*

e → a
fermeca

farmec, farmeci, farmecă, fermecăm, fermecați, farmecă, să farmece,
fermecam, fermecai, fermecasem, fermecat, fermecând

ie → ia
mieuna

miaun, miauni, miaună, mieunăm, mieunați, miaună, să miaune,
mieunam, mieunai, mieunasem, mieunat, mieunând

e → ea
scheuna scheaun, scheauni, scheaună, scheunăm, scheunați, scheaună, să scheaune,
scheunam, scheunai, scheunasem, scheunat, scheunând

Similarly: *fremăta (tu freamăți, să freamăte).*

e → ea, e, ea
rezema reazem, rezemi, reazemă, rezemăm, rezemați, reazemă, să rezeme,
rezemam, rezemai, rezemasem, rezemat, rezemând

o → oa
forfeca foarfec, foarfeci, foarfecă, forfecăm, forfecați, foarfecă, să foarfece,
forfecam, forfecai, forfecasem, forfecat, forfecând

unstressed *ă → e*
cumpăra cumpăr, cumperi, cumpără, cumpărăm, cumpărați, cumpără, să cumpere,
cumpăram, cumpărai, cumpărasem, cumpărat, cumpărând

Similarly: *apăra, astâmpăra, curăța, număra, prenumăra, răscumpăra* and *supăra.*

ă → a, unstressed *ă → e*
scăpăra scapăr, scaperi, scapără, scăpărăm, scăpărați, scapără, să scapere,
scăpăram, scăpărai, scăpărasem, scăpărat, scăpărând

Similarly: *căpăta (tu capeți), dăpăra, dărăpăna (or dărăpăn, dărapeni, dărapănă, să dărăpăne), încăibăra, recăpăta (tu recapeți), scăpăra, scăpăta (tu scapeți)* and *scărmăna.*

e → ea, unstressed *ă → e*
semăna semăn, semeni, seamănă, semănăm, semănați, seamănă, să semene,
semănam, semănai, semănasem, semănat, semănând

Similarly: *asemăna, depăna, depăra, legăna, lepăda (tu lepezi)* and *trepăda (tu trepezi).*

e → ea, unstressed *ă → e*
zgrepțăna zgreapțăn, zgreapțăni, zgreapțănă, zgrepțănăm, zgrepțănați, zgreapțănă,
să zgrepțene
zgrepțănam, zgrepțănai, zgrepțănasem, zgrepțănat, zgrepțănând

ie → ia, unstressed *ă → e*
pieptăna pieptăn, piepteni, piaptănă, pieptănăm, pieptănați, piaptănă, să pieptene,
pieptănam, pieptănai, pieptănasem, pieptănat, pieptănând

o → oa, unstressed *ă → e*
șchiopăta șchiopăt, șchioapeți, șchioapătă, șchiopătăm, șchiopătați, șchioapătă, să șchioapete,
șchiopătam, șchiopătai, șchiopătasem, șchiopătat, șchiopătând

Or *-ez.*

unstressed *e → ă*
enumera enumăr, enumeri, enumără, enumerăm, enumerați, enumără, să enumere,
enumeram, enumerai, enumerasem, enumerat, enumerând

Irregular endings

Verbs with stems ending in cons. + *l/r*

intra   intru, intri, intră, intrăm, intraţi, intră, să intre,
            intram, intrai, intrasem, intrat, intrând

            Similarly: *afla, bosumfla, consacra, contempla, dezumfla, insufla, răsufla, reafla, reintra, sufla, umbla, umfla, urla.*

str → ştr
mustra   mustru, muştri, mustră, mustrăm, mustraţi, mustră, să mustre,
            mustram, mustrai, mustrasem, mustrat, mustrând

ă → a
lătra   latru, latri, latră, lătrăm, lătraţi, latră, să latre,
            lătram, lătrai, lătrasem, lătrat, lătrând

Verbs ending in -*ia*

Cons. + *i*

îmbia   îmbii, îmbii, îmbie, îmbiem îmbiaţi, îmbie, să îmbie,
            îmbiam, îmbiai (îmbie), îmbiasem, îmbiat, îmbiind, îmbie!

            Similarly: *adia, învia* (or -*ez*), *reînvia* (or -*ez*).

apropia   apropii, apropii, apropie, apropiem, apropiaţi, apropie, să apropie,
            apropiam, apropiai (apropie), apropiasem, apropiat, apropiind, apropie!

            Similarly: *dezmânia, împrăştia, înfuria, înjunghia, întârzia, junghia, mânia, peria, sfâşia, speria* and *zgâria.*

Vowel + *i*

încuia   încui, încui, încuie, încuiem, încuiaţi, să încuie,
            încuiam, încuiai (încuie), încuiasem, încuiat, încuind, încuie!

            Similarly: *descheia, descuia, încheia, răzgâia.*

mângâia   mângâi, mângâi, mângâie, mângâiem, mângâiaţi, mângâie, să mângâie,
            mângâiam, mângâiai (mângâie), mângâiasem, mângâiat, mângâind, mângâie!

            Similarly: *ţuţuia* (or -*ez*), *zvăpăia.*

ă → a
tăia   tai, tai, taie, tăiem, tăiaţi, taie, să taie,
            tăiam, tăiai (tăie), tăiasem, tăiat, tăind, taie!

            Similarly: *întretăia* and *strătăia.*

o → *oa*

înfoi_a_   înf_oi_, înf_oi_, înfo_a_ie, înfoi_e_m, înfoi_a_ți, înfo_a_ie, să înfo_a_ie,
înfoi_a_m, înfoi_a_i (înfoi_e_), înfoi_a_sem, înfoi_a_t, înfo_i_nd, înfo_a_ie!

Similarly: *descovoia, desfoia, destoia* and *încovoia.*

u → *o, o, oa*

mui_a_   m_oi_, m_oi_, mo_a_ie, mui_e_m, mui_a_ți, mo_a_ie, să mo_a_ie,
mui_a_m, mui_a_i (mui_e_), mui_a_sem, mui_a_t, mu_i_nd, mo_a_ie!

Similarly: *despuia* and *înmuia.*

Ib: LUCRA

Indicative

Present	Imperfect	Perfect	Simple perf.	Pluperfect
lucrez	lucram	am lucrat	lucrai	lucrasem
lucrezi	lucrai	ai lucrat	lucraşi	lucraseşi
lucrează	lucra	a lucrat	lucră	lucrase
lucrăm	lucram	am lucrat	lucrarăm	lucraserăm
lucraţi	lucraţi	aţi lucrat	lucrarăţi	lucraserăţi
lucrează	lucrau	au lucrat	lucrară	lucraseră

Future	Future Perfect
voi lucra	voi fi lucrat
vei lucra	vei fi lucrat
va lucra	va fi lucrat
vom lucra	vom fi lucrat
veţi lucra	veţi fi lucrat
vor lucra	vor fi lucrat

Conjunctive

Present	Perfect	Conditional Present	Perfect
să lucrez	să fi lucrat	aş lucra	aş fi lucrat
să lucrezi	să fi lucrat	ai lucra	ai fi lucrat
să lucreze	să fi lucrat	ar lucra	ar fi lucrat
să lucrăm	să fi lucrat	am lucra	am fi lucrat
să lucraţi	să fi lucrat	aţi lucra	aţi fi lucrat
să lucreze	să fi lucrat	ar lucra	ar fi lucrat

Presumptive

Present	Perfect	Imperative Affirmative	Negative
voi fi lucrând	voi fi lucrat		
vei fi lucrând	vei fi lucrat	lucrează	nu lucra
va fi lucrând	va fi lucrat		
vom fi lucrând	vom fi lucrat		
veţi fi lucrând	veţi fi lucrat	lucraţi	nu lucraţi
vor fi lucrând	vor fi lucrat		

Infinitive

Present	Perfect
a lucra	a fi lucrat

Gerund	Participle	Supine
lucrând	lucrat, lucrată, lucraţi, lucrate	de lucrat

Verbs ending in -*ia*

studia: studiez, studiezi, studiază, studiem, studiați, studiază, să studieze,
            studiam, studiai (studie), studiasem, studiat, studiind

Verbs ending in -*che, -ghe*

urechea   urechez, urechezi, urechează, urechem, urecheați, urechează, să urecheze,
            urecheam, urecheai (ureche), urecheasem, urecheat, urechind

veghea   veghez, veghezi, veghează, veghem, vegheați, veghează, să vegheze,
            vegheam, vegheai (veghe), vegheasem, vegheat, veghind

Verbs ending in -*c, -g*

arca   parchez, parchezi, parchează, parcăm, parcați, parchează, să parcheze,
            parcam, parcai, parcasem, parcat, parcând

dialoga   dialoghez, dialoghezi, dialoghează, dialogăm, dialogați, dialoghează, să dialogheze,
            dialogam, dialogai, dialogasem, dialogat, dialogând

II: VEDEA

Indicative

Present	Imperfect	Perfect	Simple perf.	Pluperfect
văd	vedeam	am văzut	văzui	văzusem
vezi	vedeai	ai văzut	văzuși	văzuseși
vede	vedea	a văzut	văzu	văzuse
vedem	vedeam	am văzut	văzurăm	văzuserăm
vedeți	vedeați	ați văzut	văzurăți	văzuserăți
văd	vedeau	au văzut	văzură	văzuseră

Future	Future Perfect
voi vedea	voi fi văzut
vei vedea	vei fi văzut
va vedea	va fi văzut
vom vedea	vom fi văzut
veți vedea	veți fi văzut
vor vedea	vor fi văzut

Conjunctive

Present	Perfect
să văd	să fi văzut
să vezi	să fi văzut
să vadă	să fi văzut
să vedem	să fi văzut
să vedeți	să fi văzut
să vadă	să fi văzut

Conditional

Present	Perfect
aș vedea	aș fi văzut
ai vedea	ai fi văzut
ar vedea	ar fi văzut
am vedea	am fi văzut
ați vedea	ați fi văzut
ar vedea	ar fi văzut

Presumptive

Present	Perfect
voi fi văzând	voi fi văzut
vei fi văzând	vei fi văzut
va fi văzând	va fi văzut
vom fi văzând	vom fi văzut
veți fi văzând	veți fi văzut
vor fi văzând	vor fi văzut

Imperative

Affirmative	Negative
vezi (irreg.)*	nu vedea
vedeți	nu vedeți

Infinitive

Present	Perfect
a vedea	a fi văzut

Gerund	Participle	Supine
văzând	văzut, văzută, văzuți, văzute	de văzut

*Other transitive verbs -*e*, intransitive verbs -*i*.

Sound changes

părea par, pari, pare, părem, păreți, par, să pară,
păream, părui, părusem, părut, părând

Similarly: *a-, com- dis-, rea-, redis-, transpărea* and *încăpea*.

tăcea tac, taci, tace, tăcem, tăceți, tac, să tacă,
tăceam, tăcui, tăcusem, tăcut, tăcând

Similarly: *complăcea, displăcea, plăcea* and *zăcea*.

putea pot, poți, poate, putem, puteți, pot, să poată,
puteam, putui, putusem, putut, putând

durea -, -, doare, -, -, dor, să doară,
durea, duru, duruse, durut, durând

cădea cad, cazi, cade, cădem, cădeți, cad, să cadă,
cădeam, căzui, căzusem, căzut, căzând

Similarly: *decădea, recădea, scădea.*

şedea şed, şezi, şade, şedem, şedeți, şed, să şadă,
şedea, şezui, şezusem, şezut, şezând

vedea văd, vezi, vede, vedem, vedeți, văd, să vadă,
vedea, văzui, văzusem, văzut, văzând, vezi!

Similarly: *între-, pre-, pro-, re-, străvedea.*

III part. -*ut*: BATE

Indicative

Present	Imperfect	Perfect	Simple perf.	Pluperfect
bat	băteam	am bătut	bătui	bătusem
bați	băteai	ai bătut	bătuși	bătuseși
bate	bătea	a bătut	bătu	bătuse
batem	băteam	am bătut	băturăm	bătuserăm
bateți	băteați	ați bătut	băturăți	bătuserăți
bat	băteau	au bătut	bătură	bătuseră

Future	Future Perfect
voi bate	voi fi bătut
vei bate	vei fi bătut
va bate	va fi bătut
vom bate	vom fi bătut
veți bate	veți fi bătut
vor bate	vor fi bătut

Conjunctive

Present	Perfect
să bat	să fi bătut
să bați	să fi bătut
să bată	să fi bătut
să batem	să fi bătut
să bateți	să fi bătut
să bată	să fi bătut

Conditional

Present	Perfect
aș bate	aș fi bătut
ai bate	ai fi bătut
ar bate	ar fi bătut
am bate	am fi bătut
ați bate	ați fi bătut
ar bate	ar fi bătut

Presumptive

Present	Perfect
voi fi bătând	voi fi bătut
vei fi bătând	vei fi bătut
va fi bătând	va fi bătut
vom fi bătând	vom fi bătut
veți fi bătând	veți fi bătut
vor fi bătând	vor fi bătut

Imperative

Affirmative	Negative
bate*	nu bate
bateți	nu bateți

Infinitive

Present	Perfect
a bate	a fi bătut

Gerund	Participle	Supine
bătând	bătut, bătută, bătuți, bătute	de bătut

*Transitive verbs -*e*, intransitive verbs -*i*.

Sound changes

a → ă

    t → ţ

    bate

        bat, baţi, bate, batem, bateţi, bat, să bată,
        băteam, bătui, bătusem, bătut, bătând

        Similarly: *a-, com-, dez-, răz-, re-, stră-, zbate.*

    şt → sc

    naşte

        nasc, naşti, naşte, naştem, naşteţi, nasc, să nască,
        năşteam, născui, născusem, născut, născând

        Similarly: *paşte, renaşte.*

e → ea

    cere

        cer, ceri, cere, cerem, cereţi, cer, să ceară,
        ceream, cerui, cerusem, cerut, cerând

        Similarly: *aşterne, cerne, concepe, deşterne, discerne, geme, începe, întrece, percepe, petrece, pricepe, reîncepe, screme, teme* and *trece.*

    d → z

    crede

        cred, crezi, crede, credem, credeţi, cred, să creadă,
        credeam, crezui, crezusem, crezut, crezând

        Similarly: *încrede.*

    s → ş

    ţese

        ţes, ţeşi, ţese, ţesem, ţeseţi, ţes, să ţeasă,
        ţeseam, ţesui, ţesusem, ţesut, ţesând

        Similarly: *întreţese.*

    şt → sc

    creşte

        cresc, creşti, creşte, creştem, creşteţi, cresc, să crească,
        creşteam, crescui, crescusem, crescut, crescând

        Similarly: *concreşte, descreşte.*

    înveşte

        învesc, învești, înveşte, înveştem, înveşteţi, învesc, să învească,
        înveşteam, învăscui, învăscusem, învăscut, învăscând

ie → ia

    d → z

    pierde

        pierd, pierzi, pierde, pierdem, pierdeţi, pierd, să piardă,
        pierdeam, pierdui, pierdusem, pierdut, pierzând

oa → o

    s → ş

    coase

        cos, coşi, coase, coasem, coaseţi, cos, să coasă,
        coseam, cusui, cususem, cusut, cosând

        Similarly: *descoase.*

şt → sc

cunoaşte   cunosc, cunoşti, cunoaşte, cunoaştem, cunoaşteţi, cunosc, să cunoască,
cunoşteam, cunoscui, cunoscusem, cunoscut, cunoscând

Similarly: *recunoaşte.*

i → â   *d → z*

vinde   vând, vinzi, vinde, vindem, vindeţi, vând, să vândă,
vindeam, vândui, vândusem, vândut, vânzând

Similarly: *revinde.*

t → ţ

fute   fut, fuţi, fute, futem, futeţi, fut, să fută,
futeam, futui, futusem, futut, futând

III part. -*s*: ARDE

Indicative

Present	Imperfect	Perfect	Simple perf.	Pluperfect
ard	ardeam	am ars	arsei	arsesem
arzi	ardeai	ai ars	arseși	arseseși
arde	ardea	a ars	arse	arsese
ardem	ardeam	am ars	arserăm	arseserăm
ardeți	ardeați	ați ars	arserăți	arseserăți
ard	ardeau	au ars	arseră	arseseră

Future	Future Perfect
voi arde	voi fi ars
vei arde	vei fi ars
va arde	va fi ars
vom arde	vom fi ars
veți arde	veți fi ars
vor arde	vor fi ars

Conjunctive

Present	Perfect
să ard	să fi ars
să arzi	să fi ars
să ardă	să fi ars
să ardem	să fi ars
să ardeți	să fi ars
să ardă	să fi ars

Conditional

Present	Perfect
aș arde	aș fi ars
ai arde	ai fi ars
ar arde	ar fi ars
am arde	am fi ars
ați arde	ați fi ars
ar arde	ar fi ars

Presumptive

Present	Perfect
voi fi arzând	voi fi ars
vei fi arzând	vei fi ars
va fi arzând	va fi ars
vom fi arzând	vom fi ars
veți fi arzând	veți fi ars
vor fi arzând	vor fi ars

Imperative

Affirmative	Negative
arde, arzi*	nu arde
ardeți	nu ardeți

Infinitive

Present	Perfect
a arde	a fi ars

Gerund
arzând

Participle
ars, arsă,
arși, arse

Supine
de ars

*Transitive verbs -*e*, intransitive verbs -*i*.

Sound changes

a → ă

[dʒʲ] → [g]
trage   trag, tragi, trage, tragem, trageți, trag, să tragă,
                    trăgeam, trăsei (trase), trăsesem, tras, trăgând

                  Similarly: *a-*, *abs-*, *con-*, *dis-*, *ex-*, *re-* and *sustrage* and *rage* (no part., simple perf., pluperf.).

d → z
rade   rad, razi, rade, radem, radeți, rad, să radă,
                    redeam, răsei (rase), răsesem, ras, răzând

e → ea

[dʒʲ] → [g]
alege   aleg, alegi, alege, alegem, alegeți, aleg, să aleagă,
                  alegeam, alesei (alese), alesesem, ales (aleasă), alegând

                  Similarly *converge, culege, diverge* (no part., simple perf., pluperf, gerund), *drege, înțelege, merge, premerge, răsînțelege, realege, reculege, subînțelege* and *șterge.*

t → ț
sumete   sumet, sumeți, sumete, sumetem, sumeteți, sumet, să sumeată,
                  sumeteam, sumesei (sumese), sumesesem, sumes (sumeasă), sumețând

d → z
accede   acced, accezi, accede, accedem, accedeți, acced, să acceadă,
                  accedeam, -, accedând

                  Similarly: *concede.*

d → z
purcede   purced, purcezi, purcede, purcedem, purcedeți, purced, să purceadă,
                  purcedeam, purcesei (purcese), purcesesem, purces (purceasă), purcezând

oa → o

[tʃʲ] → [k]
toarce   torc, torci, toarce, toarcem, toarceți, torc, să toarcă,
                  torceam, torsei (toarse), torsesem, tors (toarsă, torși, toarse), torcând

                  Similarly: *destoarce, răstoarce, întoarce, reîntoarce* and *stoarce.*

t → ț
scoate   scot, scoți, scoate, scoatem, scoateți, scot, să scoată,
                  scoteam, scosei (scoase), scosesem, scos (scoasă, scoși, scoase), scoțând

d → z
roade   rod, rozi, roade, roadem, roadeți, rod, să roadă,
                  rodeam, rosei (roase), rosesem, ros (roasă, roși, roase), rozând

[dʒʲ] → [g]

ajunge   ajung, ajungi, ajunge, ajungem, ajungeți, ajung, să ajungă
ajungeam, ajunsei (ajunse), ajunsesem, ajuns, ajungând

Similarly: *atinge, concurge, constrânge, convinge, curge, decurge, deplânge, descinge, disjunge, distinge, distruge, exige* (no part., simple perf., pluperf., gerund), *evinge* (no part., simple perf., pluperf., gerund), *inflige* (no part., simple perf., pluperf., gerund), *împinge, împunge, încinge, întinge, învinge, linge, mulge, ninge, ocurge, parcurge, plânge, prelinge, recurge, respinge, restrânge, scurge, smulge, stinge, străpunge, strânge* and *unge*.

d → z

decide   decid, decizi, decide, decidem, decideți, decid, să decidă,
decideam, decisei (decise), decisesem, decis, decizând

Similarly: *aprinde, arde* (no vowel change!), *ascunde, circumcide, coincide, conchide, corespunde, cuprinde, depinde, deprinde, deschide, descinde, desfide* (no part., simple perf., pluperf.), *desprinde, destinde, divide* (no part., simple perf., pluperf., gerund) *exclude, extinde, include, închide, întinde, întredeschide, întrepătrunde, întreprinde, pătrunde, pretinde, prinde, răspunde, râde, reaprinde, redeschide, reînchide, subîntinde, surâde, surprinde, tinde* and *tunde*.

t → ț

admite   admit, admiți, admite, admitem, admiteți, admit, să admită,
admiteam, admisei (adimise), admisesem, admis, admițând

Similarly: *comite, compromite, demite, emite, omite, permite, promite, remite, readmite, retransmite, retrimite, transmite* and *trimite*.

III part. -*t*: RUPE

Indicative

Present	Imperfect	Perfect	Simple perf.	Pluperfect
rup	rupeam	am rupt	rupsei	rupsesem
rupi	rupeai	ai rupt	rupseși	rupseseși
rupe	rupea	a rupt	rupse	rupsese
rupem	rupeam	am rupt	rupserăm	rupseserăm
rupeți	rupeați	ați rupt	rupserăți	rupseserăți
rup	rupeau	au rupt	rupseră	rupseseră

Future	Future Perfect
voi rupe	voi fi rupt
vei rupe	vei fi rupt
va rupe	va fi rupt
vom rupe	vom fi rupt
veți rupe	veți fi rupt
vor rupe	vor fi rupt

Conjunctive / Conditional

Present	Perfect	Present	Perfect
să rup	să fi rupt	aș rupe	aș fi rupt
să rupi	să fi rupt	ai rupe	ai fi rupt
să rupă	să fi rupt	ar rupe	ar fi rupt
să rupem	să fi rupt	am rupe	am fi rupt
să rupeți	să fi rupt	ați rupe	ați fi rupt
să rupă	să fi rupt	ar rupe	ar fi rupt

Presumptive / Imperative

Present	Perfect	Affirmative	Negative
voi fi rupând	voi fi rupt		
vei fi rupând	vei fi rupt	rupe*	nu rupe
va fi rupând	va fi rupt		
vom fi rupând	vom fi rupt		
veți fi rupând	veți fi rupt	rupeți	nu rupeți
vor fi rupând	vor fi rupt		

Infinitive

Present	Perfect
a rupe	a fi rupt

Gerund	Participle	Supine
rupând	rupt, ruptă, rupți, rupte	de rupt

*Transitive verbs -*e*, intransitive verbs -*i*.

No sound changes

rupe   rup, rupi, rupe, rupem, rupeți, rup, să rupă
            rupeam, rupsei (rupse), rupsesem, rupt, rupând

            Similarly: *corupe, erupe, irupe* and *întrerupe*.

Sound changes

a → ă

      [ʤʲ] → [g]
      sparge   sparg, spargi, sparge, spargem, spargeți, sparg, să spargă,
                    spărgeam, spărsei (sparse), spărsesem, spart, spărgând

ie → ia

      fierbe   fierb, fierbi, fierbe, fierbem, fierbeți, fierb, să fiarbă,
                    fierbeam, fiersei (fierse), fiersesem, fiert (fiartă), fierbând

                    Similarly: *răsfierbe* and *refierbe*.

oa → o

      [ʧʲ] → [k]
      coace   coc, coci, coace, coacem, coaceți, coc, să coacă,
                  coceam, copsei (coapse), copsesem, copt (coaptă, copți, coapte), cocând

                  Similarly: *recoace* and *răscoace*.

[ʤʲ] → [g]

      frige   frig, frigi, frige, frigem, frigeți, frig, să frigă,
                frigeam, fripsei (fripse), fripsesem, fript, frigând

                Similarly: *înfige* and *suge*.

      frânge   frâng, frângi, frânge, frângem, frângeți, frâng, să frângă,
                frângeam, frânsei (frânse), frânsesem, frânt, frângând

                Similarly: *înfrânge* and *răsfrânge*.

IVa -*i*: FUGI

Indicative

Present	Imperfect	Perfect	Simple perf.	Pluperfect
fug	fugeam	am fugit	fugii	fugisem
fugi	fugeai	ai fugit	fugiși	fugiseși
fuge	fugea	a fugit	fugi	fugise
fugim	fugeam	am fugit	fugirăm	fugiserăm
fugiți	fugeați	ați fugit	fugirăți	fugiserăți
fug	fugeau	au fugit	fugiră	fugiseră

Future	Future Perfect
voi fugi	voi fi fugit
vei fugi	vei fi fugit
va fugi	va fi fugit
vom fugi	vom fi fugit
veți fugi	veți fi fugit
vor fugi	vor fi fugit

Conjunctive

Present	Perfect
să fug	să fi fugit
să fugi	să fi fugit
să fugă	să fi fugit
să fugim	să fi fugit
să fugiți	să fi fugit
să fugă	să fi fugit

Conditional

Present	Perfect
aș fugi	aș fi fugit
ai fugi	ai fi fugit
ar fugi	ar fi fugit
am fugi	am fi fugit
ați fugi	ați fi fugit
ar fugi	ar fi fugit

Presumptive

Present	Perfect
voi fi fugind	voi fi fugit
vei fi fugind	vei fi fugit
va fi fugind	va fi fugit
vom fi fugind	vom fi fugit
veți fi fugind	veți fi fugit
vor fi fugind	vor fi fugit

Imperative

Affirmative	Negative
fugi*	nu fugi
fugiți	nu fugiți

Infinitive

Present	Perfect
a fugi	a fi fugit

Gerund	Participle	Supine
fugind	fugit, fugită, fugiți, fugite	de fugit

*Transitive verbs -*e*, intransitive verbs -*i*.

Sound changes

e → ea

z → d
repezi reped, repezi, repede, repezim, repeziți, reped, să repeadă,
repezeam, repezii, repezisem, repezit, repezind

ie → ia

ș → s
ieși ies, ieși, iese, ieșim, ieșiți, ies, să iasă,
ieșeam, ieșii, ieșisem, ieșit, ieșind

Similarly: *reieși.*

o → oa

dormi dorm, dormi, doarme, dormim, dormiți, dorm, să doarmă,
dormeam, dormii, dormisem, dormit, dormind

Similarly: *absorbi, adormi, adsorbi, readormi, resorbi* and *sorbi.*

z → d
slobozi slobod, slobozi, sloboade, slobozim, sloboziți, slobod, să sloboadă,
slobozeam, slobozii, slobozisem, slobozit, slobozind
s → ș
mirosi miros, miroși, miroase, mirosim, mirosiți, miros, să miroasă,
miroseam, mirosii, mirosisem, mirosit, mirosind

ă → a

sări sar, sari, sare, sărim, săriți, sar, să sară,
săream, sării, sărisem, sărit, sărind

Similarly: *năzări, răsări* and *tresări.*

ț → t
împărți împart, împarți, împarte, împărțim, împărțiți, împart, să împartă,
împărțeam, împărții, împărțisem, împărțit, împărțind

Similarly: *desparți, reîmpărți* and *subîmpărți.*

u → o, o, oa

muri mor, mori, moare, murim, muriți, mor, să moară,
muream, murii, murisem, murit, murind

t → ț

învârti învârt, învârți, învârte, învârtim, învârtiți, învârt, să învârtă,
învârteam, învârtii, învârtisem, învârtit, învârtind

Also *-esc.*

ţ → t

minţi   minţ, minţi, minte, minţim, minţiţi, minţ, să minţă,
minţeam, minţii, minţisem, minţit, minţind

Similarly: *ascuţi, asmuţi, consimţi, dezminţi, împuţi, înghiţi, presimţi, puţi, resimţi* and *simţi.*

z → d

auzi   aud, auzi, aude, auzim, auziţi, aud, să audă,
auzeam, auzii, auzisem, auzit, auzind, auzi!

[dʒʲ] → [g]

fugi   fug, fugi, fuge, fugim, fugiţi, fug, să fugă,
fugeam, fugii, fugisem, fugit, fugind

Vowel stems

Verbs with a stem ending in a vowel are conjugated like *distribui*. Stress in the stem-stressed forms is on the penultimate syllable of the stem:

distribui   distribui, distribui, distribuie, distribuim, distribuiţi, distribuie, să distribuie,
distribuiam, distribuii, distribuisem, distribuit, distribuind, distribuie!

Exceptions (stem stress on the ultimate syllable of the stem):

sui   sui, sui, suie, suim, suiţi, suie, să suie,
suiam, suii, suisem, suit, suind, suie!

o → oa
îndoi   îndoi, îndoi, îndoaie, îndoim, îndoiţi, îndoaie, să îndoaie,
îndoiam, îndoii, îndoisem, îndoit, îndoind, îndoaie!

Similarly: *dezdoi.*

u → o, oa
jupui   jupoi, jupoi, jupoaie, jupuim, jupuiţi, jupoaie, să jupoaie,
jupuiam, jupuii, jupuisem, jupuit, jupuind, jupoaie!

-Ă-verbs

acoperi   acopăr, acoperi, acoperă, acoperim, acoperiți, acoperă, să acopere,
acopeream, acoperii, acoperisem, acoperit, acoperind, acoperă!

           Similarly: *descoperi, reacoperi, redescoperi* and *suferi*.

oferi   ofer, oferi, oferă, oferim, oferiți, oferă, să ofere,
oferem, oferii, oferisem, oferit, oferind, oferă!

           Similarly: *conferi, deferi, diferi, referi, absolvi* and *solvi* (or *-esc*).

sprijini   sprijin, sprijini, sprijină, sprijinim, sprijiniți, sprijină, să sprijine,
sprijineam, sprijinii, sprijinisem, sprijinit, sprijinind, sprijină!

           Similarly: *înăbuși*.

-E-verbs

ciocăni   ciocăn, ciocăni, ciocăne, ciocănim, ciocăniți, ciocăne, să ciocăne,
ciocăneam, ciocănii, ciocănisem, ciocănit, ciocănind, ciocăne!
(or *-esc*)

           Similarly: *bocăni, bombăni, ciocăni* (or *-esc*), *clănțăni* (or *-esc*), *cloncăni* (or *-esc*), *crănțăni*
           (or *-esc*), *croncăni* (or *-esc*), *dăngăni* (or *-esc*), *măcăni, țăcăni* (or *-esc*) and *zdroncăni*.

băuni: băun/baun, băuni/bauni, băune/baune, băunim, băuniți, băune/baune,
să băune/să baune,
băuneam, băunii, băunisem, băunit, băunind, băune/baune!

IVb -*i*: CITI

Indicative

Present	Imperfect	Perfect	Simple perf.	Pluperfect
citesc	citeam	am citit	citii	citisem
citești	citeai	ai citit	citiși	citiseși
citește	citea	a citit	citi	citise
citim	citeam	am citit	citirăm	citiserăm
citiți	citeați	ați citit	citirăți	citiserăți
citesc	citeau	au citit	citiră	citiseră

Future	Future Perfect
voi citi	voi fi citit
vei citi	vei fi citit
va citi	va fi citit
vom citi	vom fi citit
veți citi	veți fi citit
vor citi	vor fi citit

Conjunctive

Present	Perfect	Conditional Present	Perfect
să citesc	să fi citit	aș citi	aș fi citit
să citești	să fi citit	ai citi	ai fi citit
să citească	să fi citit	ar citi	ar fi citit
să citim	să fi citit	am citi	am fi citit
să citiți	să fi citit	ați citi	ați fi citit
să citească	să fi citit	ar citi	ar fi citit

Presumptive

Present	Perfect	Imperative Affirmative	Negative
voi fi citind	voi fi citit		
vei fi citind	vei fi citit	citește	nu citi
va fi citind	va fi citit		
vom fi citind	vom fi citit		
veți fi citind	veți fi citit	citiți	nu citiți
vor fi citind	vor fi citit		

Infinitive

Present	Perfect
a citi	a fi citit

Gerund	Participle	Supine
citind	citit, citită, citiți, citite	de citit

Vowel stems

The verbs with a stem ending in a vowel are conjugated like *trăi*:

trăi   trăiesc, trăiești, trăiește, trăim, trăiți, trăiesc, să trăiască,
       trăiam, trăii, trăisem, trăit, trăind

However, the verbs with a stem ending in -*i* are conjugated like *pustii*:

pustii   pustiesc, pustiești, pustiește, pustiim, pustiiți, pustiesc, să pustiască,
         pustiam, pustiii, pustiisem, pustiit, pustiind

Similarly: *albii, înmii, prii, sfii,* and *zapcii.*

Other irregularities

tuli   imper. tule!/tulește!

The other forms are regular.

IVa -î: VÂRÎ

Indicative

Present	Imperfect	Perfect	Simple perf.	Pluperfect
vâr	vâram	am vârât	vârâi	vârâsem
vâri	vârai	ai vârât	vârâși	vârâseși
vâră	vâra	a vârât	vârî	vârâse
vârâm	vâram	am vârât	vârârăm	vârâserăm
vârâți	vârați	ați vârât	vârârăți	vârâserăți
vâră	vârau	au vârât	vârâră	vârâseră

Future	Future Perfect
voi vârî	voi fi vârât
vei vârî	vei fi vârât
va vârî	va fi vârât
vom vârî	vom fi vârât
veți vârî	veți fi vârât
vor vârî	vor fi vârât

Conjunctive

Present	Perfect
să vâr	să fi vârât
să vâri	să fi vârât
să vâre	să fi vârât
să vârâm	să fi vârât
să vârâți	să fi vârât
să vâre	să fi vârât

Conditional

Present	Perfect
aș vârî	aș fi vârât
ai vârî	ai fi vârât
ar vârî	ar fi vârât
am vârî	am fi vârât
ați vârî	ați fi vârât
ar vârî	ar fi vârât

Presumptive

Present	Perfect
voi fi vârând	voi fi vârât
vei fi vârând	vei fi vârât
va fi vârând	va fi vârât
vom fi vârând	vom fi vârât
veți fi vârând	veți fi vârât
vor fi vârând	vor fi vârât

Imperative

Affirmative	Negative
vâră	nu vârî
vârâți	nu vârâți

Infinitive

Present	Perfect
a vârî	a fi vârât

Gerund

vârând

Participle

vârât, vârâtă, vârâți, vârâte

Supine

de vârât

Sound changes

o → oa

coborî   cobor, cobori, coboară, coborâm, coborâți, coboară, să coboare,
         coboram, coborâi, coborâsem, coborât, coborând

         Similarly: *doborî, oborî, omorî* and *pogorî.*

ă → a

tăbărî   tabăr, taberi, tabără, tăbărâm, tăbărâți, tabără, să tabere,
         tăbăram, tăbărâi, tăbărâsem, tăbărât, tăbărând

IVb -î: HOTĂRÎ

Indicative

Present	Imperfect	Perfect	Simple perf.	Pluperfect
hotărăsc	hotăram	am hotărât	hotărâi	hotărâsem
hotărăști	hotărai	ai hotărât	hotărâși	hotărâseși
hotărăște	hotăra	a hotărât	hotărî	hotărâse
hotărâm	hotăram	am hotărât	hotărârăm	hotărâserăm
hotărâți	hotărați	ați hotărât	hotărârăți	hotărâserăți
hotărăsc	hotărau	au hotărât	hotărâră	hotărâseră

Future	Future Perfect
voi hotărî	voi fi hotărât
vei hotărî	vei fi hotărât
va hotărî	va fi hotărât
vom hotărî	vom fi hotărât
veți hotărî	veți fi hotărât
vor hotărî	vor fi hotărât

Conjunctive

Present	Perfect
să hotărăsc	să fi hotărât
să hotărăști	să fi hotărât
să hotărască	să fi hotărât
să hotărâm	să fi hotărât
să hotărâți	să fi hotărât
să hotărască	să fi hotărât

Conditional

Present	Perfect
aș hotărî	aș fi hotărât
ai hotărî	ai fi hotărât
ar hotărî	ar fi hotărât
am hotărî	am fi hotărât
ați hotărî	ați fi hotărât
ar hotărî	ar fi hotărât

Presumptive

Present	Perfect
voi fi hotărând	voi fi hotărât
vei fi hotărând	vei fi hotărât
va fi hotărând	va fi hotărât
vom fi hotărând	vom fi hotărât
veți fi hotărând	veți fi hotărât
vor fi hotărând	vor fi hotărât

Imperative

Affirmative	Negative
hotărăște	nu hotărî
hotărâți	nu hotărâți

Infinitive

Present	Perfect
a hotărî	a fi hotărât

Gerund	Participle	Supine
hotărând	hotărât, hotărâtă, hotărâți, hotărâte	de hotărât

Similarly: *amărî, borî, chiorî, coptorî, cosorî, deszăvorî, izvorî, mohorî, ocărî, ogorî, oţărî, pârî, ponorî, posomorî, scociorî, stoborî, tătărî, târî, urî, viforî, zădărî, zămorî, zăporî* and *zăvorî.*

Appendix 3: Irregular verbs

Apart from the traditional irregular verbs (*avea, bea, da, fi, la, lua, mânca, sta, usca, vrea*), this appendix also includes the conjugation models of some other irregular verbs.

avea   'to have'

present	am, ai, are, avem, aveţi, au
imperfect	aveam, aveai, avea, aveam, aveaţi, aveau
simple perfect	avui, avuşi, avu, avurăm, avurăţi, avură *or*
	avusei, avuseşi, avuse, avuserăm, avuserăţi, avuseră
pluperfect	avusesem, avuseseşi, avusese,
	avuseserăm, avuseserăţi, avuseseră
conjunctive	am, ai, aibă, avem, aveţi, aibă
imperative	ai, aveţi
gerund	având
participle	avut, avută, avuţi, avute

Auxiliary verb of the perfect:	am, ai, a, am, aţi, au
Auxiliary verb of the conditional:	aş, ai, ar, am, aţi, ar

azvârli   'to throw'

present	azvârl, azvârli [-ⁱ], azvârle, azvârlim, azvârliţi, azvârlă
imperfect	azvârleam, azvârleai, azvârlea, azvârleam, azvârleaţi, azvârleau
simple perfect	azvârlii, azvârlişi, azvârli, azvârlirăm. azvârlirăţi, azvârliră
pluperfect	azvârlisem, azvârliseşi, azvârlise,
	azvârliserăm, azvârliserăţi, azvârliseră
conjunctive	azvârl, azvârli [-ⁱ], azvârle, azvârlim, azvârliţi, azvârle
imperative	azvârle, azvârliţi
gerund	azvârlind
participle	azvârlit, azvârlită, azvârliţi, azvârlite

Only the present and conjunctive are irregular. Similarly conjugated is the non-standard form *zvârli*. However, the indicative present can also regular (3rd person plural *zvârlă/zvârl*).

bea   'to drink'

present	beau, bei, bea, bem, beți, beau
imperfect	beam, beai, bea, beam, beați, beau
simple perfect	băui, băuși, băù, băurăm, băurăți, băură
pluperfect	băusem, băuseși, băuse, băuserăm, băuserăți, băuseră
conjunctive	beau, bei, bea, bem, beți, bea
imperative	bea, beți
gerund	bând
participle	băut, băută, băuți, băute

continua   'to continue'

present	continui[114], continui, continuă, continuăm, continuați, continuă
imperfect	continuam, continuai, continua, continuam, continuați, continuau
simple perfect	continuai, continuași, continuă, continuarăm, continuarăți, continuară
pluperfect	continuasem, continuaseși, continuase, continuaserăm, continuaserăți, continuaseră
conjunctive	continui, continui, continue, continuăm, continuați, continue
imperative	continuă, continuați
gerund	continuând
participle	continuat, continuată, continuați, continuate

Only the present and conjunctive are irregular.

da   'to give'

present	dau, dai, dă, dăm, dați, dau
imperfect	dădeam, dădeai, dădea, dădeam, dădeați, dădeau
simple perfect	dădui, dăduși, dădu, dădurăm, dădurăți, dădură
pluperfect	dădusem, dăduseși, dăduse, dăduserăm, dăduserăți, dăduseră
conjunctive	dau, dai, dea, dăm, dați, dea
imperative	dă, dați
gerund	dând
participle	dat, dată, dați, date

Similarly conjugated are *răzda* 'to give much (rare)' and *reda* 'to give back, to return'. The verbs *a se deda* 'to get accustomed', *preda* 'to hand over; to teach' and *reda* 'to describe, to reproduce' are conjugated like *da* in the indicative present and the conjunctive present, while the other forms are regular (imperfect *dedam*, simple perfect *dedai*, pluperfect *dedasem*).

---

[114] The recommended form for the indicative and conjunctive first person singular used to be *continuu*. In 2007 (DOOM[2]) the normative form was changed into *continui*. However, DEX (2009) gives both the forms.

deochea　'to cast an evil eye'

present de_o_chi, de_o_chi, deo_a_che, deoch_e_m, deoche_a_ţi, deo_a_che
imperfect deoche_a_m, deoche_a_i, deoche_a_, deoche_a_m, deoche_a_ţi, deoche_a_u
simple perfect deoche_a_i, deoche_a_şi, deoche_, deoche_a_răm, deoche_a_răţi, deoche_a_ră
pluperfect deoche_a_sem, deoche_a_seşi, deoche_a_se,
　　　　　deoche_a_serăm, deoche_a_serăţi, deoche_a_seră
conjunctive de_o_chi, de_o_chi, deo_a_che, deoch_e_m, deoche_a_ţi, deo_a_che
imperative deo_a_che, deoche_a_ţi
gerund deoch_i_nd
participle deoche_a_t, deoche_a_tă, deoche_a_ţi, deoche_a_te

duce　'to take'

present d_u_c, d_u_ci, d_u_ce, d_u_cem, d_u_ceţi, d_u_c
imperfect duce_a_m, duce_a_i, duce_a_, duce_a_m, duce_a_ţi, duce_a_u
simple perfect dus_e_i, dus_e_şi, d_u_se, d_u_serăm, d_u_serăţi, d_u_seră
pluperfect dus_e_sem, dus_e_seşi, dus_e_se, dus_e_serăm, dus_e_serăţi, dus_e_seră
conjunctive d_u_c, duci, d_u_că, d_u_cem, d_u_ceţi, d_u_că
imperative d_u_, d_u_ceţi
gerund duc_â_nd
participle d_u_s, d_u_să, d_u_şi, d_u_se

Similarly conjugated are *conduce, deduce, induce introduce, produce, reduce, readuce, reintroduce, reproduce, retraduce, seduce* and *traduce*. The imperative form of the verb *aduce* has the word stress on the first syllable (*_a_du!*, before the pronoun *o _a_d-o!/_a_du-o!*), otherwise it is conjugated like *duce.*

face　'to do'

present f_a_c, f_a_ci, f_a_ce, f_a_cem, f_a_ceţi, f_a_c
imperfect făce_a_m, făce_a_i, făce_a_, făce_a_m, făce_a_ţi, făce_a_u
simple perfect făc_u_i, făc_u_şi, făc_u_, făc_u_răm, făc_u_răţi, făc_u_ră
pluperfect făc_u_sem, făc_u_seşi, făc_u_se, făc_u_serăm, făc_u_serăţi, făc_u_seră
conjunctive f_a_c, f_a_ci, f_a_că, f_a_cem, f_a_ceţi, f_a_că
imperative f_ă_, f_a_ceţi
gerund făc_â_nd
participle făc_u_t, făc_u_tă, făc_u_ţi, făc_u_te

Only the imperative is irregular. Similarly conjugated are *contraface, desface, preface, reface* and *satisface.*

fi   'to be'

present[115]	sunt, ești [jeʃtⁱ], este ['jeste] *(unstressed:* e [je], *colloq.:* -i [i̯]), suntem, sunteți, sunt
imperfect	eram, erai, era, eram, erați, erau [je'ram, je'raj, je'ra, je'ram, je'ratsⁱ, je'rau̯]
simple perfect	fui, fuși, fu, furăm, furăți, fură *or* fusei, fuseși, fuse, fuserăm, fuserăți, fuseră
pluperfect	fusesem, fuseseși, fusese, fuseserăm, fuseserăți, fuseseră
conjunctive	fiu, fii, fie, fim fiți, fie
imperative	fii, fiți
neg. imperative	nu fi, nu fiți
gerund	fiind
participle	fost, fostă, foști, foste

The colloquial 3rd person singular *-i* is used after words ending in a vowel: *nu-i aici* 'he's not here', *cine-i acolo?* 'who's there?'. The present has also the non-standard and regional forms *îs, -s* (= *sunt*), *îi* (= *e*).

la   'to wash'

present	lau, lai, lă, lăm, lați, lau
imperfect	lam, lai, la, lam, lați, lau
simple perfect	lăui, lăuși, lău, lăurăm, lăurăți, lăură
pluperfect	lăusem, lăuseși, lăuse, lăuserăm, lăusrăm, lăuserăți, lăuseră
conjunctive	lau, lai, lea/leie/laie, lăm, lați, lea/leie/laie
imperative	lă, lați
gerund	lând
participle	lăut, lăută, lăuți, lăute

This verb belongs to non-standard speech.

lua   'to take'

present	iau, iei, ia, luăm, luați, iau
imperfect	luam, luai, lua, luam, luați, luau
simple perfect	luai, luași, luă, luarăm, luarăți, luară
pluperfect	luasem, luaseși, luase, luaserăm, luaserăți, luaseră
conjunctive	iau, iei, ia, luăm, luați, ia
imperative	ia, luați
gerund	luând
participle	luat, luată, luați, luate

Similarly conjugated are *prelua* and *relua*.

---

[115] Before the orthographic renewal of 1993 the present indicative forms were *sînt, ești, este, sîntem, sînteți, sînt.* In the first and second person plural the word stress could also be on the ending: *sîntem, sînteți*

mânca   'to eat'

present	mănânc, mănânci, mănâncă, mâncăm, mâncați, mănâncă
imperfect	mâncam, mâncai, mânca, mâncam, mâncați, mâncau
simple perfect	mâncai, mâncași, mâncă, mâncarăm, mâncarăți, mâncară
pluperfect	mâncasem, mâncaseși, mâncase, mâncaserăm, mâncaserăți, mâncaseră
conjunctive	mănânc, mănânci, mănânce, mâncăm, mâncați, mănânce
imperative	mănâncă, mâncați
gerund	mâncând
participle	mâncat, mâncată, mâncați, mâncate

mânea   'to spend the night'

present	mân/mâi, mâi, mâne, mânem, mâneți, mân
imperfect	mânea, mâneai, mânea, mâneam, mâneați, mâneau
simple perfect	măsei, măseși, mase, maserăm, maserăți, masără
pluperfect	măsesem, măseseși, măsese, măseserăm, măseserăți, măseseră
conjunctive	mân/mâi, mâi, mână/mâie, mânem, mâneți, mână/mâie
imp	mâi, mâneți
gerund	mânând/mâind
participle	mas, masă, mași, mase

This verb belongs to non-standard speech.

oua   'to lay eggs'

present	ouă, ouă
imperfect	oua, ouau
simple perfect	ouă, ouară
pluperfect	ouase, ouaseră
conjunctive	ouă, ouă
gerund	ouând
participle	ouat, ouată, ouați, ouate

Only the conjunctive is irregular.

pieri   'to perish'

present	pier, pieri, piere, pierim, pieriți, pier
imperfect	pieream, piereai, pierea, pieream, piereați, piereau
simple perfect	pierii, pieriși, pieri, pierirăm, pierirăți, pieriră
pluperfect	pierisem, pieriseși, pierise, pieriserăm, pieriserăți, pieriseră
conjunctive	pier, pieri, piară, pierim, pieriți, piară
imperative	piei, pieriți
gerund	pierind
participle	pierit, pierită, pieriți, pierite

Only the imperative is irregular.

ploua   'to rain'

present	plouă, plouă
imperfect	ploua, plouau
simple perfect	plouă, plouară
pluperfect	plouase, plouaseră
conjunctive	plouă, plouă
gerund	plouând
participle	plouat, plouată, plouați, plouate

Only the conjunctive is irregular.

preceda   'to precede'

present	preced, precezi, precedă, precedăm, precedați, precedă
imperfect	precedam, precedai, preceda, precedam, precedați, precedau
simple perfect	precedai, precedași, precedă, precedarăm, precedarăți, precedară
pluperfect	precedasem, precedaseși, precedase, precedaserăm, precedaserăți, precedaseră
conjunctive	preced, precezi, preceadă, precedăm, precedați, preceadă
imperative	precedă, precedați
gerund	precedând
participle	precedat, precedată, precedați, precedate

Only the conjunctive is irregular. Similarly conjugated is *succeda* 'to succeed'.

pune   'to put'

present	pun, pui, pune, punem, puneţi, pun
imperfect	puneam, puneai, punea, puneam, puneaţi, puneau
simple perfect	pusei, puseşi, puse, puserăm, puserăţi, pusdeă
pluperfect	pusesem, pusesceşi, pusese, puseserăm, puseserăţi, puseseră
conjunctive	pun, pui, punǎ, punem, puneţi, punǎ
imperative	pune, puneţi
gerund	punând
participle	pus, pusǎ, puşi, puse

Similarly conjugated are *apune, antepune, binedispune, compune, depune, descompune, dispune, expune, impune, indispune, interpune, juxtapune, opune, postpune, prepune, predispune, presupune, propune, răpune, recompune, repune, spune, suprapune, supune, suprapune, supraexpune* and *transpune*.

rămâne   'to stay'

present	rămân, rămâi, rămâne, rămânem, rămâneţi, rămân
imperfect	rămâneam, rămâneai, rămânea, rămâneam, rămâneaţi, rămâneau
simple perfect	rămăsei, rămăseşi, rămase, rămaseră, rămaserăţi, rămaseră
pluperfect	rămăsesem, rămăseseşi, rămăsese,
	rămăseserăm, rămăseserăţi, rămăseseră
conjunctive	rămân, rămâi, rămânǎ, rămânem, rămâneţi, rămânǎ
imperative	rămâi, rămâneţi
gerund	rămânând
participle	rămas, rămasǎ, rămaşi, rămase

scrie   'to write'

present	scriu, scrii, scrie, scriem, scrieţi, scriu
imperfect	scriam, scriai, scria, scriam, scriaţi, scriau
simple perfect	scrisei, scriseşi, scrise, scriserăm, scriserăţi, scriseră
pluperfect	scrisesem, scriseseţi, scrisese, scriseserăm, scriseserăţi, scriseseră
conjunctive	scriu, scrii, scrie, scriem, scrieţi, scrie
imperative	scrie, scrieţi
gerund	scriind
participle	scris, scrisǎ, scrişi, scrise

Similarly conjugated are *circumscrie, conscrie, descrie, exînscrie, înscrie, prescrie, proscrie, rescrie, retranscrie, subscrie* and *transcrie*.

sta   **'to stand'**

present   stau, stai, stă, stăm, stați, stau
imperfect   stăteam, stăteai, stătea, stăteam, stăteați, stăteau
simple perfect   stătui, stătuși, stătu, stăturăm, stăturăți, stătură
pluperfect   stătusem, stătuseși, stătuse, stătuserăm, stătuserăți, stătuseră
conjunctive   stau, stai, stea, stăm, stați, stea
imperative   stai, stați
gerund   stând
participle   stat, stată, stați, state

The verb *consta* (only third person singular and plural) is conjugated like *sta* in the indicative and conjunctive present, but the other forms are regular: present *constă, constau*, imperfect *consta, constau*, simple perfect *constă, constară*, pluperfect *constase, constaseră*, conjunctive *constea*.

şti   **'to know'**

present   știu, știi, ştie, ştim, știți, știu
imperfect   știam, știai, știa, știam, știați, știau
simple perfect   știui, știuși, știu, știurăm, știurăți, știură
pluperfect   știusem, știuseși, știuse, știuserăm, știuserăți, știuseră
conjunctive   știu, știi, ştie, ştim, știți, ştie
imperative   știi, știți
gerund   știind
participle   știut, știută, știuți, știute

trebui   **'must, to have to'**

The verb *trebui* occurs usually only in the third person singular and plural:

present   trebuie, trebuie *(colloq.:* tre')
imperfect   trebuia, trebuiau
simple perfect   trebui, trebuiră
pluperfect   trebuise, trebuiseră
conjunctive   trebuiască, trebuiască
gerund   trebuind
participle   trebuit, trebuită, trebuiți, trebuite

In the structure *a trebui să* 'must, have to' the subject of the subordinate clause is usually placed before *trebui*. The plural form is used only in the third person plural, while in all other persons the third person singular is used:

eu trebuia să merg	I had to go
tu trebuia să mergi	you had to go
el trebuia să meargă	he had to go

noi trebuia să mergem   we had to go
voi trebuia să mergeți   you had to go
ei trebuia*u* să meargă   they had to go
(*or*: trebuia ca ei să meargă)

The other tenses are formed similarly: e.g. *eu va trebui, eu a trebuit, eu trebuise,*
but: *ei vor trebui, ei au trebuit, ei trebuiseră* etc.

In the meaning 'to need', *trebui* agrees with the grammatical subject:

Îmi trebuia cartea aceasta.   I needed this book.
Îmi trebuiau cărțile aceste.   I needed these books.
Ne trebuiți.   We need you.

This verb also has the *-esc*-forms, that are now old-fashioned:

Îmi trebuiești.   I need you.

ține   'to hold'

present   țin, ții, ține, ținem, țineți, țin
imperfect   țineam, țineai, ținea, țineam, țineați, țineau
simple perfect ținui, ținuși, ținu, ținurăm, ținurăți, ținură
pluperfect   ținusem, ținuseși, ținuse, ținuserăm, ținuserăți, ținuseră
conjunctive   țin, ții, țină, ținem, țineți, țină
imperative   ține, țineți
gerund   ținând
participle   ținut, ținută, ținuți, ținute

Only the present and conjunctive are irregular. Similarly conjugated are *abți-*
ne, aparține, aține, conține, deține, întreține, menține, obține, reține and *susține.*

umple   'to fill'

present   umplu, umpli, umple, umplem, umpleți, umplu
imperfect   umpleam, umpleai, umplea, umpleam, umpleați, umpleau
simple perfect umplui, umpluși, umplu, umplurăm, umplurăți, umplură
pluperfect   umplusem, umpluseși, umpluse,
               umpluserăm, umpluserăți, umpluseră
conjunctive   umplu, umpli, umple, umplem, umpleți, umple
imperative   umple, umpleți
gerund   umplând
participle   umplut, umplută, umpluți, umplute

Only the present and conjunctive are irregular. Similarly conjugated is *re-*
umple 'refill'.

ucide   'to kill'

present	ucid, ucizi, ucide, ucidem, ucideți, ucid
imperfect	ucideam, ucideai, ucidea, ucideam, ucideați, ucideau
simple perfect	ucisei, ucisesi, ucise, uciserăm, uciserăți, ucisera
pluperfect	ucisesem, ucisesesi, ucisese, uciseserăm, uciseserăți, ucisesera
conjunctive	ucid, ucizi, ucidă, ucidem, ucideți, ucidă
imperative	ucide, ucideți
gerund	ucigând
participle	ucis, ucisă, ucisi, ucise

Only the gerund is irregular. Similarly conjugated is *sinucide* 'to commit suicide'.

usca   'to dry'

present	usuc, usuci, usucă, uscăm, uscați, usucă
imperfect	uscam, uscai, usca, uscam, uscați, uscau
simple perfect	uscai, uscași, uscă, uscarăm, uscarăți, uscară
pluperfect	uscasem, uscasesi, uscase, uscaserăm, uscaserăți, uscasera
conjunctive	usuc, usuci, usuce, uscăm, uscați, usuce
imperative	usucă, uscați
gerund	uscând
participle	uscat, uscată, uscați, uscate

veni   'to come'

present	vin, vii, vine, venim, veniți, vin
imperfect	veneam, veneai, venea, veneam, veneați, veneau
simple perfect	venii, venisi, veni, venirăm, venirăți, venira
pluperfect	venisem, venisesi, venise, veniserăm, veniserăți, venisera
conjunctive	vin, vii, vină, venim, veniți, vină
imperative	vino, veniți
gerund	venind
participle	venit, venită, veniți, venite

Similarly conjugated are *contraveni, conveni, cuveni, deveni, interveni, parveni, preveni, proveni, reveni, redeveni* and *surveni*.

vrea (voi)   'to want'

The imperfect form of *vrea* is normally replaced by the verb *voi* (*-esc*), which can also be used is some forms of the simple perfect and in the pluperfect. In the imperative, only *voi* is used. In all the other forms *vrea* is preferred.

present	vreau, vrei, vrea, vrem, vreți, vor
	(voiesc, voiești, voiește, voim, voiți, voiesc)
imperfect	voiam, voiai, voia, voiam, voiați, voiau
	(vream, -, vrea, -, -, vreau)
simple. perfect	vrui, vruși, vru, vrurăm, vrurăți, vrură
	-, -, voi, voirăm, voirăți, voiră
pluperfect	vrusem, vruseși, vruse, vruserăm, vruserăți, vrusera
	voisem, voiseși, voise, voiserăm, voiserăți, voiseră
conjunctive	vreau, vrei, vrea, vrem, vreți, vrea
	(voiesc, voiești, voiască, voim, voiți, voiască)
imperative	voiește, voiți
gerund	vrând
	(voind)
participle	vrut, vrută, vruți, vrute
	(voit, voită, voiți, voite)

Auxiliary verb of the future: voi, vei, va, vom, veți, vor

Mixed forms that start with *vroi-* (e.g. the imperfect *vroiam*) are colloquial and they are not recommended, even though they are quite frequent even in print.

As an auxiliary verb, *vrea* has colloquially shorter forms *oi, ăi (ei, îi, oi), o (a), om, ăți (eți, îți, oți),* or, which are not used in the standard language.

Dialectally, the simple perfect also has a longer form: *vrusei, vruseși, vruse, vruserăm, vruserăți, vrusera.* In the pluperfect the longer forms (*vrusesem, vrusesești, vrusese, vruseserăm, vruseserăți, vruseseră*) are more acceptable[116], but they should not be used in the standard language.

---

[116] In some grammar books (e.g. Goga) the short form (*vrui*) is used in the simple perfect, but the longer form (*vrusesem*) in the pluperfect. The grammar of Academia Română from 1966 gave the shorter form in the pluperfect singular, but the longer form in the plural: *vrusem, vruseși, vruse, vruseserăm, vruseserăți, vruseseră.*

zgândări   'to irritate, to anger'

present	zgândăr, zgândări, zgândăre, zgândărim, zgândăriți, zgândăr
imperfect	zgândăream, zgândăreai, zgândărea,
	zgândăream, zgândăreați, zgândăreau
simple perfect	zgândării, zgândăriși, zgândări,
	zgândărirăm, zgândărirăți, zgândăriră
pluperfect	zgândărisem, zgândăriseși, zgândărise,
	zgândăriserăm, zgândăriserăți, zgândăriseră
conjunctive	zgândăr, zgândări, zgândăre, zgândărim, zgândăriți, zgândăre
imperative	zgândăre, zgândăriți
gerund	zgândărind
participle	zgândărit, zgândărită, zgândăriți, zgândărite

Only the conjunctive is irregular. This verb can also be conjugated regularly according to the conjugation IVb (-*esc*)[117].

zice   'to say'

present	zic, zici, zice, zicem, ziceți, zic
imperfect	ziceam, ziceai, zicea, ziceam, ziceați, ziceau
simple perfect	zisei, ziseși, zise, ziserăm, ziserăți, ziseră
pluperfect	zisesem, ziseseși, zisese, ziseserăm, ziseserăți, ziseseră
conjunctive	zic, zici, zică, zicem, ziceți, zică
imperative	zi, ziceți
gerund	zicând
participle	zis, zisă, ziși, zise

Similarly conjugated are *contrazice, dezice, interzice, prezice* and *răszice*.

---

[117] DOOM². DEX (2009) gives only *zgândăresc*.

Appendix 4: Conjugation of reflexive verbs

Reflexive pronoun in the accusative

Indicative

Present	Imperfect	Perfect	Simple perf.	Pluperfect
mă deștept	mă deșteptam	m-am deșteptat	mă deșteptai	mă deșteptasem
te deștepți	te deșteptai	te-ai deșteptat	te deșteptași	te deșteptaseși
se deșteaptă	se deștepta	s-a deșteptat	se deșteptă	se deșteptase
ne deșteptăm	ne deșteptam	ne-am deșteptat	ne deșteptarăm	ne deșteptaserăm
vă deșteptați	vă deșteptați	v-ați deșteptat	vă deșteptarăți	vă deșteptaserăți
se deșteaptă	se deșteptau	s-au deșteptat	se deșteptară	se deșteptaseră

Future	Future Perfect
mă voi deștepta	mă voi fi deșteptat
te vei deștepta	te vei fi deșteptat
se va deștepta	se va fi deșteptat
ne vom deștepta	ne vom fi deșteptat
vă veți deștepta	vă veți fi deșteptat
se vor deștepta	se vor fi deșteptat

Conjunctive

Present	Perfect
să mă deștept	să mă fi deșteptat
să te deștepți	să te fi deșteptat
să se deștepte	să se fi deșteptat
să ne deșteptăm	să ne fi deșteptat
să vă deșteptați	să vă fi deșteptat
să se deștepte	să se fi deșteptat

Conditional

Present	Perfect
m-aș deștepta	m-aș fi deșteptat
te-ai deștepta	te-ai fi deșteptat
s-ar deștepta	s-ar fi deșteptat
ne-am deștepta	ne-am fi deșteptat
v-ați deștepta	v-ați fi deșteptat
s-ar deștepta	s-ar fi deșteptat

Presumptive

Present	Perfect
mă voi fi deșteptând	mă voi fi deșteptat
te vei fi deșteptând	te vei fi deșteptat
se va fi deșteptând	se va fi deșteptat
ne vom fi deșteptând	ne vom fi deșteptat
vă veți fi deșteptând	vă veți fi deșteptat
se vor fi deșteptând	se vor fi deșteptat

Imperative

Affirmative	Negative
deșteaptă-te	nu te deștepta
deșteptați-vă	nu vă deșteptați

Infinitive

Present	Perfect
a mă deștepta	a mă fi deșteptat
a te deștepta	a te fi deșteptat
a se deștepta	a se fi deșteptat
a ne deștepta	a ne fi deșteptat
a vă deștepta	a vă fi deșteptat
a se deștepta	a se fi deșteptat

Gerund

deșteptându-mă
deșteptându-te
deșteptându-se
deșteptându-ne
deșteptându-vă
deșteptându-se

Reflexive pronoun in the dative

Indicative

Present	Imperfect	Perfect	Simple perf.	Pluperfect
îmi amintesc	îmi aminteam	mi-am amintit	îmi amintii	îmi amintisem
îţi aminteşti	îţi aminteai	ţi-ai amintit	îţi amintişi	îţi amintiseşi
îşi aminteşte	îşi amintea	şi-a amintit	îşi aminti	îşi amintise
ne amintim	ne aminteam	ne-am amintit	ne amintirăm	ne amintiserăm
vă amintiţi	vă aminteaţi	v-aţi amintit	vă amintirăţi	vă amintiserăţi
îşi amintesc	îşi aminteau	şi-au amintit	îşi amintiră	îşi amintiseră

Future	Future Perfect
îmi voi aminti	îmi voi fi amintit
îţi vei aminti	îţi vei fi amintit
îşi va aminti	îşi va fi amintit
ne vom aminti	ne vom fi amintit
vă veţi aminti	vă veţi fi amintit
îşi vor aminti	îşi vor fi amintit

Conjunctive

Present	Perfect		
să-mi amintesc	să-mi fi amintit		
să-ţi aminteşti	să-ţi fi amintit		
să-şi amintească	să-şi fi amintit		
să ne amintim	să ne fi amintit		
să vă amintiţi	să vă fi amintit		
să-şi amintească	să-şi fi amintit		

Conditional

Present	Perfect
mi-aş aminti	mi-aş fi amintit
ţi-ai aminti	ţi-ai fi amintit
şi-ar aminti	şi-ar fi amintit
ne-am aminti	ne-am fi amintit
v-aţi aminti	v-aţi fi amintit
şi-ar aminti	şi-ar fi amintit

Presumptive

Present	Perfect
îmi voi fi amintind	îmi voi fi amintit
îţi vei fi amintind	îţi vei fi amintit
îşi va fi amintind	îşi va fi amintit
ne vom fi amintind	ne vom fi amintit
vă veţi fi amintind	vă veţi fi amintit
îşi vor fi amintind	îşi vor fi amintit

Imperative

Affirmative	Negative
aminteşte-ţi	nu-ţi aminti
amintiţi-vă	nu vă amintiţi

Infinitive

Present	Perfect
a-mi aminti	a-mi fi amintit
a-ţi aminti	a-ţi fi amintit
a-şi aminti	a-şi fi amintit
a ne aminti	a ne fi amintit
a vă aminti	a vă fi amintit
a-şi aminti	a-şi fi amintit

Gerund

amintindu-mi
amintindu-ţi
amintindu-şi
amintindu-ne
amintindu-vă
amintindu-şi

Appendix 5: Passive conjugation

Passive (masculine)

Indicative

Present	Imperfect	Perfect	Simple perf.	Pluperfect
sunt iubit	eram iubit	am fost iubit	fu(se)i iubit	fusesem iubit
ești iubit	erai iubit	ai fost iubit	fu(se)și iubit	fuseseși iubit
este iubit	era iubit	a fost iubit	fu(se) iubit	fusese iubit
suntem iubiți	eram iubiți	am fost iubiți	fu(se)răm iubiți	fuseserăm iubiți
sunteți iubiți	erați iubiți	ați fost iubiți	fu(se)răți iubiți	fuseserăți iubiți
sunt iubiți	erau iubiți	au fost iubiți	fu(se)ră iubiți	fuseseră iubiți

Future	Future Perfect
voi fi iubit	voi fi fost iubit
vei fi iubit	vei fi fost iubit
va fi iubit	va fi fost iubit
vom fi iubiți	vom fi fost iubiți
veți fi iubiți	veți fi fost iubiți
vor fi iubiți	vor fi fost iubiți

Conjunctive

Present	Perfect	Conditional Present	Perfect
să fiu iubit	să fi fost iubit	aș fi iubit	aș fi fost iubit
să fii iubit	să fi fost iubit	ai fi iubit	ai fi fost iubit
să fie iubit	să fi fost iubit	ar fi iubit	ar fi fost iubit
să fim iubiți	să fi fost iubiți	am fi iubiți	am fi fost iubiți
să fiți iubiți	să fi fost iubiți	ați fi iubiți	ați fi fost iubiți
să fie iubiți	să fi fost iubiți	ar fi iubiți	ar fi fost iubiți

Presumptive

Present	Perfect	Imperative Affirmative	Negative
voi fi fiind iubit	voi fi fost iubit		
vei fi fiind iubit	vei fi fost iubit	fii iubit	nu fi iubit
va fi fiind iubit	va fi fost iubit		
vom fi fiind iubiți	vom fi fost iubiți		
veți fi fiind iubiți	veți fi fost iubiți	fiți iubiți	nu fiți iubiți
vor fi fiind iubiți	vor fi fost iubiți		

Infinitive

Present	Perfect	Gerund
a fi iubit	a fi fost iubit	fiind iubit
a fi iubiți	a fi fost iubiți	fiind iubiți

Passive (feminine)

Indicative

Present	Imperfect	Perfect	Simple perf.	Pluperfect
sunt iubită	eram iubită	am fost iubită	fu(se)i iubită	fusesem iubită
eşti iubită	erai iubită	ai fost iubită	fu(se)şi iubită	fuseseşi iubită
este iubită	era iubită	a fost iubită	fu(se) iubită	fusese iubită
suntem iubite	eram iubite	am fost iubite	fu(se)răm iubite	fuseserăm iubite
sunteţi iubite	eraţi iubite	aţi fost iubite	fu(se)răţi iubite	fuseserăţi iubite
sunt iubite	erau iubite	au fost iubite	fu(se)ră iubite	fuseseră iubite

Future	Future Perfect
voi fi iubită	voi fi fost iubită
vei fi iubită	vei fi fost iubită
va fi iubită	va fi fost iubită
vom fi iubite	vom fi fost iubite
veţi fi iubite	veţi fi fost iubite
vor fi iubite	vor fi fost iubite

Conjunctive

Present	Perfect
să fiu iubită	să fi fost iubită
să fii iubită	să fi fost iubită
să fie iubită	să fi fost iubită
să fim iubite	să fi fost iubite
să fiţi iubite	să fi fost iubite
să fie iubite	să fi fost iubite

Conditional

Present	Perfect
aş fi iubită	aş fi fost iubită
ai fi iubită	ai fi fost iubită
ar fi iubită	ar fi fost iubită
am fi iubite	am fi fost iubite
aţi fi iubite	aţi fi fost iubite
ar fi iubite	ar fi fost iubite

Presumptive

Present	Perfect
voi fi fiind iubită	voi fi fost iubită
vei fi fiind iubită	vei fi fost iubită
va fi fiind iubită	va fi fost iubită
vom fi fiind iubite	vom fi fost iubite
veţi fi fiind iubite	veţi fi fost iubite
vor fi fiind iubite	vor fi fost iubite

Imperative

Affirmative	Negative
fii iubită	nu fi iubită
fiţi iubite	nu fiţi iubite

Infinitive

Present	Perfect
a fi iubită	a fi fost iubită
a fi iubite	a fi fost iubite

Gerund

fiind iubită
fiind iubite

Passive (neuter)

Indicative

Present	Imperfect	Perfect	Simple perf.	Pluperfect
este iubit	era iubit	a fost iubit	fu(se) iubit	fusese iubit
sunt iubite	erau iubite	au fost iubite	fu(se)ră iubite	fuseseră iubite

Future	Future Perfect
va fi iubit	va fi fost iubit
vor fi iubite	vor fi fost iubite

Conjunctive		Conditional	
Present	**Perfect**	**Present**	**Perfect**
să fie iubit	să fi fost iubit	ar fi iubită	ar fi fost iubit
să fie iubite	să fi fost iubite	ar fi iubite	ar fi fost iubite

Presumptive

Present	Perfect
va fi fiind iubit	va fi fost iubit
vor fi fiind iubite	vor fi fost iubite

Infinitive		Gerund
Present	**Perfect**	
a fi iubit	a fi fost iubit	fiind iubit
a fi iubite	a fi fost iubite	fiind iubite

Appendix 6: Word order of the verbal structure

The negative adverb *nu*, the unstressed accusative and dative pronouns and the adverbs *mai, tot, cam, prea, și* are placed in front of the verb in the following order:

1. Conjunctive, infinitive and supine markers *să, a, de.*
2. Negative adverb or prefix.
3. Unstressed dative pronoun.
4. Unstressed accusative pronoun.
5. The auxiliary verbs *avea* and *vrea.*
6. Adverbs *mai, tot, cam, prea, și.*
7. Auxiliary verb *fi.*
8. Main verb.

	1	2	3	4	5	6	7	8
Ind. present		nu	i	-l		mai		fac
Ind. perf.		nu	i	-l	am	mai		făcut
Ind. fut.		nu	i	-l	voi	mai		face
Ind. fut. perf.		nu	i	-l	voi	mai	fi	făcut
Neg. imper.		nu	i	-l		mai		face!
Conj. present	să	nu	i	-l		mai		fac
Conj. perf.	să	nu	i	-l		mai	fi	făcut
Cond. present		nu	i	-l	ar	mai		făcea
Cond. perf.		nu	i	-l	ar	mai	fi	făcut
Presumpt. pres.		nu	i	-l	voi	mai	fi	făcând
Inf. present	a	nu	i	-l		mai		face
Inf. perf.	a	nu	i	-l		mai	fi	făcut
Part.		ne...				...mai...		făcut
Gerund		ne...				...mai...		făcând
Supine	de	ne...				...mai...		făcut
Pass. ind. present		nu				mai	este	făcut
Pass. ind. perf.		n-			a	mai	fost	făcut
Pass. cond. pres.		n-			ar	mai	fi	făcut
Pass. cond. perf.		n-			ar	mai	fi fost	făcut

Exceptions:

When the auxiliary verb (*avea* or the colloquial forms of *vrea*) starts with a vowel, the feminine third person singular accusative pronoun *o* is placed after the main verb. This happens in the indicative perfect, the present and perfect conditional, the colloquial indicative future and some forms of the presumptive:

> n-am mai făcut-o
> n-ar mai face-o
> n-ar mai fi făcut-o
> n-oi mai face-o (colloq.) = n-o voi mai face.
> n-ar mai fi făcând-o

The semiadverb *şi* always comes immediately before the main verb:

> voi fi şi făcut   a fost şi făcut
> să fi şi făcut   ar fi fost şi făcut
> ar fi şi făcut

With compound future forms formed with the conjunctive, the negative adverb is placed before the auxiliary verb, while the pronouns and semiadverbs are added to the conjunctive form:

> n-am să-l mai fac
> n-o să-l mai fac

The pronouns are placed after a gerund or an affirmative imperative:

> nemaifăcându-l
> mai fă-l!

Index of verbs

Index of grammatical points